C000151950

Bail in Criminal Proceedings

Bail in Criminal Proceedings

Neil Corre
Solicitor-Advocate (Higher Courts Criminal)

David Wolchover
of Gray's Inn, Barrister

BLACKSTONE
PRESS LIMITED

First published in Great Britain 1999 by Blackstone Press Limited,
Aldine Place, London W12 8AA. Telephone 0181–740 2277

© N. Corre, D. Wolchover, 1999

ISBN: 1 85431 921 3

British Library Cataloguing in Publication Data
A CIP catalogue record for this book is available from the British Library

Typeset by Style Photosetting Limited, Mayfield, East Sussex
Printed by Livesey Ltd, Shrewsbury, Shropshire

All rights reserved. No part of this book may be reproduced or transmitted in any
form or by any means, electronic or mechanical, including photocopying, recording, or any information storage or retrieval system without prior permission from
the publisher.

Contents

1.1 The origins of the right to bail   1.1.1 The early Norman period   1.1.2 Obtaining release by royal writ   1.1.3 The Statute of Westminster I of 1275 1.1.4 Developments through to the 16th century   1.1.5 The Bail Statute of 1554 1.1.6 The 17th century and onwards   1.1.7 Bail in murder: the duelling cases and other aspects   1.2 The statutory general right to bail   1.2.1 Enactment of the general right in section 4 of the Bail Act 1976   1.2.2 Meaning of 'bail in criminal proceedings'   1.2.3 Applicability of the general right in section 4   1.2.4 Homicide and rape charges where defendants have previous convictions for those offences   1.3 Exceptions to the right to bail in Schedule 1 to the Bail Act 1976 1.3.1 Exceptions in the case of imprisonable offences: Part I of Schedule 1   1.3.2 Exceptions in the case of non-imprisonable offences: Part II of Schedule 1 1.4 Aspects of the statutory considerations for assessing whether to invoke the principal exceptions   1.4.1 Nature and seriousness of the offence   1.4.2 Strength of the evidence   1.4.3 Character, antecedents, associations and community ties 1.4.4 Previous bail history   1.4.5 Any other relevant matters   1.5 Applying the exceptions to bail   1.5.1 'Substantial grounds' (original main exceptions – imprisonable offences)   1.5.2 Failure to surrender   1.5.3 Commission of offences while on bail   1.5.4 Interfere with witnesses or otherwise obstruct the course of justice   1.5.5 Defendant already on bail   1.5.6 Own protection or welfare 1.5.7 Insufficient information   1.5.8 'Impracticable to prepare report or make inquiries'   1.5.9 Non-imprisonable offences   1.6 Requirement to explain and record bail decisions   1.6.1 Obligation of the court to state reasons for refusing

6 Police Bail 152

7 The Jurisdiction of the Magistrates' Court   170

8 The Jurisdiction of the Crown Court   207

authority accommodation with no security requirement   11.1.9 Remand to secure accommodation   11.1.10 Application by local authority to keep in secure accommodation a 'child' whom they are looking after   11.1.11 Prosecution right of appeal in respect of bail   11.1.12 Abolition of power to commit juveniles with view to sentence of detention in a young offender institution   11.1.13 Time spent in custody to count towards sentence   11.2 Persons affected by adverse mental condition 11.2.1 Remand to hospital for report on the accused's mental condition 11.2.2 Remand by Crown Court of accused persons to hospital for treatment 11.2.3 Committal to the Crown Court under sections 43 and 44 of the Mental Health Act 1983 with a view to a restriction order   11.2.4 Removal to hospital of mental patients

12.1 Background   12.2 Overall time limits   12.2.1 Power of Secretary of State to set time limits   12.2.2 Provisions for overall time limits not yet implemented 12.3 Custody time limits in the magistrates' court   12.3.1 Either-way offences 12.3.2 Either-way offences tried summarily   12.3.3 Indictable only offences 12.3.4 Old-style committal   12.3.5 Transfers   12.3.6 Meaning of first appearance in magistrates' court   12.3.7 Application of custody time limits to young persons 12.4 Custody time limits in the Crown Court   12.4.1 The general rule   12.4.2 Separate committals   12.4.3 Voluntary bill following committal   12.4.4 Where indictment contains a new count   12.4.5 Application of the Regulations to transfers for trial   12.4.6 Meaning of start of trial in the Crown Court   12.4.7 Custody time limit does not end with arraignment   12.4.8 Measurement of the custody time limit   12.4.9 Each offence attracts its own custody time limit 12.4.10 Substitution of new charge   12.5 Extension   12.5.1 Application for the extension of custody time limits   12.5.2 An application for extension must be made before expiry of the custody time limit   12.5.3 Applications and orders must be made clearly   12.5.4 Method of application   12.5.5 Reasons to be given for making an extension order   12.5.6 Standard of proof   12.5.7 Grounds for extension or further extension of a custody time limit   12.5.8 Judicial review 12.6 Appeal   12.6.1 By the defendant   12.6.2 By the prosecution   12.6.3 Procedure   12.6.4 Abandonment of appeal   12.7 Effect of expiry of custody time limit   12.7.1 Modification of Bail Act 1976   12.7.2 Crime and Disorder Act 1998 12.7.3 Commencement of proceedings   12.8 Custody time limits in practice 12.8.1 Routine extension   12.8.2 Empirical findings

13.1 The prosecuting advocate   13.1.1 Duty irrespective of whether objection is raised against bail   13.1.2 Raising objections and duties in contrast with the position in relation to sentencing   13.1.3 Duty of disclosure to the defence 13.1.4 Mode of presenting objections   13.1.5 Duty to reply when appropriate

13.2 The defending advocate   13.2.1 Professionalism   13.2.2 Special difficulties involved in bail applications   13.2.3 The duty to present the client's case without knowingly misleading the court   13.2.4 The difficulty over previous convictions 13.2.5 Influence on performance of costs regulations   13.2.6 Reluctance to make unmeritorious applications   13.2.7 Preparation   13.2.8 The hearing   13.2.9 Advocate's duty where client fails to attend court

Preface

In about 1988 we discussed the possibility of collaborating together on some sort of joint project, of which a manual on bail was one of the favoured options. In the event, we did not pursue the project and Neil Corre went ahead on his own to write the first edition, published in 1990. Then, about two years ago, we met by chance at a seminar and the happy outcome of that casual encounter was the idea of taking up where we had left off, joining forces in producing jointly a new edition of the original work.

Our initial intention was to keep broadly to the same format, structure and length as the first edition. However, as the research and writing proceeded it became obvious that with the enormous volume of legislation since 1990 a much more detailed and extensive text was not only required but also inevitable. Although significant parts of the original text have been retained, in many respects this new edition is very different from the first and there has been substantial restructuring, rewriting and additional composition and analysis. In keeping with requests from numerous practitioners and court clerks we have included throughout the text a comprehensive treatment of Rules of Court and relevant secondary legislation. We are grateful to the many readers who have taken the trouble to write to Neil Corre with constructive criticism and valuable suggestions. We have also included much more research and empirical data than previously to give the reader a perspective as to how the law in action is sometimes different from the law in theory. In conformity with the publisher's house style we have been pleased to avoid the use of gender-specific language in general. To that end we have wherever possible paraphrased the terms of statutory provisions. However, it has occasionally been necessary to cite the exact terms of statutory measures; and where this has been unavoidable we have tried our best to quote the statutory language as little as possible in order to avoid the male pronoun. We have of course dispensed with such restraints in covering those provisions of s. 23 of the Children and Young Persons Act 1969 (as amended by s. 28 of the Crime and Disorder Act 1998) which deal with male defendants over the age of 15 years.

We are grateful to the Research and Statistics Directorate of the Home Office for providing so much information and to those at Blackstone Press who were so helpful in the preparation of this work. Thanks are also due to Stefan Corre and

John Mays for their assistance in reading the proofs and to our family members for their forbearance during the many hours in which we isolated ourselves from their company. Lastly, we wish to record our gratitude to the importers of Darjeeling and the *cafeicultores do Brasil*, without whose products this book could never have been written!

Neil Corre
David Wolchover
February 1999

Table of Cases

Table of Statutes

List of Abbreviations

BA 1976   Bail Act 1976
BAA 1993   Bail (Amendment) Act 1993
CA 1989   Children Act 1989
CAA   Criminal Appeal Act (1968 and 1995)
CAR 1968   Criminal Appeal Rules 1968
CCR 1982   Crown Court Rules 1982
CDA 1998   Crime and Disorder Act 1998
CJA   Criminal Justice Act (1948, 1961, 1967, 1972, 1982, 1987, 1988, 1989, 1991)
CJPOA 1994   Criminal Justice and Public Order Act 1994
CLA 1977   Criminal Law Act 1977
CPIA 1996   Criminal Procedure and Investigations Act 1996
CPS   Crown Prosecution Service
CYPA   Children and Young Persons Act (1933 and 1969)
MCA 1980   Magistrates' Courts Act 1980
MCR 1981   Magistrates' Courts Rules 1981
MHA 1983   Mental Health Act 1983
PACE 1984   Police and Criminal Evidence Act 1984
PCCA 1973   Powers of the Criminal Courts Act 1973
POA 1985   Prosecution of Offences Act 1985
RSC 1965   Rules of the Supreme Court 1965
SCA 1981   Supreme Court Act 1981

Introduction

The gaoler's office of a London magistrates' court used to display a notice that read 'PLEASE DO NOT ASK FOR BAIL AS A REFUSAL OFTEN OFFENDS'. At the same court, the brief facts of a case were concluded with the words: 'He was arrested and cautioned, to which he replied, "Will I get bail?".' Practitioners will know of clients who accept with resignation a custodial sentence but campaign with all their energy for the grant of bail. It seems that the adage 'If you can't do the time, don't do the crime' does not apply to remands in custody. Bail is not only a subject of importance to defendants; it is also a matter of constitutional importance. Lord Hailsham of St Marylebone, addressing the Gloucester branch of the Magistrates' Association on 11 September 1971 in his capacity as Lord Chancellor, described the refusal of bail as '. . . the only example in peace-time where a man can be kept in confinement without a proper sentence following conviction after a proper trial. It is therefore the solitary exception to the Magna Carta'.

The attempt of the judiciary to check the monarch's power of arbitrary arrest and detention without trial formed an important aspect of the constitutional conflicts of the 17th century. The decision in *Darnel's Case* or *The Five Knights' Case* (1627) 3 St Tr 1, that there was no right to a writ of habeas corpus where the prisoner was detained *per speciale mandatum regis* (by special order of the King), and the general issue of the powers of the royal prerogative were not finally resolved until the passing of the Bill of Rights in 1688 and the nascency of the modern doctrine of constitutional monarchy. The right to habeas corpus continued to be suspended during times of political unrest. The statute 34 Geo III, c.54, for example, prohibited any person imprisoned under a warrant signed by a Secretary of State on a charge of high treason from insisting upon being discharged or put on trial.

Until recent times, the only admissible ground for refusing bail was that the defendant would fail to surrender to custody. For that reason the requirement of sureties for attendance was the only condition which could be attached to bail. More recently – in the period immediately after the Second World War – the risk that a defendant would commit an offence if released on bail was acknowledged judicially as imposing a duty on courts to refuse bail. With the acceptance of that basis for objection the ground was cleared for the introduction of conditions apart from surety. Statutory authority for these was given by the Criminal Justice Act 1967, during the passage of which the Minister of State told the House of Commons:

> It is hoped that the court will keep in mind that the purpose of the provision is to save some people being kept in prison and not to burden those who will in any event be given bail by the adding of conditions. There should be no question of imposing special conditions [as they were then called] as a matter of course.

It is arguable that this exhortation has not been heeded, and that many conditions or grants of conditional bail do not fulfil the statutory criterion of being 'necessary'. It certainly appears that conditions have become ever more elaborate. The chief clerk of a London magistrates' court has reported that a defendant actually applied for a variation so that he could 'attend his hairdresser by prior appointment on seven days' prior notice to the CPS [Crown Prosecution Service] and the police' ((1990) 154 *Justice of the Peace* 107).

The importance of the bail decision

The Home Office Working Party on magistrates' courts bail procedures observed:

> The importance of the bail decision can hardly be exaggerated. It involves balancing the liberty of the individual who (in the case of remand before conviction) has been found guilty of no offence against the need to ensure that accused persons are duly brought to trial and the public protected. Quite apart from depriving him of his liberty, a remand in custody may often have other harmful effects. . . . On the other hand, it is rightly a matter of serious concern if a person granted bail absconds or commits offences while on bail. (*Bail Procedures in Magistrates' Courts, Report of the Working Party*, London: HMSO, 1974, p. 17)

Conditions of remand prisoners

Remand prisoners are subject to overcrowding and the indignities of slopping out, and have little opportunity for work or recreational activities (Morgan, R., 'Remands in Custody: Problems and Prospects' [1989] Crim LR 481, at p. 485, citing *Report of the Chief Inspector of Prisons, 1984*, London: HMSO, 1985, paras 2.11–2.13, Chief Inspector of Prisons, *Prison Sanitation*, London: Home Office, 1989, *passim*).

Remand prisoners are subject to the uncertainty of the legal process and cannot plan for the future. Nor, as Lord Windlesham, a former Chairman of the Parole Board, has stated, can they settle down to serving a finite term of imprisonment (quoted in Cavadino, P. and Gibson, B., *Bail: The Law, Best Practice and the Debate*, Winchester: Waterside Press, 1993, p. 71, and Hucklesby, A., 'Bail or Jail? The Magistrates' Decision', unpublished PhD thesis, University of Glamorgan, 1994, pp. 11–12).

Remand prisoners are often held in worse conditions than convicted prisoners. 'Because they are not in prison as a punishment the regime for remands should be better than that for sentenced prisoners. . . . Unhappily, the position is often the reverse' (Woolf LJ, *Prison Disturbances April 1990: Report of an Inquiry*, Cmnd. 1456, London: HMSO, 1991, p. 246). 'The explanation for this travesty of justice is partly that it is the natural inclination of the prison service to devote proportionately more of its resources to the inmates who are longest in custody' (*ibid.*). Morgan puts the same point rather more starkly: 'The reason why the dictates of moral as well as legal logic have been inverted by the prison department – untried prisoners get the worst conditions while sentenced, generally longer term, prisoners get the best – stems from the organisational goals and managerial convenience of the prison system' ('Remands in Custody: Problems and Prospects', *supra*).

The effect of legal representation

The 1976 Cobden Trust study, *The Effect of a Duty Solicitor Scheme*, compared Hendon Magistrates' Court, which had a duty solicitor scheme, with Harrow Magistrates' Court, which did not. At the time of the research, the two courts fell within the same petty sessional area. During the first 16 months of the scheme at Hendon, the proportion of defendants granted bail on their first appearance rose by 4 per cent, while at Harrow the proportion fell by 1.5 per cent.

By way of contrast, another study found that while 80 per cent of represented defendants were granted bail, the figure for unrepresented defendants was 86 per cent (Zander, M., 'The Operation of the Bail Act in London Magistrates' Courts' *New Law Journal*, 1979, vol. 129, pp. 108–111). A 1985 study also found that defendants who were legally represented were less likely to be granted bail than unrepresented defendants (Doherty, M. and East, R., 'Bail Decisions in Magistrates' Courts' (1985) 25(3) *British Journal of Criminology* 251–66). The proportion of represented defendants granted bail was 78 per cent, while the corresponding proportion for unrepresented defendants was 94 per cent. This may be due to the fact that persons charged with serious offences are more likely to be represented, and the authors of the study argue that the discrepancy may be due to the fact that the police objected to bail in 19 per cent of cases where the defendant was represented but in only 6 per cent of cases where the defendant was unrepresented. A more recent study found that 94 per cent of defendants were legally represented and that magistrates and clerks made every effort to persuade unrepresented defendants to seek legal advice (Hucklesby, *supra*, p. 147). The study found no cases of an unrepresented defendant being remanded in custody.

Know your tribunal

The cardinal rule of advocacy – know your tribunal – applies as much to the bail decision as it does to trials and pleas in mitigation. Courts are reputed to be either 'hard' or 'soft' on bail. Writing before the introduction of the Crown Prosecution Service (CPS), James Morton described a facet of court life that will be remembered with less than fondness by many older practitioners (although possibly mitigated by the sense of nostalgia for anything that tends to be associated with lost youth):

> One of the greatest difficulties in applying for bail is that rules may vary from town to town and even from courtroom to courtroom. Some magistrates accept a statement by the prosecution or even the Court Inspector by way of objections to bail. Some agree that the officer in the case should give evidence and submit to cross-examination. Some will not allow it . . . Some courts will even make the defendant apply for bail without hearing the prosecution evidence or even the grounds for their objections' ('Why the Bail Lottery Needs Reform', *Guardian*, 10 November 1980)

It is now unusual for police officers to attend magistrates' courts on remand hearings, and the objections or observations on bail are in most cases given by the crown prosecutor. This is sometimes expressed in a bland or even dull manner, and means that the defence has no scope for cross-examination.

The anecdotal evidence of practitioners regarding variation between courts is supported by empirical evidence which shows that a defendant is ten times more likely to be refused bail at some magistrates' courts than at others (Winfield, M., *Lacking Conviction: The Remand System in England and Wales*, London: Prison Reform Trust, 1984). Variations have also been found in the proportion of defendants remanded in custody, ranging from 7 per cent in Bedfordshire to 37 per cent in North Yorkshire (Jones, P., 'Remand Decisions in Magistrates' Courts', in Moxon, D. (ed.), *Managing Criminal Justice*, London: HMSO, 1985, p. 117).

The Home Office has recognised the disparate nature of bail decisions and has urged courts to be more consistent:

> In the interests of justice and public confidence, the approach adopted by courts when taking decisions on bail should be reasonably consistent, subject of course to differing mixes of offences and defendants encountered in its courts . . . But, as a general principle, the decision on whether the defendant is remanded in custody or bailed ought not to depend upon the particular attitude of the bench before which he appears. (Home Office circular 25/1988, para. 4)

Court culture

Hucklesby has suggested that the variation in the bail/custody rate cannot be fully explained by differences in the types of cases and defendants appearing in different courts (Hucklesby, A., 'Court Culture: An Explanation of Variations in the Use of Bail by Magistrates' Courts', *Howard Journal*, May 1997, vol. 36, No. 2, pp. 129–145). She argues that the variation may be explained by the culture of the court. By this she means that the reputation of the court and of individual magistrates influences the expectations of the participants, which in turn influences their working practices. Prosecutors and defence advocates adjust their approach to bail according to their view of the court's likely response. This feeds back into the reputation of the court as lenient or hard and perpetuates the culture of the court.

Are the objectives of the remand decision contradictory?

Hucklesby has argued that the objectives of the remand decision are contradictory (1994 unpublished PhD thesis, *supra*, p. 124). She identifies a due process objective (every defendant (to whom s. 4 of the Bail Act 1976 applies) has the right to bail) and a crime control objective (the protection of the public). It is arguable that many of the changes to the Bail Act since its original enactment have shifted the emphasis from the first objective to the second. The most striking example is the exclusion of bail in cases of homicide or rape where the defendant has a previous conviction for any such offence (s. 25 of the Criminal Justice and Public Order Act 1994, now ameliorated by s. 56 of the Crime and Disorder Act 1998: see Chapter 1, para. 1.2.4). The provision as originally enacted is also an illustration of the movement from judicial decision-making to executive decision-making. The amendment introduced by s. 56 of the Crime and Disorder Act 1998, which creates a rebuttable presumption that bail will not be granted in such cases in place of an absolute exclusion of bail, retains the same objective. As the Solicitor-General, Lord Falconer, has stated: 'We see this new provision as allowing some flexibility to prevent injustice, while ensuring that the protection of the public remains the primary concern and providing a tough additional safeguard against bad bail decisions in these particularly serious circumstances' (HL Deb vol. 588, cols. 239–240, 31 March 1998).

The Bail (Amendment) Act 1993 takes the shift in emphasis a stage further. The statute has the effect of allowing the prosecution to overturn the presumption in favour of bail pending the determination of its application to the Crown Court, even though the magistrates' court, by its decision to grant bail, found that none of the exceptions to bail applied (Hucklesby, A., 'Unnecessary Legislative Change,' *New Law Journal*, 1993, vol. 143, pp. 233–34 and 255). Arguably the Act also removes from prosecutors the character of 'ministers of justice assisting in the administration of justice' (*per* Avory J in *R v Banks* [1916] 2 KB 621, at 623) and puts the prosecution firmly in the arena. Fears that the CPS will lose its independence have been heightened by a recommendation in the Glidewell Report 'to bridge the gulf between the police and the CPS' (Glidewell, Sir Iain, *The Review of the Crown Prosecution Service*, Cm. 3972, London: HMSO, 1998, para. 28).

An illustration of a shift in the opposite direction – towards the presumption in favour of bail – is to be found in *R* v *Rafferty*, *The Times*, 9 April 1998, in which the Court of Appeal held that a defendant's bail status on committal for sentence should remain as it was prior to the hearing at which he is committed for sentence. The effect of the decision is to extend the presumption in favour of bail to circumstances for which it was never intended. The clear authority in s. 4(2) of the Bail Act 1976 is that the general right to bail does not apply after conviction. The explanation for this unprincipled approach is probably, as James Richardson has suggested, a 'desire to provide as many inducements as possible to defendants to plead guilty and to do so as quickly as possible' (*Criminal Law Week*, CLW/98/14/32).

Does reform achieve its objectives?

Writing in 1996, the late Lord Chief Justice, Lord Taylor of Gosforth, observed:

> We have had more Criminal Justice Acts in the past six years than in the preceding sixty. . . . It is not just the volume of legislation that has become alarming, with each successive Criminal Justice Act treading on the last one's heels. It is also the haste with which each is prepared. Significant and complex reforms are introduced by way of amendment halfway through the progress of a Bill through Parliament. As a result, inconsistencies and lacunae have to be cured in the Court of Appeal or even by yet more legislation. (*The Times*, 7 March 1996)

Research findings on sch. 1, Part I, para. 2A to the Bail Act 1976, as inserted by s. 26 of the Criminal Justice and Public Order Act 1994 (exception to the right to bail for persons accused or convicted of an indictable or either-way offence committed whilst on bail) suggest that the reform has not had its intended effect (see Chapter 1, para. 1.5.3).

A further illustration is provided by the power of the police to impose conditions after charge (s. 3A of the Bail Act 1976, as inserted by s. 27 of the Criminal Justice and Public Order Act 1994). This was no doubt a well-intentioned measure designed to avoid the overnight detention of persons considered by the police to be suitable for conditional bail. In theory, the measure should provide savings to police staffing of custody suites, to the maintenance of police cells, to forensic medical examiner call-outs and to prisoner transport, as well as to the CPS, probation service and the court. In practice, initial research conducted for the Home Office indicates that the provision imposes additional resource costs in such areas as:

- *legal aid* – solicitors spend more time in police stations negotiating conditions
- *court time* – courts spend additional time establishing what conditions were imposed by the police

- *police time* – in considering conditions, checking the defendant's circumstances and additional paperwork
- *police training*
- *police monitoring* of conditions imposed.

(See Raine, J. and Willson, J., *Police Bail with Conditions – The Cost/Savings Effect of the New Power – Report to the Home Office, 1996*, unpublished, pp. 5–8, read by the authors with kind permission of the Home Office.) The authors of the report conclude that the data are open to two possible, and contrasting, interpretations. Conditional police bail may be seen as a valuable instrument of crime control, or it may draw defendants further into the criminal justice system by making them liable to further trouble if caught in breach of the conditions imposed. Thus, observe Raine and Willson, 'the imposition of bail conditions may be questionable both in terms of justice and crime control' (*ibid.*, p. 12).

Legal reform may also have more subtle, unintended consequences. It has been suggested that the Bail (Amendment) Act 1993 may have the following effects:

(a) Prosecution expectations may be based not only on the culture of the magistrates' court but also on expectations of the judge's decision.

(b) The prosecution will be more confident in opposing bail because of the possibility of appeal.

(c) Magistrates may be more reluctant to grant bail in the face of prosecution objections for fear of a successful prosecution appeal.

(d) Conversely, in some cases where they are unsure, magistrates may grant bail in the knowledge that if the prosecution appeal, the decision will be made by a Crown Court judge.

(Hucklesby, A., 'Court Culture: An Explanation of Variations in the Use of Bail by Magistrates' Courts', *Howard Journal*, May 1997, vol. 36, No. 2, pp. 129–45 at p. 142; article written before the implementation of the Bail (Amendment) Act 1993.)

Reducing Remand Delays

It was argued in the first edition of this book (Corre, N. *Bail in Criminal Proceedings*, London: Fourmat Publishing, 1990, p. 151) that reforms designed to reduce custodial waiting time are as important as those designed to reduce the number of receptions into custody. A number of recent reforms are designed to reduce remand delays:

- the abolition of 'live' old-style committals (s. 47 of, and sch. 1 to the Criminal Procedure and Investigations Act 1996)
- the power of the judge to order a preparatory hearing (s. 29 of the Criminal Procedure and Investigations Act 1996)

- the abolition of committal proceedings for indictable-only offences (s. 51 of the Crime and Disorder Act 1998)
- the duty of custody officers to bail a defendant to the first sitting of a court after charge (s. 47(3A) of the Police and Criminal Evidence Act 1984, as inserted by s. 46 of the Crime and Disorder Act 1998)
- the extension of custody time limits to the start of trial (s. 22(11A) and (11B) of the Prosecution of Offences Act 1985, as inserted by s. 71 of the Criminal Procedure and Investigations Act 1996)
- the power of the court to impose conditions to ensure that a defendant attends an interview with a legal representative (s. 3(6)(e) of the Bail Act 1976, as inserted by s. 54(2) of the Crime and Disorder Act 1998)
- plea before venue (s. 17A of the Magistrates' Courts Act 1980, as inserted by s. 49(2) of the Criminal Procedure and Investigations Act 1996)
- the imposition of overall time limits and the power of the Secretary of State to set different time limits for different types of case, different areas, and different classes of person (s. 22(2) of the Prosecution of Offences Act 1985, as substituted by s. 43(1) of the Crime and Disorder Act 1998)
- additional time limits for defendants under the age of 18 (s. 22A of the Prosecution of Offences Act 1985, as inserted by s. 44 of the Crime and Disorder Act 1998)
- the more restricted grounds for extending a time limit (s. 22(3) of the Prosecution of Offences Act 1985, as substituted by s. 43(2) of the Crime and Disorder Act 1998)
- the power of a youth court to remit a person who subsequently attains the age of 18 to the magistrates' court (s. 47(1) of the Crime and Disorder Act 1998)
- the power of a youth court to commit related offences to the crown court along with grave crimes (s. 24(1A) of the Magistrates' Courts Act 1980, as inserted by s. 47(3) of the Crime and Disorder Act 1998)
- the presumption against adjourning youth court cases solely on the ground that the defendant is committed to the Crown Court in respect of a separate offence, or the accused is charged with another offence (s. 10(3A) of the Magistrates' Courts Act 1980, as inserted by s. 47(2) of the Crime and Disorder Act 1998)

Measures designed to ensure the attendance of the defendant

In 1997, an estimated 11 per cent of defendants bailed failed to appear. More than 44,000 offenders were found guilty at magistrates' courts of failing to attend. Some 4,000 bench warrants were issued at the Crown Court and 6 per cent of defendants on bail to the Crown Court failed to appear (*Criminal Statistics England and Wales 1997*, Cm. 4162, London: HMSO, 1998, paras 8.1–8.12, pp. 181–182).

Some recent reforms are designed to ensure the defendant's attendance at court. The court now has the power to impose a security in all cases when it is considered necessary – not just where it appears that the defendant will not remain in Great Britain (s. 54(1) of the Crime and Disorder Act 1998). Recognizances are now liable to forfeiture upon the defendant's failure to appear (s. 120(1A) of the Magistrates' Courts Act 1980, as inserted by s. 55(1) of the Crime and Disorder Act 1998).

As has previously been argued, legislative reform does not always achieve its intended purpose. These measures may lead to an increase in the remand population if securities are imposed in cases where they cannot be met, and if the fear of immediate forfeiture results in fewer people being willing to stand surety.

The remand population

The remand population in 1996 was 11,600 (*The Prison Population in 1996*, Home Office Statistical Bulletin No. 18/97, London: Home Office, 1997). Research predicts that the remand population could be as high as 13,300 by the year 2000 and 15,900 by 2005, or as low as 12,300 by 2000 and 12,400 by 2005 (White, P. and Powah, I., *Revised Projections of Long-Term Trends in the Prison Population to 2005*, Home Office Statistical Bulletin No. 2/1998, London: Home Office, 1998). Using the regression method, the prediction is 13,400 by 2000 and 15,400 by 2005.

The European Convention on Human Rights

It is worth mentioning that Article 5 of the European Convention for the Protection of Human Rights and Fundamental Freedoms, Cm. 8969, 1950 provides:

(1) Everyone has the right to liberty and security of the person. No one shall be deprived of his liberty save in the following cases and in accordance with a procedure prescribed by law . . .

(c) the lawful arrest or detention of a person effected for the purpose of bringing him before the competent legal authority on reasonable suspicion of having committed an offence or when it is reasonably considered necessary to prevent his committing an offence or fleeing after having done so . . .

(3) Everyone arrested or detained in accordance with the provisions of paragraph (1)(c) of this Article shall be brought promptly before a judge or other officer authorised by law to exercise judicial power and shall be entitled to trial within a reasonable time or to release pending trial. Release may be conditioned by guarantees to appear for trial.

Persons charged with an offence must be released pending trial unless the state can show that there are 'relevant and sufficient' reasons to justify their continued detention: *Wemhoff* v *FRG*, 1 EHRR 55. There are four categories of acceptable reasons:

1. *Risk that the accused will fail to appear for trial*
The refusal of bail on the ground that the accused will fail to appear for trial requires 'a whole set of circumstances . . . which give reason to suppose that the

consequences and hazards of flight will seem to the accused to be a lesser evil than continued imprisonment': *Stögmüller* v *Austria* [1969] 1 EHRR 155. Relevant considerations may be 'the character of the person involved, his morals, his home, his occupation, his assets, his family ties, and all kinds of links with the country in which he is being prosecuted': *Neumeister* v *Austria* 1 EHRR 91. The severity of the likely sentence, although an important consideration, is not an independent ground, and cannot itself justify the refusal of bail: *ibid*; *Letellier* v *France* 14 EHRR 83, and see *W* v *Switzerland* [1993] 17 EHRR 60; and *Mansur* v *Turkey* 20 EHRR 535.

2. *Interference with the course of justice*
Bail may properly be refused where there is a well-founded risk that the accused, if released, would take action to prejudice the administration of justice, for example by interfering with witnesses, warning other suspects, or destroying evidence: *Wemhoff* v *FRG, supra*; *Letellier* v *France, supra*. However, the risk must be identifiable and supported by evidence and a generalised risk would be insufficient: *Clooth* v *Belgium*, 14 EHRR 717.

3. *Prevention of other offences*
Where there are good reasons to believe that the accused, if released, would be likely to commit offences, the public interest in crime prevention may justify refusal of bail: *Matznetter* v *Austria*, 1 EHRR 198; *Toth* v *Austria*, 14 EHRR 551.

4. *Preservation of public order*
Temporary detention of the accused on remand may be justified where the nature of the crime alleged and the likely public reaction are such that the release of the accused may give rise to public disorder: *Letellier* v *France, supra*, where the court stressed that this was confined to offences of particular gravity.

The principle of 'equality of arms,' *i.e.* the primacy of a fair trial guaranteed by Art. 6, also applies to bail proceedings: *Woukam Moudefo* v *France* 13 EHRR 549. This includes a right to disclosure of prosecution evidence for the purposes of making a bail application: *Lamy* v *Belgium*, 11 EHRR 529. Reasons for refusing bail should be given: *Tomasi* v *France* 15 EHRR 1. Renewed applications should be entertained at reasonable intervals: *Bezicheri* v *Italy* 12 EHRR 210.

Permissible conditions of bail include a requirement to surrender travel documents and driving documents (*Stögmuller* v *Austria, supra*; *Schmid* v *Austria*, 44 DR 195), a residence requirement (*Schmid* v *Austria*), and the provision of a surety or security (*Wemhoff* v *FRG, supra*). Where a financial condition is imposed, the figure must be gauged by reference to the accused's means, if it is a security, or to that of the person standing surety, and must take account of the relationship between the two: *Neumeister* v *Austria, supra*; *Schertenleib* v *Switzerland*, 23 DR 137.

1 The Right to Bail

1.1 THE ORIGINS OF THE RIGHT TO BAIL

1.1.1 The early Norman period

The right to to be bailed,' Sir James Stephen observed, 'is as old as the law of England itself, and is explicitly recognised by our earliest writers' (*A History of the Criminal Law of England*, 3 vols, London: Macmillan, 1883 (hereafter *HCL*), vol. i, p. 233). He notes, for example, that Glanville recognised the right 'in curt and general terms' (*Tractatus de Legibus et Conseutudinibus Regni Angliae*, xiv, c. 1). In early English criminal justice there was no preliminary inquiry prior to the holding of the sheriff's tourn or, in more serious cases, the commission of oyer and terminer and general gaol delivery. Since there might be long delays, even of years, before the king's itinerant justices arrived to undertake that commission it was important for defendants to be able to obtain a provisional release from custody. In the early Norman period sheriffs asserted a discretion of releasing on pledge to sureties, anyone appealed of grave crime, including even homicide, and discretionary release seems to have become the norm. Imprisonment was costly and inconvenient, escape was easy, there were serious consequences for sheriffs in permitting escape, and they preferred to avoid the responsibility of keeping accused persons secure by handing them over to their friends or relatives pending trial (see Pollock, Sir F., and Maitland, F.W., *The History of English Law before the Time of Edward I*, 2 vols, Cambridge: Cambridge University Press, 1st ed. 1895; 2nd ed. 1898 (1911 printing); reissued 1968 with additional material, vol. ii, 584; De Haas, E., *Antiquities of Bail: origin and historical development in criminal cases to the year 1275*, New York: Columbia University Press, 1940 (noting consequences for the sheriffs in permitting escape)). In 1166 the Assize of Clarendon established the jury of presentment as the principal means of initiating prosecution and the sworn certainty of the appeal of felony thus gave way to accusation upon suspicion (Langbein, I.L., 'The Jury of Presentment and the Coroner', *Columbia Law Review*, 1933, vol. 33, p. 1329). With arrest upon conjecture, release on bail proved all the more necessary as a factor in obtaining justice (De Haas, *op. cit.*).

The general practice of release is described by Glanville, but he also refers to a prohibition on bail in cases of homicide, presumably introduced by some now unidentified ruling or ordinance: 'in all pleas of felony, the accused is generally dismissed on pledge, except in a plea of homicide, where for the sake of striking terror it is otherwise decreed' (*Tractatus, loc. cit.*). There were also exceptions in the case of forest offences and imprisonment by special command of the king or his chief justiciar. The exceptions must have been introduced before 1190 (the year of Glanville's death) but it is not known whether the homicide exception was introduced before or after 1179, the year in which, Radolph de Diceto tells us, Henry II decreed hanging as the punishment for homicide (*Opera Historica*, i, 434, Rolls series.) It is not possible to say for certain therefore whether it was the introduction of the death penalty which caused bail to be forbidden in homicide cases. Moreover, Henry I had decreed hanging for some thefts without banning locally authorised bail in such cases. When hanging replaced mutilation for most major felonies during the late 12th and 13th centuries there was no commensurate prohibition of local bail.

1.1.2   Obtaining release by royal writ

Bail was certainly not unobtainable in the situations designated as 'irreplevisable', that is where the accused was not eligible for 'replevin', i.e. release on bail. Release could be secured by means of various types of writ issued in the King's courts. Central records such as the *Rotuli litterarum clausarum*, the Close Rolls and the Calendar of Close Rolls, contain hundreds of instances in which the central office ordered the sheriff, constable or other local official, holding a man for homicide, to release him to the care of sureties or 'mainpernors'. Feudal lords were always anxious to maintain their labour force, and virtually anyone who could pay for a writ from Chancery would benefit. Moreover, the vagueness of a law which gave sheriffs an almost limitless discretion over bail meant that even where bail was plainly called for there was no certainty it would be granted, and royal writs became available to redress the problem of the unjust withholding of bail by requiring sheriffs or other relevant officials to do their duty.

Most important of the several forms of royal writ issuing out of Chancery were the writ *de homine replegiando*, the writ *de manucaptione*, and the writ *de odio et atiâ*. Under the procedure for all of them, if the first writ issued was disobeyed, a second, called an 'alias', was issued and a fine could be levied for delay. If the alias was disobeyed, a third, called a 'pluries', was issued and, similarly, a fine for delay could be levied. The final remedy was an attachment by which the recalcitrant officer was imprisoned.

Even a brief historical introduction to the subject of bail would be incomplete without some account at least of the three writs. It has been observed, however, that they could never have been of the first importance and must soon have fallen into disuse (Stephen, *HCL*, i, pp. 242–43). The reason is probably that from the earliest times the superior courts and the Lord Chancellor had available a simpler and more straightforward means of achieving the same object, namely the writ of habeas corpus, a procedure which is addressed elsewhere in the present work.

1.1.2.1 *De homine replegiando*   One of the first records for the purchase of this writ is located in the Pipe Roll records for 1165–1166 (the year of the Assize of Clarendon, which permitted arrest on conjecture). The writ applied to cases in which a person was imprisoned before trial for an offence bailable under 3 Edw. 1, c. 12 and to cases in which a person was unlawfully detained by anyone not having legal authority to do so. It was not available in homicide. The sheriff might respond to the writ that the detained person had been 'eloigned' – carried off too far to be located – in which event a further writ might require the sheriff to imprison the captor until he produced the detained person.

1.1.2.2 *De manucaptione*   This writ, known as the writ of mainprise, was issued in cases in which a person arrested on suspicion of felony had tendered 'manucaptors', or 'mainpernors', who had been rejected. Although the terms 'bail' and 'mainprise' came to be used interchangeably there were apparently technical differences described by Hale (*Pleas of the Crown*, 2 vols, London 1736, ii, 140). Stephen found the differences so described 'very obscure' (*HCL*, i, 241).

1.1.2.3 *De odio et atiâ*   This writ was restricted to cases of homicide and, according to Stephen, had 'an odd history' and 'a singularly clumsy procedure' (*ibid.*). The writ is described by Bracton (*De Legibus et Consuetudinis Angliae*, 2 vols, 1250–56, ii, pp. 292–96) in a passage which seems to provide for bail where the prosecutor was moved by hatred or malice. Stephen suggests that the true issue to be examined was the evidence of the guilt of the accused, and that the 'odium et atya' were mere legal figments by which the presence or absence of reasonable cause of suspicion was obscurely denoted (*HCL*, i, 241). If a man hated another, Stephen explained, because he had been seen committing a murder, his hatred would be no reason why he should not prosecute the criminal. If the prosecutor was unable to assign any cause for the prosecution, it would not be unnatural to say that he must hate the person imprisoned. If there was evidence, malice was immaterial. If there was no evidence malice was inferred. Hence, the sufficiency of the evidence, being the real point, was inquired into under the pretence of inquiring into the malice. The effect of the writ, therefore, was to occasion a preliminary inquiry in cases of homicide, the result of which determined whether the accused should be admitted to bail or held in custody until he was finally tried. If malice was established he was admitted to bail on finding 12 sureties. It was unclear when the writ was abolished, but in any event it largely fell into disuse.

1.1.3   The Statute of Westminster I of 1275

The strict enforcement of the prohibition of local bail in cases of homicide, forest offences and imprisonment by royal command presupposes a degree of centralisation which was not reached until after the Statute of Westminster I of 1275 (3 Ed. I, c. 12). There are in the Assize Rolls of Yorkshire for 1218–1219 some examples of bail being granted in homicide without reference to central government (*Rolls of the Justices in Eyre, Being the Rolls of Pleas and Assizes for Yorkshire in 3*

Henry III, London: Seldon Society Publications, 1937, vol. 56 (pleas 865, 871, 895, 918 and 967)). These cases appear to have been outright breaches of the rule against local bail in homicide, suggesting that some such practice as extortion must have been at work. But even in less extreme instances chicanery appears to have been commonplace. Although Bracton (d. 1268) advised that in exercising their discretion sheriffs ought to have regard to the gravity of the charge, the accused's character and the weight of the evidence (*De Corona*, p. 302), beyond this terse guidance the discretion was ill-defined and the general practice of release led to widespread abuses uncovered by the Hundred Inquest investigations. Measures aimed at ending these were eventually introduced by the Statute of Westminster I, an enactment which served as the main foundation of the law of bail for the next 550 years. The preamble recited that sheriffs and others had released on replevin those who were not replevisable and had kept in prison those who were replevisable 'because they would gain of the one part and grieve the other'. Pointing out that apart from homicide, imprisonment by command of the King or his justices and forest offences, the law had not hitherto stated in which cases the accused was replevisable and in which not, the statute proceeded to furnish a list of cases, apparently in addition to the existing categories, in which the accused was not to be replevisable either by the 'common writ or without writ' and others in which prisoners might be released 'by sufficient surety, whereof the sheriff will be answerable, and that without giving ought of their goods'. Those offences (chief amongst which was homicide) which were not replevisable by the common writ or without writ could be made the subject of bail in the superior courts at Westminster, or by habeas corpus. Hawkins noted that the statute made no distinction between homicide of malice, misadventure or self-defence and that the justices of the peace who had power to bail a man arrested for a 'light suspicion of homicide' could not bail any person for manslaughter 'or even excusable homicide' if he was plainly guilty (*Pleas of the Crown*, ii, 95, 105).

The extended prohibition was to apply, *inter alia*, to the outlawed and those who had abjured the realm, to approvers who had confessed, known thieves accused by approvers, felonious arsonists, counterfeiters, excommunicants arrested on a bishop's request, and to those accused of manifest offences, of breaching the King's prison or of treason touching the King himself. The statute permitted bail to those accused of larceny on indictment at the sheriffs' tourn or court leet, or on light suspicion, or of petty larceny not exceeding 12*d*, if not previously convicted of larceny, or of accessory before or after a felony, or of misdemeanour (i.e. trespass not punishable with death or dismemberment), or on accusation by an approver who had died where the accused was not a common thief.

1.1.4 Developments through to the 16th century

Between 1275 and 1444 the function of the sheriffs in admitting prisoners to bail was gradually and largely transferred to the justices of the peace by a series of enabling statutes. The latter date marks the final statute regulating the sheriffs' bail function (23 Hen. 6, c. 9) and required the sheriffs in certain cases to grant bail, in terms which Stephen suggested seem to imply that their refusal to do so had become a well-known abuse (*HCL*, i, 236). In 1330 the statute 4 Edw. 3, c. 1, enacted that persons indicted or arrested by the keepers of the peace should not be let to mainprise (bail) by a sheriff. In 1360 the statute 34 Edw. 3, c. 1, in very general terms gave the justices a power to grant bail. It seems that this must have been taken to apply only to prisoners indicted at the sessions, because the statute 1 Rich, 3, c. 3, of 1485 recited that many people had been daily arrested and imprisoned, some out of malice and sometimes on the basis of 'light suspicion', and empowered justices of the peace to admit such persons to bail as though they were indicted of record before the same justices in their sessions. In 1487, 3 Hen. 7, c. 3, recited that as a result of being admitted to bail by justices of the peace against due form of law many murderers and felons had escaped. It therefore enacted that bail could only be granted by a minimum of two justices, who were required at the next general sessions of the peace or next general gaol delivery to certify that they had done so. The statute also enacted that sheriffs and all other officials having the responsibility for detaining felony prisoners in gaol were to certify the names of all such prisoners who were in custody pending the next gaol delivery. Of itself the requirement for two justices may have afforded little more than a rather limited safeguard against abuse. But the new provisions were probably effective in curtailing the opportunities which had previously allowed offenders to gain complete impunity as a result of there being nothing to warn the court of trial that a single justice had granted bail on little or no security. The new measures formed part of the rigorous administration of justice by which Henry VII grappled with the disorders arising from the Wars of the Roses (see Stephen, *HCL*, i, 237).

1.1.5   The Bail Statute of 1554

The régime introduced by the bail statute of 1554 (1 & 2 Philip and Mary, c. 13) was much more stringent. In cases of felony where the accused was to be given bail pending trial, it made compulsory the complex system of preliminary inquiry and record keeping which had been developing piecemeal over the previous century or two. A modified structure which the committal statute of 1554–55, 2 & 3 P and M, c. 10, made compulsory in all felony, whether bail or custody cases, was to become the fundamental model of pre-trial criminal procedure until the 19th century. (For the definitive study of the bail and committal statutes, see Langbein, J. H., *Prosecuting Crime in the Renaissance*, Cambridge, Massachusetts: Harvard University Press, 1974.) But the original main purpose of the bail statute was to tackle the problem of collusive releases which had recently arisen once again, possibly as a result of Wyatt's rebellion and the attempt to put Lady Jane Grey on the throne. Reciting that 'often times by sinister labour and means . . . the greatest and notablest offenders such as be not replevisable by the laws of the realm' had been set at large, the statute explained how the two justice requirement of 1487 was being evaded. One justice of the peace would grant bail in his own name and that of a companion justice without making that other justice party or privy to the case, and then to 'hide their affections' would signify the cause of the accused's arrest as mere suspicion of felony.

To curtail the abuse the statute laid down that in cases where the accused was bailed depositions were to be taken from the witnesses and transmitted to the court of trial. Fines were imposed for breach. London and other corporate towns and the county of Middlesex were exempted from the Act, for in the great towns where there were aldermen and other magistrates by charter, and a considerable population, the danger of collusion would be less than in the country. There was obviously no need for such precautions in cases in which the accused was held in custody, but in the following year the committal statute introduced measures applicable in all cases of felony which required the taking of depositions, examination of the prisoner, and transmission of the dossier to the trial court. The statute also prohibited justices from bailing persons not eligible for local bail under the Statute of Westminster I.

1.1.6   The 17th century and onwards

The 17th and 18th centuries saw the enactment of numerous statutes regulating bail in relation to a wide variety of specific offences. However, as a matter of general principle the refusal or delay by any judge or magistrate to grant bail to any person entitled to be bailed constituted a violation of the Habeas Corpus Act 1679 and of the Bill of Rights 1688. According to Blackstone, writing in the 18th century, it was also a common law offence against the liberty of the subject (*Commentaries*, 297). However, it was held in the 19th century that the bail decision was a judicial one and not ministerial or administrative, and therefore no action could lie against a magistrate without proof of malice for refusing to admit to bail a person charged with an offence: *R* v *Badger* (1843) 4 QB 468; *Linford* v *Fitzroy* (1849) 13 QB 247; *Osborne* v *Gough* 3 B & P 551. In *R* v *Rose* (1898) 78 LT 119, Lord Russell said 'It cannot be too strongly impressed on the magistracy that bail is not to be withheld as a punishment'. Since this is a truism which needs no expressing, it can hardly be imagined that it would not be malicious for any magistrate or judge to deny bail out of such a motive.

The numerous bail provisions of the 17th and 18th centuries relating to specific offences were all repealed by s. 32 of the Criminal Law Act 1826 (7 Geo. 4, c. 64), a general measure which made new provisions on bail and brought the law of bail and preliminary procedure under a single umbrella. It placed the grant of bail on an entirely new footing, and instead of requiring the decision to be determined by reference to the nature of the offence charged (effectively the test since 1275) made it contingent on the weight of the evidence. Section 1 provided that on an accusation of felony or suspicion of felony where the evidence was positive or credible such as raised, in the words of the section, a 'strong presumption' of guilt, the accused was to be detained in custody. If, however, it merely showed sufficient ground for judicial inquiry into the issue of guilt, the accused, on going before two justices, could be granted bail under s. 2. Later on, the statute 5 & 6 Will. IV, c. 33, s. 3, broadened still further the progressive nature of the thinking behind the new statutory regime by enacting that bail was permitted even after a confession, a reflection of the mood of suspicion which the common law felt towards self-incrimination.

The 1826 statute was superseded by the Indictable Offences Act 1848 (11 & 12, Vict. c. 42) which remained in force until itself replaced by succeeding legislation in the 20th century. A single justice was permitted to act on matters of bail. Section 25 referred to the two standards in the Act of 1826 and provided that, even if the evidence only came up to the lower standard in the 1826 Act, the accused could still be committed to prison. However, s. 23 gave the committing justice or justices an unfettered discretion to grant bail or to withhold it (although the latter option was not expressly mentioned) in the case of any felony or of any common misdemeanour. In cases of libel, conspiracy to commit a number of specific misdemeanours listed in the Act, unlawful assembly, night poaching and seditious offences, and in misdemeanours created by special acts, bail could not be refused. In cases of high treason bail was impermissible except by order of a Secretary of State or by the High Court. (This provision perpetuated the principle in 34 Geo. III, c. 54, which had prohibited any person imprisoned under a warrant signed by a Secretary of State on a charge of high treason from insisting upon being discharged under habeas corpus.) The 1848 Act contained a series of provisions (ss. 23 and 24) governing the granting of bail after committal, with sureties.

The independence of the courts in determining whether or not to grant bail has always been reflected in the principle under common law that, provided they act judicially, they enjoy a discretion to grant bail despite objection by the prosecution and to refuse bail even though the prosecution raise no objection. It was formerly said that the requirements of bail were merely to secure the attendance of the defendant at trial (*R* v *Rose* (1898) 78 LT 119). This is plainly no longer the case, since in *R* v *Phillips* (1947) 32 Cr App R 47 the likelihood that the offence might be repeated if bail were granted was acknowledged to be a vital consideration. However, although no longer the exclusive consideration in granting bail, securing attendance remains the primary concern and there is little doubt, therefore, that the discretion is to be exercised on the basis of criteria harking back to at least Bracton (see para. 1.1.3,). These are:

    (a)   the nature of the accusation: see *Re Barronet and Allain* (1852) 1 E & B 1;
    (b)   the nature of the evidence in support of the accusation: see *Re Robinson* (1854) 23 LJQB 286; and
    (c)   the severity of the punishment on conviction: *ibid.*

The importance of these was reiterated in *R* v *Phillips*. The independence of the sureties and the question of whether they are to be indemnified by the accused are essential concerns: *Herman* v *Jeuchner* (1885) 15 QBD 561; *Consolidated*

Exploration and Finance Company v *Musgrave* [1900] 1 Ch 37; *R* v *Porter* [1910] 1 KB 369 (see further Chapter 2, para. 2.1.17). They are conventionally addressed obliquely by the courts through a routine inquiry into the means of the proposed surety.

1.1.7   Bail in murder: the duelling cases and other aspects

It has been seen that throughout the history of bail since the middle ages there has run a consistent thread of concern about granting bail to persons accused of homicide. The issue was highlighted in two cases four years after the 1848 Act which gave justices a complete discretion in all cases of felony regardless of the nature of the offence. Both arose out of duelling incidents involving expatriate French citizens. In *Re Barronet and Allain* (above) a writ of habeas corpus was sought to release the French seconds in a fatal duel. On behalf of the application it was submitted that the duel had been fair, and although it involved murder, the sentence was unlikely to be enforced against two foreigners, ignorant of English law, who were refugees from a country where duelling was legal. Reference was made to *Re Allen* (1782) *The Annual Register*, Chronicle, 211, at p. 213, in which the applicant had killed a man in a duel and, so it was reported, had been bailed to stand trial. In rejecting the application Lord Campbell CJ observed that it was not clear that the report was accurate in stating that the accused had 'surrendered' himself at the Old Bailey; but that even if it was accurate, the justice of the peace who had bailed him had acted unlawfully. It is not clear why Lord Campbell made this assumption, since there was no reason to assume that the accused was not granted bail by order of a judge of the Queen's Bench. In *Re Barthelemy* (1852) 1 E & B 8, the decision also involved two seconds in a duel between Frenchmen, but there had been no admissions of guilt as had been the case in *Re Barronet*. Reliance was placed on two duelling case rulings in favour of bail, which it appears were cited from newspaper reports. These were *Re Gulliver* (1843), in which the surgeon in attendance at a fatal duel was committed for trial on bail, and the *Earl of Cardigan's case*, in which the shooting was non-fatal and Lord Cardigan, despite having confessed to a magistrate, was bailed with his second, a commoner. Nevertheless, while conceding that the principle of bail in murder had never been denied, Lord Campbell rejected the application on the ground that there was clear evidence that a murder had been committed and a strong indication of guilt.

Even before the abolition of the death penalty for murder, the admission of defendants to bail on murder charges was not unknown. In 1938 a woman appeared on bail at Leeds Assizes for the murder of her mentally handicapped son, aged five, believing it to be her duty in the eyes of God (see 'Some Notes on Bail' ((1938) 2 JCL 316). There had been no suggestion before the committing magistrate of mental disorder, but it was probably taken for granted that the accused would never go to the gallows. In creating the special category of non-capital murder, the Homicide Act 1957 inevitably established a climate for admitting some defendants to bail in such cases, and within a short time Thomas

James Harding was bailed pending trial for non-capital murder at Liverpool Crown Court, where he was acquitted and discharged on 6 November 1957 (see Morris, T., and Blom-Cooper, L., *A Calendar of Murder*, London: Michael Joseph, 1964, p. 13). Following the abolition of capital punishment for murder by the Murder (Abolition of Death Penalty) Act 1965, it was not unexpected that some defendants accused of murder would be admitted to bail. In *R v Carr* it was reported that the defendant, charged with murder, was admitted to bail by the Liverpool stipendiary magistrate (*The Times*, 8 February 1966; see also *McLaren v HM Advocate* [1967] Crim LR 422, commentary). The prosecution had stated that the accused had been subjected to an unprovoked assault by his son and had stabbed him in the course of defending himself. In 1970, six youths appeared at Balham magistrates' court charged with the murder of a ticket collector at Balham railway station ((1970) 34 JCL 218). Three were granted bail with sureties and at the subsequent remand hearing no evidence was offered against them. Of a total of 287 persons proceeded against for murder in England and Wales in 1969, as many as 24 were admitted to bail (*Criminal Statistics, England and Wales 1969*, Cmnd 4398, London: HMSO, 1970, Table Ia, p. 14). In recent years there have been reported in the popular press relatively so many murder trials in which defendants have been on bail that the practice may be treated as a commonplace.

1.2   THE STATUTORY GENERAL RIGHT TO BAIL

1.2.1   Enactment of the general right in section 4 of the Bail Act 1976

Two decades ago the general law on bail was addressed by Parliament in a dedicated statute, the Bail Act 1976 (BA 1976), the central feature of which, contained in s. 4, was to declare a general right to bail, usually cited as 'the presumption in favour of bail'. This is sometimes regarded as a corollary to the presumption of innocence, although its historical roots are quite different. The report of the Home Office Working Party on bail procedures in magistrates' courts recommended that there should be a presumption in favour of bail, that the onus should not be on the defendant to apply for bail but that the court should of its own volition consider on each occasion when it remands an accused whether the remand should be on bail or in custody (*Bail Procedures in Magistrates' Courts, Report of the Home Office Working Party*, London: HMSO, 1974). The Working Party attempted to codify good practice, and, as its recommendations were embodied in the Bail Act, the statute itself may be regarded as a codification of existing good practice. Some commentators have argued that it was unnecessary to enact a presumption in favour of bail because it was already implicit. Thus, Eric Crowther, a metropolitan stipendiary magistrate, observed:

> Although I do remember one court in the 1960s where the chairman always used to say, 'if the police say there will be no bail, there will be no bail' (that court at least had the virtue of consistency), I would have thought that such an attitude

had disappeared by the mid-1970s after a decade of compulsory training for justices. (Crowther, E., *Advocacy for the Advocate*, 2nd ed., Harlow: Longman, 1990, p. 110, in Chap. 10, 'To bail or not to bail')

Again, Michael Mott, a judge of the Crown Court, declared in a letter to the *Criminal Law Review* that the Bail Act was 'not a great seachange' ([1989] Crim LR 849).

Although the authority of these commentators can hardly be denied, it must be stressed that the aim and achievement of the Bail Act was to rationalise the bail decision by distinguishing the exceptions to the right to bail from the reasons for applying those exceptions. Although this may have been good practice before the Act it was not universally followed and was lacking in statutory authority. Section 18(5) of the Criminal Justice Act 1967 had laid down exceptions for refusing bail when dealing with offences punishable with not more than six months' imprisonment, but otherwise the court had unlimited discretion. Bail would be refused for a number of reasons, such as the fact that the defendant was of no fixed abode, that he had previous convictions, that there were further police inquiries or that the alleged offence was serious.

1.2.2 Meaning of 'bail in criminal proceedings'

Section 1(1) of the BA 1976 provides that the expression 'bail in criminal proceedings' means in the context of the Act:

(a) bail grantable in or in connection with proceedings for an offence to a person who is accused or convicted of the offence; or

(b) bail grantable in connection with an offence to a person who is under arrest for the offence or for whose arrest for the offence a warrant (endorsed for bail) is being issued.

The word 'bail' means bail grantable under the law (including common law) for the time being in force: s. 1(2). Section 1 does not apply to bail in or in connection with *proceedings* outside England and Wales (s. 1(3)), but it does apply (i) whether the offence was committed in England or Wales or elsewhere, and (ii) whether it is an offence under the law of England and Wales, or of any other country or territory (s. 1(5)). It is provided that bail in criminal proceedings shall be granted (and in particular shall be granted unconditionally or conditionally) in accordance with the Act: s. 1(6).

1.2.3 Applicability of the general right in section 4

1.2.3.1 Circumstances in which section 4 is applicable Section 4 defines the ambit of the applicability of the general right to bail. Subject to various exceptions it applies to the following categories of person:

(a)   Unconvicted persons. It applies to any defendant who is accused of an offence and appears or is brought before a magistrates' court or the Crown Court in the course of or in connection with proceedings for the offence (s. 4(2)(a)).

(b)   Unconvicted persons applying for bail. It applies to any defendant accused of an offence who applies to the court for bail or for a variation of the conditions of bail in connection with the proceedings (s. 4(2)(b); 'variation' in relation to bail means the imposition of further conditions after bail is granted, or the variation or rescinding of conditions: s. 2(2)).

(c)   Convicted persons in breach of community sentences. It applies to any person who, having been convicted of an offence, appears or is brought before a magistrates' court to be dealt with under Part II of sch. 2 to the Criminal Justice Act 1991 (CJA 1991) for breach of requirement of a probation, community service, combination or curfew order (s. 4(3), as amended by the CJA 1991, s. 100 and sch. 11, para. 21).

(d)   Convicted persons remanded for reports. It applies to any person convicted of an offence whose case is adjourned by the court for the purpose of enabling reports to be made to assist the court in dealing with the offender for the offence (s. 4(4)).

1.2.3.2   Right to bail exists independently of application for bail   The right to bail applies to any defendant who is accused of an offence and appears or is brought before a magistrates' court or the Crown Court in the course of or in connection with proceedings for the offence. Although there will be many occasions when the prosecution apply for a defendant to be remanded in custody and the defence make no application for bail, the defendant will nevertheless still enjoy the right to bail unless any of the statutory exceptions applies. It follows that even though no application for bail is made the court is still obliged to consider whether the right to bail applies in the particular case irrespective of the defence stance. In other words, the consent to a remand in custody is not equivalent to the resolution of a potential issue in litigation by consent between the parties which the court is bound to accept. In cases where the statutory right to bail does not apply and there is no application for bail, the court enjoys a discretion whether or not to grant bail.

1.2.3.3   Meaning of 'court'   The expression 'court' includes a judge of a court and a justice of the peace and, in the case of a specified court, includes a judge or (as the case may be) justice having powers to act in connection with proceedings before that court: s. 2(2). In sch. 1, the term 'court' in the expression 'sentence of the court' includes a service court as defined in s. 12(1) of the Visiting Forces Act 1952: Part III, para. 4.

1.2.3.4   Presence of accused in court   Section 4(2) of the BA 1976 enacts that the right to bail 'applies to a person who is accused of an offence when:

(a)   he appears or is brought before a magistrates' court or the Crown Court in the course of or in connection with proceedings for the offence, or

(b)   he applies to a court for bail or for a variation of the conditions of bail in connection with the proceedings.'

Where an enactment (whenever passed) which relates to bail in criminal proceedings refers to the person bailed *appearing* before a court it is to be construed unless the context otherwise requires as referring to the person surrendering into the custody of the court (s. 2(3); see para. 1.2.3.1). The disjunction in s. 4(2)(a) between a person who 'appears' before the court and one who is 'brought' before the court obviously expresses the contrast between arriving there at liberty and arriving in custody. The subsection evidently enacts that the statutory right to bail, where the accused does not actually apply for bail, is contingent on physical presence at court. A prisoner on remand who is not produced and does not apply for bail either through a legal representative in court or in writing, would seem therefore to enjoy no statutory right to bail. In such a case the court would not be bound to consider the question of bail of its own motion. By contrast with s. 4(2)(a), under s. 4(2)(b) the right to bail is enjoyed by an unconvicted accused who applies to a court for bail. However, the right of an unconvicted accused to apply for bail is not unlimited. It is subject to the restriction imposed by the rule against renewed applications for bail (see generally Chapter 5). Further, although it is not precisely established if the right to apply is contingent on the accused's presence in court, it was observed by the Divisional Court in *Baxter* v *Chief Constable of the West Midlands Police, Independent*, 15 June 1998, that there was no section in any statute which expressly provided that an applicant for bail needed to be personally present in the court at the hearing of a bail application. In fact, as the court noted, s. 122 of the Magistrates' Courts Act 1980 (MCA 1980) pointed to the contrary. The section provides:

(1)   A party to any proceedings before a magistrates' court may be represented by counsel or solicitor.

(2)   Subject to subsection (3) below, an absent party so represented shall be deemed not to be absent.

(3)   Appearance of a party by counsel or solicitor shall not satisfy any provision of any enactment or any condition of a recognizance expressly requiring his presence.

On the other hand, the court observed, the normal practice was that the accused should appear in person. Constructive attendance by means of a video link has now been enacted for by s. 57 of the Crime and Disorder Act 1998, which provides:

(1)   In any proceedings for an offence a court may, after hearing representations from the parties, direct that the accused shall be treated as present in court for any particular hearing before the start of the trial, if, during that hearing—

(a) the accused is held in custody in a prison or other institution; and

(b) whether by means of a live television link or otherwise, the accused is able to see and hear the court and to be seen and heard by it.

(2) A court shall not give a direction under subsection 57(1) unless—

(a) it has been notified by the Secretary of State that facilities are available for enabling persons held in custody in the institution in which the accused is or is to be so held to see and hear the court and to be seen and heard by it; and

(b) the notice has not been withdrawn.

(3) If in a case where it has power to do so a magistrates' court decides not to give a direction under subsection 57(1), it shall give its reasons for not doing so.

1.2.3.5 Meaning of 'conviction' In the BA 1976, unless the context otherwise requires, the term 'conviction' includes:

(a) a finding of guilt;

(b) a finding that a person is not guilty by reason of insanity;

(c) a finding under s. 30(1) of the Magistrates' Courts Act 1980 (remand for medical examination) that the person in question did the act or made the omission charged; and

(d) a conviction of an offence for which an order is made placing the offender on probation or discharging the offender absolutely or conditionally,

and 'convicted' is construed accordingly: s. 2(1), amended by the MCA 1980, sch.7.

1.2.3.6 Circumstances in which section 4 is inapplicable The right does not apply in the following cases:

(a) Convicted persons. It does not apply to defendants after conviction, except when remanded for reports: s. 4(2).

(b) Fugitive offenders. It does not apply as respects proceedings against a fugitive offender: s. 4(2). Proceedings against a fugitive offender are those under the Extradition Act 1989, or s. 2(1) or s. 4(3) of the Backing of Warrants (Republic of Ireland) Act 1965: s. 2(2), BA 1976, as amended by the Extradition Act 1989, s. 36(3).

(c) Treason. The section is subject to s. 41 of the MCA 1980, which provides that persons charged with treason may be granted bail only by a judge of the High Court or a Secretary of State: s. 4(7), as amended by the MCA 1980, sch.7.

1.2.4 Homicide and rape charges where defendants have previous convictions for those offences

Section 25 of the Criminal Justice and Public Order Act 1994 (CJPOA 1994) not only deprives an accused of the *right* to bail where that accused falls into one of the relevant categories, but in general *prohibits* bail from being granted in any such case. The measure was enacted in response to concerns arising from a number of cases, the most notorious of which was that of Winston Silcott who was on bail for murder when he was charged with another murder. He was subsequently convicted of both offences, although the second one resulted in a successful appeal against conviction. As originally enacted, s. 25(1) and (3) together provided that where a person in any proceedings was charged with or convicted of murder, attempted murder, manslaughter, rape or attempted rape, it was absolutely forbidden to grant bail if that person had been previously convicted by or before a court in any part of the United Kingdom of any of those offences or of culpable homicide (an offence under Scots law), and in the case of a previous conviction of manslaughter or of culpable homicide, if the person was then sentenced to imprisonment, or, if at the time a child or young person, sentenced to long-term detention under any of the relevant enactments as defined in s. 25(5).

Article 5(3) of the European Convention for the Protection of Human Rights and Fundamental Freedoms (1950) (Cmnd 8969) requires that a person charged with an offence must be released pending trial unless the state can show that there are 'relevant and sufficient' reasons to justify the continued detention: *Weinhoff* v *FRG* (1968) 1 EHRR 155. (For the Convention provisions on bail, see *Archbold: Criminal Pleading and Practice*, London: Sweet & Maxwell, 1999, Appendix E, paras E-20 to E-25.) In a number of cases pending before the European Commission on Human Rights, s. 25 as originally enacted is under challenge for violating the Article (see e.g., *CC* v *United Kingdom* 32819/96; *BH* v *United Kingdom* 30307/96). These were recently communicated to the Government (see Emmerson, B., 'The Human Rights Bill: its effect on Criminal Proceedings (Part II)', *Archbold News*, 9 April 1998). Apparently in order to avoid an adverse judgment at the European Court of Human Rights at Strasbourg the Government has secured the amelioration of s. 25 by s. 56 of the Crime and Disorder Act 1998 (CDA 1998). Section 25 is modified by the removal of the absolute prohibition on granting bail as originally enacted. Instead, it allows that bail may be granted in cases to which s. 25 relates, but only if the court or, as the case may be, the constable considering the grant of bail is satisfied that there are exceptional circumstances which justify it. In introducing the modifying measure as a Government amendment during the Third Reading of the Bill in the House of Lords, the Solicitor-General stated:

> The offences concerned here are very serious . . . [b]ut to remove the ability of the police and the courts to make [the decision as to bail or custody] is not in the interests of justice. It cannot be right to fetter the judicial discretion of the court in this way. (HL Deb, vol. 588, cols 239–240, 31 March 1998)

Section 25 applies whether or not an appeal is pending against conviction or sentence: s. 25(4). For the purposes of the section, 'conviction' includes a finding that a person is not guilty by reason of insanity, a finding in a case of unfitness to plead that the person did the act or made the omission charged, and a conviction of an offence for which an order is made placing the offender on probation or granting an absolute or conditional discharge: s. 25(5).

1.3 EXCEPTIONS TO THE RIGHT TO BAIL IN SCHEDULE 1 TO THE BAIL ACT 1976

Section 4 of the BA 1976 enacts that bail must be granted by a court to a person accused of an offence, or remanded for inquiries or a report, or brought before the court for breach of a requirement of probation, community service, combination or curfew order, *if none of the exceptions specified in sch. 1 applies.*

1.3.1 Exceptions in the case of imprisonable offences: Part I of Schedule 1

The exceptions to the right to bail which are set out in Part I of sch. 1 are those which apply where the offence or one of the offences of which the defendant is accused or convicted in the proceedings is punishable with imprisonment. The question whether an offence is punishable by imprisonment is determined without regard to any enactment prohibiting or restricting imprisonment of young offenders or first offenders: BA 1976, sch.1, Part III, para. 1.

1.3.1.1 Principal exceptions in the Bail Act 1976 as originally enacted: defendant will abscond, commit an offence on bail or obstruct justice Schedule 1, Part I, para. 2, provides that in the case of any offence punishable with imprisonment bail need not be granted if the court is satisfied that there are substantial grounds for believing that if released on bail (whether subject to conditions or not) the defendant would:

(a)   fail to surrender to custody; or
(b)   commit an offence while on bail; or
(c)   interfere with witnesses or otherwise obstruct the course of justice, whether in relation to the defendant or any other person.

1.3.1.2 Principal exception subsequently incorporated in the 1976 Act: defendant 'already' on bail Section 26 of the CJPOA 1994 inserts an additional principal exception in the BA 1976, sch. 1, Part I. The inserted measure, para. 2A, provides that a defendant need not be granted bail if:

(a)   the offence is an indictable offence or an offence triable either way; and
(b)   it appears to the court that the defendant was on bail in criminal proceedings on the date of the offence.

1.3.1.3 Considerations in determining whether any of the principal exceptions applies In determining whether any of the exceptions in paras 2 and 2A applies, Part I, para. 9 provides that the court must have regard to such of the following considerations as appear to be relevant:

(a)   The offence in question. The court must have regard to the nature and seriousness of the offence or default (and the probable method of dealing with it).

(b)   Social background. The court must have regard to the character, antecedents, associations and community ties of the defendant.

(c)   Past bail record. The court must have regard to the defendant's record as respects the fulfilment of any obligations under previous grants of bail. References in sch. 1 to previous grants of bail in criminal proceedings include references to bail granted before the coming into force of the Act (Part III, para. 2).

(d)   Strength of the evidence. Except in the case of a defendant whose case is adjourned for inquiries or a report, the strength of the evidence that the defendant committed the offence or defaulted.

(e)   Any other relevant considerations. The court must also have regard to any other considerations which appear to be relevant.

'Default' means the default for which the defendant is to be dealt with (i.e., breach of a requirement of a probation, community service, combination or curfew order) under s. 101(2) and sch. 13 of the CJA 1991, which replaced s. 6 or s. 16 of the Powers of the Criminal Courts Act 1973: BA 1976, sch. 1, Part III, para. 4. The 1991 Act enacts no express amendment to s. 6 and s. 16 of the 1973 Act but the editors of *Archbold: Criminal Pleading and Practice*, London: Sweet & Maxwell, 1999, contend, at para. 3-52, that this was presumably an oversight as similar references in s. 4(3) of the Bail Act 1976 (see para. 1.2.3.1) were expressly dealt with. The editors submit that the provisions of the Interpretation Act 1978, s. 17(2)(a) cover the situation and that the references to the repealed provisions should be construed as references to Part II of sch. 2 to the CJA 1991.

1.3.1.4   Subsidiary exceptions   Schedule 1, Part I, paras 3 to 7, provide for the following further exceptions to the right to bail in cases of an imprisonable offence:

(a)   Own protection. Bail need not be granted if the court is satisfied that the defendant should be kept in custody for his or her own protection, or, in the case of children or young persons, for their own welfare (para. 3).

(b)   Serving prisoner. Bail need not be granted if the defendant is in custody in pursuance of the sentence of a court or of any authority acting under any of the Service Acts (para. 4).

(c)   Insufficient information. Bail need not be granted where the court is satisfied that it has not been practicable to obtain sufficient information for the purpose of taking a decision about bail through want of time since the proceedings were instituted (para. 5).

(d)   Arrest for failing to surrender or for breach of a bail condition. Bail need not be granted if, having been released on bail in or in connection with the proceedings for the offence, the defendant has been arrested, in pursuance of s. 7 of the Act, for having failed to surrender or having breached a condition of bail, or because it is believed on reasonable grounds that failing to surrender or the

breach of a condition is likely or because a surety has given written notice that the defendant is unlikely to surrender and wishes for that reason to withdraw as surety (para. 6).

(e) Adjournment for inquiries or report. Bail need not be granted where the defendant's case is adjourned for inquiries or a report, if it appears to the court that it would be impracticable for these to be accomplished without keeping the defendant in custody (para. 7).

As to (b), a sentence does not include committal for default of payment of any sum of money, or for want of sufficient distress to satisfy any sum of money, or failure to do or abstain from doing anything required to be done or left undone: MCA 1980, s. 180. The Service Acts in question are the Army Act 1955, the Air Force Act 1955 and the Naval Discipline Act 1957: BA 1976, sch. 1, Part III, para. 4.

1.3.2 Exceptions in the case of non-imprisonable offences: Part II of Schedule 1

Schedule 1, Part II, paras 1 to 5, provide that where the offence, or every offence, charged is not punishable with imprisonment, defendants need not be granted bail in the following circumstances:

(a) Previous failure to surrender. Bail need not be granted if it appears to the court that the defendant has previously failed to surrender to custody in accordance with obligations under the grant of bail and in view of that failure it is believed that if released on bail (whether subject to conditions or not) the defendant would fail to surrender (para. 2).

(b) Own protection. Bail need not be granted if the court is satisfied that the defendant should be kept in custody for his or her own protection, or, in the case of children or young persons, for their own welfare (para. 3).

(c) Serving prisoner. Bail need not be granted if the defendant is in custody in pursuance of the sentence of a court or of any authority acting under any of the Service Acts (para. 4).

(d) Arrest for failing to surrender or for breach of a bail condition. Bail need not be granted if, having been released on bail in or in connection with the proceedings for the offence, the defendant has been arrested in pursuance of s. 7 of the Act (para. 5; see above para. 1.3.1.4 (d)).

1.4 ASPECTS OF THE STATUTORY CONSIDERATIONS FOR ASSESSING WHETHER TO INVOKE THE PRINCIPAL EXCEPTIONS

It is important to stress that the four statutory criteria (BA 1976, sch.1, Part 1, para. 9) for determining whether to invoke the principal exceptions to the right to bail may each be relevant to each of the exceptions. For example, the nature and seriousness of the offence may be relevant not only to the question whether the accused will abscond but also to the risk of the commission of offences on bail. An editorial in [1987] Crim LR 437, drew attention to the 'disjunction between the considerations set out in para. 9 and the three "exceptions to the right to bail"'. It was suggested that 'wayward decisions' could be produced by such disjunction:

> If the question which the court has to answer is, are there substantial grounds for believing that this defendant would commit an offence whilst on bail? the court needs to know about his criminal record, whether the evidence against him is strong, how frequently this type of defendant offends whilst on bail, and any special evidence relating to this defendant. It is difficult to see how, strictly speaking, it is relevant to any of the three 'exceptions to the right to bail' to consider how the defendant might be dealt with if convicted. Perhaps it should be relevant. Perhaps the 'exceptions' are too restrictive. Or perhaps this 'consideration' leads courts to remand in custody where the offence appears serious, without focusing on the probability or otherwise of an offence being committed whilst he is on bail.

1.4.1 Nature and seriousness of the offence

1.4.1.1 Distinction between nature and seriousness Nature and seriousness are arguably distinct and separate, but it is also important to distinguish between the nature of an offence *as a class* and that of a particular offence. Some offences defined by class may be inherently grave in their nature, for example murder, while the gravity of other categories of offence, not necessarily grave in their nature, will be determined by the particular facts. An analogy is provided by the Police and Criminal Evidence Act 1984 (PACE 1984), s. 116, which provides that certain arrestable offences are always serious, while others are serious if they lead to serious consequences. The nature of a particular offence, considered *on its facts*, will determine its gravity. In determining whether to grant or refuse bail, only the particular facts will be relevant. It is arguable, therefore, that the word 'seriousness' is superfluous. However, the nature of a particular offence will bear relevance in determining whether or not to grant bail in respects distinct from those of its gravity and so the use of the two terms in the Act is sensible.

1.4.1.2 Impact of gravity on likelihood of absconding Objectively considered, there is an undoubted correlation between the gravity of the offence charged and the temptation to abscond. The more serious the offence, the longer the sentence is likely to be and therefore the greater the incentive to avoid attending court. This may be particularly compelling where the defendant is subject to a court order for which a conviction will constitute a breach. An outstanding suspended sentence may be regarded as an especially strong reason for believing that a person will fail to surrender. The graver the alleged offence the greater will be the likelihood that the defendant will avoid the risk of a lengthy sentence by absconding.

1.4.1.3 Nature of offence can influence absconding It is not only offence gravity which will determine the absconding risk. That risk will also be influenced by the nature of the offence. For example, the prevalence of a given class of offence in a particular district may be influential in determining whether on principles of general deterrence a sentence is likely to be more severe than it might otherwise be if the offence were not particularly prevalent. Although the CJA 1991, s. 2(2)(a), appears to exclude deterrence as a sentencing principle, the Court of Appeal took a different view in *R* v *Cunningham* [1993] 1 WLR 183.

1.4.1.4 Nature and seriousness of the offence and commission of offences while on bail Notwithstanding the editorial opinion expressed in the *Criminal Law Review* cited above, it is submitted that the seriousness of the offence may well be relevant to the likelihood that the defendant if granted bail will commit an offence or offences while on bail. Someone facing the certainty of a long sentence may well be tempted to resort to crime in order to establish a nest egg for eventual release, or to provide for a spouse, children or other dependent relatives during the years of incarceration. The nature of the offence charged may well have a very significant bearing on this calculation. For example, if the offence charged bears all the hallmarks of a professional burglary, this may well suggest that the defendant is a professional burglar with little or no compunction about committing such offences while on bail. Together with a history of committing such offences and with the fact that the defendant is a family man, the nature of the instant offence, being one for which the detection rate is notoriously low, may well justify the supposition that the defendant will commit burglaries if released on bail. By way of contrast with professional burglary, a domestic murder, although very grave, is in its nature unlikely to pose any risk of repetition and if the risk of absconding is perceived as negligible it may well be considered safe to grant bail in such a case (see *Bail Procedures in Magistrates' Courts, Report of the Home Office Working Party*, London: HMSO, 1974, para. 57, and see Chatterton, C., *Bail: Law and Practice*, London: Butterworths, 1986, p. 46).

1.4.1.5 View that seriousness should not be conclusive As a rule of thumb, the more serious the case the greater must be the hesitation to grant bail, especially where the evidence is strong or there are admissions. This was the view of Lord Hailsham, then Lord Chancellor, when, addressing the Magistrates' Association in 1984, he said:

> I would be slow to grant bail in cases where the charge was murder, attempted murder, rape or attempted rape, or wounding, or other grave crimes. This list is not exhaustive. . . . If the exceptions and restrictions provided by the Schedule to the Act were properly applied, only in exceptional cases would one expect to see bail granted to a person charged with murder, rape, wounding, or other grave crimes.

Section 25 of the CJPOA 1994 is an attempt to incorporate Lord Hailsham's thinking into legislation. However, the seriousness of an offence should not be, and is not, treated as conclusive. The Home Office Working Party on bail procedures in magistrates' courts observed at para. 61 of their report that a defendant who was likely to receive a custodial sentence ought not necessarily to be refused bail, and they did not accept as conclusive the argument that where a defendant was likely to receive a custodial sentence it was doing no kindness to allow a preliminary period of liberty. They pointed out that if the sentence was likely to be short the period on remand might exceed it, and that the likely sentence ought to be considered more in relation to the risk of absconding than as a factor in its own right. They also pointed out (at para. 60) that although it was wrong to assume that where a custodial remand was followed by a non-custodial sentence bail should have been granted initially, it was clearly desirable that, where an eventual custodial sentence was unlikely, bail should be granted unless there were strong grounds for a remand in custody. In borderline cases, the Working Party suggested, the court might give the defendant the benefit of the doubt, if a non-custodial sentence seemed the likeliest outcome.

1.4.2   Strength of the evidence

Aligned with the previous consideration is the strength of the evidence. Section 48 of the Criminal Law Act 1977 requires the prosecution to supply advance disclosure of its case to the defence so that, in either-way matters, all parties should at a comparatively early stage in the proceedings be in a position to have regard to this question when bail is considered. In any event, by the time of committal the defence and the court will know the strength of the case (see the Working Party's report, para. 58). The strength of the evidence is important, because if it is strong the defendant is more likely to be convicted and therefore more likely to abscond. Conversely, if it is weak, it is unnecessary to refuse bail as the defendant will be unlikely to be convicted and will have little to fear by standing trial. It may be argued that it is unjust to refuse bail to a person who is unlikely to be convicted. Amongst the factors that the court will consider under this head are:

(a)   Is it alleged that the defendant has made admissions?
(b)   Is identification in issue?
(c)   Was the defendant found in recent possession of stolen property?
(d)   Is there scientific evidence linking the defendant with the offence?
(e)   Was the defendant caught in the act of committing the offence or arrested as a result of inquiries?
(f)   Are the witnesses reliable, or may they be reluctant or hostile?

1.4.3   Character, antecedents, associations and community ties

The defendant's character, antecedents, associations and community ties are all clearly relevant to the bail decision.

1.4.3.1 Character The reference to character means, essentially, whether or not the defendant has previous convictions and, if so, the range, variety, number and rate of offences. Previous convictions are relevant in general to the risk of absconding and that of the commission of offences on bail. The worse a defendant's record of convictions the more likely will the court be to impose a custodial sentence, or the longer an inevitable custodial sentence is likely to be. Convictions for offences of a similar nature to the one charged will be more significant than if the offences are different. Convictions for similar offences suggest persistence, which is likely to warrant a more severe penalty for the offence than might otherwise be the case, and which is likely therefore to provide a greater temptation to abscond than otherwise, or else the commission of offences for the kind of reasons discussed above. Persistence also points to a risk of repetition while on bail. It has been suggested that it is inadvisable to grant bail to offenders with a bad criminal record: *R* v *Gentry* (1955) 39 Cr App R 195, CCA; *R* v *Wharton* [1955] Crim LR 565, CCA. This is a very general statement, although since any exercise in gauging the risk factors against the details of the allegation and the defendant's past record is an inexact 'science', there may be an understandable tendency by courts to err on the side of caution. It has been observed that a long string of petty offences does not automatically justify a remand in custody (see Chatterton, C., *Bail: Law and Practice*, London: Butterworths, 1986, p. 47, citing the Working Party report, para. 59).

1.4.3.2 Antecedents The term 'antecedents' has a wide meaning and embraces offences taken into consideration and the whole of the defendant's past history: *R* v *Vallet* [1951] 1 All ER 231.

1.4.3.3 Associations A defendant who habitually consorts with known criminals may justifiably be supposed to make a living from crime and may continue to do so if granted bail. Evidence of association may be inferred from the facts of the offence or offences charged, or may derive from police intelligence based on a combination of hearsay and conjecture which for the purposes of trial would be plainly inadmissible, but which for the purposes of bail are conventionally taken into account.

1.4.3.4 Community ties The issue of community ties involves the following questions: Does the defendant have a fixed address? If so, for how long has he or she had it? Is there a spouse or other partner? Are there children? Does the defendant have employment? If so, what is the nature of the work and how long has the job been held? The rationale behind this is that the stronger a person's community ties, in the form of home, family and employment, the less reason there is to abscond. This is not to say that these considerations must be followed like an actuarial formula. People with strong community ties do sometimes fail to surrender, and unemployed and homeless people do answer to their bail. Indeed, a Home Office Circular issued on 8 October 1975 (which drew the attention of the courts to the Working Party report) advised courts not to give undue weight to the fact that the defendant was of no fixed abode. While acknowledging that this was a material consideration, the Working Party expressed the view that it was important that courts should ascertain the precise circumstances (report, para. 65). It is clearly important to establish whether the defendant is sleeping rough, staying with friends, residing in a hostel or in bed and breakfast accommodation, travelling around in a trailer or motor caravan, living in a fixed mobile home on a registered pitch at an official 'caravan dwellers' site, or lodging in digs or in a furnished bed-sit.

1.4.4   Previous bail history

Whether or not defendants have complied with obligations under any previous grant of bail will be an important factor in deciding whether there are substantial grounds for believing that they will fail to surrender to their bail. Where defendants have always answered to bail in the past, particularly if the charges have been serious, it may be argued that there are no substantial grounds for believing that they will abscond if granted bail in the present case. Conversely, where there has been a previous failure to surrender, this may furnish grounds for fearing (i.e. believing) that repetition will occur. On the other hand, the judgment is one of fine balance and the failure must be examined in the context of the overall history. Where the defendant has a history of having been on bail facing a succession of serious charges over a number of years in the past and has always complied to the letter with bail conditions, but has once or twice failed to surrender in relation to comparatively minor charges, it might be oppressive to deny bail on the basis of an assessment of the bail history, particularly where there is a reasonable explanation for those failures.

Apart from any past occasion when defendants may have been prosecuted under s. 6 of the BA 1976 for failing to surrender to bail, courts will generally have no means of judging from defendants' records of conviction their history as regards compliance with obligations under previous grants of bail. Convictions under s. 6 are recorded, but beyond that criminal records rarely show whether in relation to a given past offence the defendant was on bail or in custody awaiting trial and independent records of this are rarely filed or preserved by the police – certainly not systematically. Moreover, no records of arrest under s. 7 for breaches of bail are systematically preserved, even in this computer age. The CPS, therefore, are rarely able to refute the proposition that in relation to a particular conviction the defendant was on bail and complied with its terms. Even a previous appearance on which the defendant was dealt with for a number of offences which plainly could not have been committed on the same occasion will not indicate that any of the offences must have been committed while the defendant was on bail for any of the other offences listed.

1.4.5   Any other relevant matters

Other matters which it has been suggested may be relevant include the mental stability of defendants, and any indications that they are liable to cause harm or injury to themselves or others (see Chatterton, C., *Bail: Law and Practice*, London: Butterworths, 1986, p. 48), although these considerations are best dealt with in relation to sch. 1, Part II, para. 3 (own protection or welfare). See also para. 1.5.3 (last sentence).

1.5 APPLYING THE EXCEPTIONS TO BAIL

1.5.1 'Substantial grounds' (original main exceptions – imprisonable offences)

After a great deal of Parliamentary discussion, the test adopted by the Act in the case of the main exceptions was 'substantial grounds for believing'. It is insufficient that there is a likelihood of any of the exceptions applying, or that there are grounds, or even strong or reasonable grounds, for so believing. The belief must be *substantial*. It has already been noted that the bail decision is judicial and not ministerial or administrative: *R v Badger* (1843) 4 QB 468; *Linford v Fitzroy* (1849) 13 QB 247. On the other hand, as Lord Hailsham pointed out, '. . . in granting or refusing bail you are bound to come to a decision on the basis of probabilities and not certainties. If you could only refuse bail on the basis of certainty, you could never refuse it at all' ('To bail or not to bail', *The Magistrate*, February 1972). Lord Hailsham's comment dates from before the BA 1976, but the effect of what he said was supported by the Divisional Court in *Re Moles* [1981] Crim LR 170. There it was held that strict rules of evidence were inherently inappropriate in a court deciding whether there were substantial grounds for believing something, such as a court considering an application under the BA 1976. This is one of the arguments against the application of the doctrine of *res judicata* to the bail decision, that the doctrine cannot apply to a prediction but only to a finding of fact. (The topic is further discussed in Chapter 5.). It is in keeping with the principle that the strict rules of evidence are inappropriate in the court's making of a determination on bail that when objections to bail are raised by the prosecution they are generally made by way of representation. In *R v Guest, ex parte Metropolitan Police Commissioner* [1961] 3 All ER 1118, Widgery J said that there was no overriding requirement that the prosecutor should adduce sworn evidence to support his application, nor was there an assumption that bail was to be granted in cases where sworn evidence connecting the accused with the offence was not given.

1.5.2 Failure to surrender

Many aspects of this exception have already been discussed in para. 1.4.1, above. It forms the subject of Chapter 4, where it is discussed in detail. The risk that the defendant will fail to surrender may be regarded as the most deeply rooted and historical reason for withholding bail. Indeed, until recent times it was still the only ground for refusing bail. In *R v Rose* (1898) 78 LT 119, Lord Russell said that 'the requirements as to bail are merely to secure the attendance of the prisoner at his trial' (see also *Re Robinson* (1854) 23 LJQB 286). In assessing the risk that a defendant may fail to surrender to bail the court must clearly balance against it, all that would inevitably be involved in absconding. A defendant with extensive family ties, a good marriage, children at school, a house with a mortgage and substantial equity, would have to suffer enormous inconvenience in electing to take on a fugitive existence in order to achieve the short-term gain of avoiding the discomfort of a prison sentence. It is perhaps a reflection of the reality of this that the actual number of defendants who fail to surrender is in fact very small. In 1988, 5 per cent of those bailed from a police station failed to appear (*Criminal Statistics, England and Wales, 1988*, Cm 847, London: HMSO, 1989), and in 1991 7 per cent of defendants granted bail by the courts failed to appear (*Criminal Statistics, England and Wales, 1991*, Cm 2134, London: HMSO, 1992). In a study several years later no significant change in the position had taken place: 7 per cent of defendants bailed by police failed to attend their first court appearance, and 9 per cent of those bailed by the court failed to attend at least one court hearing (Brown, D., *Offending on Bail and Police Use of Conditional Bail*, Home Office Research and Statistics Directorate, Research Findings No. 72, London: Home Office, 1998, p. 1).

Failure to surrender is the only exception to the right to bail to which all the considerations in the BA 1976, sch. 1, Part I, para. 9, appear to be relevant.

1.5.3 Commission of offences while on bail

The risk that the accused will commit an offence while on bail is an exception to the right to bail which is of comparatively recent origin. It is often referred to by the shorthand title 'further offences', an unfortunate misnomer which implies that the offence before the court is a proved offence rather than an offence charged or an alleged offence. It probably owes its origin to *dicta* by Lord Goddard CJ in a series of appeals in which he criticised courts for having given bail to defendants with bad records and in which he laid down the principle that bail should be withheld if the defendant were likely to commit 'further offences'. In *R v Pegg* [1955] Crim LR 308, Lord Goddard declared that it was 'no kindness to the prisoner' to grant bail to any person who had a bad criminal record and who ought to be denied 'the opportunity of committing further offences' while on bail (see also *R v Gentry* (1955) 39 Cr App R 195, CCA; *R v Wharton* [1955] Crim LR 565, CCA). The risk posed to the community when housebreakers were granted bail was adverted to in *R v Phillips* (1947) 32 Cr App R 47, an appeal in fact presided over by Lord Goddard in which judgment was delivered by Atkinson J, who said (at p. 48):

> Some crimes are not at all likely to be repeated pending trial and in those cases there may be no objection to bail; but some are, and housebreaking particularly is a crime which will very probably be repeated if a prisoner is released on bail, especially in the case of a man who has a record for housebreaking such as the

applicant had. It is an offence which can be committed with a considerable measure of safety to the person committing it . . . To turn such a man loose on society until he had received his punishment for an undoubted offence, an offence which was not in dispute, was, in the view of the Court, a very inadvisable step.

Eric Crowther remembers that '[a] Court of Criminal Appeal presided over long ago by Lord Goddard roundly condemned justices who had granted bail to a professional burglar pending his appearance at a higher court, thereby enabling him to commit many more burglaries so as to "set his family up" during the period that he anticipated being away' (Crowther, E., *Advocacy for the Advocate*, 2nd ed., Harlow: Longman, 1990, p. 115, in Chap. 10, 'To bail or not to bail'). The case to which the author appears to have been referring was in fact a decision of the Divisional Court. This was *R* v *Whitehouse, sub nom HM Postmaster-General* v *Whitehouse* (1951) 35 Cr App R 8, in which Lord Goddard CJ observed:

The [High] Court will exercise the power [to grant bail] with extreme care and will require to see what is the prisoner's previous history of convictions, because, as we have pointed out in cases in the Court of Criminal Appeal, bail ought to be sparingly granted in cases where prisoners have long records of convictions, since it very often results, when such a person obtains bail, he commits offences while on bail, sometimes telling the Court afterwards that he did it so as to get money to enable him to be represented at Quarter Sessions, in other cases saying that he had to make some provision for his wife and children while he was in prison. We have pointed this out in the Court of Criminal Appeal on more than one occasion.

Lord Goddard may be regarded not only as the originator of the misnomer 'further offences', but also as the originator of the reason for remanding in custody on the basis that the defendant will commit an offence while on bail. The reason (but not the misnomer) first found statutory form in the Criminal Justice Act 1967, s. 18(5). It did not take long for this exception to assume a greater significance in the view of the courts than the more deeply-rooted exception of failure to surrender. By 1978, the year in which the Bail Act came into force, the Home Office Statistical Department found that 'the commission of an offence' was given as a reason for refusing bail in 63 per cent of the magistrates' court cases it monitored, while the comparable figure for 'failing to surrender' was 51 per cent.

In a study conducted by the Home Office the comparatively small proportion of 8 per cent of those granted bail were found to have committed at least one offence while on bail (*Estimates of Offending by Persons on Bail*, Home Office, London: HMSO, 1981). Furthermore, the study revealed that the figure for those granted bail in spite of police objections was as high as 25 per cent, showing that the police are relatively good at predicting who such persons might be.

Different studies of the proportion of defendants who re-offend while on bail have produced different results, depending on the methodology used. The study 'Re-offending on Bail in Avon and Somerset' (Bristol: Avon and Somerset

Constabulary, 1991) measured the number of defendants who were arrested for a further offence while on bail. A court survey showed the proportion to be 28 per cent, while CID and custody officer questionnaires showed the proportion to be 27 per cent and 12 per cent respectively. The study also found a correlation between further arrest and the following factors:

(a) *Age of defendant.* Defendants aged between 17 and 20 were twice as likely to commit an (alleged) offence on bail than those aged 26 and over.

(b) *Type of offence.* Defendants charged with vehicle-related crime and burglary were the most likely to be re-arrested while on bail.

(c) *Number of previous convictions.*

A study entitled *Bail and Multiple Offending*, (Newcastle: Northumbria Police, 1991) used data collected from custody records, detected crime records and court files. It reported that 23 per cent of arrests involved persons who were on bail when they were arrested, but the figures included persons who were subsequently acquitted. Studies which excluded acquittal produced lower figures. Ennis and Nichols found that 12 per cent of those granted bail by courts were convicted of offences committed while they were on bail (Ennis, J., and Nichols, T., *Offending on Bail*, Metropolitan Police Directorate of Management Services Report No. 16/90, London: Metropolitan Police, 1991). Studies by Henderson and Nichols and by Morgan found the corresponding figure to be 10 per cent (Henderson, P., and Nichols, T., *Offending While on Bail*, Home Office Research Bulletin No. 32, London: Home Office, 1992; Morgan, P.M., *Offending While on Bail: A Survey of Recent Studies*, Home Office Research and Planning Unit Paper 65, London: Home Office, 1992).

Very recent research has shown that 24 per cent of people on bail committed one or more offences while on bail (Brown, D., *Offending on Bail and Police Use of Conditional Bail*, Home Office Research and Statistics Directorate, Research Findings No. 72, London: Home Office, 1998, p. 1). The highest rates were among those on bail for vehicle-related crime (44 per cent) and theft by shoplifting (40 per cent). Juveniles are more than twice as likely as adults to commit an offence while on bail and they offend more persistently. Amongst the factors shown to be important in another very recent study (Morgan, P., and Henderson, P., *Remand Decisions and Offending on Bail: Evaluation of the Bail Process Project*, Home Office Research Study 184, London: Home Office, 1998, p. 45) were the following:

• persons with no fixed abode (42 per cent offended on bail), although the number of such defendants in the sample was small (only 97 defendants or 4 per cent of the whole sample)
• those who waited more than six months before trial or sentence (32 per cent offended on bail)
• those charged with theft of cars or unauthorised taking (32 per cent), burglary (29 per cent) or robbery (23 per cent)

- those with at least one previous breach of bail (27 per cent), i.e. they had failed to appear at court in the past, had breached bail conditions in the past, or were on bail when charged with the current offence
- those who had served a previous custodial sentence (28 per cent)
- those under 18 (29 per cent)
- those who were unemployed or were not on the workforce (i.e. at school, retired, etc – 21 per cent).

The lowest rates of offending on bail were found for:

- persons who waited less than one month before trial or sentence (4 per cent)
- those who were employed (7 per cent)
- those charged with sex offences (6 per cent), assault (7 per cent) or fraud (8 per cent).

Some commentators have seen the shift in emphasis from securing attendance to preventing offences as an inroad into traditional liberties and the presumption of innocence (see e.g. Zander, M., 'Bail: A Reappraisal' [1967] Crim LR 25; Vogler, 'The Changing Nature of Bail', *LAG Bulletin*, February 1983; Dworkin, R., *Taking Rights Seriously*, London: Duckworth, 1987). It is undoubtedly true that the requirement of 'substantial grounds for belief' is a far less rigid test than the strict rules which are applicable to the recognised form of 'preventive detention' in the nature of a term longer than that commensurate with the seriousness of the offence for violent and sexual offences (CJA 1991, s. 2(1)(b)). However, it is also arguable that the courts have an overriding duty to protect the public and that one of the aims of any penal system must be to prevent crime. Less ambitious than prevention as an aim of the criminal law, but also one more capable of realisation in practice than prevention, is that of reducing the incidence of types of behaviour prohibited by the criminal law, an aim for which Nigel Walker coined the term 'reductivism' (*Sentencing in a Rational Society*, Harmondsworth: Penguin Books, 1969, Chap. 1). The issue is of course whether reductivism should be obtained at the remand stage, or whether it should be reserved until after conviction. However, it is certainly arguable that an implied condition of every grant of bail is that the defendant shall be of good behaviour. In *R v Ellis, Independent (CS)*, 15 January 1990, the Court of Appeal held that where defendants have a history of committing offences while on bail, it was neither fair to the community in which they live nor to defendants themselves to go on releasing them on bail. The occasions on which bail should be granted in respect of an offence alleged to have been committed while the defendant was on bail for another offence should be very infrequent.

In deciding whether the exception of an offence on bail applies, the relevant considerations will be the strength of the evidence, the defendant's record under previous grants of bail and, most importantly, his character, antecedents, associations and community ties.

As regards the strength of the evidence, it is arguable that if the evidence is strong there is a greater likelihood that defendants will commit an offence while on bail. But courts will always have regard to the presumption of innocence, and if evidence is weak defendants are less likely to be guilty and it follows that this must lessen the grounds for believing that they will commit an offence if given bail. It is sometimes argued that defendants who know they are likely to be convicted will having nothing to lose by committing an offence on bail. If the offence for which they are on bail is a serious one and they are facing a custodial sentence, it may be said that they have still less to lose by committing another offence.

The previous record of defendants in fulfilling their obligations under grants of bail in the past will be relevant only to the extent that it is possible to show whether they have in fact previously committed offences while on bail. It will rarely be possible to give a positive answer to this question from an interpretation of the criminal record sheet, and unless the police can point to some independent file entry dealing specifically with the point – information which is seldom available – the court may have to accept assertions by the defence advocate. It will, however, usually be possible to establish whether the defendant is on bail for some other alleged offence, and this will clearly be relevant in assessing any risk of the commission of offences if bail is granted.

The question whether defendants have previous convictions will be relevant in two ways. Previous convictions may make a custodial sentence more likely or may increase the likely length of such a sentence, and this may go to the issue of the risk of absconding. People with bad records may be more inclined to commit offences regardless of whether or not they are on bail; in other words, they may be less in awe of courts and less inhibited by proceedings which are pending. The court will want to ask various questions: For what sort of offence does the accused have previous convictions? How recent were they? Are there any significant gaps in the record?

Considerations of community ties in the form of employment, home and family are probably less relevant in this context than in the context of deciding whether there are substantial grounds for believing that defendants will fail to surrender. However, the court may conclude that persons of no fixed abode and with no community ties are under less pressure to obey the law as they have less to lose in the event of a conviction. Conversely, it could be argued that in cases of dishonesty a defendant with no family to support will have less motive to fend for them by crime before receiving an inevitable prison sentence. On the other hand, it is sometimes argued in relation to cases of dishonesty, that an unemployed defendant who has no means of support other than the proceeds of crime is likely to commit an offence if granted bail. Where defendants are addicted to hard drugs and have no sufficient means of financing their dependence, the court may find that they are likely to commit offences of dishonesty – or even trafficking – in order to do so, and at the very least that they will commit an offence of unlawful possession. Where the alleged offence involves violence, the court will have regard to any grudge or grievance the defendant may have against the complainant in deciding whether there is a risk of the commission of an offence if bail is granted. In the case of sexual offences, the court will have regard to the mental condition of defendants in deciding whether they are able to control themselves or whether the condition is such that they are likely to commit an offence on bail. In this context 'character' has a wider meaning than 'previous convictions'.

1.5.4   Interfere with witnesses or otherwise obstruct the course of justice

The risk of interference with witnesses or other obstruction of the course of justice is an important exception to the right to bail because any system of justice must depend on witnesses being free from fear of intimidation or bribery and upon evidence being properly obtained. The most common manifestations of the behaviour contemplated by this exception are cases in which:

(a)   the defendant has allegedly threatened witnesses;

(b)   the defendant has allegedly made admissions that he intends to do so;

(c)   the witnesses have a close relationship with the defendant, for example in cases of domestic violence or incest;

(d)   the witnesses are especially vulnerable, for example where they live near the defendant, or are children or elderly people;

(e)   it is believed that the defendant knows the location of inculpatory documentary evidence and would destroy it, or has hidden stolen property or the proceeds of crime and would dispose of it beyond hope of recovery;

(f)   it is believed that the defendant will intimidate or bribe jurors;

(g)   other suspects are still at large and may be warned by the defendant.

The exception will not apply merely because there are further police inquiries or there are other suspects who have yet to be apprehended. Although interfering with witnesses or otherwise obstructing the course of justice will almost always involve the commission of an offence, such as assault or perverting the course of justice, the exception nevertheless stands in its own right. In assessing the risk the relevant considerations will be the strength of the evidence, any history of interference with witnesses or obstructing justice which the defendant might have under previous grants of bail, and general character and associations. It is commonly applied to a person who has previously been, or is alleged presently to be, engaged in organised crime, but it is also frequently applied to impulsive offenders who have close connections with a complainant. It may be instructive to quote the following opinion of the Home Office Working Party, (*Bail Procedures in Magistrates' Courts, Report of the Working Party*, London: HMSO, 1974, para. 69):

The possibility of the defendant interfering with witnesses arises less frequently and will usually be relevant only when the alleged offence is comparatively serious *and* there is some other indication, such as a past record of violence or threatening behaviour by the defendant. Where there is a substantial ground for fearing such interference, this seems to us to be a very strong reason for refusing bail. (emphasis supplied)

It is to be noted that s. 51 of the CJPOA 1994 creates new offences of doing anything intended to intimidate or harm a person who is assisting or has assisted in the investigation of an offence or who is, will be, òr has been a witness or juror in any criminal proceedings. Further, a new trial may be ordered where a person has been acquitted of an offence and a person has been convicted of an administration of justice offence involving interference with or intimidation of a juror or a witness or potential witness: Criminal Procedure and Investigations Act 1996, s. 54(1); see Corre, N., *A Practical Guide to the Criminal Procedure and Investigations Act 1996*, London: Callow Publishing, 1996, p. 56.

1.5.5 Defendant already on bail

The BA 1976, sch. 1, Part I, para. 2A (inserted by CJPOA 1994, s. 26) raises a slight difficulty. It provides that bail need not be granted in the case of an indictable offence or an offence triable either way if it appears to the court that the defendant was on bail in criminal proceedings on the *date* of the offence. Presumably it is not intended that the application of the exception should literally depend on the date of the offence. Suppose a defendant is on bail, is acquitted or discharged and is then arrested the same day for allegedly committing an offence after leaving court. The provision is surely intended to be confined to the situation in which the defendant was on bail for another offence *at the time* of the instant offence.
Research indicates that the main effects of s. 26 of the CJPOA 1994 have been:

(a)   an increase in the use of conditional bail for those defendants who allegedly commit an offence while on bail (although this may be attributable to the police power to impose conditions which came into force at the same time);
(b)   the proportion of defendants known to have committed an offence while on bail who were remanded in custody has only marginally increased since the implementation of s. 26. It has been pointed out that 'section 26 has not changed court remand decisions in those cases which already were deemed to be serious. In addition, it may simply mean that courts were already using other exceptions, typically risk of further offences, to remand defendants in custody when they deemed it necessary' (Hucklesby, A., and Marshall, E., *Tackling Offending on Bail: the impact of the Criminal Justice and Public Order Act 1994*, unpublished, London: Home Office, 1996, p. 45, summarised in Morgan, P., and Henderson, P., *Remand decisions and offending on bail: evaluation of the Bail Process Project*, Home Office Research and Statistics Directorate Research Findings 184, London: Home Office, 1998, p. 81; the authors of the present work have perused the full report with the kind permission of the Home Office).

Section 26 has not had a measurable effect on the decision-making process of the court (Hucklesby and Marshall, *op. cit.*, p. 45). However, s. 26 has led to a greater likelihood of a remand in custody for persons charged with serious offences who have more than four previous convictions, have served a custodial sentence and have a bail history (Warren, J., *Monitoring the Effects of Section 26 of the Criminal Justice and Public Order Act 1994 in Bournemouth Magistrates' Court*, final report to the Home Office, unpublished, London: Home Office, p. 15, summarised in Morgan and Henderson, *op. cit.*, p. 83; the authors of the present work have read the full report with the kind permission of the Home Office).

1.5.6 Own protection or welfare

The need for defendants to be kept in custody for their own protection, or in the case of children or young persons, for their own welfare, will usually apply where:

(a)   defendants need protection from themselves, for example where they are mentally unstable, suicidal, alcoholic, or drug addicted;
(b)   defendants are in need of protection from others, for example where they are accused of an offence which has aroused public anger such as child abuse.

As to the position in (a), it should be noted that pre-trial medical reports are inappropriate unless there is doubt about a defendant's fitness to plead or unless there exists the possibility of an order under s. 37(3) of the Mental Health Act 1983 (MHA 1983) without conviction. As to (b), the need to protect the defendant from others, this is 'Montero's Aim' in imposing a criminal justice sanction (after the Spanish jurist who described it), the need to protect offenders and suspected offenders from unofficial retaliation (see Walker, N., *Sentencing in a Rational Society*, Harmondsworth: Penguin Books, 1969, Chap. 1). There is a wider aim in the case of children or young persons since the exception then applies for their own welfare. This is in accordance with the principle laid down in the Children and Young Persons Act 1933 (CYPA 1933), s. 44 of which provides:

Every court in dealing with a child or young person who is brought before it, either as an offender or otherwise, shall have regard to the welfare of the child or young person and shall in a proper case take steps for removing him from undesirable surroundings and for securing that proper provision is made for his education and training.

1.5.7 Insufficient information

A court may refuse bail if it has insufficient information to take a bail decision through want of time since the proceedings were instituted, but this exception usually applies only on the defendant's first appearance in court on the first morning after detention for inquiries under PACE 1984 have concluded. There may be doubt about the defendant's identity, address or previous convictions. The advantage of applying this exception from the defendant's point of view is that it does not preclude a further application for bail since full argument cannot have been heard previously: *R* v *Calder Justices, ex parte Kennedy* (1992) 156 JP 716. It has been suggested that where a first appearance application for bail is unsuccessful the defence should actually invite the court to specify the ground of refusal of bail as that of 'insufficient information' in order to keep their options open for a later application (see Chatterton, C., *Bail: Law and Practice*, London: Butterworths, 1986, p. 55). Renewed applications form the subject matter of Chapter 5.

1.5.8 'Impracticable to prepare report or make inquiries'

The exception to the right to bail where it appears to the court to be impracticable to complete inquiries or prepare a report without keeping the defendant in custody is generally used as a last resort. The defendant will normally have failed to keep appointments or to cooperate in some other way. The requirement is that the preparation of reports or the making of inquiries must be *impracticable*, not merely difficult or inconvenient.

1.5.9 Non-imprisonable offences

The historical reason for refusing bail is preserved here, but with the proviso that the belief that the defendant will fail to surrender must be based on a previous failure to surrender. The belief need not be based on reasonable grounds. The provisions as to the defendant's own protection or welfare, serving prisoners and following an arrest pursuant to the BA 1976, s. 7, also apply to non-imprisonable offences.

1.6   REQUIREMENT TO EXPLAIN AND RECORD BAIL DECISIONS

1.6.1   Obligation of the court to state reasons for refusing bail or imposing conditions on grant of bail

1.6.1.1   Fundamental principles involved   It is an essential element of a defendant's right to bail that where an exception applies warranting suspension or limitation of that right the defendant should be allowed to know the reasons. This is a clear application of the fundamental principle of open government in a fair and democratic society, that individuals should normally be informed of the reasons for official decisions affecting their lives – particularly where those decisions relate to the liberty of the subject. However, there is a further reason for the right to know why bail is refused. It is to enable the defendant to challenge the decision before a higher court, for without knowing the ostensible reasons the higher court can make no rational judgment on their validity.

1.6.1.2 Statutory duty of the court to give reasons The right of the defendant to be informed of the reasons for refusal of bail is enshrined in the BA 1976, s. 5(3). The subsection provides that where a magistrates' court or the Crown Court:

(a) withholds bail in criminal proceedings; or
(b) imposes conditions in granting bail in criminal proceedings; or
(c) varies any conditions of bail or imposes conditions in respect of bail in criminal proceedings;

and the general right to bail applies, then the court must, with a view to enabling the defendant to consider making an application in the matter to another court, give reasons for withholding bail or for imposing or varying those conditions.

1.6.2 Court's duty to give reasons for granting bail in certain classes of serious crime

The converse of the need in certain cases for a court to state its reasons for refusing bail or imposing conditions on granting bail is that there are circumstances in which the public have a right to know the reasons why a court has granted bail. The 16th-century Statute of Bail is the first instance of this concern being expressed in an Act of Parliament. As described in the historical account at the beginning of the present chapter, the statute was enacted to prevent collusive release of felony prisoners, and it sought to achieve this aim by obliging magistrates to record the depositions of witnesses in order to furnish a check on the strength of the case and on whether it was therefore safe to admit the accused to bail.

During the 1980s public anxiety was provoked by a number of high-profile cases in which defendants charged with a serious offence were released on bail only to commit a fresh offence of gravity while on bail. Parliament in consequence enacted s. 153 of the Criminal Justice Act 1988, which inserted in sch. 1, Part I to the BA 1976 a new paragraph, para. 9A, which provided that:

(a) where a person is charged with murder, manslaughter, rape, attempted murder, or attempted rape; and
(b) representations are made as to the exceptions to the right to bail; and
(c) the court decides to grant bail;

the court must state the reasons for the decision.

1.6.3 Requirement to record bail decision and reasons

The right to be informed of the reasons for a decision to refuse bail or otherwise impose conditions for granting it, the duty to give those reasons, and the duty to give reasons for granting bail in the special classes of serious case referred to in the last paragraph will have little effect without an obligation on the part of the court to record those reasons. Accordingly, the BA 1976 contains various provisions requiring such decisions to be recorded.

1.6.3.1 Circumstances in which a bail decision must be recorded Section 5(1) of the BA 1976, as amended by the CJPOA 1994, s. 27(4) and sch. 3, para. 1, provides that in any of the following cases in which a bail decision is made the decision must be recorded:

(a) where a court or constable grants bail in criminal proceedings;
(b) where a court withholds bail in criminal proceedings from a person entitled to the general right to bail;
(c) where a court, officer of a court, or constable appoints a time or place, or a court or officer of a court appoints a different time or place for a person granted bail in criminal proceedings to surrender to custody; or
(d) where a court or constable varies conditions or imposes conditions of bail in criminal proceedings.

1.6.3.2 Copy of record to be given to person to whom bail decision relates on request Further, as soon as practicable after the decision has been recorded a copy of the record must be given to the person in relation to whom the bail decision was taken if that person so requests: BA 1976, s. 5(1).

1.6.3.3 Requirement to record reasons for bail decision Where by virtue of s. 5(3) of the BA 1976 (see para. 1.6.1.2) a magistrates' court or Crown Court is required in respect of a defendant entitled to the general right to bail to give reasons for withholding bail, imposing conditions for granting bail, or varying or imposing any conditions of bail, the court must include a note of those reasons in the record of its decision: s. 5(4).

1.6.3.4 Note of reasons to be given to the defendant Where by virtue of s. 5(4) a note of the reasons for a bail decision is required to be included in the record of the court's decision, then in the case of a decision in the magistrates' court or in the case of an unrepresented defendant in the Crown Court, a copy of the note must be given to the defendant, but the Crown Court need not give a copy of the note of the reasons for its decision to defendants represented by counsel or a solicitor unless counsel or the solicitor so requests: s. 5(4) and (5).

1.6.3.5 Reasons for granting bail in certain serious cases to be recorded Reference was made above, at para. 1.6.2, to the provision of para. 9A of sch. 1, Part I to the BA 1976 requiring the court to state the reasons for granting bail in cases of murder, manslaughter, rape, attempted murder or attempted rape where representations are made as to the exceptions to the right to bail. Paragraph 9A further requires those reasons to be included in the record of the proceedings.

1.7   TIME SPENT IN CUSTODY PRIOR TO SENTENCE

It is important to remember that as with any entrenched constitutional right, the right to bail under the BA 1976 is distinct from a 'privilege' accorded as a favour. The deprivation of bail for reasons of expedience or necessity is legitimately to be regarded therefore as a 'regrettable' incursion on that constitutional right. In a fair and just society the loss of any right – even where demanded by expediency – must be compensated in some way. In this chapter on the right to bail it is appropriate, therefore, to include consideration of the mechanism by which the law makes restitution for the deprivation of that right. It does not do so by awarding financial compensation to the acquitted defendant. It does so by discounting any time served on remand against the sentence imposed.

1.7.1   Applicability

1.7.1.1   General rule   Section 67(1) and (1A) of the Criminal Justice Act 1967 (CJA 1967) provide that the length of any sentence of imprisonment is reduced by any period during which the offender was:

(a)   in police detention within the meaning of the PACE 1984, or detained under s. 14 of the Prevention of Terrorism (Temporary Provisions) Act 1989;

(b)   in custody by reason only of having been committed to custody by order of a court in connection with any proceedings relating to that sentence or the offence for which it was passed or any proceedings from which those proceedings arose (i.e., on remand) or so committed in custody and having been concurrently detained otherwise than by order of a court; or

(c)   in connection with the offence for which the sentence was passed, or remanded to local authority accommodation by virtue of an order under s. 23 of the Children and Young Persons Act 1969 (CYPA 1969) in accommodation provided for the purpose of restricting liberty.

1.7.1.2   Young persons   The reference to an offender being committed to custody by an order of a court includes a reference to the offender's being remanded or committed to a remand centre or prison under s. 23 of the CYPA 1969 but does not include a reference to the offender's being remanded or committed to local authority accommodation under s. 23 or s. 37 unless the young person was remanded or committed in accommodation provided for the purpose of restricting liberty (see para. 1.7.1.1, above). Special provision is made where a young offender is sentenced to a Detention and Training Order under s. 73, CDA 1998. Section 74(5) of the CDA 1998 provides that in determining the term of a detention and training order for an offence, the court shall take account of any period for which the offender has been remanded in custody in connection with the offence, or any other offence the charge for which was founded on the same facts or evidence. Section 74(6) provides that the reference to an offender being remanded in custody is a reference to the offender being—

(a)   held in police detention;
(b)   remanded in or committed to custody by an order of a court;
(c)   remanded or committed to local authority accommodation under s. 23,
CYPA 1969, and placed and kept in secure accommodation;
(d)   remanded, admitted or removed to hospital under ss. 35, 36, 38, or 48 of
the Mental Health Act 1983.

1.7.1.3   Concurrent sentences arising out of different committals   Where an
offender is sentenced to a combination of individual sentences, whether consecutive or concurrent, time spent in custody in connection with any of the offences is
deducted from the aggregate sentence, subject always to the rule that time could
never be counted more than once: *R* v *Governor of Brockhill Prison, ex parte
Evans*; *R* v *Onley Young Offender Institution, ex parte Reid* [1997] 2 WLR 236.
Where an offender has been remanded in custody in respect of two separate
offences and is sentenced to imprisonment for one such offence, the sentence may
be treated as reduced by the length of the remand period only once, even if the
first sentence has been served by the time sentence is passed for the second offence
(*R* v *Secretary of State for the Home Department, ex parte Kitaya*, *The Times*, 20
January 1998, DC). James Richardson has argued that the use of the word 'only'
in s. 67(1)(b), CJA 1967, constitutes a significant restriction on the provision
(*Criminal Law Week*, CLW/98/03/2). He contends that the key issue is not whether
there are two or more separate offences, but whether there are two or more separate
sets of proceedings:

> If an offender appears before a magistrates' court charged with two offences and
> he is remanded in custody, he would (in relation to each offence) be in custody
> 'by reason only of having been committed to custody by an order of a court
> made in connection with any proceedings relating to that sentence or the offence
> for which it was passed.' In the normal course of events, both matters would be
> dealt with by the same court, and any sentence passed would be automatically
> reduced by the period on remand. This would apply whether or not there was a
> conviction of both offences or of one only. In the unusual event of the offences
> being separated, with the offender being tried and sentenced for the first offence
> before trial of the second offence, sentence for the first offence would be reduced
> by operation of s. 67. If there were an acquittal at the first trial and a conviction
> at the second trial, it is submitted that any sentence imposed would similarly be
> reduced by operation of s. 67. If there were convictions at both trials, logic
> suggests that s. 67 applies to both sentences (the language of the section not
> having changed).

Richardson suggests that the court appears to have got round this conclusion, first
by saying, in reliance on *R* v *Governor of Brockhill Prison, ex parte Evans*; *R* v
Onley YOI, ex parte Reid, above, that there is an embargo on double-counting, and
secondly by resorting to s. 41(2), CJA 1991. This provides that any period by

which a sentence is reduced under s. 67 is to be treated as having been served as part of the sentence. The court therefore concluded that an offender was in custody not only as a result of the remand but also because he was serving the sentence imposed for the first offence. A prisoner whose release date has been delayed because it was wrongly determined by the application of what at the time was held to be the correct intepretation of the statutory provisions is entitled to damages for false imprisonment: *R* v *Governor of Brockhill Prison, ex parte Evans (No. 2)*, *sub nom Evans* v *Governor of Brockhill Prison, The Times*, 6 July 1988. Time spent in custody on remand for certain offences while also serving a sentence of imprisonment for those offences, even where the sentence for the earlier offence has already been reversed on appeal: *R* v *Governor of Wandsworth Prison, ex parte Sorhaindo, The Times*, 5 January 1999.

1.7.1.4 Power of the court to make directions regarding time spent in custody The Crime (Sentences) Act 1997, s. 9(1) and (3) provide that where a court sentences an offender to imprisonment and that offender has been remanded in custody in connection with the offence or an offence founded on the same facts or evidence (a 'related offence'), the court may direct that the number of days for which the offender was remanded in custody in connection with the offence or a related offence shall count as time served by the offender as part of the sentence. Section 9 of the 1997 Act had not been brought into force at the time of writing.

1.7.1.5 Extradited prisoners Section 47 of the CJA 1991 allows a court dealing with an offender who has been extradited to order that part or the whole of the time spent in foreign custody should count towards sentence. Earlier authorities indicate that an offender who has deliberately prolonged the period in custody abroad should not be given credit for the full period: see e.g. *R* v *Scalise and Rachel* (1984) 7 Cr App R (S) 395. In *R* v *Vincent* [1996] 2 Cr App R (S) 6, the Court of Appeal reduced the term of the sentence rather than exercise the power under s. 47.

1.7.1.6 Life sentences In the case of an offender sentenced to life imprisonment with a period specified under s. 34 of the CJA 1991, any period spent in custody in relation to the offence for which the sentence was passed will count as part of the specified period. Neither this provision nor s. 47 (see para. 1.7.1.5 above) applies to an extradited prisoner who is sentenced to life imprisonment. In such a case the court may reduce the specified period by such amount as it considers appropriate: *R* v *Howard* [1996] 2 Cr App R (S) 273.

1.7.2 Inapplicability

1.7.2.1 General The effect of s. 67 of the CJA 1967 is that time spent in custody on remand is not deducted from a sentence of imprisonment or other custodial sentence if the offender is in custody in connection with other matters (for example, concurrently serving a sentence for an unrelated offence, or a term of imprisonment in default of payment of a fine). However, this exception does not apply, and the time in custody will discount, where the offender is simultaneously in custody otherwise than by order of a court (for example, where detained under the Immigration Act 1971).

1.7.2.2 Suspended sentence Where a suspended sentence is activated time is not deducted from any period spent in custody before the suspended sentence was passed: CJA 1967, s. 67(1). Accordingly, it has been held that where a suspended sentence is passed, the sentencing court should make allowance for time spent in custody on remand, as this time will not be deducted from the sentence if it is eventually activated: *R* v *Williams* (1989) 11 Cr App R (S) 152. Where an offender has been in custody on remand for a period which would be equivalent to the appropriate sentence, the sentencer should not pass a suspended sentence but should impose an immediate sentence; this will enable the offender to have the benefit of the time spent in custody so that it counts towards the sentence: *R* v *McCabe* (1988) 10 Cr App R (S) 134, followed in *R* v *Peppard* [1990] Crim LR 446 and *R* v *Helder* (1991) 13 Cr App R (S) 611, CA. These cases pre-date the implementation of s. 5 of the CJA 1991, which restricts the imposition of a suspended sentence to cases of 'exceptional circumstances'.

1.7.2.3 Sentence for breach of non-custodial orders Where under sch. 2, para. 8, to the CJA 1991 a custodial sentence is imposed for breach of a probation order, a community service order, an order for conditional discharge, or other community order, time is not deducted for any period spent in custody before the order was made: CJA 1967, s. 67(1) and (5). The Court of Appeal has held that the custodial sentence imposed in such circumstances should be reduced by an appropriate amount to compensate the offender for this time. In relation to probation orders, this point was stressed in *R* v *McDonald* (1988) 10 Cr App R (S) 458; *R* v *Gyorgy* (1989) 11 Cr App R (S) 1; and *R* v *Needham*, (1989) 11 Cr App R (S) 506. In relation to community service orders it was made in *R* v *McIntyre* (1985) 7 Cr App R.(S) 196; but in *R* v *MacKenzie* (1988) 10 Cr App R (S) 229, the Court of Appeal refused to interfere with a sentence passed in place of a community service order and held that the extent to which time spent in custody in such cases could be taken into account was a matter for judicial discretion. The importance of judicial discretion was emphasised in *R* v *Henderson* [1997] 2 Cr App R (S) 266. However, in *R* v *McCleod*, unreported, November 27 1998, CA (98/05728 W4), (cited in CLW/99/4/14) the Court of Appeal reduced the sentence by double the amount of time spent on remand where the judge stated in accordance with *Practice Direction (Custodial Sentences: Explanations)* [1998] 1 WLR 278, that any time spent in custody would count towards the sentence but failed to make any allowance for time spent in custody prior to the imposition of the community service order.

1.7.2.4 Remand in custody for breach will discount against subsequent custodial sentence The effect of s. 67 of the CJA 1967 is that where an offender is in custody before being dealt with for breach of a probation order, community service order, or suspended sentence, time is deducted from any sentence of imprisonment imposed or ordered to be served subsequently.

1.7.2.5 Offences subsequently taken into consideration In *R* v *Towers* (1987) 9 Cr App R (S) 333, CA, the appellant spent about 18 days in custody after being arrested for an offence which was subsequently taken into consideration. It was held that this time was not deductible from the sentence by virtue of s. 67, but 'as an act of mercy . . . on the special facts' of the case sentence was reduced by one month.

1.8 DEFERRED SENTENCE

Bail must not be imposed upon deferment of a sentence: *R* v *Ross* (1988) 86 Cr App R 337. Section 1(6A) of the Powers of Criminal Courts Act 1973 states that notwithstanding any enactment, a court which under the section defers passing sentence shall not on the same occasion remand the offender.

2 Surety and Security

2.1 SURETY FOR ATTENDANCE

2.1.1 Nature of suretyship

2.1.1.1 General aspects In contrast with the power, created by statute in 1967, to impose unspecified conditions of bail, the requirement to find a surety or sureties as a condition for release on bail is as old as bail itself. Indeed, historically sureties are instrinsic to the very term 'bail'; in the 17th century Hale defined the latter as 'the delivery of a person out of custody into the custody of sureties' (*Pleas of the Crown*, 2 vols, i, 96; the treatise was first printed in 1736 from a manuscript by the author, who died in 1680). The word 'surety' means a person who undertakes to be made responsible for another, and sureties for bail are required to undertake to be responsible for the surrendering of the bailed person to custody on pain of being liable to forfeit the sum of money fixed beforehand by the bailing authority as a condition of releasing the person on bail. The undertaking is known as a *recognizance*, that is an acknowledgement, or recognition, of liability. The BA 1976 clearly states that the purpose of a surety is to 'secure [the accused's] surrender to custody' (s. 3(4)) and that purpose is given effect by the obligation of the surety to guarantee surrender. The failure of the accused to surrender will generally (although not necessarily) imply a failure on the part of the surety, the cost of which will be an order for the forfeiture of a portion or the whole of the sum assured, or liability to imprisonment in default. In *R v Southampton Justices, ex parte Green* [1976] QB 11, Lord Denning MR set out the characteristics of a recognizance. It is in the nature of a bond, the breach of which gives rise to a civil debt. It is different from other civil debts in that it may be enforced by a warrant of distress or a committal to prison. The difference is only in the manner of enforcement; the nature of the debt is simply a civil debt upon a bond.

2.1.1.2 Authorities empowered to grant bail in criminal proceedings Criminal courts and courts exercising criminal law jurisdiction are vested with the power generally to impose the requirement of sureties as a condition of granting bail to defendants facing criminal proceedings. However, it is not only criminal courts which have this power. In exercising their discretion to grant bail to persons who are in custody during the initial stages of the criminal process the police also have the authority to impose sureties. Section 47(1) of PACE 1984, which is captioned 'bail after arrest', provides that where a person is released on bail under Part IV of the Act (the detention for inquiries provisions) such a release is 'a release on bail granted in accordance with [s.]3 . . . of the BA 1976 as [it] appl[ies] to bail granted by a constable'. Section 47(3) provides that the granting of bail in the context is subject to a duty:

(a)   to appear before a magistrates' court at such time and such place; or
(b)   to attend at such police station at such time, as the custody officer may appoint.

Section 3(4) of the BA 1976 provides that persons granted bail in criminal proceedings may be required, before release on bail, to provide a surety or sureties to secure their surrender to custody. It follows that when a person in detention under Part IV of PACE 1984 is granted bail, sureties may be imposed conditional on the person surrendering to court or to the police station. Confirmation of the power of the police to impose sureties when a person is bailed after charge to surrender in due course to the magistrates' court is furnished by s. 43 of the MCA 1980. Section 38(1) of PACE 1984 provides that a person charged by the police with an offence may be released from detention with or without bail. Where persons are charged and released on bail they will usually be required to surrender to custody at a magistrates' court on a given date, although there is nothing in PACE 1984 to prevent the police from granting bail to a charged person to return to the police station for inquiries into other matters. Where a person who has been charged is required to surrender to court in due course it is clear from s. 43 of the MCA 1980 that the police have a power to impose sureties. The section provides that where a person is granted bail under Part IV of PACE 1984 subject to a duty to appear before a magistrates' court, the court before which the person is to appear may appoint a later time as the time for appearance and 'may enlarge the recognizances of any sureties'. Although it is not unknown for the police to require sureties when a defendant is charged and bailed pending appearance in court, it is virtually unknown in practice for sureties to be required when suspects, not being charged, are given police bail to return to the police station for further inquiries into the offence being investigated.

2.1.2   Abolition of personal recognizances

Prior to the Bail Act 1976, defendants in criminal proceedings could be admitted to bail on their own recognizance, with or without sureties. The Act abolished the power to take a personal recognizance as a condition of granting bail (s. 3(2)), replacing it with the imposition on the accused of a duty to surrender to custody, such duty being enforceable (s. 3(1)). The removal by s. 54(1) of the CDA 1998 of the former restriction on the provision of a security for attendance to cases in which there is a risk that the defendant will leave Great Britain effectively restores the old power of the court to require defendants to be bound in their own recognizance. There are, of course, elements of distinction between own recognizance and security. First, the security has to be lodged in an account controlled by the court, whereas a recognizance is merely an undertaking to be bound to pay the sum involved in the event of a failure to surrender. Secondly, the source of the security is immaterial; it may be lodged by the defendant or on the defendant's behalf. The defendant's recognizance was a personal undertaking. This may have very significant implications for the development of bail procedures on the light of the 1998 Act, which are discussed later in this chapter (see para. 2.2, below).

2.1.3   Excessive bail must not be demanded

It was pointed out in Chapter 1 that refusal of bail to any person who should properly be granted bail is a violation of the Habeas Corpus Act 1679 and of the Bill of Rights 1688. The Bill of Rights also declares the corollary of that principle, that is: 'Bail must not be excessive.' It is wrong, in other words, to demand a recognizance which is excessive having regard to the gravity of the crime, the evidence against the accused, and the personal circumstances of the accused. By prohibiting the setting of bail at unjustifiably high levels the statute clearly sought to prevent courts from affecting the cosmetic appearance of observing fairness while at the same time depriving accused persons of the proper right to the presumption of innocence, reflected in their liberty pending trial. Until courts were prohibited by the Bail Act from granting bail on the defendant's own recognizance the amount of bail which could be considered reasonable bore a direct relation to the defendant's assets. However, although that linkage was severed with the BA 1976, there was always an indirect relationship in reality between the monetary worth of defendants and that of their sureties. Just as rich people were likely to have wealthy kin or friends, so people in humble circumstances were unlikely to be able to offer sureties other than from a similar station in life to their own. To demand of defendants amounts of surety significantly in excess of those likely to be available among their friends and family was arguably to undermine the Bill of Rights. It has been said to be fallacious to argue that the amount set for a surety should be reduced on account of the surety's means because, otherwise, persons of very limited means could be put forward as sureties in all serious cases and the sanction against absconding would be severely devalued and open to abuse (see Chatterton, *Bail: Law and Practice*, London: Butterworth, 1986, p. 109). The argument is unconvincing. In general terms a defendant of known or reputed means will be presumed to have family or one or two friends, at least, of broadly similar wealth. For such a defendant to claim to be unable to find sureties in sums comparable or proportionate to his or her own wealth, if a genuine protestation, speaks only to a lack of community ties, which is a good reason in itself for believing the person will fail to surrender.

The principle that bail must not be excessive was relied upon in an application for habeas corpus in *Ex parte Thomas* [1956] Crim LR 119, DC. The applicant was charged with the robbery of 3 shillings on Clapham Common. He was granted bail in his own recognizance of £100 with a surety in £500. The applicant was quite unable to find a surety in that amount and sought habeas corpus on the grounds that the imposition of such excessive bail amounted to a grant of no bail, contravened the Bill of Rights 1688 and thus made his imprisonment unlawful. It was held that the correct procedure had been followed and that in the 18th and early 19th centuries habeas corpus was often used for the purpose of obtaining bail. The application was adjourned until after the further hearing in the magistrates' court in order that notices might be served. Counsel was asked to request the magistrate either to reduce the amount of bail sought, or to acquaint the High Court with his reasons for imposing such high bail. The magistrate reduced the surety to that in £100 and the application for habeas corpus was dismissed. (See commentary, *ibid.*, and see *Ex parte Speculand* [1946] KB 48 and *R* v *Manning* (1888) 5 TLR 139.)

2.1.4 Obligations of the surety

Bail may have been defined in the 17th century as 'the delivery of a person out of custody into the custody of sureties' (*per* Hale; see para. 2.1.1.1) but whether the role of surety ever implied such a duty there is certainly no existing rule that sureties must literally keep the accused in their custody. Their responsibility is restricted to guaranteeing the accused's surrender to court or police custody (where they are required to ensure the latter). In meeting that obligation there must be more than a mere wish to prevent the accused from absconding. To 'get wind' of the accused's intent to abscond but to do nothing is to abdicate responsibility. Active steps must be taken: *R* v *Salford Stipendiary Magistrate, ex parte Monaghan, The Times*, 18 July 1984. Short of insisting on residence in the surety's home, the very least the surety must do is to keep in close and frequent contact with the accused and to keep abreast of any variations in conditions of bail. Yet this will seldom guarantee the discovery of a secret intent to abscond, and in practice there will be little a surety can do, even exercising all due diligence, to prevent a determined effort by the accused to abscond. On the other hand, where the surety is alerted to an impending escape, prevention will not necessarily involve the surety being required to deploy physical restraint, although the surety's use of reasonable force will plainly be lawful. (In some United States jurisdictions the use of 'deadly force' is permitted.) In *Consolidated Exploration and Finance Company* v *Musgrave* [1900] 1 Ch 37, 64 JP 89, Lord Alverstone CJ said of the relationship between sureties and the accused that 'they may seize his person at any time or at any place so as to carry him to a justice to find new sureties or be committed in discharge'. In practice, however, the surety will usually be advised to enlist the assistance of the police. Provided the surety at the earliest possible opportunity alerts them to the impending disappearance of the accused, that should

be enough to discharge the obligation of suretyship. In *R* v *Porter* [1910] 1 KB
369, at p. 373, Lord Alverstone CJ said:

> It is to the interest of the public that criminals should be brought to justice and,
> therefore, that it should be made as difficult as possible for a criminal to
> abscond; for many years it has been held that not only are [persons who go] bail
> responsible on their recognizance for the due appearance of the person charged,
> but that if it comes to their knowledge that he is about to abscond, they should
> at once inform the police of the fact. [The words in brackets were omitted from
> the report as the result of a misprint. They were included in a version of the
> same passage in [1909–10] All ER 78, at p. 80.]

Standing as a surety involves a very serious obligation and it is only fair and
proper that a prospective surety should be made aware officially of the burden. A
Home Office circular (206/1977, p. 7) advises courts of the importance of ensuring
that the proposed surety is made aware both of the responsibilities and of the
consequences if the surety should abscond. However, there appears to be no legal
obligation on courts to give any such advice to proposed sureties. In *R* v *Ebbw
Vale and Merthyr Tydfil Justices, ex Parte Raynsford and Campbell*, unreported,
20 October 1980 (cited in *Justice of the Peace*, vol. 145, No. 1, p. 1, 3 January
1981), two men accused of drug offences were granted bail on condition *inter alia*
that they should each provide a surety in £1,000 and their *de facto* wives
volunteered. The men were subject to suspended sentences also for drug offences
and, bearing in mind that if convicted they would, or might, be facing long prison
sentences, the magistrates were very careful to give a clear warning to the women
as to the risks involved. They were not put off and the magistrates then went even
further and instructed their clerk to advise the women that if at any time they had
reason to feel that they could no longer undertake the duties and obligations of
sureties they were to notify the police, and upon the men surrendering to their bail
or being arrested, they would be able to terminate their suretyship. Having been
granted bail the two men, without any indication to the women, made an excuse
that they were going off on a social visit, left the scene and failed subsequently to
reappear at court. It was argued on behalf of the women that it was impracticable
for them to follow the men about all day long, as shadows, and report to the police
the moment they acted in any way suspiciously. They were seeing the men every
evening, living in the same house, and there was nothing further they could have
done. The magistrates did give some thought to the existence of a conspiracy
between the women and the men but accepted the women's account. Having done
so they decided that if they were to do other than order the whole bail to be
estreated they would undermine the purpose of requiring sureties. Giving the
judgment of the Divisional Court upholding the magistrates' decision, Donaldson
LJ said that what the magistrates did in warning the women was right, helpful and
clearly very sensible, but that in doing so *they were probably going almost beyond
their duty*.

2.1.5 Suitability of sureties

2.1.5.1 Statutory factors to be considered Section 8(2) of the BA 1976 provides that in considering the suitability of a proposed surety as a condition for releasing a person on bail, regard may be had (amongst other things) to the surety's:

(a)   financial resources;

(b)   character and any previous convictions; and

(c)   proximity (whether in point of kinship, place of residence or otherwise) to the person to be bailed.

It is expressly provided that these three factors are not exhaustive. It will be for the court or the constable to decide which factors are most important.

2.1.5.2 Primary consideration: sufficiency of proposed surety's resources The principal consideration which the court must determine in assessing the suitability of sureties is the question whether they have sufficient financial resources to answer for the sum in which they are to be bound: Hawkins, *Pleas of the Crown*, 1716, c.15, s. 5. It is for magistrates or judges in their discretion to determine whether the surety has sufficient funds: *R v Saunders* (1849) 2 Cox CC 249. Since proposed sureties may only be required to enter into a recognizance for sums which it is within their ability to pay, it has been observed that the recognizance must come out of the surety's personal property, not out of any joint property or the matrimonial home: *R v Southampton Justices, ex parte Green* [1976] QB 11. Although the court will always be rigorous in inquiring into the means of proposed sureties, this does not exempt sureties from responsibility in the assessment of their means. In *R v Waltham Forest Justices, ex parte Parfrey* (1980) 2 Cr App R (S) 208, Donaldson LJ said (at p. 211): 'There is an obligation on a surety to be fully satisfied that he or she can meet the liability which will arise if the accused person does not surrender to bail.' The Home Office circular HO 206/1977 advises at p. 6 that '[i]t is for the court to decide what extent the means of the individuals put forward as sureties should affect the amount in which they stand'. It is irresponsible, and possibly a matter for consideration by a professional disciplinary body, for lawyers or legal executives to tender anyone as a surety unless they have reasonable grounds for believing that the surety would, if necessary, be able to meet his financial undertaking: *R v Birmingham Crown Court, ex parte Rashid Ali and another*; *R v Bristol Magistrates' Court, ex parte Davies*; *R v Immigration Appellate Authority, ex parte Davies, The Times*, 16 October 1998. Unless the surety has had separate legal advice, a court clerk should make some inquiries so as to be satisfied that the surety would, if necessary, be able to pay: *ibid.*

2.1.5.3 Character and criminal record The character or any previous convictions of a surety will *prima facie* be highly material. A person with convictions will not automatically be rejected, particularly where the convictions are old and in a category different from that involved in the instant case, but it is usually advisable to find sureties with a clean record in order to avoid objections being raised on that ground.

2.1.5.4 Proximity The proximity of the surety to the accused in terms of kinship or friendship may be an advantage or a disadvantage depending on the circumstances. In one case the existence of a close relationship may deter the accused from treating the surety's stake as expendable. In another case it may increase the risk of connivance and collusion. Geographical proximity will generally be an advantage through making it easier and more convenient for the surety to monitor or supervise the accused. Relatives or friends living at a distance from the accused would be less acceptable to a court than those residing in the same district.

2.1.5.5 Persons debarred from standing as surety There are a number of categories of person who are not permitted to stand as surety. They are:

(a)   the defendant's solicitor (not precluded by law, but it has been held that it is not expedient for solicitors to act as surety for their clients: *R* v *Scott-Jarvis*, *The Times*, 20 November 1876, QBD);

(b)   a minor (by analogy with the general law of contract, although there is no direct authority on the point);

(c)   a person in custody (since this will preclude the exercising of control of the accused);

(d)   a person who has been indemnified by the accused.

2.1.5.6 Irrelevant factors The political opinions of the proposed surety are irrelevant: *R* v *Badger* (1843) 4 QB 468, in which the Divisional Court criticised magistrates who refused to accept Chartists as sureties for people arrested in Chartist disturbances. If political opinions are irrelevant, then *a fortiori* regard may not be had to the race, religion, or sex of a proposed surety. Disability may be a relevant consideration, but only if it might result in the proposed surety being unable to exercise control over the defendant.

2.1.5.7 Determining suitability A proposed surety may be examined on oath as to means: see *R* v *Hall* (1776) 2 WB1 110. The court may in its discretion order that reasonable notice must be given to the prosecutor and the police to enable them to inquire into or object to the sufficiency of the surety. A proposed surety must understand the nature of the obligations of suretyship and should be asked the following questions, either in court, or by the person taking the recognisance if it is taken elsewhere (for example at a police station):

(a)   Are you willing to stand surety for the defendant in the sum the court is proposing to fix?

(b)   What is your relationship to the defendant?

(c) Do you understand what it means to stand surety?

(d) Are you worth the sum proposed after all your debts if any are paid?

(e) How would you find that sum if called upon to do so at short notice?

(f) Do you appreciate that if the defendant failed to attend court you might have to pay all or part of that sum of money?

(g) Do you realise that if the defendant failed to attend and you were unable to pay, you would be liable to be sent to prison yourself?

(h) What degree of control are you able to exercise of the defendant?

Where the recognizance is taken by a court, these questions are usually put to the proposed surety on oath.

2.1.6 Postponement of the taking of sureties

2.1.6.1 Surety amount must be fixed where court grants bail Section 8(3) of the BA 1976 provides that where a court grants bail on condition that the accused furnishes a surety or sureties but is unable to release the defendant because no surety or suitable surety is available, the court must fix the amount in which the surety is to be found and the recognizance may be entered into subsequently. Only a court may exercise the power to postpone the taking of a surety's recognizance. A court as defined includes a judge and a justice of the peace: BA 1976, s. 2(2). The police have no powers of postponement.

2.1.6.2 Officials before whom the postponed recognizance may be taken Section 8(4) of the BA 1976 provides that where the taking of a recognizance for surety is postponed, the recognizance may be taken by such of the following persons or descriptions of persons as the court may by order specify, or, if it makes no such order, before any of the following persons:

(a) where the decision is taken by a magistrates' court, before a justice of the peace, a justices' clerk or a police officer who either is of the rank of inspector or above or is in charge of a police station, or, if magistrates' courts rules so provide, by a person of such other description as is specified in the rules;

(b) where the decision is taken by the Crown Court, before any of the persons specified in (a) above or, if Crown Court rules so provide, by a person of such other description as is specified in the rules (r. 20(2) of the Crown Court Rules 1982 (SI 1882 No. 1109; CCR 1982) authorises the recognizance to be taken before an officer of the Crown Court);

(c) where the decision is taken by the High Court or the Court of Appeal, before any of the persons specified in (a) above or, if Supreme Court rules so provide, by a person of such other description as is specified in the rules;

(d) where the decision is taken by the Courts-Martial Appeal Court, before any of the persons specified in (a) above or, if Courts-Martial Appeal Court rules so provide, by a person of such other description as is specified in the rules.

It is provided that where an amount of surety required as a condition of bail has been previously fixed, the recognizance may be entered into, where the accused is in a prison or other place of detention, before the governor or keeper of the prison or place: Magistrates' Court Rules 1981 (SI 1981 No. 552; MCR 1981), r. 86(1)(a); CCR 1982, r. 20(2); Rules of the Supreme Court 1965 (SI 1965 No. 1776; RSC 1965), Ord. 79, r. 9(6A). Home Office circular HO 206/1977, p. 7, advises courts that the proposed surety may enter into the recognizance before any of the persons listed as authorised for that purpose unless the court has limited the power to accept the recognizance to one or more of the personages or persons listed in (a) to (d) above. Such an order may mean that in some cases the proposed surety has to travel further to enter into a recognizance than if no limitation were imposed, and courts have been invited to use this power only when justified by particular circumstances (see Chatterton, *Bail: Law and Practice*, London: Butterworths, 1986, p. 110).

2.1.6.3 Accused granted bail must remain in custody until surety enters into recognizance Where defendants are granted bail subject to finding a surety, they must remain in custody until arrangements can be made for the surety to enter into the recognizance: MCA 1980, s. 128(2). The period of remand must not exceed the statutory time limit for such a remand.

2.1.6.4 Responsibilities attaching to postponed recognizance are the same as when entered into before a court Where a recognizance is entered into otherwise than in court, the same responsibilities attach to it as if it had been entered into before the court: BA 1976, s. 8(7); MCA 1980, s. 119(2); Criminal Justice Administration Act 1914, s. 24. See also Home Office circular HO 206/1977, p. 7. It is essential, therefore, for the official taking the recognizance to advise the surety of the responsibilities involved and the consequences should the defendant abscond.

2.1.6.5 Procedure for taking postponed recognizance Section 8(4) of the BA 1976 enacts that the rules of magistrates' courts, the Crown Court, the Supreme Court, or the Courts-Martial Appeal Court may prescribe the manner in which a postponed recognizance may be entered into and enforced and the persons by whom it may be enforced. The MCR 1981 provide a comprehensive code of procedures as they apply to magistrates' courts. The relevant rules are r. 86 and r. 87 (both amended by the Magistrates' Courts (Amendment) Rules 1984 (SI 1984 No. 1552)) and r. 88. The provisions for Crown Court practice are contained in CCR 1982, r. 20 and those relating to bail granted by the High Court are contained in RSC 1965, Ord. 79, r. 9, but for reasons which are unclear the rules relating to magistrates' courts procedure are more comprehensive than are those relating to the Crown Court and the High Court. Each of the statutory procedures in the following list is shown with the relevant rules which provide for it:

(a)   Court certificate to be issued showing amount of recognizance. The clerk of the magistrates' court which has fixed the amount in which a surety is to be bound by a recognizance as a condition for a person's release on bail must issue a certificate in the prescribed form showing the amount of the recognizance (MCR 1981, r. 86(2)).

(b)   Recognizance not to be taken without production of the certificate. A person authorised to take the recognizance shall not be required to take or do it without production of the certificate issued by the magistrates' court showing the amount and conditions, if any, of the recognizance (MCR 1981, r. 86(2)).

(c)   Court fixing an amount of surety must send certificate of notice to prison governor or keeper, etc. Where a court has fixed the amount in which any surety for bail is to be bound, the clerk of the court must give notice to the governor or keeper of the prison or place where the defendant is detained by sending a certificate required by r. 86(2): MCR 1981, r. 87(a).

(d)   Proposed surety in respect of bail granted by the Crown Court to give one day's notice to the prosecutor. A person who, in pursuance of an order made by the Crown Court, or as the case may be a judge of the High Court, for the grant of bail in criminal proceedings, proposes to enter into a recognizance must unless the Crown Court or, as the case may be, the High Court judge, otherwise directs, give notice to the prosecutor at least 24 hours before entering into the recognizance: CCR 1982, r. 20(5); RSC 1965, Ord. 79, r. 9(7) – in the latter case in Form No. 100 in Appendix A to the Rules of 1965.

(e)   Recognizance must be sent to the relevant court. Where the recognizance of any surety of a person committed to custody by a court is taken by any person outside the court which committed the accused to custody, the person taking the recognizance must send it to the clerk of that court, except where the accused has been committed in custody to the Crown Court for trial or for sentence or otherwise to be dealt with, in which case the person taking the recognizance must cause it to be transmitted to the appropriate officer of the Crown Court: MCR 1981, r. 86(4); RSC 1965, Ord. 79, r. 9(8)(a) and (b). Where in pursuance of an order of the Crown Court, a recognizance is entered into before any person, the recognizance must be sent forthwith to the appropriate Crown Court Officer: CCR 1982, r. 20(6). Home Office Circular No. 104/1972 advises that when a duly authorised person has taken a surety's recognizance, the prison governor should immediately be notified by telephone that this has been done in cases where it would be impracticable (e.g., because of the distance involved) for the surety's copy of the notice that recognizances have been taken to be presented at the prison in time to secure the prisoner's release that day. The governor should be advised that written confirmation in the prescribed form is being despatched by first class post to the prison.

(f)   Surety taken by prison governor or keeper, etc. If any person proposed as a surety for a person committed to custody by a magistrates' court produces to the governor or keeper of the prison or other place of detention in which the person so committed is detained, a certificate in the prescribed form to the effect that the

proposed surety is acceptable as such, signed by any of the justices composing the court or the clerk of the court and signed in the margin by the person proposed as a surety, the governor or keeper must take the recognizance of the person so proposed: MCR 1981, r. 86(3).

(g)   Person taking the recognizance must send notice thereof to the prison governor or keeper, etc. Where a court has fixed the amount in which any surety for bail is to be bound, any person authorised to take the recognizance must, on taking it, send notice thereof by post to the governor or keeper of the prison or place where the defendant is detained in the prescribed form (in the case of bail granted by the Crown Court, it is a copy of the recognizance which must be sent at the same time as the recognizance is sent to the appropriate Crown Court officer): MCR 1981, r. 87(b); CCR 1982, r. 20(6); RSC 1965, Ord. 79, r. 9(8).

(h)   Copy of recognizance-taker's notice to prison governor or keeper, etc, to be given to surety. The person authorised to take the recognizance must give to the surety a copy of the notice required to be sent by (f) above: MCR 1981, r. 87(b); RSC 1965, Ord. 79, r. 9(8).

(i)   Release of person bailed from custody when recognizance of surety has been taken. Where a court has, with a view to release on bail of a person in custody, fixed the amount in which a surety must be bound and has given notice thereof to the governor or keeper of the prison or place where that person is detained, the governor or keeper must, when satisfied that the recognizances of all sureties required have been taken, release the person detained, unless that person is in custody for some other cause (MCR 1981, r. 88). Home Office Circular No. 104/1972 advises that where the taking of a recognizance is confirmed by a telephone call to the prison governor from the person taking the recognizance and the governor is satisfied that the information is authentic and that the necessary written notice is being despatched by first class post, arrangements should be made for the immediate release of the prisoner on bail without awaiting the written notification.

2.1.6.6   Directions by court   The lack of comprehensiveness of the CCR 1982 and RSC 1965 by comparison with the MCR 1981 may be compensated for by the provision in all three that where under the BA 1976, s. 3(6), a requirement is imposed to be complied with before a person's release on bail, the court or the judge in chambers, as the case may be, may give directions as to the manner in which the requirement may be complied with: MCR 1981, r. 85; CCR 1982, r. 20(3); and RSC 1965, Ord. 79, r. 9(6B). Section 3(6) of the BA 1976 provides for the imposition, before release on bail, of such requirements as appear to the court to be necessary to secure, *inter alia*, that the person to be bailed surrenders to custody. If this embraces the power to require a surety, it would follow that r. 85, r. 20(3) and r. 9(6B) above confer the discretion to make *ad hoc* directions. The difficulty is that it is BA 1976, s. 3(4) which makes provision for the requirement, before release on bail, of a surety or sureties to secure the person's surrender to custody, the implication being that s. 3(6) is intended to provide for the imposition of conditions *apart from surety*. However, there is nothing in the terms of s. 3(6) which necessarily so restricts its application. That it may include a power to require a surety for attendance is suggested by the fact that s. 3(4) is a general power which may be exercised by the police as well as by courts. Section 3(6) conditions may be imposed by a court only and the provision for the postponed taking of recognizances applies exclusively to those required by courts.

2.1.7 Refusal of surety

Where a person in one of the categories listed under the last preceding head is not satisfied of the surety's suitability and refuses therefore to take a surety, the surety may apply to:

(a) the court which fixed the amount of the recognizance; or

(b) a magistrates' court for the petty sessions area in which the surety resides, for that court to take the recognizance;

and if the court is satisfied that the surety is suitable, it will take the recognizance: BA 1976, s. 8(5).

2.1.8 Option to make surety continuous

The surety's obligation may apply only to the hearing immediately following the taking of the recognizance or it may be continuous. A continuous surety will be responsible for the attendance of the accused at every time and place to which during the course of the proceedings the hearing may from time to time be adjourned. Section 128(1) and (4) of the MCA 1980 provide that when bail is granted by a magistrates' court, the court may direct that the recognizance be conditioned for the appearance of the accused:

(a) before that court at the end of the period on remand; or

(b) at every time and place to which during the course of the proceedings the hearing may be from time to time adjourned, and also before the Crown Court in the event of a committal for trial.

This is without prejudice to the power of the court to vary the order at any subsequent hearing: Criminal Justice Administration Act 1914, s. 19, as amended by Sch. 2 to the BA 1976. Indeed, nothing may deprive the court of the power at a subsequent hearing to remand the accused afresh: MCA 1980, s. 128(5). The power of a magistrates' court to make a surety continuous to the Crown Court arises only during an inquiry into an alleged offence. This means that the magistrates must be sitting as examining justices, that is, after the court has declined jurisdiction or the defendant has elected trial, or where the alleged offence is indictable only. Where the accused is committed for trial, and the recognizance of the surety has been made continuous to trial, the court may, in the absence of the surety, enlarge the recognizance so obliging the surety to secure that the person committed for trial also appears before the Crown Court: s. 129(4). Rule 84(2) of the MCR 1981 provides that if a magistrates' court, under s. 129(4) of the 1980 Act, enlarges the recognizance of a surety for a person committed for trial, it must give the surety notice thereof. Ultimately, however, it is for sureties to keep themselves informed of any bail conditions: *R v Wells St Magistrates' Court, ex parte Albanese* [1982] QB 333, in which it was said that sureties can help themselves by entering into recognizances only from one remand to the next. In that way they will learn of any variations of bail.

2.1.9   Variation of sureties and recognizances

A surety for attendance previously accepted by a court may apply to the court to be discharged from the obligation. Alternatively an application may be made for a variation of the bail terms with regard to recognizances. The court will inquire whether there has been any change of circumstances warranting an order for discharge or variation. For example, discharge would be appropriate where the surety intended leaving the neighbourhood and would be unable to exercise sufficient control over the defendant. A surety's assets may have diminished in value and it may be sought to vary the terms of bail by substituting one surety with two each in a lesser sum. Where bail has been granted by the High Court or the Crown Court, magistrates have no power to alter the amount of any recognizances. While the Crown Court may consider an application for bail from a person remanded in custody by magistrates (CCR 1982, r. 19) it may not consider an application to vary requirements of bail, including the requirement of sureties. Such an application may only be dealt with by a judge in chambers.

2.1.10   Enlargement of recognizance

Where a defendant has been remanded on bail to appear in court again on a particular date but does not do so, and the court is satisfied that this is because of illness or accident, the absent defendant may be further remanded and the recognizance of any surety conditioned for the defendant's appearance may be enlarged: MCA 1980, s. 129. If a magistrates' court before which any defendant is bound by a recognizance to appear enlarges the recognizance to a later time under s. 129 in the absence of the defendant, it must give the defendant and any sureties notice accordingly: MCR 1981, r. 84(1). Where a magistrates' court alters the time at which a defendant on bail is to appear or further remands a defendant who is absent under s. 129, it must give the defendant and any sureties notice thereof: MCR 1981, r. 91. The latter rule would seem to apply where a surety has previously been made continuous.

2.1.11   Existing surety not bound by Crown Court order renewing bail on same terms made in absence of surety's consent

Where a magistrates' court commits a person for trial on bail the bail ceases when the defendant surrenders to the Crown Court, whether for the purposes of arraignment or otherwise. If the Crown Court releases the defendant on bail thereafter, it is duty bound to consider the suitability of any conditions afresh, including the position of a surety. Where, therefore, a judge granted bail 'as heretofore' without considering the position of a surety required by the magistrates, this was ineffective for the purpose of renewing the suretyship as a condition of bail: *R* v *Kent Crown Court, ex parte Jodka*, (1997) 161 JP 638, DC.

2.1.12 Surety residing in Scotland

2.1.12.1 Suitable surety to be taken in Scotland before a constable If the court is satisfied of the suitability of a proposed surety residing in Scotland, it may direct that arrangements be made for the recognizance to be taken in Scotland before any constable, within the meaning of the Police (Scotland) Act 1967, having charge at any police office or station in like manner as the recognizance would be entered into in England or Wales: BA 1976, s. 8(6).

2.1.12.2 Suitability inquiries by the Scottish police The Scottish police should be asked to make inquiries about the suitability of the proposed surety. The request should be made by the English police on behalf of the court. The Scottish police will report back to the court, who will alone determine whether the person is suitable. The Scottish police will make inquiries only and will make no decision as to suitability. If the court decides that the proposed surety is suitable, the clerk should write to the Scottish police explaining the procedure for the taking of a recognizance and enclosing the necessary forms. A specimen letter for the use of courts has been agreed with the Scottish authorities. Three copies of the appropriate forms must accompany the letter (no stocks being held in Scotland): see the Magistrates' Courts (Forms) Rules 1981, SI 1981 No. 553. Home Office circular HO 11/1978 advises that the court should complete each of the forms, leaving the Scottish police officer simply to obtain the surety's signature, to witness the signing, and to dispatch the appropriate documents in accordance with the instructions in the letter.

2.1.12.3 Estreatment of Scottish surety If the recognizance of the Scottish surety is subsequently estreated (forfeited) the enforcement arrangements will be the same as those applicable in an English or Welsh court for a fine imposed on someone resident in Scotland: see Home Office circular HO 206/1977, p. 7.

2.1.13 Withdrawal by a surety

2.1.13.1 Right of withdrawal on likelihood of failure to surrender It is not clear if sureties enjoy an unfettered right to withdraw from their obligations whenever they so desire. The BA 1976 provides for a right to withdraw where sureties learn that the person for whom they are standing bail is unlikely to surrender and they wish to be relieved of their obligations: s. 7(3). Whether the common law affords a right to withdraw even if the surety has no reason to believe that the bailed person is unlikely to surrender is uncertain. Loss of assets would undoubtedly oblige the surety to inform the court that the recognizance could no longer be honoured. But if the surety's attitude to the accused ceased to be amicable, whether for reasons connected with the case or not, it is a moot point whether withdrawal would be permissible. It is arguable that a recognizance is a solemn undertaking concerning the liberty of the subject, and that once having entered into it a surety should not lightly be relieved of the obligation involved.

2.1.13.2   Police power of arrest when surety wishes to withdraw   If a surety notifies a constable in writing that the person on bail is unlikely to surrender to custody and that the surety wishes to be relieved of the obligations of standing bail, the constable may arrest the person without warrant: BA 1976, s. 7(3). Presumably the surety's anxiety would have to be assessed as a reasonable one to justify the arrest. It would be oppressive to make an arrest because the surety held an irrational fear that the bailed accused was going to abscond.

2.1.13.3   Requirement to produce arrested person before a court   As soon as practicable and in any event within 24 hours of being arrested under s. 7(3), the person arrested must be brought before a justice of the peace for the petty sessions area in which the arrest was made. Where the arrest is made less than 24 hours before the time originally appointed for the surrender to custody, the person must be brought before the court at which that surrender was to be made: BA 1976, s. 7(4).

2.1.13.4   Powers of the court to deal with the arrested person   If the justice of the peace is of the opinion that the person is not likely to surrender to custody, bail may be refused or granted subject to the same or to different conditions: BA 1976, s. 7(5). If the justice of the peace is not of the opinion that the person is not likely to surrender to custody, bail must be granted subject to the same conditions as were originally imposed: s. 7(5).

2.1.14   Forfeiture of recognizance: substantive principles

2.1.14.1   Forfeiture and discharge, remission or mitigation   At common law the recognizance was automatically forfeited if the accused failed to surrender. This reflected the belief that it was only the certainty of forfeiture which ultimately underwrote the probability that the accused would surrender to custody. The underlying incentive at work was well described by Lord Widgery CJ in *R* v *Southampton Justices, ex parte Corker* (1976) 120 SJ 214, DC, when he observed: 'The real pull of bail, the real effective force that it exerts, is that it may cause the offender to attend his trial rather than subject his nearest and dearest who has gone surety for him to undue pain and discomfort.'

Forfeiture in the Crown Court is no longer automatic. The Powers of the Criminal Courts Act 1973 (PCCA 1973), s. 31(1)(c), provides for the discharging of a recognizance or the reduction of the amount due thereunder. Provision for the estreatment of a recognizance entered into in respect of a person granted bail to appear before a Crown Court is also made by CCR 1982, r. 21(1) as amended by the Crown Court (Amendment) Rules 1998 (SI 1998 No. 2168), where it appears to the court that a default has been made in performing the conditions of the recognizance other than by failing to appear before the Crown Court in accordance with any such condition. It has been held that 'default' means 'failure', and that the court therefore enjoys a discretion under the rule to discharge or remit part of the sum otherwise due: *R v Warwick Crown Court, ex parte Smalley (No. 2)* [1987] 1 WLR 237. The possibility of making an application under s. 31 of the 1973 Act for an order discharging a recognizance or reducing the amount due thereunder after the Crown Court has forfeited it was considered in *R v Central Criminal Court, ex parte Naraghi and Binji* [1980] 2 Cr App R (S) 104, DC. (See also *R v Wood Green Crown Court, ex parte Howe* (1992) 93 Cr App R 213, DC.)

The effect of the MCA 1980, s. 120(1) and (3), as originally enacted was to give magistrates' courts a discretionary power to declare a recognizance to be forfeited in whole or in part or not at all. However, nothing in that Act or any other statute prescribed any particular procedure to be followed by the court in making a decision. In practice courts would usually make no order immediately but would set a date for the surety to appear to show cause why the recognizance should not be forfeit. As there was no requirement to order the surety's attendance, a surety might well disappear before a subsequent forfeiture order could be made, with the result that there might be no means of enforcing it. Forfeiture in cases of surety for attendance has now been placed on a much more formalised footing. Section 55 of the CDA 1998 replaces s. 120(1) – and s. 120(2), which relates to recognizances for good behaviour – with new subsection (1) and (1A), the effect of which is to impose on the court a strict requirement to make a forfeiture order *forthwith*. Further, the court is now required to issue a summons directed to persons bound by the recognizance as surety, requiring them to appear before the court on a date specified in the summons to show cause why they should not be ordered to pay the sum in which they are bound. On the date so specified, the court may proceed in the absence of any surety if satisfied that the summons has been served on the surety. Section 120 of the MCA 1980 as originally enacted was silent as to the machinery by which forfeiture proceedings in cases of sureties for attendance were to be instituted. It was only in relation to forfeiture of recognizances for good behaviour that the court was required to proceed by order made on complaint. The contrast appears to remain unchanged. An order for whole or part remission must be entered in the court register or in a separate dedicated register: MCR 1981, r. 65. The recognizance must come out of the surety's personal property, not out of any joint property or the matrimonial home or property belonging to another: see *R v Southampton Justices, ex parte Green* [1976] QB 11. (See further, para. 2.1.14.5)

2.1.14.2 Forfeiture ineffective unless surety valid To be valid the recognizance must have been entered into properly, a state of affairs that will generally be presumed (see *Ex parte Jeffreys* (1888) 52 JP 280). Since a recognizance has no validity without a solemn consent by the surety to be so bound, there can be no forfeiture where the surety gave no such consent. It has already been noted (see para. 2.1.11, above) that where a Crown Court renews a defendant's bail it is duty bound to consider the suitability of any conditions afresh, including the position of a surety; where, therefore, a judge granted bail 'as heretofore' without considering the position of a surety required by the committing magistrates, this was ineffective for the purpose of renewing the suretyship as a condition of bail: *R v Kent Crown Court, ex parte Jodka* (1997) 161 JP 638. Accordingly, there could be no order of forfeiture. *Ex parte Jodka* was distinguished in *R v Harrow Crown Court, ex parte Lingard* [1998] COD 254, where the surety had renewed her commitment by signing surety forms at the Crown Court after the court had re-admitted the defendant to bail on the same terms as before.

2.1.14.3   Accused's failure to surrender must be proved   There can clearly be no forfeiture unless it is strictly proved that the accused failed to surrender.

2.1.14.4   Notice of forfeiture hearing in the Crown Court   Rule 21(2) of the CCR 1982 provides that where the Crown Court is to consider making an order under r. 21(1) for a recognizance to be estreated, the appropriate officer of the court must give notice to that effect to the person by whom the recognizance was entered into indicating the time and place at which the matter will be considered; and no such order may be made before the expiry of seven days after the required notice has been given. Notice may be given by personal service, or sent by post to the surety's last usual or last known residence or place of business in England or Wales: r. 28. (Section 7 of the Interpretation Act 1978 provides that 'unless the contrary intention appears, the service is deemed to be effected by properly addressing, pre-paying and posting a letter containing the document, and unless the contrary is proved, to have been effected at the time at which the letter would be delivered in the ordinary course of the post'.) By contrast with Crown Court procedure there is no formal procedure in the magistrates' court for bringing a surety before the court to show why the recognizance should not to be forfeited. However, it has been observed that the rules of natural justice would require the giving of adequate notice of the time and place of the application for forfeiture (Chatterton, *Bail: Law and Practice*, p. 116).

2.1.14.5   Question whether forfeiture can be ordered in the absence of the surety   It would follow from the presumption of service adverted to in the last preceding paragraph that an absent surety against whom forfeiture is sought can be presumed to have received valid notice of the hearing and that an order for forfeiture in those circumstances ought to be lawful. In *R v Central Criminal Court, ex parte Naraghi and Binji* (1980) 2 Cr App R (S) 104, DC, the statutory rules on service of notice had been infringed and Stocker J observed (at p. 107):

It would seem to me that in a matter where the liberty of the subject is involved, as well as the question of estreating a large sum of money, the rule [as to giving notice] should be complied with, at least to the extent that notice should be delivered to the address [which the surety had given to the court]. It also would seem to me that this is the sort of situation which requires the presence before the court of a person whose recognizance is to be estreated. It has been suggested that that might impose an unduly onerous burden upon the prosecuting authorities or the officers of the court since circumstances may well arise in which a surety has absconded himself deliberately, possibly in company with the accused in respect of whose attendance he has made himself responsible. That seems to be a difficulty perhaps without any real substance in it, for in those circumstances it is improbable, to say the least, that the money due under the recognizance could be successfully obtained.

These comments have been said to leave in some doubt the question whether a court may forfeit a recognizance in the absence of the person bound (see Chatterton, *Bail: Law and Practice*, p. 116). Yet it is difficult to see where the supposed doubt lies. The court was merely stressing the need for compliance with notice procedures. It was not being said that even where proper notice had been given it was nevertheless desirable to have the surety present. (The fact that an absconding surety might have no money worth chasing was beside the point. Sureties who deliberately keep out of the way of the court can hardly be heard to complain that they have been deprived of a fair hearing.) Prior to the CDA 1998 there were no statutory provisions for notice as to forfeiture proceedings in magistrates' courts. Where a recognizance was conditioned for the appearance of a person before a magistrates' court and the recognizance appeared to the court to be forfeited, s. 120(1) of the MCA 1980 provided that 'the court may . . . declare the recognizance to be forfeited and adjudge the persons bound thereby . . . to pay the sum in which they are respectively bound'. Section 55 of the CDA 1998 replaced the relevant part of s. 120(1) with measures contained in a new subsection, s. 120(1A), which provides:

If, in the case of a recognizance which is conditioned for the appearance of an accused before a magistrates' court, the accused fails to appear in accordance with the condition, the court shall—
    (a)   declare the recognizance to be forfeited;
    (b)   issue a summons directed to each person bound by the recognizance as surety, requiring him to appear before the court on a date specified in the summons to show cause why he should not be adjudged to pay the sum in which he is bound;
and on that date the court may proceed in the absence of any surety if it is satisfied that he has been served with the summons.

The Crown Court (Amendment) Rules (SI 1998 No. 2168) apply the provisions for immediate forfeiture of a recognizance to the Crown Court. Section 120(1A) was added during Third Reading of the Bill in the House of Lords by a Government amendment moved by the Solicitor-General, who stated:

> [T]his clause seeks to strengthen the use of sureties in bail cases. . . . The new measure gives the magistrates' court a new power to declare a recognizance – that is, the agreed sum – to be forfeited immediately and automatically where a defendant fails to appear at a court hearing. The new clause deals only with the procedure in the magistrates' courts only because it is only those courts to which the existing provisions apply. Forfeiture of a surety's recognizance in other courts is dealt with by rules of court, which may be amended by subordinate legislation. (HL Deb, vol. 588, cols 236–237, 31 March 1998)

The Government's justification for the new measure is set out in *The Crime and Disorder Bill [HL] [Bill 167 of 1997–98]; Youth Justice, Criminal Procedures and Sentencing*, House of Commons Library Research Paper, 98/43, at p. 82:

> At present, when a defendant fails to answer to bail the court must first consider the extent to which the surety was at fault before deciding whether the sum shall be forfeited and whether the person bound should pay the whole sum or only part of it. In some cases we believe that this approach may encourage the surety to enter into this contract recklessly, perhaps in the belief that he will easily be able to persuade the court that he did all that he could and that his money is never in danger. . . . [T]he onus for establishing lack of culpability is shifted fairly and squarely onto the surety.

2.1.14.6 Requirement for court to observe elementary procedures going to the root of administrative justice It is implicit that in determining whether to order forfeiture or allow discharge or remission of the recognizance a court must observe those elementary procedures which lie at the root of administrative justice: see *R v McGregor* [1945] 2 All ER 180. Thus sureties against whom a breach of recognizance is alleged must be told the exact nature of the obligations involved in standing as a surety and the precise nature and manner of failing to comply with the undertaking. Further, they must be asked:

(a)   whether they wish to give evidence and explain their conduct;
(b)   whether they prefer to give an explanation from the dock; and
(c)   whether they have any witnesses to call.

2.1.14.7 Forfeiture will normally be ordered It has already been noted that in *R v Southampton Justices, ex parte Green* [1976] QB 11, Lord Denning MR pointed out that a recognizance is in the nature of a bond. As such it gives rise to a civil debt, which although different from the ordinary civil debt in its manner of enforcement, is in essence of the same nature. Accordingly, the forfeiture of a recognizance is not a criminal cause or matter and estreatment of a recognizance is not a trial of the surety for culpability the aim of which is punishment. In *R* v *Waltham Forest Justices, ex parte Parfrey* [1980] Crim LR 571, Donaldson LJ stressed that as the recognizance is a civil debt it is no different to a guarantee given on a civil contract and courts are not expected to remit that sort of obligation. Although forfeiture is no longer mandatory the general principle remains that where the defendant fails to appear, the full sum should normally be forfeited: *R* v *Uxbridge Justices, ex parte Heward-Mills* [1983] 1 All ER 530. In *R* v *Horseferry Road Magistrates' Court, ex parte Pearson* [1976] 2 All ER 264, DC, the court emphasised how important it was for sureties to realise that they were entering into a very serious obligation, a point which was reiterated by Donaldson LJ in *R* v *Ebbw Vale and Merthyr Tydfil Justices, ex parte Raynsford and Campbell* unreported, 20 October 1980 (cited in *Justice of the Peace*, vol. 145, No. 1, p. 1, 3 January 1981):

> It cannot I think be emphasized too much that . . . 'going bail', as it is put . . . for somebody accused of offences is a very serious matter, and one which carries with it a high degree of risk in all cases . . . it is only in the wholly exceptional cases that they can really expect the court to make any reduction in the amount which they have agreed shall be forfeit if the person concerned does not turn up for his trial.

Donaldson LJ also stressed the seriousness of the obligation in *R* v *Waltham Forest Justices ex parte Parfrey*, (above) when he observed that the failure to surrender was not a theoretical possibility, although the surety might think that it was. The event happened frequently; there was a real risk and no one should think the obligation could be entered into lightly. The burden of satisfying the court that the full sum should not be forfeited was a very heavy one and no one should think that they could appear before a court and tell some hard luck story to which the court would say 'Well, be more careful in the future'. In *ex parte Raynsford and Campbell* the two sureties claimed that they saw the two defendants each evening, they were living in the same house, and the defendants had absconded following a pretext that they were going out on a social visit. Acknowledging that they could have done no more, Donaldson LJ, dismissing the appeal, said: 'That is the story of all sureties where the man or woman concerned absconds; it is no answer.' In *R* v *Maidstone Crown Court, ex parte Lever and Connell* [1996] 1 Cr App R 524, the applicants stood surety in the sums of £19,000 and £40,000 for the defendant who failed to attend his trial. Although the judge at first instance found that there had been no culpability in either surety, he ordered them to forfeit £16,000 and £35,000 respectively. The Divisional Court refused their applications for judicial review and, in dismissing their appeals to the Court of Appeal, Butler-Sloss LJ stated that the governing principle was that reducing the financial obligation of a surety must be the exception rather than the rule and that it might be granted only in really deserving cases. Giving the judgment of the court she observed (at p. 526):

The general principle is that the purpose of a recognizance is to bring the defendant to court for trial. The basis of estreatment is not as a matter of punishment of the surety, but because he has failed to fulfil the obligation which he undertook. The starting point on the failure to bring a defendant to court is the forfeiture of the full recognizance.

2.1.14.8   Applicable factors in exercising discretion to waive forfeiture or reduce sum to be forfeited   The following factors appear to apply not only to magistrates' courts but also to all courts exercising their discretion in dealing with a breach of recognizance:

(a)   The question of means. In *R* v *Waltham Forest Justices, ex parte Parfrey*, above, it was pointed out that in *R* v *Horseferry Road Magistrates' Court, ex parte Pearson* [1976] 2 All ER 264, DC, the court had made it quite clear that, where there was no question raised as to the ability to pay, the magistrates were under no obligation to inquire as to the ability of the surety to pay. In the latter case it was acknowledged by the court that although forfeiture should be approached 'on the footing that the surety has seriously entered into a serious obligation' the question of the surety's means was a factor which in exceptional circumstances could be taken into account in determining whether it would be fair and just to allow the payment of a smaller sum. Apparently giving a slightly more charitable slant, Lord Denning MR, in *R* v *Southampton Justices, ex parte Green* [1976] QB 11, said that the surety's means *ought* to be taken into account in deciding whether all or part of the recognizance should be forfeited. In *R* v *Wood Green Crown Court, ex parte Howe* (1993) 93 Cr App R 213, DC, it was held that reference in the authorities to consideration of means implied that the court should have some regard to ability to pay and to the consequences for the surety of ordering payment in an amount which would inevitably lead to a term of imprisonment in default. Thus, if the surety's assets have diminished since the recognizance was taken it may be appropriate, after inquiring into the current state of means, to order a lesser sum to be forfeited commensurate with the surety's reduced circumstances (see Chatterton, *Bail: Law and Practice*, London: Butterworths, 1986, p. 121).

It has been argued that while the courts are bound, on the authorities, to consider the means of a surety, they should scrutinise claims of inability to pay with the greatest care, since it is the invariable practice to ask intending sureties how they would raise the money in the event of a default and to explain that the likely consequence of non-appearance and non-payment is imprisonment: *Archbold*, para. 3–143a. Sureties who mislead the court as to their means would be most unlikely to receive sympathetic treatment: *R* v *Bow Street Magistrates' Court, ex parte Hall, The Times*, 27 October 1996, CA in which it was observed that such a surety acted in a way which caused to the court to do that which it would not otherwise have done and struck at the roots of the surety system.

(b)   Bankruptcy. An order of discharge in bankruptcy does not release the bankrupt from any debt on the recognizance: Bankruptcy Act 1914, s. 28(1)(a).

Even though a surety dies, the recognizance would appear to subsist: *R* v *Kettle, ex parte Ellis* [1905] 1 KB 212.

(c) Culpability versus due diligence. Since the surety's debt is a civil one and proceedings for forfeiture supposedly involve no element of punishment, the absence of any obloquy or negligence on the part of the surety ought necessarily to be irrelevant. Yet the question whether or not the surety has shown 'culpability' in failing to prevent the person bailed from absconding is one which the courts have conceded might make a difference when it comes to deciding whether to order full forfeiture or, to a greater or lesser extent, partial remission of the recognizance. In *R* v *Southampton Justices, ex parte Green* [1976] QB 11, Lord Denning MR seemed to incline to a liberal approach, in that he appeared to stress the absence of connivance on the part of the surety in the defendant's disappearance as a factor which might warrant mitigation of the whole sum. This is to be inferred from the fact that he expressed the view that where the surety had been involved in such connivance it would be proper to forfeit the whole sum, whereas if the surety was merely wanting in 'due diligence' it *might* be proper to forfeit the whole or a substantial part of the recognizance (implying the propriety of *some* mitigation in the absence of connivance). In cases where the surety was not guilty of want of diligence and used every effort to secure the appearance of the accused, it might be proper to remit the sum entirely (but not necessarily), although entire remittal would be appropriate only in wholly extreme and exceptional cases. In Lord Denning's view the surety in that case, who had stood for her husband, 'did as much as any wife might be expected to do'. In *R* v *Maidstone Crown Court, ex parte Lever and Connell* [1996] 1 Cr App R 524, the Court of Appeal, in affirming that the presence or absence of culpability was a factor to be considered in remitting part or all of the recognizance, observed that the *dicta* of Lord Denning MR in *R* v *Southampton Justices, ex parte Green* and of Lawton LJ in *R* v *Bow Street Magistrates' Court ex parte Hall*, above, were misleading insofar as they gave the impression that the surety's degree of culpability was the guiding principle in the exercise of the discretion. This may be right if culpability is synonymous with connivance. If it means a lack of due diligence in the sense that the surety made less than every possible effort in the circumstances, it would be wrong. However, the former meaning is to be preferred and is consistent with the pattern of thinking in the authorities.

It was said in *Consolidated Exploration and Finance Company* v *Musgrave* [1900] 1 Ch 37, 64 JP 89, that a surety who believes that the accused is about to abscond is authorised to pre-empt this by the use of reasonable force. It is open to argument whether sureties must be prepared to use this power if they are to avoid forfeiture or whether it may be sufficient in such a situation to warn the police. In *R* v *Ipswich Crown Court, ex parte Reddington* [1981] Crim LR 618 the surety became worried that the accused was unreliable and reported her anxieties to the police but the Crown Court judge apparently treated this as inadequate. Criticising him for ignoring her efforts and misdirecting himself that she had been wrong to go to the police, the Divisional Court held that a surety who informs the police of fears that the defendant will fail to surrender may well be acting with due diligence warranting reduction of liability. However, they cautioned that sureties are not automatically relieved of their responsibilities by notifying the police in accordance with s. 7(3)(c) of the BA 1976 (see para. 2.1.13, *supra*). On the other hand, applying Lord Denning's dictum in *R* v *Southampton Justices, ex parte Green* that 'she did as much as any wife might be expected to do', it is arguable that a surety who acts in accordance with s. 7(3)(c) has done so in accordance with due diligence.

(d)   Surety warning police of a breach of a condition of residence. A surety who informs the police that the defendant is not complying with a condition of residence may be acting with due diligence: *R* v *Waltham Forest Justices, ex parte Parfrey* [1980] Crim LR 571. The applicant had told the police of her brother's whereabouts when she discovered that he was wanted by the police in connection with an alleged offence. He was arrested as a result of this information and granted bail with a surety and a condition of residence at his mother's home. The applicant stood surety. When her brother failed to arrive at the mother's home, she informed the police and told them of possible addresses to which he might go. She sought to withdraw her surety and her brother failed to surrender. The justices ordered her to forfeit the entire sum of the recognizance. The Divisional Court made an order of *certiorari* quashing the justices' decision. It would not have done so if, after hearing the applicant, the justices had been unable to find anything in her conduct which justified remitting the recognizance. The justices had gone much further and found a conspiracy between the surety and the defendant of which there was no evidence. This was therefore an application of the principle under para. 2.1.14.13, below.

(e)   Failure of court to warn surety of return date may be relevant. In *R* v *Reading Crown Court, ex parte Bello* (1992) 92 Cr App R 303, CA (Civ Div), it was said that a court should always notify sureties when a hearing date was fixed, and, if no date was fixed, notify them as to dates between which the case was likely to be listed. Such a warning should be given as far in advance as possible. A surety undertook to ensure the appearance of the accused at court when required. Ignorance of the date, however, would not always be an answer to proceedings for forfeiture. Each case would depend upon its own facts.

(f)   Relevance of bail variation to the due diligence issue. A particular application of the general principle that the court is under a duty to investigate whether the surety exercised due diligence or was negligent (see *R* v *Southampton Justices, ex parte Green*, above; *R* v *Knightsbridge Crown Court, ex parte Newton* [1980] Crim LR 715) is that a variation in conditions of bail may be relevant in determining whether the full recognizance should be forfeited: *R* v *Wells Street Magistrates' Court ex parte Albanese* (1981) 74 Cr App R 180, DC. There it was held that in entering into a recognizance, sureties have a duty to keep in touch with the bailed prisoner and to keep themselves informed of the conditions of bail so as to ensure that the defendant surrenders to bail. Where bail is made continuous, the court has no obligation to notify a surety that it is proposing to vary the

conditions of bail or to obtain the surety's consent to a variation. Accordingly, the order varying the conditions is valid and does not affect the recognizance entered into by the applicant. It was suggested that sureties can, if they wish, help themselves to keep informed of any variation in bail conditions, by entering into a recognizance only from one remand to the other. Although the court is under no duty to notify sureties of any changes, the fact that the surety had no knowledge of a variation might be relevant to the exercise of the discretion to order forfeiture. It is for the justices to determine the degree of neglect attributable to a surety in not knowing of the variation and to decide whether the surety would have acted differently had the variation been known. (See also *R v Inner London Crown Court, ex parte Springall and another* (1987) 85 Cr App R 214, DC.) It has been suggested that in many cases that fact would carry no weight because it could not have affected the action of the surety. The same commentator has suggested that sureties might be expressly warned, possibly on the appropriate form, that conditions of bail may be varied by the court without notice and the surety should not sign for continuous bail if concerned about the bail conditions, which might in themselves be usefully endorsed on the recognizance (Chatterton, *Bail: Law and Practice*, London: Butterworths, 1986, p. 120).

(g) *Complete absence of blame.* While the surety is under a duty to keep in contact with the accused and to be aware of conditions of bail, in extreme circumstances the surety may be wholly free of any blame. In *R v Berry: Re Serruys and Hopper* [1985] Crim LR 300, one of the defendant's conditions of bail was to surrender his passport. When it was inadvertently returned to him and he left the country, the sureties were held not to be bound by their recognizances. But in examining the facts of many of the reported cases it is not always easy to see the reasoning behind the court's refusal to discharge the recognizance. In *R v Salford Stipendiary Magistrate, ex parte Monaghan, The Times*, 18 July 1984, the defendant was on bail with sureties and absconded because he knew he was likely to be arrested for a much more serious offence. It was held that there was no duty on the authorities (i.e. the court, the police or the prosecuting authority) to inform the sureties of the warrant, so as to enable them to seek to be discharged of their obligation in advance of the defendant's failure to attend court. Accordingly there was no basis for treating their obligations as discharged. It has been observed that such a duty would, in many cases, be unworkable and would reverse the role of the surety, which is to take active steps to ensure that a defendant does not abscond (Chatterton, *Bail: Law and Practice*, p. 120). The argument smacks of an apologia for official complacency. Whereas it would have been a simple act of prudence on the part of the authorities to have alerted the sureties about the warrant, it is difficult to see why it should ever have occurred to the sureties that a warrant might have issued. The first instance decision in *Re Evans* (unreported) Kingston Crown Court, 21 March 1995, deserves mention. The defendant had been committed for trial on various charges in connection with motor vehicles and was granted bail with his uncle standing surety. He failed to attend court, and a warrant was issued for his arrest, but he told his uncle that he had been given a community penalty.

It was not disputed that he continued to live at the same address and to drive the same vehicle he had originally been arrested in, that he frequently visited the uncle, who lived in the same neighbourhood, and that he remained at large for nearly two years until he was arrested on new matters. It was conceded that the failure of the surety personally to ensure that the defendant originally attended court warranted forfeiture of a proportion of the recognizance. However, it was submitted that in the light of the failure of the police to execute the warrant despite the defendant's brazenness, it was only too natural that the surety should have assumed that his nephew had told him the truth and that he had no reason to take further action. The Crown Court judge nonetheless ordered the whole sum forfeited. In *R* v *Bristol Justices, ex parte Nisar Ahmed* [1997] COD 12, QBD, the surety acted in accordance with his solicitor's advice to make exhaustive efforts to discover the whereabouts of a defendant who had absconded. The justices' decision to forfeit the full amount of the recognizance was held to be perverse, the lower court having found the surety blameworthy in not having contacted the police when he knew the defendant had absconded.

2.1.14.9 Burden on surety to show that forfeiture should not be ordered
The burden of satisfying the court that the sum should not be forfeited rests on the surety, whose obligation it is to lay before the court evidence of means and want of culpability: *R* v *Uxbridge Justices, ex parte Heward-Mills* [1983] 1 All ER 530; *R* v *Maidstone Crown Court, ex parte Lever and Connell* [1996] 1 Cr App R 524.

2.1.14.10 Unrepresented surety In *R* v *Waltham Forest Justices, ex parte Parfrey* [1980] Crim LR 571, it was pointed out that in *R* v *Horseferry Road Magistrates' Court, ex parte Pearson* [1976] 2 All ER 264, DC, the court had made it clear that where a surety is unrepresented courts should bear in mind the possibility that there may be a problem of means and that the surety may not be aware of the importance of raising the question. Courts should try to be as helpful as possible. In *R* v *Uxbridge Justices, ex parte Heward-Mills*, above, it was observed that when a surety is unrepresented the court should explain the principles to be applied in ordering forfeiture in ordinary language and should give the surety the opportunity to call evidence and advance argument: As to the particular duty to inquire into all the circumstances in the case of an unrepresented surety, see *R* v *Reading Crown Court, ex parte Bello* (1992) 92 Cr App R 303, CA (Civ Div).

2.1.14.11 Unavailability of legal aid Criminal legal aid is not available to enable a surety to be represented in connection with forfeiture proceedings: *R* v *The Chief Clerk Maidstone Crown Court, ex parte Clark* [1995] 2 Cr App R 617, DC, but civil legal aid may be. Further, the Legal Advice and Assistance (Scope)(Amendment) Regulations 1997 (SI 1997 No. 997) make advice by way of representation (ABWOR) available to persons at risk of imprisonment for failure to obey a court order. Moreover, the Legal Aid Board Duty Solicitor Arrangements 1997, para. 30(2)(6), provide that a duty solicitor at a magistrates' court shall where necessary provide advice and representation to a defendant who is before the court as a result of failure to pay a fine or other sum ordered or to obey an order of the court, and such failure may lead to the defendant being at risk of imprisonment. This provision was made in response to the decision in *Benham* v *UK* (1996) 22 EHRR 293; *The Times*, 24 June 1996, that denial of legal aid to a poll tax defaulter at a hearing before magistrates was a breach of Art. 6 of the European Convention for the Protection of Human Rights and Fundamental Freedoms (1950) (Cmnd 8969) – hereafter referred by its popular title, the 'European Convention on Human Rights'. Article 6(1) provides that '[i]n the determination . . . of any criminal charge against him, everyone is entitled to a fair . . . hearing' and Art. 6(3) provides that '[e]veryone charged with a criminal offence has the . . . right . . . if he has not sufficient means to pay for legal assistance, to be given it free when the interests of justice so require'. The words 'criminal charge' in Art 6. bear an autonomous meaning, independent of the categorisation under domestic law.

2.1.14.12 Order for forfeiture must not be premature In *R* v *Inner London Crown Court, ex parte Springall and another* (1987) 85 Cr App R 214, the Divisional Court described as premature an order for forfeiture where the question had been considered in advance of a fixed date for trial. The defendant had gone abroad in breach of his bail conditions and it was held that the matter should have been considered once it was known that he would not appear to stand trial.

2.1.14.13 Tribunal must act judicially and on evidence As the estreatment of a recognizance is not a conviction, no right of appeal lies to the Crown Court against a magistrates' court order for forfeiture: *R* v *Durham Justices, ex parte Laurent* [1945] KB 33. However, forfeiture orders by magistrates' courts and Crown Courts are not immune from judicial review under s. 23(3) of the Supreme Court Act 1981 (SCA 1981): *Re Smalley* [1985] AC 622, HL, overruling *R* v *Sheffield Crown Court, ex parte Brownlow* [1980] QB 530 (see, further, Chapter 10, para. 10.3.4). The Divisional Court will determine whether the justices, for example, in exercising their discretion to order forfeiture under MCA 1980, s. 120, acted judicially and on the basis of evidence and not speculation: *R* v *Waltham Forest Justices, ex parte Parfrey* [1980] Crim LR 571. If the justices failed to exercise their discretion, or exercised it on wrong principles or following an erroneous finding of the facts, the Divisional Court will intervene. This is an application of the so-called '*Wednesbury* principles', laid down in *Associated Provincial Picture Houses Ltd* v *Wednesbury Corporation* [1948] 1 KB 223, in which it was held that in exercising a discretion:

(a)   regard must be had to any matter which ought to be taken into account;

(b)   regard must not be had to any matter which ought not to be taken into account; and

(c)   the conclusion reached must not be one which no reasonable tribunal could reach.

In *R* v *Tottenham Magistrates' Court, ex parte Riccardi* (1978) 66 Cr App R 150, the Divisional Court gave guidance as to the attitude which the court should adopt with regard to forfeiture orders made by magistrates, and held that there was no power to interfere by way of *certiorari* unless it could be said that no reasonable bench properly instructed could have reached the decision made.

Although a judge's discretionary power to forfeit a recognizance is extraordinarily wide, the Divisional Court will interfere where a decision is plainly wrong. In *R* v *York Crown Court, ex parte Coleman and How* (1988) 86 Cr App R 151, DC, the sureties had ensured the defendant's attendance at each preliminary hearing and at the committal hearing. The defendant surrendered on the morning of his trial but failed to return to the court after the case had been adjourned to 2.00 pm. The Divisional Court held that the judge's decision to forfeit the entire amount of the recognizances was plainly wrong. Compare *R* v *Warwick Crown Court, ex parte Smalley (No. 2)* [1987] 1 WLR 237, in which the Divisional Court refused to interfere with the judge's discretion in a case where it could not be said that the judge's decision was so unreasonable that no reasonable judge could have made it.

2.1.15   Enforcement of forfeiture

2.1.15.1   Surety becomes a debtor to the Crown   Where the defendant fails to answer bail and the recognizance entered into by the surety is ordered to be forfeited, the surety becomes a debtor to the Crown for that sum: *R* v *Southampton Justices, ex parte Green* [1976] QB 11, CA, at pp. 15 and 19.

2.1.15.2   Recognizance analogous to fine for enforcement purposes   Although the estreatment of a recognizance is not a conviction (*R* v *Durham Justices, ex parte Laurent* [1945] KB 33), the powers of enforcement in relation to a recognizance are analogous to those in relation to a fine. Where a recognizance conditioned for a person's appearance before a magistrates' court is ordered to be forfeited, payment of any such sum may be enforced as if it were a fine and as if the adjudication were a summary conviction of an offence not punishable with imprisonment: MCA 1980, s. 120(4). This will also be the case in respect of a recognizance conditioned for a person's appearance in the higher courts (see para. 2.1.15.5). The effect of the words 'summary conviction of an offence not punishable by imprisonment' is that magistrates may not commit a surety to prison for non-payment of a forfeited recognizance on the ground that the surety has sufficient means to pay forthwith without inquiring whether the surety does have such funds. This may involve the court exercising its powers to order a personal search (see further para. 2.1.15.10).

2.1.15.3   Remission of forfeited sum   A court which declares a recognizance to be forfeited may, instead of adjudging any person liable to pay the whole sum, order the person to pay part only of it or may remit the whole sum: MCA 1980,

s. 120(3). The provision of s. 85 of the MCA 1980 empowering a court to remit the whole or a part of a fine or to commit the offender to prison for non-payment applies to a forfeited recognizance, but the power of remission applies only after a term of imprisonment has been imposed on the surety in default and at any time before the issue of a warrant of commitment to enforce payment of the sum, or before the sale of goods under a warrant of distress to satisfy the sum: s. 120(4). Such remission may be absolute or on such conditions as the court thinks just.

2.1.15.4 No transmission to Crown Court of recognizance entered into before a magistrates' court A recognizance entered into before a magistrates' court shall not be transmitted to the Crown Court, nor shall its forfeiture be certified to that court: MCA 1980, s. 120(5).

2.1.15.5 Recognizance forfeited by the Crown Court, Court of Appeal (Criminal Division) or the House of Lords A recognizance forfeited by the Crown Court is treated for the purposes of collection, enforcement and remission as having been forfeited by a magistrates' court specified in an order made by the Crown Court, or, if no such order is made, by the magistrates' court by which the offender in question was committed to the Crown Court to be tried or dealt with: PCCA 1973, s. 32(1). For the same purposes a recognizance forfeited by the Criminal Division of the Court of Appeal, or by the House of Lords on appeal from that division is treated as a recognizance forfeited by the Crown Court: s. 32(3) and (5). A magistrates' court may not remit the whole or part of any forfeited recognizance transferred to it from the Crown Court, the Court of Appeal or the House of Lords, without the consent of the Crown Court.

2.1.15.6 No power to order costs against surety As forfeiture of recognizances in bail cases has no statutory footing and is not a procedure by way of complaint, it appears that there is no power to order costs against a surety in proceedings brought to estreat a recognizance (see Chatterton, *op. cit.*, para. 5.22, p. 122).

2.1.15.7 Payment deferred Statutory provision is made for courts to allow time for the payment of an amount due under a forfeited recognizance: PCCA 1973, s. 31(1)(a) (Crown Court); MCA 1980, s. 75(1), (magistrates' courts); MCA 1980, s. 75(2), (further time). Written notice must be given to the surety of the terms, where time to pay is allowed or where the surety was absent from the proceedings: MCR 1981, r. 46(1).

2.1.15.8 Payment by instalments Statutory provision is made for courts to allow the payment of an amount due under a forfeited recognizance to be made by instalments: PCCA 1973, s. 31(1)(b) – order by the Crown Court for payment by instalments 'of such amounts and on such dates respectively as may be specified in the order'; MCA 1980, s. 75(1) – magistrates' courts. Where a magistrates' court has ordered payment by instalments and default is made in the payment of any one instalment, proceedings may be taken as if the default had been made in the payment of all the instalments then unpaid: MCA 1980, s. 75(3). Written notice must be given to the surety of the terms, where payment by instalments is allowed or where the surety was absent from the proceedings: MCR 1981, r. 46(1).

2.1.15.9 Modes of enforcement not involving imprisonment A court may make a number of orders not involving the imprisonment of the surety. Thus, orders may be made for attachment of earnings, supervision of payment, issuing of a distress warrant, and up to four days' detention in default of payments.

2.1.15.10 Enforcement by imprisonment in default of payment Where a Crown Court forfeits the recognizance it is duty bound to make an order fixing a term of imprisonment, or of detention in the case of a person aged between 17 and 20, which the surety is to undergo if any sum liable to be paid is not duly paid or recovered: PCCA 1973, s. 31(2). Section 31(3) of the 1973 Act, applicable to Crown Courts, and s. 82(1) of the MCA 1980, applicable to magistrates' courts, both provide that where the recognizance of a surety is forfeited by a court the surety must not be committed to prison unless:

(a) the surety appears to the court to have sufficient means to pay the sum forthwith;

(b) it appears to the court that the surety is unlikely to remain long enough at a place of abode in the United Kingdom to enable the sum to be enforced by other methods; or

(c) on the same occasion the court imposes on the surety an immediate custodial sentence or the surety is already serving a custodial sentence.

Once a surety is committed to custody in default of payment of the recognizance, the court can then exercise the general powers of remission provided in respect of fines and remit part or all of the sums due. As mentioned in para. 2.1.15.5 above, a recognizance forfeited by order of the Crown Court is treated for the purposes of collection and enforcement as having been forfeited by the magistrates' court. Therefore the question whether the surety against whom forfeiture has been ordered by the Crown Court has sufficient means to pay the sum forfeited will be determined, as in the case of a forfeiture order made by a magistrates' court, in a means inquiry conducted by the magistrates' court. Although magistrates' courts are responsible for enforcing the collection of recognizances, and may presumably therefore order a personal search to be made for the purposes of establishing whether the defaulting surety is in possession of cash which may be applied to the payment, the PCCA 1973, s. 34A (inserted by the Criminal Law Act 1977, s. 49) provides that where the Crown Court orders the forfeiture of a recognizance, then if the surety is before it, the Crown Court may order the surety to be searched and any money so found applied to payment of the recognizance. This power is presumably available to the Crown Court, although it is magistrates' courts which bear the responsibility for collection, because if the surety is before the Crown Court it would be absurd to remit the case back to the Crown Court for enforcement.

2.1.15.11 Postponement of imprisonment in default A term of imprisonment may be postponed on condition that agreed terms of payment are complied with. It was formerly supposed that such a suspended sentence could not be varied, but in *R v Colchester Justices, ex parte Wilson, The Times*, 29 March 1985, the House of Lords held that the power to postpone a custodial term for non-payment may be exercised from time to time and as often as the court concerned considers that the occasion requires. This was because of s. 12(1) of the Interpretation Act 1978, which provides that where an act confers a power or imposes a duty, it is implied, unless the contrary intention appears, that the power may be exercised, or the duty is to be performed, from time to time as the occasion requires.

2.1.16 Arguments in favour of and against the surety system

2.1.16.1 In favour The arguments in favour of the system as it is are as follows:

(a) *Well established.* The system is so well established that it is favoured by courts and therefore enables more people to be released on bail.

(b) *Compliance before release.* The imposition of a surety is one of the few conditions that must be complied with before release on bail.

(c) *Members of the public involved in policing it.* It involves members of the public in a policing role and therefore relieves pressure on the police.

(d) *More effective than other conditions.* It is more effective than other conditions since it imposes a legal obligation on the surety and a moral obligation on the defendant.

(e) Unlike other conditions it goes to the heart of the concern that the accused will fail to surrender.

2.1.16.2 Against Against the surety system it can be said:

(a) *Only the Crown should be the accused's gaoler.* The role of pre-trial gaoler should be assumed exclusively by the Crown and not by individuals.

(b) *Impecunious defendants discriminated against.* Poor defendants are likely to be without friends or family of substance and the system therefore discriminates against impecunious defendants. There should be no place for 'cheque-book justice'.

(c) *System fails to cater for the inadequate and mentally ill.* The system fails to address the problem of the inadequate or the mentally ill, who may be unlikely to surrender but also unlikely to be able to find a surety.

(d)   Unfair burden placed on families and friends. It places an unfair burden on the family and friends of the accused, who are often under pressure to stand surety as they know that the alternative may be a remand in custody.

(e)   Effective physical control not generally feasible. Few people have sufficient control over another to ensure that the condition is effective.

(f)   System is over-used. The system is over-used and many who are subject to a surety could safely have been granted unconditional bail.

(g)   Proper sanction is a Bail Act prosecution. The proper sanction for failing to surrender ought to be a charge under s. 6 of the BA 1976 and the knowledge that bail will subsequently be withheld.

2.1.17   Indemnifying a surety

2.1.17.1   The offence   It had long been an offence under common law for a person to agree with another to indemnify that other against any liability which might be incurred as surety for attendance: see *R* v *Porter* [1910] 1 KB 369, where the defendant was held liable to be convicted of the conspiracy even though there was no 'wrongful intent', that is, no intent that the bailed defendant should abscond. (An agreement to indemnify is clearly invalid: *Consolidated Exploration and Finance Company* v *Musgrave* [1900] 1 Ch 37, 64 JP 89.) It is now an offence triable either way under s. 9(1) of the BA 1976 (see MCA 1980, ss. 18 to 21 for the procedure relating to triable either-way offences). The offence is committed whether the person for whom the surety is standing is convicted, unconvicted, or under arrest: s. 9(1). By s. 9(2) the offence is committed:

(a)   whether the agreement is made before or after the person to be indemnified becomes a surety; and

(b)   whether or not that person becomes a surety; and

(c)   whether the agreement contemplates compensation in money or money's worth.

Both parties to the agreement are guilty of the offence.

2.1.17.2   Jurisdiction and penalties   A person guilty of the offence is liable:

(a)   on summary conviction, to imprisonment for a term not exceeding three months or to a fine not exceeding the prescribed sum or to both; or

(b)   on conviction on indictment or following a committal for sentence, to imprisonment for a term not exceeding 12 months or to a fine or to both: BA 1976, s. 9(4).

The reference to 'prescribed sum' was substituted by s. 32(2) of the MCA 1980. The prescribed sum is currently £5,000.

2.1.17.3 Committal for purposes of sentence The BA 1976, s. 9(3), provides that a person convicted by a magistrates' court of the offence of indemnifying bail may be committed on bail or in custody to the Crown Court for sentence if the court thinks:

(a) that the circumstances of the offence are such that greater punishment should be inflicted than is in the court's power; or

(b) in a case where it commits that person for trial to the Crown Court for another offence, that it would be appropriate for the person to be dealt with for the offence of indemnifying by the court before which the other offence is to be tried.

2.1.17.4 Authority to prosecute Proceedings for the offence may be taken only by or with the consent of the Director of Public Prosecutions: BA 1976, s. 9(5).

2.1.18 Personation of a surety

Section 34 of the Forgery Act 1861 provides that:

Whosoever, without lawful authority or excuse (the proof whereof shall lie on the party accused), shall, in the name of any other person, acknowledge any recognizances or bail . . . being convicted thereof shall be liable to imprisonment for any term not exceeding seven years.

2.2 SECURITIES FOR ATTENDANCE

2.2.1 The statutory power

When special conditions of bail were first permitted by the CJA 1967, s. 21, a number of courts used the new measure as an opportunity to introduce the practice of requiring defendants or their sureties to deposit a sum of money with the court as a condition of bail (see Notes of the Week, *Justice of the Peace*, vol. 145, p. 573, 26 September 1981). However in *R* v *Harrow Justices, ex parte Morris* (1972) 136 JP 868, it was held that there was no power under that provision or otherwise to require a surety to deposit money with the court. Section 3(5) of the BA 1976 went some way in providing such a power. As originally enacted, the subsection that if it appeared that the defendant was unlikely to remain in Great Britain until the time appointed for surrendering to custody, the defendant might be required by the police or by the courts, before release on bail, to give a security for surrender to custody. The CDA 1998, s. 54(1), removes the qualification that a security may be imposed only if it appears that the defendant is unlikely to remain in Great Britain. The amendment allows a security to be imposed in every case where it is considered necessary to secure the defendant's attendance. The redrawn s. 3(5) states that the person to be bailed 'may be required, before release on bail, to give security for his surrender to custody'. The security may be given 'by him or on his behalf'. It has been suggested that it must be within the means of a defendant to provide a security and the requirement must not be oppressive (Chatterton, *Bail: Law and Practice*, London: Butterworths, 1986, p. 146). This is presumably meant to be consistent with the principle of the Bill of Rights 1688 that excessive bail ought not to be demanded. Although the security may be provided on the person's behalf, the principle that excessive bail ought not to be demanded will be applicable to the advancement of a sum by another on the basis that station in life is usually reflected in the wealth of relatives, friends and associates.

The practice of cash bail has the considerable incidental advantages that when the case is concluded and the defendant is sentenced to a fine or another financial liability is imposed, the court already has at its disposal a sum of the defendant's money from which the fine or other liability can be levied (see Notes of the Week, *Justice of the Peace*, vol. 145, p. 574).

2.2.2 Security not defined

The term 'security' is not defined in the BA 1976, but it may be in the form of money or money's worth. Home Office circular 206/1977, issued on 18 November 1977, described it as:

> . . . cash, travellers cheques or any other article of value. In exercising their discretion in a particular case, courts or the police should have regard to the ease with which the security could be held and converted into pounds sterling in the event of forfeiture. For example, it would be unwise to accept any perishable articles or any article that would create problems of storage or valuation.

Home office circular 34/1998, issued on 10 August 1998, states, at para. 7:

> The courts and the police retain their existing discretion to decide as to the form of the security although it is suggested that the security should usually be in the form of cash or a banker's draft to avoid problems of valuation, storage or conversion.

2.2.3 Sources of the security

The security may be given by the person to be bailed or on that person's behalf: BA 1976, s. 3(5). This raises the interesting question whether s. 54(1) of the CDA 1998 will occasion the introduction of commercial 'bail bond' enterprises of the sort which are intrinsic to the criminal justice system in the United States. Where a court 'posts' bail in a certain sum the defendant may contract with a 'bailbondsman' whereby, in return for the payment of a fee, or premium, usually 10 per cent of the amount of the bail, the bail agent assumes responsibility for payment of the full sum to the court. If the defendant fails to surrender, the agent may avoid forfeiture by apprehending the defendant, and indeed the pursuit and arrest of defaulting defendants forms a key part of the bail agent's business activities. Bailbond companies either pursue the wanted person themselves or hire independent agents to do so. The latter are widely referred to as 'bounty hunters' since their primary business is capturing the fugitive. However, the term is inappropriate to describe bailbond companies, whether those pursuing the wanted accused themselves or those contracting out, since their primary aim in capturing an absconding defendant is merely to redeem the stake. (For an informative news report, see 'Bounty hunters kill two in hunt for bail-jumper', *Daily Telegraph*, 3 September 1997.)

It is an interesting question whether there might be any legal impediment to the establishment of similar enterprises in England and Wales. Since the security is lodged on behalf of the defendant its source is immaterial. There can be no question, as in the case of a surety, of the donor of the security being indemnified, since the source of the security is legally irrelevant. Yet an agreement to indemnify was regarded as a form of conspiracy to cause a public mischief (see *R* v *Porter* [1910] 1 KB 369). The question which may be asked is whether an agreement to purchase the lodging of a security with a premium would be likely to be regarded also as such a conspiracy.

If that hurdle were cleared it would still remain to be seen if the courts would be prepared routinely to redeem all or most of the sum liable to be forfeited if the defendant who had failed to surrender were arrested and subsequently brought to court by the supplier of the 'bond'. Otherwise, the enterprise would not be commercially viable. The difficulty is that since the security is lodged on behalf of the accused and the donor is irrelevant, action by the donor to rectify the estreatment might equally be seen to be irrelevant. Arguably, the authorities might be reluctant to encourage the involvement of private individuals in what might be regarded as a form of vigilante-ism. On the other hand, it would not amount to privatisation of law enforcement in the first instance but would constitute no more than an extension of custodial operations, now very widely undertaken by private enterprise under contract. In fact, it is noteworthy that the Government has recently announced plans to permit private street patrols working in conjunction with the police (see *The Times*, 17 July 1998).

2.2.4 Permissible directions

Where, under the BA 1976, s. 3(5), a magistrates' court, a Crown Court, or a High Court judge in chambers, as the case may be, imposes a requirement for the lodging of a security to be complied with before a person is released on bail, the court may give directions as to the manner in which and the person or persons before whom the requirement may be complied with: MCR 1981, r. 85; CCR 1982, r. 20(3); RSC 1965, Ord. 79, r. 9(6B).

2.2.5 Procedures involved in postponed compliance with a condition requiring the lodging of a security

For reasons which are unclear, there is little uniformity in the provisions of the MCR 1981, the CCR 1982 and the RSC 1965, Ord. 79, governing postponed compliance with a requirement under s. 3(5) of the BA 1976 for the giving of a security for the bailed person's surrender to custody. As with the postponed taking of sureties, the MCR 1981 provide the most comprehensive code of procedure, but there are provisions in the CCR 1982 and the RSC 1965 which find no counterpart in the MCR 1981.

2.2.5.1 Issue of statement of requirement for a security The clerk of a magistrates' court which has imposed any requirement for a security under the BA 1976, s. 3(5) to be complied with must, before a person's release on bail, issue a certificate in the prescribed form containing a statement of the requirement: MCR 1981, r. 86(2).

2.2.5.2 No obligation to officiate over compliance requirement without production of statement of requirement A person authorised to do something in relation to the compliance with a requirement to provide a security for the defendant's surrender to custody is not required to do it without production of the certificate under r. 86(2): MCR 1981, r. 86(2).

2.2.5.3 Notice of imposition of requirement of security to be given to governor of prison, etc Where a magistrates' court has, with a view to the release on bail of a person in custody, imposed a requirement for security for attendance under s. 3(5) of the BA 1976, to be complied with before the defendant's release, the clerk must give notice thereof to the governor or keeper of the prison or place where that person is detained by sending a such certificate as is mentioned in r. 86(2): MCR 1981, r. 87(a).

2.2.5.4 Person proposing to give security in respect of bail granted by the Crown Court to give one day's notice to the prosecutor A person who, in pursuance of an order made by the Crown Court, or as the case may be by a judge of the High Court, for the grant of bail in criminal proceedings, proposes to give security must, unless the Crown Court or, as the case may be, the High Court judge, otherwise directs, give notice to the prosecutor at least 24 hours before giving the security: CCR 1982, r. 20(5); RSC 1965, Ord. 79, r. 9(7) – in the latter case in Form No. 100 in Appendix A to the Rules of 1965.

2.2.5.5 Compliance with court order to be transmitted to appropriate officer of the Crown Court or court clerk, as the case may be Where, in pursuance of an order of the Crown Court, a requirement for a security must, under s. 3(5) of the BA 1976, be complied with before a person's release on bail and it is complied with before some person, a statement of the requirement must be transmitted by that person forthwith to the appropriate officer of the Crown Court: CCR 1982, r. 20(6). Where in pursuance of an order by a High Court judge in chambers under RSC 1965, Ord. 79, r. 9, a requirement for a security is complied with before a person, it is that person's duty to cause a statement of the requirement complied with to be transmitted forthwith, where the defendant has been committed to the Crown Court for trial or to be sentenced or otherwise dealt with, to the appropriate officer of the Crown Court, or, in any other case, to the clerk of the court which committed the defendant to custody: Ord. 79, r. 9(8)(a).

2.2.5.6 Notice of compliance to be sent to prison governor, etc Where a magistrates' court, with a view to the release on bail of a person in custody, has imposed a requirement for security for attendance under s. 3(5) of the BA 1976 to be complied with before the defendant's release, any person authorised to do anything in relation to the compliance with the requirement must, on doing it, send notice thereof by post to the said governor or keeper in the prescribed form: MCR 1981, r. 87(b). Where, in pursuance of an order of the Crown Court, a requirement for a security must, under s. 3(5) of the BA 1976, be complied with before a person's release on bail and it is complied with before some person, that person must cause a copy of the statement of the requirement to be sent forthwith to the governor or keeper of the prison or other place of detention in which the person named in the order is detained: CCR 1982, r. 20(6). Where in pursuance of an order by a High Court judge in chambers under RSC 1965, Ord. 79, r. 9(7), a requirement for a security is complied with before some person authorised, it is that person's duty to cause a copy of the statement of the requirement complied with to be transmitted forthwith to the governor or keeper of the prison or other place of detention in which the defendant is detained: Ord. 79, r. 9(8).

2.2.5.7 Release when a requirement for a security has been met Where a magistrates' court has, with a view to the release on bail of a person in custody, imposed a requirement for a security under s. 3(5) of the BA 1976 to be complied with before release and given notice in accordance with the MCR 1981 to the governor or keeper of the prison or place where the person is detained, the governor must, when satisfied that the requirement for security has been complied with, release the person: MCR 1981, r. 88.

2.2.6 Forfeiture on failure to surrender

2.2.6.1 Forfeiture where no reasonable cause Where a person has given security and a court is satisfied that that person has failed to surrender to custody, the court may order the security to be forfeited unless it appears that there was a reasonable cause for the failure: BA 1976, s. 5(7).

2.2.6.2 Forfeiture of less than the full sum If a court orders the forfeiture of a security, it may declare that the forfeiture extends to such amount less than the full value of the security as it thinks fit to order: BA 1976, s. 5(8).

2.2.6.3 Forfeiture of a money security to be treated as a fine Where a forfeiture order is made, if the security consists of money, it must be accounted for and paid in the same manner as a fine: BA 1976, s. 5(9)(a). If it does not consist of money, it may be enforced by the magistrates' court specified in the order: s. 5(9)(b).

2.2.6.4 Time of taking effect An order for forfeiture, unless it is previously revoked, takes effect at the end of 25 days beginning with the day on which the order is made: BA 1976, s. 5(8A), inserted by sch. 12 to the Criminal Law Act 1977. This provision gives the person against whom the order was made sufficient time to lodge an appeal.

2.2.6.5 Showing cause for failure to surrender A court which has ordered forfeiture of a security may, if satisfied on an application made by or on behalf of the person who gave it that that person did after all have reasonable cause for failing to surrender to custody, by order remit the forfeiture or declare that it extends to such amount less than the full value of the security as it thinks fit to order: BA 1976, s. 5(8B), inserted by sch. 12 to the Criminal Law Act 1977.

2.2.6.6 Time for applying to show cause An application to show reasonable cause for a failure to surrender may be made before or after the order for forfeiture has taken effect, but will not be entertained unless the court is satisfied that the prosecution were given reasonable notice of the applicant's intention to make it: BA 1976, s. 5(8C), inserted by sch. 12 to the 1977 Act.

2.2.6.7 Application granted after taking effect of an order
Where an application made under BA 1976, s. 5(8B) is granted after a forfeiture order has taken effect, any money which has been paid by the person who gave security will be repaid to him: BA 1976, s. 9A, inserted by sch. 12 to the 1977 Act.

2.3 SURETY FOR GOOD BEHAVIOUR

2.3.1 Existence of power in contention and variation of practice

Whether the courts enjoy a power to impose sureties for good behaviour as a condition of bail is uncertain and contentious. The Home Office rejected a recommendation by the Home Affairs Committee (Session 1983–84, HC 252/1, para. 47) that the courts should be empowered to require the defendant or a third party to stand surety for the defendant's good behaviour. It has been argued that the power to require a third party to stand surety for good behaviour already exists (Neil Corre, 'Bail or Custody: A Contemporary Problem and an Ancient Solution' [1984] Crim LR 162).

Lawyers tend to be divided between those who 'believe' in sureties for good behaviour as a condition of bail and those who do not. Some judges, stipendiary magistrates and justices' clerks will readily accept sureties for good behaviour as a bail condition. Others will reject any such application without hearing argument.

Opinion is so divided that the issue is often decided on the basis of belief rather than following dispassionate consideration of the law. For this reason it is worth examining the arguments on both sides of the question.

2.3.2 Arguments in favour of existence in law

2.3.2.1 Conditions permitted to prevent commission of an offence The BA 1976, s. 3(6) and sch. 1, Part I, para. 8, empower a court to impose conditions to secure, *inter alia*, that the defendant does not commit an offence while on bail.

2.3.2.2 Ancillary power of criminal courts to impose a bind-over Any court of record having a criminal jurisdiction has, as ancillary to that jurisdiction, the power to bind over to keep the peace, and power to bind over to be of good behaviour, a person who or whose case is before the court, by requiring the person to enter a personal recognizance or to find sureties or both and to make an order of committal to prison for failure to comply: Justices of the Peace Act 1968, s. 1(7), as amended by sch. 5, Part I, to the Administration of Justice Act 1973. This is subject to the prohibition in s. 3(2) of the BA 1976 on the taking of a personal recognizance as a condition of bail.

2.3.2.3 Order under the Justices of the Peace Act 1361 permitted at any stage of proceedings Although an order for binding over under s. 116 of the MCA 1980 may be made only after the case is completed, an order under the Justices of the Peace Act 1361 may be made at any stage of the proceedings: *R v Aubrey-Fletcher, ex parte Thompson* [1969] 2 All ER 846.

2.3.2.4 No actual or apprehended breach necessary A surety for good behaviour may be imposed even where there is no actual or apprehended breach of the peace: *R v Sandbach, ex parte Williams* [1935] 2 KB 192, in which Avory J relied on the following passage from Blackstone, *Commentaries*, IV, 251:

> This preventive justice consists in obliging those persons for whom there are probable grounds to suspect of future misbehaviour, to stipulate with and to give full assurance to the public, that such offence as is apprehended shall not happen; by finding pledges or securities for keeping the peace, or for their good behaviour.

Similarly it is not essential for the imposition of a surety for good behaviour that the defendant should have caused any individual person to go in bodily fear: *Lansbury v Riley* [1914] 3 KB 229. A distinction must be made between a surety to keep the peace, which requires evidence that there might be a breach of the peace in the future (*R v Aubrey-Fletcher, ex parte Thompson*), and a surety for good behaviour, which does not require any such evidence.

2.3.2.5 Previous convictions admissible Although a bind-over may only be made on admissible evidence (*Brooks and Breen* v *Nottingham Police* [1984] Crim LR 677) such evidence may take the form of the defendant's previous convictions.

2.3.2.6 Practice too well established to be questioned The practice of ordering sureties for good behaviour is too well established to be questioned: *Lansbury* v *Riley*, above. In *R* v *Justices of Queen's County* (1882) 10 LR Ir 294, at p. 301, Fitzgerald J held: 'It may be described as a branch of preventive justice, in the exercise of which magistrates are vested with large judicial discretionary powers for the maintenance of order and the preservation of the public peace.'

2.3.2.7 Good behaviour surety more potent than common conditions designed to prevent offences A surety for good behaviour will be more effective than such conditions as residence, reporting and curfew, as it will mean that a member of society will have a stake in an accused person's future good conduct.

2.3.3 Arguments against existence of power in law

2.3.3.1 Bail Act contains no specific enabling provision There is no specific provision in the BA 1976 for the imposition of such a condition.

2.3.3.2 Power to impose sureties nominally confined to the purpose of securing attendance The BA 1976, s. 3(6)(b) enables a court to impose such conditions as appear to the court to be necessary to prevent the commission of an offence while the accused is on bail, and it might be argued that the unrestricted nature of this power therefore provides a sound basis for imposing sureties for good behaviour in a suitable case. However, s. 3(4) and sch 1, Part. I, para. 8, stress that the purpose of a surety is to secure surrender to custody only and since this is a specific limitation it may be argued that s. 3(6)(b), which is expressed in general terms, ought to be read subject to s. 3(4).

2.3.3.3 Bind-over requires evidence of future risk of breach of the peace A bind-over may be made only if there is evidence that there might be a breach of the peace in the future: *R* v *Aubrey-Fletcher, ex parte Thompson* [1969] 2 All ER 846.

2.3.3.4 Bind-over requires admissible evidence A bind-over may be made only on admissible evidence and not on the assertions of an advocate or the hearsay evidence of a police officer: *Brooks and Breen* v *Nottingham Police* [1984] Crim LR 677. Bail conditions may be imposed on the strength of material which would not necessarily constitute admissible evidence.

2.3.3.5 Surety for good behaviour superfluous and wrong in principle It may be argued that the proper sanction for criminal behaviour should be the law itself and that a surety for good behaviour is not only superfluous but wrong in principle. As to the superfluity argument, it may be observed that the failure to surrender to custody is a criminal offence (BA 1976, s. 6), yet s. 3(4) gives the responsibility of ensuring compliance with the law to another person by allowing sureties for attendance. As to the argument that it is wrong in principle to take a surety for good behaviour while the accused is on bail, this is an argument against using bind-overs for good behaviour in general and it is not generally contended that the taking of sureties for good behaviour (apart from bail) is other than well established in law as an instrument of preventive justice.

2.3.3.6 Offence on bail itself provides grounds for revocation of bail A person who commits an offence while on bail may have his bail revoked as there may then be substantial grounds for believing he will commit an offence. This is arguably a better deterrent than the risk of forfeiture.

2.3.3.7 Breach of the condition will be difficult to detect The breach of a condition of providing sureties for the defendant's good behaviour will be difficult to detect as no central record is kept of sureties. Information should be more readily available since the issuing of *Practice Direction (Crime: Antecedents)* [1997] 4 All ER 350 (see para. 13.2.4).

2.3.3.8 Bind-over ineffective to maintain a surety's control over the bailed defendant The condition will be ineffective since there can be few people with sufficient control over a person to prevent that person committing an offence.

2.3.4 Another option: bind-over independent of bail

The uncertainty over whether there is a lawful discretionary power to impose sureties for good behaviour as a condition of bail can be circumvented by another option which is open to the court. This is as follows:

(a) The court grants bail with or without conditions.

(b) Concurrently but independently of the granting of bail the court imposes a bind-over with a surety for good behaviour in accordance with the Justices of the Peace Act 1361.

(c) The defendant who cannot comply with the order to provide a surety will be committed to prison for that failure subject to the defendant being given an opportunity to make representations in relation to the imposition of a surety: *R v Clerkenwell Stipendiary Magistrate, ex parte Hooper* [1998] 4 All ER 193, DC.

The imposition of the surety is not a condition of bail and so the term of the suretyship may exceed the period of the remand.

2.3.5 Forfeiture

The principles set out in s. 120 of the MCA 1980 as amended by CDA 1998, s. 55 (see para. 2.1.14) and *mutatis mutandis* in the decided cases, apply to sureties for good behaviour. The only difference is that the court must not declare the recognizance forfeited except by order made on complaint: MCA 1980, s. 120(2). It has been argued that costs may be ordered in respect of forfeited recognizances taken in respect of persons bound over to keep the peace or to be of good behaviour because the procedure in such cases is by way of 'complaint', as contrasted with forfeiture of recognizances of sureties for attendance (Chatterton, *Bail: Law and Practice*, London: Butterworths, 1986, p. 123).

3 Conditions other than Surety or Security

3.1. INTRODUCTION

The imposition of 'requirements' with which a defendant must comply as a condition for being admitted to bail is such an everyday occurrence in the criminal courts that it is easy to lose sight of the fact that the power to impose such requirements other than sureties is of comparatively recent origin. The power to attach special conditions (as they were then known) to the granting of bail was introduced by s. 21 of the CJA 1967. The aim was to reduce the number of defendants in custody by providing a means of restricting defendants' liberty while still allowing them bail. The courts were comparatively slow in taking up their new powers. In 1969 special conditions were imposed in 8 per cent of a sample monitored in a Home Office study (Simon, F., and Weatheritt, M., *The Use of Bail and Custody by London Magistrates' Court before and after the Criminal Justice Act 1967*, Home Office Research Unit, London: HMSO 1974). But the numbers were growing. A 1971 study found that 15 per cent of defendants were granted conditional bail (King, M., *Bail or Custody*, London: Cobden Trust, 1971). In 1978 conditions were imposed on 20 per cent of those bailed by London magistrates' courts (*Criminal Statistics, England and Wales, 1978*, Cmnd 7670, London: HMSO, 1979, paras 8, 11–12). By 1979, one-third of those bailed by the London magistrates' courts monitored by Zander were subject to conditions (Zander, M., 'Operation of the Bail Act in London magistrates' courts' *New Law Journal*, 1979, vol. 129, p. 109). In 1984 the figure, according to Home Office research, was back to 20 per cent (*Remands in Custody: A Consultation Document*, London: Home Office, 1985), but according to another study it had grown apace to 38 per cent (East, R., and Doherty, M., 'The practical operation of bail,' *Legal Action*, March 1984).

Statute did not and does not define the categories of permissible conditions of bail apart from sureties and there was some initial doubt as to the ambit of conditions which might be imposed. In *R* v *Aubrey-Fletcher, ex parte Thompson* [1969] 2 All ER 846, the applicant was charged with two offences of using insulting words whereby a breach of the peace may have been occasioned, contrary to s. 54 of the Metropolitan Police Courts Act 1839. The trial of the first alleged offence was adjourned part-heard, whereupon the prosecution sought a condition of bail prohibiting the applicant from participating in meetings at Speakers' Corner. The defence opposed the application and submitted that such a condition would be invalid. The stipendiary magistrate accepted this submission and instead of imposing a condition, made an order binding over the applicant to keep the peace, under the Justices of the Peace Act 1361. The application to the Divisional Court was concerned with this order, but in pointing out that the order binding over the applicant was used as an alternative to a condition of bail which the magistrate had accepted could not validly be made, Lord Parker CJ expressly declined to decide if the condition was one which could validly be made. However, within a few years the Divisional Court had no difficulty in upholding the validity of much more sweeping conditions in *R* v *Mansfield Justices, ex parte Sharkey and others* [1985] 1 QB 613; [1985] Crim LR 148, a case under the regime of the BA 1976 which is considered below.

Research conducted over a three-year period (1990–1993) in three magistrates' courts in South Wales found that 34 per cent of defendants were granted conditional bail, 44 per cent were granted unconditional bail and 21 per cent were remanded in custody (Hucklesby, A., 'The Use and Abuse of Conditional Bail', *The Howard Journal*, 1994, vol. 33, pp. 258–70; it is understood from the author that the remaining 1 per cent was made up of 0.6 per cent who were subject to a further detention warrant and 0.4 per cent who were granted technical bail in that they were in custody for other matters when granted bail on the matter for which they were appearing). The research identified several problems associated with the operation of conditional bail, as follows:

(a)   Conditional bail is not always used as an alternative to custody but may sometimes be used in cases where unconditional bail may have been appropriate.

(b)   Conditions may not be relevant to the grounds for objecting to bail. For example, a curfew is sometimes imposed to ensure attendance rather than to prevent offences.

(c)   Specific conditions do not always attain their objectives. For example, surrendering a passport does not prevent people leaving the country.

(d)   Conditions are difficult to enforce, the police are not always aware of conditions imposed, and persons arrested for breach of bail conditions do not usually suffer any punishment.

3.2   BAIL ACT PROVISIONS RELATING TO CONDITIONS

3.2.1   The basic provisions

As already mentioned, statute does not define the categories of bail conditions and this allows courts some flexibility and innovative discretion to meet special circumstances and local needs. Rather, the scheme of s. 3(6) of the BA 1976, as expanded by s. 3A of the Act (inserted by s. 27(3) of the CJPOA 1994) is simply to empower courts or the police in granting bail to impose such requirements as appear to be necessary to secure that defendants:

(a)   surrender to custody;
(b)   do not commit an offence while on bail; or
(c)   do not interfere with witnesses or otherwise obstruct the course of justice whether in relation to themselves or any other person.

The CJPOA 1994 for the first time gives custody officers the authority to impose requirements, apart from surety, as a condition of granting police bail after charge. The text of s. 3(6) of the BA 1976 has been amended accordingly by deleting the parenthesised phrase '(but only by a court' from the words 'He may be required (but only by a court) to comply, before release on bail or later, with such requirements as appear . . .'. However, curiously, the subsection continues to employ the wording 'as appear *to the court* to be necessary to secure that . . .'.

In addition to the requirements which may be imposed for securing the objectives (a) to (c) above, a court may impose such requirements as appear to be necessary to secure that defendants make themselves available for the purpose of enabling inquiries or a report to be made to assist the court in dealing with them for the offence: BA 1976, s. 3(6)(d). Conditions may be imposed only if they are considered necessary to secure attendance, to prevent offences, to prevent interference with witnesses or other obstruction of the course of justice, or to enable a report or inquiries to be made: BA 1976, s. 3(6) as amended and sch. 1, Part I, para. 8. Except as provided by s. 3, no requirement (apart from security or sureties) may be imposed as a condition of bail: s. 3(3). (The CJA 1988 inserted s. 3(6ZA), which provides for compliance with the rules of a bail or probation hostel where the defendant is required to reside in such a hostel: see para. 3.4.3.) The CDA 1998, s. 54, makes provision for a condition to attend an interview with a legal representative (see para. 3.4.5).

3.2.2   Application of the provisions

3.2.2.1   Meaning of 'necessary'   The meaning of 'necessary' in BA 1976, s. 3(6) was considered in *R v Mansfield Justices, ex parte Sharkey and Others* [1985] QB 613. The applicants were striking Yorkshire coal miners who picketed collieries in the East Midlands. Some were charged with threatening behaviour and others with obstructing a police officer in the execution of his duty. They were granted bail on condition that they did not visit any premises or place for the purpose of picketing or demonstrating in connection with the then current trade dispute between the National Union of Mineworkers and the National Coal Board, other than peacefully to picket or demonstrate at their usual place of employment. They sought orders of *certiorari* to quash the condition and of *mandamus* to admit them to unconditional bail. The Divisional Court dismissed their applications and, giving judgment, Lord Lane CJ, at p. 625, explained the contrast between the statutory grounds for refusing bail and those for imposing conditions:

> The justices, when the defendant is going to be bailed, are not concerned with paragraph 2 of the Schedule to the Bail Act 1976 which deals with the refusal of bail. They are concerned with section 3(6) and with paragraph 8(1) of the Schedule. The reference to 'any of the events mentioned in paragraph 2' is to sub-paragraphs (a), (b) and (c), namely failure to surrender, commit an offence on bail, or interfere with witnesses, etc. There is a duplication between paragraph 8 and section 3(6) due to indifferent drafting, but the intention of the legislature emerges as the logical wish to impose less rigorous requirements when a defendant is being admitted to bail than when an unconvicted man is being refused bail altogether.

It was held that in contrast with the test for refusing bail, which is that *substantial grounds* must exist for believing that any of the adverse events listed in the Act might happen, in considering whether to impose *conditions of bail* the magistrates were not obliged to find substantial grounds for believing that any of those adverse events might follow if the accused were released on bail. Instead, the test laid down for the justices to apply was that '. . . it is enough if they perceive a real and not fanciful risk of an offence being committed [or the defendant absconding or interfering with witnesses, etc.] (*ibid.*).

The *ratio* in the above case was based on the finding that large numbers of pickets are likely to lead to intimidation of those wishing to work and thus to an offence of threatening behaviour contrary to s. 5 of the Public Order Act 1936. The position would presumably be the same under s. 5 of the Public Order Act 1986. The condition was therefore considered necessary because there was a real risk of an offence unless the number of pickets was reduced. The decision is not limited to its own peculiar facts and 'necessary' has now been given the *per curiam* definition of real and not fanciful risk. It applies by analogy not only to the risk of offences, but also to the other reasons for which conditions may be imposed.

3.2.2.2 The court's discretion   The effect of the 'real and not fanciful risk' test, in the view of the Divisional Court, is that BA 1976, s. 3(6) and sch. 1, Part I, para. 8 give tribunals a wide discretion to inquire whether the proposed condition is necessary. As to the exercise of that discretion, Lord Lane CJ cited (at p. 625) the following passage from the judgment of Lord Greene MR in *Associated Provincial Picture Houses Ltd* v *Wednesbury Corporation* [1948] 1 KB 223, at p. 229:

> [D]iscretion must be exercised reasonably. . . . It has frequently been used and is frequently used as a general description of things that must not be done. For instance, a person entrusted with discretion must . . . direct himself properly in law. He must call his own attention to matters which he is bound to consider.

He must exclude from his consideration matters which are irrelevant to what he has to consider. If he does not obey those rules, he may truly be said, and often is said, to be acting 'unreasonably'.

3.2.2.3 Standard of evidence It was further held in *Mansfield Justices* that although a court must have sufficient material before it before imposing conditions, there is no requirement for formal evidence to be given (see *Re Moles* [1981] Crim LR 170). It is sufficient for the facts to be related to the magistrates at second hand, for example by a police officer.

3.2.2.4 Local knowledge may be applied in determining necessity It was held in *Mansfield Justices* that the magistrates were entitled to use their knowledge of events in the locality relating to the industrial dispute during preceding weeks, because it was only on the basis of that knowledge, *inter alia*, that they could properly reach a conclusion as to the necessity of imposing conditions.

3.2.2.5 Character of accused In *Mansfield Justices* it was held that the fact that the defendants were men of good character did not affect the likelihood that they might breach their conditions of bail.

3.2.2.6 Defendants' cases should not be considered en bloc It was held in *Mansfield Justices* that a court determining whether to impose conditions of bail should not put several defendants in the dock at the same time when they have been arrested at different times or places. Giving judgment, Lord Lane CJ said (at p. 628):

> Putting into the dock, together, defendants who have been arrested on different occasions or at different places makes it difficult to avoid the appearance of 'group justice'. We appreciate that these justices faced an uphill task of dealing with literally hundreds of cases over and above their normal list. We sympathise with them in their task. However, whatever pressures a court is subject to, the practice is one to be discouraged. Nor does it do the bench credit if their clerk continues to affix standard conditions of bail to bail forms even while applications are being made for unconditional bail, as happened in some of the instant cases.

3.2.3 Consent not required

It is not necessary to ask defendants if they consent to proposed conditions. Conditional bail is not an order that requires consent, as used to be the case with regard to probation or community service orders (until the requirement for consent to such orders was abolished by the Crime (Sentences) Act 1997, s. 38). A defendant who signifies an intent to refuse to comply with a condition may be arrested under s. 7 of the BA 1976. Alternatively, the expression of consent may be made a condition *per se*, since s. 3(6) of the 1976 Act empowers the court to require the defendant to comply with conditions 'before release on bail or later'.

3.2.4   Conditions must be capable of implementation and enforcement

The person to be bailed must be capable of complying with a proposed condition. To impose a condition with which it would plainly be impossible for the accused to comply would be tantamount to an unwarranted refusal of bail. A condition must also be capable of enforcement. (See, generally, Chatterton, *Bail: Law and Practice*, London: Butterworths, 1986, p. 143, and Archbold, *Criminal Pleading, Evidence and Practice*, London: Sweet & Maxwell, 1999, para. 3–4(ii)). The Home Office in its circular HO 206/1977, issued on 18 November 1977, advises:

> Courts should ensure both that the accused is able to comply with any conditions they intend to impose under s. 3(6) and any such conditions are enforceable. Difficulty has been encountered where, for example, a court has required residence at a particular address, without first checking that accommodation was available there; a court has delegated the approval of a place of residence to the police or probation service; a court has required the defendant not to enter any licensed premises for the period of bail; a court has imposed a reporting condition without specifying the police station or has named a station without checking that it is continuously manned.

3.2.5   Imprisonable and non-imprisonable offences

3.2.5.1   Conditions may be imposed in cases of non-imprisonable offences
Conditions of bail may be imposed in relation to non-imprisonable offences as with imprisonable ones. In this respect the BA 1976 in general makes no distinction between the two categories of offence. In *R* v *Bournemouth Magistrates' Court, ex parte Cross and Others* [1989] Crim LR 207; 89 Cr App R 90, DC, the applicants had been arrested and proceeded against in connection with their activities as anti-hunting protestors, and they sought judicial review of the decision of the magistrates to impose a condition of bail in relation to a non-imprisonable offence. It was held that ss. 3(3)(c) and 3(6) of the 1976 Act restrict conditions which may be applied in *all* cases where bail is granted. Although sch. 1, Part I, para. 8 to the Act is expressly limited to cases involving imprisonable offences, in the court's view it adds nothing to s. 3(6). The absence of a similar paragraph from Part II of sch. 1, which deals with non-imprisonable offences, is of no significance. The reference to 'conditions' in para. 2(b) of Part II of sch. 1 suggests that conditions may be imposed in cases involving non-imprisonable offences, and s. 3 therefore applies fully in such cases.

3.2.5.2   Exception in the case of adjournment for reports   There is a difference between imprisonable and non-imprisonable offences in relation to the ground set out in BA 1976, s. 3(6)(d), that is, the necessity of securing the availability of the defendant for the purposes of enabling inquiries or a report to be made to assist the court in dealing with the defendant for the offence. Part I of sch. 1 to the Act, which relates to imprisonable offences, provides, in para. 8(1), that in the case of a condition under s. 3(6)(d), no condition shall be imposed unless it is necessary to enable inquiries or a report to be made into the defendant's physical or mental condition. No such restriction to medical reports applies in the case of non-imprisonable offences. Accordingly, for imprisonable offences it appears that requirements may not be imposed for the sole purpose of obtaining pre-sentence reports.

3.2.5.3 Incongruity in the case of non-imprisonable offences The power to impose conditions in the case of non-imprisonable offences involves an apparent incongruity. Schedule 1, Part II, provides that bail may be refused in respect of non-imprisonable offences only where:

(a)   in view of an apparent previous failure to surrender it is believed that a defendant will fail to surrender; or

(b)   the court is satisfied that a remand in custody is necessary for the defendant's own protection or, in the case of a child or young person, own welfare;

(c)   the defendant is a serving prisoner; or

(d)   the defendant has been arrested in pursuance of s. 7 of the Act.

In the case of non-imprisonable offences, the court may not refuse bail even if there are substantial grounds for believing that the exceptions which justify refusal of bail in respect of imprisonable offences apply (see Chapter 1, para. 1.3.2). However, conditions may be imposed to prevent the occurrence of any of the events which would justify the refusal of bail in the case of imprisonable offences (i.e. failure to surrender, commission of an offence, interference with witnesses or other obstruction of the course of justice; and non-availability for the purposes of enabling inquiries or a report to be made to assist the court in dealing with the accused for the offence: s. 3(6)). Therefore, although conditions can be imposed in non-imprisonable cases to reduce the risk that one of those eventualities will occur, bail cannot be refused because of that risk. This presumably means that even if the accused breaks a condition designed to prevent, for example, the commission of an offence on bail (substantial grounds for fearing which would justify the refusal of bail in respect of an imprisonable offence), bail must not be withdrawn on the grounds that the breach affords a substantial reason for believing that the defendant will commit an offence if released on bail again. However, the withdrawal of bail in such a case may be achieved by an indirect route. It may be withdrawn in consequence of the defendant's arrest in pursuance of s. 7 for breaching a condition of bail. (The commission of an offence on bail contrasts with the repetition of a failure to surrender which, by virtue of sch. 1, Part II, para. 2, would justify withdrawal of bail without resort to the s. 7 limb.) An illustration may be helpful.

A woman is charged with soliciting for the purposes of prostitution (a non-imprisonable offence). She has never previously failed to surrender to bail and none of the exceptions to bail in the case of non-imprisonable offences applies. In order to prevent the commission of an offence while on bail, the court imposes a curfew, for breaching which she is arrested in pursuance of s. 7 of the BA 1976. She may be refused bail because she has been arrested for breaching the curfew condition (sch. 1, Part II, para. 5) but not because the court has substantial grounds for believing she will commit an offence. If the court fears that the defendant will commit an offence while on bail it may impose conditions but if it is of the view that there are no conditions which will prevent offences, it must release her on bail (unless resort is made to the fact of a s. 7 arrest).

3.2.5.4 Criteria for imposing requirements do not apply to surety and security requirement in the case of non-imprisonable offences Part I of sch. 1 to the Act, which relates to imprisonable offences, provides, in para. 8(1), that where the defendant is granted bail, no conditions shall be imposed under s. 3(4) to (7) unless they are necessary for the purpose of preventing the occurrence of any of the adverse events mentioned in s. 3(6). To recapitulate, these are: failure to surrender; commission of an offence; interference with witnesses or other obstruction of the course of justice; and non-availability for the purposes of enabling inquiries or a report to be made to assist the court in dealing with the accused for the offence. (In the case of the last purpose, the inquiries or report must be into the accused's physical or mental condition.) Sections 3(4) and (5) make provision for release on bail with surety and security, respectively. Thus, in the case of imprisonable offences a requirement for surety or security must be for the purposes of securing the avoidance of the events mentioned in s. 3(6). Chatterton has pointed out (see *Bail: Law and Practice*, London: Butterworths, 1986, p. 145) that by contrast, there is apparently no such restriction written into the Act in the case of non-imprisonable offences, in relation to which surety and security may be imposed without reference to the criteria of necessity mentioned in s. 3(6). It is this distinction, together with that relating to adjournment for inquiries and a report, etc., which occasioned Chatterton's critique of the relevant drafting as 'over-complex' and adding 'nothing to the value' of the provision. In his view it would have been simpler to have had one statutory criterion for both imprisonable and non-imprisonable offences. In practice, however, there is no distinction of merit as regards surety and security because s. 3(4) and s. (5) themselves restrict the purpose of such conditions to securing the defendant's surrender to custody and *ipso facto* the other grounds (for example, prevention of further offences) are irrelevant.

3.2.5.5 Police powers to impose conditions wider than that of the courts
Originally, the police had no power under the BA 1976 to impose conditions apart from surety. Section 27(3) of the CJPOA 1994 inserted into the 1976 Act a new section, s. 3A, which gives the police the power to impose conditions subject to appropriate modifications, notably the express withholding of the power to impose

a condition of residence in a bail hostel (s. 3A(2)) and, self-evidently, a condition requiring the availability of the person for the purpose of enabling inquiries or a report to be made to assist a court in dealing with the person (s. 3A(3)) (see para. 6.5.1). Significantly, conditions can be imposed in the case of all offences for the purpose of preventing failure to surrender to custody, commission of offences and interference with witnesses, etc. The restrictions imposed on the power of the courts by sch. 1, Part II, in relation to non-imprisonable offences are not carried over to bail by the police, which means that the police now have a wider power than do the courts to impose conditions in respect of non-imprisonable offences.

3.2.6. Recording of conditions and of reasons for imposing them

3.2.6.1 Requirement to record decision Where a court or constable decides to impose or to vary any condition in respect of bail in criminal proceedings a record of the decision must be made in the prescribed manner and containing the prescribed particulars: BA 1976, s. 5(1)(d) as amended by s. 27(4) of the CJPOA 1994. The prescribed manner is that laid down by the MCR 1981, rr. 66 and 90 (and see Forms 149–153), the CCR 1982, r. 19, and the RSC 1965, Ord. 79, r. 9(13), or, in relation to a decision by a constable, prescribed by direction of the Secretary of State: BA 1976, s. 5(10).

3.2.6.2 Requirement to furnish copy of record of the decision If requested by the person in relation to whom the decision to impose or vary conditions of bail has been taken, the court or constable must cause a copy of the record of the decision to be given to the person as soon as practicable after the record is made: BA 1976, s. 5(1).

3.2.6.3 Requirement to give reasons Where in respect of a person to whom the statutory right to bail applies, a magistrates' court or the Crown Court imposes or varies conditions of bail in criminal proceedings, the court must with a view to enabling the person to consider making an application in the matter to another court, give reasons for imposing or varying the conditions: BA 1976, s. 5(3). The Home Office circular HO 11/1978 issued on 17 February 1978, advises that detailed statements of reasons are not required but that there may be occasions where more precise information would be helpful to a later court which reconsiders the matter. Where a custody officer imposes or varies any conditions of bail in criminal proceedings, the custody officer must, with a view to enabling that person to consider requesting that or another custody officer, or making an application to a magistrates' court, to vary the conditions, give reasons for imposing or varying the conditions: BA 1976, s. 5A(2), inserted by s. 27(4) of the CJPOA 1994, and sch. 3, para. 2.

3.2.6.4 Note of reasons to be filed and furnished A court which is required by virtue of s. 5(3) of the 1976 Act to give reasons for its decision must include a note of those reasons in the record of its decision and must give a copy of the note to the person who is to be bailed, except that the Crown Court need not give a copy of the note to a person who is represented by counsel or a solicitor unless counsel or the solicitor requests the court to do so: BA 1976, s. 5(4) and (5). A custody officer who is by virtue of s. 5A(2) required to give reasons for the imposition or variation of conditions of bail must include a note of those reasons in the custody record and must give a copy of that note to the person in relation to whom the decision was taken: BA 1976, s. 5A(3), inserted by s. 27(4) of the 1994 Act, and sch. 2, para. 2.

3.2.7   Procedures involved in postponed compliance with a requirement

There is little uniformity in the provisions of the MCR 1981, the CCR 1982 and the RSC 1965, Ord. 79, governing postponed compliance with a requirement under s. 3(6) and (6A) of the BA 1976 to be complied with before a person is released on bail or any condition of bail imposed under those subsections. As with the postponed taking of sureties and lodging of security, the MCR 1981 provide the most comprehensive code of procedure but there are provisions in the CCR 1982 and the RSC 1965 which find no counterpart in the MCR 1981.

3.2.7.1   Court power to make directions for compliance with requirements before release   Where a court, under s. 3(6) of the BA 1976, imposes any requirement to be complied with before a person's release on bail, it may give directions as to the manner in which and the person or persons before whom the requirement may be complied with: MCR 1981, r. 85; CCR 1982, r. 20(3); RSC 1965, Ord. 79, r. 9(6B).

3.2.7.2   Issue of statement of requirement or condition   The clerk of a magistrates' court which, under the BA 1976, s. 3(6) or (6A), has imposed:

(a)   any requirement, to be complied with before a person is released on bail; or
(b)   any condition of bail;
must issue a certificate in the prescribed form containing a statement of the requirement or condition of bail: MCR 1981, r. 86(2).

3.2.7.3   No obligation to officiate over compliance requirement without production of statement of requirement or condition   A person authorised to do something in relation to the compliance with a requirement under BA 1976, s. 3(6) or (6A) is not required to do it without production of the certificate required to be issued under r. 86(2): MCR 1982, r. 86(2).

3.2.7.4   Notice of imposition of requirement or condition to be given to governor of prison, etc   Where a magistrates' court has, with a view to the release on bail of a person in custody, under s. 3(6) or (6A) of the BA 1976 imposed:

(a)   a requirement to be complied with before the defendant's release; or

(b)   a condition of bail;

the clerk of the court must give notice thereof to the governor or keeper of the prison or place where that person is detained by sending such a certificate as is mentioned in r. 86(2): MCR 1981, r. 87(a).

3.2.7.5   Compliance with Crown Court order to be transmitted to appropriate officer of the Crown Court   Where, in pursuance of an order of the Crown Court, a requirement imposed under s. 3(6) of the BA 1976 is complied with (being a requirement to be complied with before a person's release on bail) before a person, a statement of the requirement must be transmitted by that person forthwith to the appropriate officer of the Crown Court: CCR 1982, r. 20(6). Similarly, where in pursuance of an order by a High Court judge in chambers under RSC 1965, Ord. 79, r. 9, a requirement is complied with before a person, it shall be that person's duty to cause a statement of the requirement complied with to be transmitted forthwith, where the defendant has been committed to the Crown Court for trial or to be sentenced or otherwise dealt with, to the appropriate officer of the Crown Court, or, in any other case, to the clerk of the court which committed the defendant to custody: Ord. 79, r. 9(8)(a).

3.2.7.6   Notice of compliance to be sent to prison governor, etc   Where a magistrates' court, with a view to the release on bail of a person in custody, has imposed a requirement under s. 3(6) or (6A) of the BA 1976 to be complied with before the defendant's release, a person authorised to do anything in relation to the compliance with the requirement must, on doing it, send notice thereof by post to the said governor or keeper in the prescribed form: MCR 1981, r. 87(b). Where, in pursuance of an order of the Crown Court, a requirement imposed under s. 3(6) of the BA 1976 is complied with (being a requirement to be complied with before a person's release on bail) before a person, that person must cause a copy of the statement of the requirement to be sent forthwith to the governor or keeper of the prison or other place of detention in which the person named in the order is detained: CCR 1982, r. 20(6). Where in pursuance of an order by a High Court judge in chambers under RSC 1965, Ord. 79, r. 9, a requirement is complied with before some person, it is that person's duty to cause a copy of the statement of the requirement complied with to be transmitted forthwith to the governor or keeper of the prison or other place of detention in which the defendant is detained: Ord. 79, r. 9(8).

3.2.7.7   Release when a requirement for a security has been met   Where a magistrates' court has, with a view to the release on bail of a person in custody, under s. 3(6) or (6A) of the BA 1976, imposed a requirement to be complied with before release and given notice in accordance with the MCR 1981 to the governor or keeper of the prison or place where the person is detained, the governor must, when satisfied that the requirement has been complied with, release the person: MCR 1981, r. 88.

3.2.8 Variation or subsequent imposition of conditions

3.2.8.1 Variation of terms by a court Where a court has granted bail in criminal proceedings, that court, or, where the court has committed a person on bail to the Crown Court for trial or to be sentenced or otherwise dealt with, that court or the Crown Court may on application by or on behalf of the person to whom bail was granted, or by the prosecutor or a constable, vary the conditions of bail or impose conditions in respect of bail which has been granted unconditionally: BA 1976, s. 3(8). Where a notice of transfer is given under a relevant transfer provision s. 3(8) shall have effect in relation to a person in relation to whose case the notice is given as if the person had been committed on bail to the Crown Court for trial: s. 3(8A). The 'relevant transfer provision' means s. 4 of the CJA 1987 (serious or complex fraud) and s. 53 of the CJA 1991 (cases involving children): 2nd subs (10) of s. 3. (See generally Chapter 7, paras 7.5 and 7.6.)

3.2.8.2 Meaning of vary 'Vary' means imposing further conditions after bail is granted, or varying or rescinding conditions: BA 1976, s. 2(2).

3.2.8.3 Magistrates' court Under the BA 1976, s. 3(8), a magistrates' court has jurisdiction to vary conditions of bail only in cases where the earlier grant of bail was made by *that* court. Further, following committal for sentence or for trial the court retains jurisdiction concurrently with the Crown Court to entertain an application for variation or imposition of conditions of bail, a parallel jurisdiction which lapses only when the defendant surrenders bail at the Crown Court: *R v Lincoln Magistrates' Court, ex parte Mawer* [1995] Crim LR 878 (see further, Chapter 7, paras 7.1.3.6, and 7.4.1.5 and 7.5.3).

3.2.8.4 Crown Court The Crown Court enjoys jurisdiction under s. 3(8) of the 1976 Act to vary conditions in cases where the accused has been committed for trial or for sentence or otherwise to be dealt with. ('Dealt with' for the purpose of legal aid means dealt with under the PCCA 1973, ss. 6, 8, 16, 17(1) or (2), 23 or 27, or the CLA 1977, s. 47(3). It also means dealt with for failure to comply with a condition of recognizance to keep the peace or be of good behaviour.) The Crown Court therefore has no power to vary conditions set by the magistrates' court on granting bail pending appeal to the Crown Court. Only a judge in chambers in the High Court may do so: RSC 1965, Ord. 79, r. 9. The Crown Court also enjoys the power to vary or impose conditions of bail where a notice of transfer has been given under a relevant transfer provision: BA 1976, s. 3(8A). Where the defendant seeks to challenge the imposition of extra conditions imposed by the Crown Court while awaiting trial on indictment application should be made to a High Court judge in chambers (RSC 1965, Ord. 79, r. 9) and not a challenge by way of judicial review: see *R v Croydon Crown Court, ex parte Cox* [1997] Crim LR 52.

3.2.9 Breach of conditions

3.2.9.1 Powers of arrest for breach of bail Section 7(3)(b) of the BA 1976 provides that a person who has been released on bail may be arrested without warrant if the arresting constable has reasonable grounds:

(a) for believing that that person is likely to break any of the conditions of bail; or

(b) for suspecting that that person has broken any of those conditions.

A defendant arrested in accordance with the provisions above need not be granted bail (BA 1976, sch. 1, Part I, para. 6, and Part II, para. 5).

3.2.9.2 Time limit on court appearance following arrest for breach Other than in cases of an arrest for breach of conditions made within 24 hours before the defendant is to appear in court in answer to bail, defendants arrested under s. 7 must be brought as soon as practicable, and in any event within 24 hours, before a justice of the peace in the petty sessional area in which the arrest was effected: BA 1976, s. 7(4)(a). The arrested person should not be taken to the court which originally granted bail, unless that is the court for the area in which the arrest was made. A person arrested in pursuance of s. 7(3) must be brought before a justice of the peace within 24 hours of arrest. In reckoning the period of 24 hours, no account is to be taken of Sunday, Christmas Day or Good Friday (added by the CLA 1977, sch. 12). It is insufficient that the person is brought within the precincts of a magistrates' court within that time. Failure to comply with this requirement will result in the release of the arrested person: *R* v *Governor of Glen Parva Young Offenders Institution, ex parte G., The Times,* 24 January 1998, DC.

3.2.9.3 Arrest within 24 hours before next due appearance Where a defendant is arrested under s. 7 for breach of bail conditions and less than 24 hours remain until the appointed time of the defendant's appearance in court in answer to bail, the defendant must be brought before that particular court: BA 1976, s. 7(4)(b).

3.2.9.4 Court disposal upon presentation for breach Section 7(5) of the BA 1976 provides that if the magistrate before whom a person arrested for breach of conditions is brought is of the opinion that the person has broken or is likely to break any condition, the magistrate may:

(a) refuse bail; or

(b) grant bail with the same or different conditions.

If the magistrate is not of the opinion that the person arrested has broken or is likely to break any conditions, the defendant must be granted bail as before. In any event the decision must be made forthwith. There is no power to adjourn the hearing for further inquiries or for evidence to be called: *R* v *Liverpool City*

Justices, ex parte DPP (1992) 95 Cr App R 222, DC. The magistrate must send a copy of the record of the proceedings to the court which made the original grant of bail, except where that court is the court for which the magistrate is acting: MCR 1981, r. 92. The statutory right to bail does not apply if the accused is arrested for breach of conditions: BA 1976, sch. 1, Part I, para. 6, and Part II, para. 5.

3.2.9.5 Manner and standard of adjudication   The test of whether the person has broken or is likely to break a condition of bail is the opinion of the court. There is no need for proof or even substantial grounds. This is a necessary concomitant of the absence of any power to adjourn the hearing, for it will often not be practicable to adduce proof by means of admissible sworn evidence of the facts supporting the complaint. On the other hand, the court can hardly form an opinion without some material in support. It is therefore good practice to ask the defendant if the breach of conditions is admitted, or if it is likely that they will be broken. Some years ago the editors of *Justice of the Peace* expressed the view that if no such admission were forthcoming, the appropriate and safest course would be for the prosecution to call evidence on oath as to the facts, where it was practicable to do so (1989, p. 49). However, the practicalities will often preclude the furnishing of evidence on oath. The officer in the case may be unavailable, being engaged on duties elsewhere, or the defendant may have been arrested in a different area and it may be difficult to arrange the attendance of witnesses to the breach at short notice. In *R v Guest, ex parte Metropolitan Police Commissioner* [1961] 3 All ER 1118, it was held that evidence was not necessary for a refusal of bail. In *Re Moles* [1981] Crim LR 170, Donaldson LJ clearly stated that the procedure upon initial applications for bail is usually by representation and not evidence:

> I am quite unable to understand why it is said that application should be dealt with in accordance with the strict rules of evidence. It seems to me that any such proposition would render the operation of the Act wholly unworkable. This is an informal inquiry conducted by magistrates to see whether there is anything to displace the prima facie entitlement of every accused person to bail. . . . They are not finding facts.

In *R v Mansfield Justices, ex parte Sharkey* [1985] 1 QB 613, Lord Lane CJ said that it was sufficient for the facts to be related to the magistrates at second hand by the police officer. Finally, in *R v Liverpool City Justices, ex parte DPP* (1992) 95 Cr App R 222, the Divisional Court set out the following guidance as to the procedure under s. 7(5) of the BA 1976:

(a)   The matter may be heard by a single justice.

(b)   Section 7 does not create an offence but creates a procedure for determining whether the arrested person is unlikely to surrender to custody, or has broken or is likely to break a condition of bail.

(c)   The justice is not required to hear evidence on oath. The police officer will state the grounds for believing that the arrested person is unlikely to surrender to custody, or has broken or is likely to break a condition of bail; this may include hearsay.

(d)   The justice should give the arrested person an opportunity to respond.

(e)   There is no power to adjourn the s. 7 procedure.

Confirmation of the absence of any power to adjourn a s. 7 hearing and of the principle that the decision need not be based on sworn evidence of a strictly admissible nature clearly rendered invalid the view of the editors of *Stone's Justices Manual* (London: Butterworths, 1986, p. 140, n. (d)) that the 'statement of the arresting constable's "reasonable grounds" may form the basis of the opinion of the JP [although i]n the circumstances . . . the period of remand should clearly be as short as possible so that an early decision may be made on the full evidence'. One commentator was therefore entirely correct to observe that this seemed to place a higher standard of proof in respect of breaches of bail than was necessary for applications for bail when the defendant first appeared before the court (Chatterton, C., *Bail: Law and Practice*, London: Butterworths, 1986, para. 6.16).

3.2.9.6   No offence to break bail conditions   Although persons who break the conditions of their bail are liable to arrest, they commit no offence. Shortly after the Bail Act came into force it was reported that some courts were actually trying and convicting defendants for breach of conditions (Cameron, N., 'The Bail Act 1976: Two inconsistencies and an imaginary offence' *New Law Journal*, 1980, vol. 130, pp. 382–383). It is still the practice – albeit bad practice – of some courts to tell defendants that they will be committing an offence if they break their bail conditions, and that they may be fined or imprisoned or both!

3.2.10   Summary of provisions

In cases of imprisonable offences, the points to be kept in mind are:

(a)   defendants have a right to bail;

(b)   the grant of bail must be unconditional, unless conditions are necessary to prevent the occurrence of any of the events set out in the BA 1976, sch. 1, Part I, para. 2;

(c)   in order for conditions to be necessary, there must be a real risk of any of the prescribed events occurring if conditions are not imposed;

(d)   if the risk is only fanciful, unconditional bail must be granted;

(e)   if there is a real risk, conditions must be to prevent the occurrence of those events;

(f)   if there are substantial grounds for believing the events will occur even if conditions are imposed, the court need not grant bail.

In practice, what usually happens is as follows:

(a)   the court is put on notice (usually by the prosecutor, but sometimes of its own motion) that bail may be inappropriate;

(b)   the court hears 'objections' or 'observations' from the prosecutor that there are substantial grounds for believing that one or more of the exceptions apply;

(c)   the defence make their 'application' by replying that this is an appropriate case for bail conditions; in so doing, the defence are implicitly acknowledging that conditions are necessary and that there is therefore a 'real risk';

(d)   the court decides either to grant unconditional bail or conditional bail, or to remand in custody.

A variation on this is where the prosecution represent that conditional bail is appropriate and the defence concur. The court will then make its decision after hearing almost identical submissions from both parties.

The distinction between substantial grounds and real risk is rarely articulated and the decision is usually taken on the basis of an overall view of the case.

3.3.   SOME COMMON CONDITIONS

3.3.1   Reporting to a police station

3.3.1.1   Securing attendance and cue for good behaviour   The usual reason for requiring a defendant to report to a police station is to secure attendance, although it is sometimes argued that reporting serves as a reminder to defendants that they are on bail and must be of good behaviour.

3.3.1.2   Argument against the efficacy of securing attendance   The obvious argument against reporting as a means of securing attendance is that it is possible to report at, say, 6 o'clock, reach an airport by 6.30 and be on an aircraft to the other side of the world at 8 o'clock. Even with a requirement to report again at 6 o'clock the following day the defendant would be well beyond the reach of the police by the time it was realised that there had been a failure to report.

3.3.1.3   Argument against the efficacy of preventing offences   As for the reminder argument – that the discipline of reporting will remind the defendant of the importance of good behaviour, at least for the duration of the case – it is doubtful whether there is any realistic hope that defendants who are blithe about committing offences while on bail are likely to be in the slightest degree influenced to the good by any 'reminder'. The White Paper *Crime, Justice and Protecting the Public*, London: HMSO, 1990, para. 2.8, pointed out: 'Much crime is committed on impulse, given the opportunity presented by an open window or unlocked door, and it is committed by offenders who live from moment to moment; their crimes as impulsive as the rest of their feckless, sad or pathetic lives. '

3.3.1.4 Pragmatic argument against reporting At some inner city police stations, especially between the popular reporting times of 6 and 8 pm, there is an enormous queue of persons waiting to report. For both the persons in the queue and the police who have to administer the system, the conclusion must be that the whole exercise is a waste of time, energy and resources. The Home Office in its circular HO 206/1977 issued on 18 November 1977, requested courts to be especially selective in requiring reporting to a police station, since this can be burdensome for the police as well as raising potential problems of identification. In 1984, the Metropolitan Police issued a directive ordering officers not to request a condition of reporting. It is surely time for the courts – particularly lay justices – to direct themselves in a similar manner. If they do not, reporting is likely to be seen as a form of pre-trial punishment – both for defendants and for the police.

3.3.2 Surrender of passport and order not to leave the country

The reason for requiring the surrender of a passport is clearly to secure attendance, although it is open to the objection that it does not prevent people absconding within the jurisdiction. Furthermore, it does not prevent people from going to countries such as the Republic of Ireland, where a passport is not needed. The editors of *Archbold* suggest (at para. 3–4(ii)) that as the condition for surrendering a passport is designed to prevent the defendant from absconding abroad it should be accompanied by a post-release condition stipulating that the defendant shall not leave Great Britain during the period of bail. In fact, it is usually accompanied by a condition obliging the defendant not to apply for travel documents, although detection of the breach of such an order will usually be too late. If the police discover that a person is about to flee the jurisdiction, an arrest under s. 7 is a perfectly adequate way of dealing with the situation.

3.3.3 Condition of residence

A requirement that the defendant is to reside at a particular address is usually imposed in order to secure attendance. (It has been pointed out that the word 'live' is more restrictive than 'reside': Chatterton, C., *Bail: Law and Practice*, London: Buterworths, 1986, p. 149, note.) Sometimes, however, it is used to keep defendants away from complainants or other witnesses, or where following committal defendants have failed to keep in touch with their solicitors and the solicitor has been driven to have the case listed before the Crown Court for non-cooperation. Very occasionally solicitors with a notion that their clients may be poor at keeping in touch with them have been known to take the initiative by using coded language to the magistrates in order to achieve the imposition of this condition. The efficacy of the condition is limited in practice by the fact that police resources are inadequate to keep a constant check on compliance. In any event, it is not unknown for defendants to live at the address given but still fail to surrender. It is a not uncommon practice to explain to defendants who are made subject to a condition of residence that they are required to 'live and sleep' at the address in question. The practice has shown no sign of declining in spite of the description of it by a certain Metropolitan Stipendiary Magistrate as unfair if the defendant should happen to suffer from insomnia.

It is bad practice, although a common one, to impose a condition of residence coupled with a condition requiring notification of any change of address. The two requirements are mutually inconsistent.

3.3.4 Not to go within a specified distance of a certain location

Courts often impose a condition prohibiting defendants from coming within a certain specified distance of a given location. This may be a county, a town, a district, an area, a street or a building. It is also used in the case of alleged pickpockets to prevent them using public transport. Its purpose is to prevent offences of the kind presently charged against the defendant, or those such as interference with witnesses who might be known to be residing at a certain address. Whether the condition achieves this purpose is open to doubt since it does not take account of the possibility of offences at other locations. The other argument against this condition is the one that appears to have been accepted by the stipendiary magistrate in *R* v *Aubrey-Fletcher, ex parte Thompson* [1969] 2 All ER 846, namely that it imposes an unfair restriction on the liberty of an unconvicted person.

3.3.5 Curfew

The imposition of a curfew – requiring a person to remain indoors between certain specified times, usually at night – might be regarded as an even more severe restriction on an unconvicted person's liberty than a location ban. It is often coupled with a condition of residence, telling the person where he must be during the hours of curfew. Its purpose is usually to prevent offences, but it leaves open the possibility of offences at times which are not subject to the curfew.

3.3.5.1 Ambit of curfew conditions The imposition of curfew as a condition of bail is to be distinguished from the curfew order which may be imposed under s. 12, CJA 1991, as amended by the Crime (Sentences) Act 1997, s. 43(1), which removed the former restriction on curfew orders to persons 'of or over the age of 16 years.' A curfew order may now be made in respect of any person convicted of an offence, fine defaulters (s. 35, Crime (Sentences) Act 1997) and persistent petty offenders (s. 37(1), Crime (Sentences) Act 1997). A curfew order may also be made in respect of a young offender for breach of a supervision order: s. 15(3)(a)(ii), CYPA 1969, as inserted by s. 72(1), CDA 1998.

3.3.5.2 Doorstep (or presenting) condition It is becoming increasingly common for courts to impose an additional condition which is designed to enforce a curfew. This is a requirement that persons subject to a curfew and a condition of residence at a specified address must present themselves to a police officer calling at the address during the hours of the curfew. It remains to be decided whether the requirement – commonly known as a 'doorstep condition' or 'presenting condition' – complies with s. 3 (6), BA 1976, or sch. 1, Part I, para. 8, (see para. 3.2.1, above) . The overlap between the section and the schedule was attributed by Lord Lane CJ in *R* v *Mansfield Justices, ex parte Sharkey* [1985] 613, at p. 625c, to 'indifferent drafting' but the negative wording of the schedule – 'no conditions shall be imposed . . . unless it appears to the court that it is necessary to do so for the purpose of preventing the occurrence of any of the events mentioned in paragraph 2' – implies that conditions will properly be imposed *only* for that purpose. On one view a condition designed to ensure compliance with another condition is not imposed 'only' for the purpose of preventing the occurrence of any of the events set out in para. 2 because it will have a collateral purpose (Support for the argument may be found in s. 3(6ZA) which makes specific provision for a condition to comply with the rules of a bail hostel in which a person is required to reside as a condition of bail.) The converse argument is that since the doorstep condition is intended to be used in conjunction with a curfew and residence condition, it is plainly intended to be used for the purpose of preventing the same events as those conditions, *and no other.* In any event, it is arguable that such a condition is open to abuse in that it gives too much discretion to the police who may make any number of visits to a defendant's home.

3.3.5.3 Electronic monitoring Section 13 of the 1991 Act makes provision for electronic monitoring of the offender's whereabouts during the curfew periods specified in the order. Section 34A, CJA 1991, as inserted by s. 99, CDA 1998, which provides for the early release of short term prisoners on licence, is subject to s. 37A, CJA 1991, as inserted by s. 100, CDA 1998. This provides that a curfew condition subject to electronic monitoring must be included in such a licence.

3.3.6 Not to contact or interfere with witnesses

It has been argued that a condition prohibiting the bailed person from contacting or interfering with witnesses is unsound both in law and practice (see Corre, N., 'Three Frequent Questions on the Bail Act' [1989] Crim LR 493). If the condition is not to *interfere with* witnesses then it is difficult to argue that it meets the criterion of being 'necessary' since any interference will itself amount to an offence of perverting or attempting to pervert the course of justice, for which a consecutive sentence will usually be appropriate: *Attorney-General's Reference No. 1 of 1990 (R* v *Atkinson)* [1990] Crim LR 754. Section 51 of the CJPOA 1994 creates specific offences of intimidating or harming witnesses.

In any event, defendants who interfere with witnesses are likely to have their bail revoked as there will then be substantial grounds for believing that this exception to bail applies. If the order is expressed in the form 'not to *contact* witnesses', it is arguably wrong in law since if it is feared that mere contact will lead to interference then we are beyond 'real risk' and into the realm of 'substantial grounds' warranting refusal of bail.

3.3.7   Incidence of the common conditions

Research conducted for the Home Office shows the proportion of use of the various common conditions invoked across a sample of cases in which such conditions are imposed (Morgan, P., and Henderson, P., *Remand Decisions and Offending on Bail: Evaluation of the Bail Process Project*, Home Office Research and Statistics Directorate Research Findings No. 184, London: Home Office, 1998, p. 42). The proportions are set out in Table 3.1.

Condition	Percentage of defendants given condition
Residence	72%
Not to contact X	41%
Not to approach Y	28%
Curfew	20%
Report to police	18%
Surety	6%
Surrender passport	3%

Table 3.1   Preportion of use of common conditions

3.4   SOME LESS COMMON CONDITIONS

3.4.1   Not to drive a motor vehicle

A person charged with driving with excess alcohol or driving while unfit through drink or drugs may be required as a condition of bail not to drive a motor vehicle. The power should be used sparingly and the court must endeavour to avoid unexpected or unjust results: *R* v *Kwame* (1974) 60 Cr App R 65. The Home Office consultation paper, *Combating Drink Driving: Next Steps*, London: HMSO,1998, paras 22–24, suggests that the disqualification imposed upon conviction might be reduced by any period of time for which the defendant was banned from driving as a condition of bail. Primary legislation would be needed for this.

It has been suggested that the imposition of such a condition may be desirable where:

(a)   the defendant has previous convictions of a similar nature;
(b)   the defendant has allegedly committed a drinking and driving offence while on bail;
(c)   the reading is very high;

(d)   the defendant is an alcoholic;

(e)   there has been a bad accident;

(f)   there appears to be no arguable defence;

(g)   in the event of conviction the defendant will be disqualified for more than the minimum period of 12 months (or three years in the case of a second conviction in ten years) so that the sentencer may take into account the condition when deciding on the period of disqualification;

(h)   there is likely to be a delay before trial, particularly if the defendant appears to be deliberately delaying the case;

(i)   the condition will be effective; if not and the defendant is likely to ignore it then a remand in custody will appear to be necessary (see Samuels, A., 'No Driving as a Requirement or Condition of Bail' [1988] Crim LR 739).

The difficulty with such a condition is that if persons cannot be trusted to drive without previously consuming excess alcohol, the court may feel that they cannot be trusted to abide by the requirement not to drive. This is an area where 'substantial grounds' and 'real risk' are so close that they become almost indistinguishable.

3.4.2   Not to enter licensed premises or a registered club

This is occasionally imposed in appropriate cases. In contrast, a condition prohibiting the defendant from consuming alcoholic drink would be too wide and incapable of enforcement.

3.4.3   To reside at a bail hostel

3.4.3.1   Purpose   The usual purpose of the condition requiring the defendant to reside in a bail hostel is to secure attendance at court, where the defendant is either of no fixed abode or else cannot return home for some reason. The condition is also used to prevent offences, where the alleged offence is connected with the home or someone in the defendant's household.

3.4.3.2   Demand for places exceeds supply   The imposition of a condition requiring residence in a bail hostel is less common than it might be for the simple reason that the demand for bail hostel places greatly exceeds the number of places available. The CJA 1972 empowered the Home Office to finance hostels for the use of persons awaiting trial. In May 1986, there were 16 hostels with 240 available places. In December 1989, there were 19 hostels with 310 places. In March 1998, there were 101 approved hostels with a total of 2,198 beds in the system, a temporary loss of 66 beds and therefore there were 2,132 available beds. Of these 61 per cent were occupied by residents on bail, 20 per cent by those on probation, 14 per cent by those on parole and 5 per cent by others (see *Approved Hostels Monthly Bulletin*, Home Office, March 1998).

3.4.3.3 Hostels primarily used for recidivists In the mid-1970s only 16 per cent of those sent to hostels were first offenders and 49 per cent had previously served a custodial sentence (Simon, F., and Wilson, S., *Field Wing Bail Hostel: the first nine months*, Home Office Research Unit Study No. 30, London: Home Office, 1975). But it may be that there has been an excessive resort to bail hostels. In the opinion of the authors of one study, 'those remanded to bail hostels would not – or, perhaps should not – have been remanded in custody' (Lewis, H., and Mair, G., *Bail and Probation Work II; The Use of London Probation/ Bail Hostels for Bailees*, Home Office Research and Planning Unit Paper 50, London: Home Office, 1988).

3.4.3.4 Bad risks usually unwelcome Bail hostels will usually refuse to take those they consider to be bad risks, such as defendants accused of (or with convictions for) arson, sexual offences, or serious assault, or those who are addicted to drink or drugs. The management committee of a hostel is required to adopt an admissions policy and to notify the courts for the area in which the hostel is situated of that policy: Approved Probation and Bail Hostel Rules 1995 (SI 1995 No. 302), r. 10(2). Admission policy means 'the policy as to the category or categories of persons whom the committee considers suitable for admission to the hostel, r. 5(1).

3.4.3.5 Hostels facilitate rehabilitative guidance One of the advantages of hostels is that they enable staff to work with residents on an informal case-work basis, in a way that is rarely achieved where the defendant is in custody. Residents are often assisted with finding accommodation, employment or medical or psychiatric treatment. It is impossible to prove this empirically, but it may be that 'further' offences are prevented by such means.

3.4.3.6 Requirement to comply with hostel rules Where a condition of residence at a bail hostel is imposed it may be expressed simply as 'to reside at [name] hostel [address]'. Some courts add the rider 'and to abide by the rules of the hostel'. It is arguable that this is unnecessary, because if the hostel managers regard a breach of house rules as sufficiently serious to justify having the resident taken back to court for the breach it is certain that they will also consider it warrants expulsion and this will therefore put the defendant in breach of the condition of residence. Be this as it may, specific provision for the rider was enacted by s. 131 of the CJA 1988. That enactment inserted in s. 3 of the BA 1976 new subs (6ZA), which provides that where a requirement is made for residence in a bail hostel or probation hostel under s. 3(6), the defendant may also be required to comply with the rules of the hostel.

3.4.3.7. Condition of residence in a bail hostel in order to assess suitability for residence in a probation hostel in pursuance of disposal for the offence Section 131 of the CJA 1988 also amends para. 8 of sch. 1, Part I to the 1976 Act, by allowing a condition of residence at a bail hostel or probation hostel where it is necessary to impose it to assess the defendant's suitability for being dealt with for the offence in a way which would involve a period of residence in a probation hostel.

3.4.4 Electronic monitoring

Electronic monitoring, popularly known as 'tagging', was used as a condition of bail in a series of field trials with voluntary participants between August and October 1989, in the petty sessional divisions of North Tyneside, Nottingham and Tower Bridge, London. A Home Office Information Release issued in January 1990 described the practical aspects of the proposed scheme:

The trials will use a 'continuous signalling' system. Participants will wear a small anklet fitted with a low powered radio transmitter which signals every few minutes to a receiver/dialler unit attached to the person's telephone. If the radio signal is not received at the appropriate time, a message is relayed via normal telephone lines to a central computer in a monitoring station. In this way the monitoring station is informed when the participant is not at home during the prescribed period of curfew as ordered by the court. When this happens, as with a normal bail violation, the police will be informed.

In a written Parliamentary answer (12 June 1989), Mr John Patten MP, Minister of State at the Home Office, told the House of Commons that participants who did not have a telephone but were otherwise suitable for electronic monitoring would have a telephone installed free of charge. It would be provided solely for communication with the central monitoring station through electronic barring at the telephone exchange.

In a reply to a question from Mr Gerald Bermingham MP, John Patten told the House of Commons on 9 February 1990: 'Electronic monitoring cannot prevent breaches of bail, which are also committed by defendants on bail subject to other conditions, but it does enable them to be detected' (HC Deb, vol. 166, col. 823).

In practical terms the distinction here between prevention and detection may have some validity. It might have been supposed that since, as seems to be the case, electronic monitoring ensures that breaches of curfew will invariably be detected, the resulting deterrent effect would guarantee breach prevention. On that basis it might well be worth the cost involved, although even then, with the cost of the three field trials amounting to £564,706 (including VAT), it is doubtful whether this is a scheme which is not simply too expensive for the benefits. However, it clearly failed to prevent breaches in a very significant number of the cases involved in the field study. Twenty-four of the 46 defendants subject to electronic monitoring either breached their conditions of bail or absconded, or were arrested for an offence while on bail (HC Deb, vol. 166, col. 166, 9 June 1990). As at 10 June 1990, of a total of 50 defendants who were subject to electronic monitoring, 17 breached their bail conditions, and eleven committed an offence while on bail (see HL Deb, vol. 520, col. 914, 19 June 1990).

A report of the pilot project on electronic monitoring found that '[m]agistrates and judges generally did not seem to have much confidence in the applicability of electronic monitoring as an alternative to a remand in custody, and commented on the difficulties of finding suitable candidates for it' (Mair, G., *Electronic Monitoring: The Trials and Their Results*, Home Office Research and Statistics Directorate Research Study No. 120, London: HMSO, 1990, p. 65). The response of the defendants subject to the trials was also somewhat negative: 'One key point to note is that, generally, those who were monitored preferred it to custody though they also found it to be restrictive and demanding. A significant minority, however, said that they would not choose monitoring again, it was too rigorous and it would not be deducted from a custodial sentence' (*op. cit.*, p. 68). This was also the finding of a later study: the trials 'were not a great success in terms of take-up, partly because of the way the new power was implemented – for example, bailees could be curfewed for up to 24 hours per day, and any time spent tagged was not taken into account in the event of a custodial sentence being imposed' (Mortimer, E., and May, C., *Electronic Monitoring in Practice: The Second Year of the Trials of Curfew Orders*, Home Office Research and Statistics Directorate, Research Study No. 177, London: Home Office, 1997, p. 1).

Curfew orders imposed as a community sentence in accordance with the CJA 1991, s. 12(1), may include requirements for electronic monitoring: CJA 1991, s. 13(1). Curfew orders may be made in respect of fine defaulters, persistent petty offenders and juveniles aged 10 to 15 years: Crime (Sentences) Act 1997, ss. 36, 37 and 43 (in force since 1 January 1998). Section 91 of the CDA 1998 inserts a new section, s. 34A, into the CJA 1991, to provide a power for prisoners over the age of 18 who are serving sentences of more than three months but less than four years to be released on a 'home detention curfew licence' to be enforced by electronic monitoring. It has been reported that '[p]lans are under way to use electronic monitoring as a condition of bail' (Mortimer, E., and May, C., *Electronic Monitoring of Curfew Orders: The Second Year of the Trials*, Home Office Research and Statistics Directorate, Research Findings No. 66, London: Home Office, 1998, p. 4).

3.4.5 Conditions necessary to secure attendance at interview with legal representative

Section 54(2)(e) of the CDA 1998 inserts into s. 3(6) of the BA 1976 a new objective. Now, s. 3(6)(e) provides that a defendant may be required to comply with such requirements as may be necessary to secure that: '. . . before the time appointed for him to surrender to custody, he attends at an interview with an authorised advocate or authorised litigator, as defined by section 119(1) of the Courts and Legal Services Act 1990.' This is a category of requirement which only a court may impose; the police are not empowered to do so: BA 1976, s. 3A(2), as amended by CDA 1998, s. 54(3). The drafting of the amendment is such as to enable a court to impose conditions to secure attendance at such an interview. The difficulty is that by adding a new paragraph to s. 3(6) the amendment is out of line with the purpose for which the other conditions may be imposed. The other reasons for the imposition of conditions in the subsection relate to the reasons for withholding bail in the case of imprisonable offences.

The purpose of the amendment is to reduce delays in the criminal justice system which are purportedly caused by solicitors not being adequately instructed. The amendment therefore has little to do with the principles underlying the BA 1976 and everything to do with the convenience of the courts. An examination of the reasons for adjournments in magistrates' courts only partially justifies the new provision. A recent study found that 20.6 per cent of cases were adjourned because the defence were unable to proceed; however, another 5.7 per cent of adjournments were caused by the failure of the CPS to provide advance information, and a further 4.9 per cent were caused by delays in applications for or decisions on legal aid (Whittaker, C., and Mackie, A., with Lewis, R., and Ponikiewski N., *Managing Courts Effectively: The Reasons for Adjournments in Magistrates' Courts*, Home Office Research and Statistics Directorate Research Findings No. 168, London: HMSO, 1997, p. 11.

The introduction of the condition raises a number of questions. Where clients who are waiting on bail for trial on indictment persistently fail to attend at their solicitors' offices to give instructions, practitioners will already be familiar with the obligation to have the case listed for 'non-cooperation'. Exactly what powers the Crown Court properly enjoys in dealing with the case in such circumstances is not clear. Obviously, defendants called to account for the first time for such insouciance are reminded of the importance of assisting in the preparation of their case but rarely if ever have their bail withdrawn. On the other hand, continued lack of cooperation might well result in such an outcome. It is not unknown for defendants to be re-released subject to a condition that they keep in contact with their solicitor and cooperate with the solicitor in preparing the defence. Such a condition can be enforced only with the cooperation of the solicitor who must become an informer against the client. This does not seem to raise any issue of client confidentiality because the failure in question involves no element of 'lawyer–client privileged communication'. Indeed, the very opposite is the case, for there has been no communication! Moreover, there is no real conflict of interest between the duty to the court and the duty to protect the client, because it can hardly be said to be in the client's interest to allow a situation to continue in which through the defendant's lack of interest the defence remains unprepared. Indeed, under the régime introduced by s. 11 of the Criminal Procedure and Investigations Act 1996 a court may draw such inferences as appear proper from the failure by the defence to furnish a statement of the defence case within the statutory period required. It may be concluded then that the condition can be enforced through the agency of the solicitor without any ethical conflict. Whether the condition can be complied with by an extra-curial chat in the corridor after court is another matter.

Home Office Circular No. 34 of 1998 makes it clear that '[t]he defendant's solicitor should not be expected to report a breach if the defendant fails to attend an interview' (para. 11).

3.5 CONDITIONS TO ENABLE MEDICAL REPORTS TO BE PREPARED

3.5.1 On a charge of murder

Subject to s. 25 of the CJPOA 1994, the statutory right to bail applies where a person is charged with murder. However, it has been said that such a person should not be granted bail until medical reports have been prepared. In *R* v *Vernege* [1982] 1 WLR 293, the Court of Appeal observed that on a charge of murder consideration ought to be given to remanding the accused in custody, in his own interests, to facilitate an examination by the prison doctor. Consideration could then be given to the various relevant matters affecting the accused's state of mind at the time of the offence, and in particular to the possibility of the defence of diminished responsibility. When such report was prepared, the accused could apply to the Crown Court for bail.

A provision inserted in the BA 1976 in 1982 states that in the case of a person accused of murder the court granting bail must, unless it considers that satisfactory reports on his medical condition have already been obtained, impose as conditions of bail:

(a) a requirement that the accused must undergo examination by two medical practitioners for the purpose of enabling such reports to be prepared; and

(b) a requirement that the accused must for that purpose attend such an institution or place as the court directs and comply with any of the directions which may be given for that purpose by either of those practitioners: s. 3(6A), inserted by s. 34 of the Mental Health (Amendment) Act 1982.

One such practitioner must be approved for the purposes of s. 12 of the MHA 1983: BA 1976, s. 3(6B). A defendant who is charged with murder and granted bail without such conditions is unlawfully at large: *R* v *Central Criminal Court, ex parte Porter* [1992] Crim LR 121. The restriction as to imposing conditions of bail does not apply: BA 1976, sch. 1, Part I, para. 8(3).

3.5.2 After summary trial

Section 30(1) of the MCA 1980 provides that if on the trial by a magistrates' court of an offence punishable on summary conviction with imprisonment, the defendant is convicted or the court is satisfied that the accused did the act or made the omission charged and the court is of the opinion that an inquiry ought to be made into the defendant's physical or mental condition before the method of disposal is determined, the court must adjourn the case to enable a medical examination and report to be made and must remand him. The adjournment must not be for more than three weeks at a time where the court remands the defendant in custody, or for more than four weeks at a time where it remands the defendant on bail. Section 30(2) provides that where on an adjournment under s. 30(1) the accused is remanded on bail, the court must impose conditions under s. 3(6)(d) of the 1976 Act and the requirements imposed as conditions under that paragraph (i.e., requiring the accused to be available for the purpose of enabling inquiries or a report to be made to assist the court in dealing with the offence) must be or must include requirements that the accused:

(a)   undergo medical examination by a fully qualified medical practitioner or, where the inquiry is into the accused's mental condition and the court so directs, two such practitioners; and

(b)   for that purpose attend such institution or place, or on such practitioner, as the court directs and, where the inquiry is into the accused's mental condition, comply with any other directions which may be given for that purpose by any person specified by the court or by a person of any class so specified.

In the case of offences not punishable with imprisonment magistrates have the power to remand an accused for medical reports (MCA 1980, s. 10; and see *Boaks v Reece* [1957] 1 QB 219) but there is no requirement to impose the statutory conditions of bail.

4   Failing to Surrender

4.1.   THE DUTY TO SURRENDER TO CUSTODY

4.1.1   Introduction

The counterpart of the right to bail is self-evidently a duty of the bailed person to surrender to custody at the appointed time, and this is expressly written into the BA 1976, s. 3(1) of which provides: 'A person granted bail in criminal proceedings shall be under a duty to surrender to custody . . .'

The duty is enforceable in two ways. The first is by arresting the absconder. A person bailed by the police under a duty to surrender to a constable may be arrested without a warrant: PACE 1984, s. 46A. Where a person who has been released on bail in criminal proceedings and is under a duty to surrender into the custody of a court fails to do so at the appointed time, the court may issue a warrant for the person's arrest: BA 1976, s. 7(1). The second means of enforcement – expressly laid down in s. 3(1) – is by prosecuting the absconder under s. 6 of the BA 1976, which makes it an offence to fail to surrender to custody without reasonable cause.

Failure to comply with the duty to surrender may have consequences beyond prosecution for an offence under the BA 1976 (see para. 4.3.2). Where a defendant on bail fails to appear for trial, which then takes place without the defendant being present, this cannot found a ground of appeal on the basis that the trial should not have taken place in the defendant's absence: *R v Donnelly* [1998] Crim LR 131, CA.

4.1.2   Statutory definition of 'surrender to custody'

Section 2(2) of the BA 1976 defines 'surrender to custody' as, in relation to a person released on bail, surrendering into the custody of the court or of the constable (according to the requirements of the grant of bail) at the time and place for the time being appointed. Where an enactment (whenever passed) which relates to bail in criminal proceedings refers to the person bailed appearing before a court, it is to be construed (unless the context otherwise requires) as referring to the person surrendering into the custody of the court: BA 1976, s. 2(3).

4.1.3   Surrender determined by particular court procedure

Whether a person has in fact surrendered to the court will depend upon the procedure adopted by the particular court. The obligation of a person on bail is to comply with the procedures of that court and to surrender to the appropriate official: *DPP* v *Richards* [1988] Crim LR 606, DC. The direction to report to an official must be made by the court and must be of a formal nature, whether orally or in writing. Where a defendant attends the court building but does not report to an official and then leaves before the case is heard, there will have been no surrender to custody: *R* v *Reader* (1987) 84 Cr App R 294. Defendants who are arraigned without previously having surrendered to custody thereby surrender to the custody of the court: *R* v *Central Criminal Court, ex parte Guney* [1996] AC 616, HL. If, therefore, a case is adjourned following arraignment, judges must address their minds to the issue of bail since a grant of bail requires a judicial decision: *R* v *Dimond* (1999) 149 NLJ 87, CA. The interpretation of 'surrender to custody' was taken one stage further in *R* v *Maidstone Crown Court, ex parte Jodka, The Times*, 13 June 1997, where it was held that any bail granted by a magistrates' court ceases when a defendant surrenders to the custody of the Crown Court, whether at an arraignment or at another hearing.

4.1.4.   Reporting to a court official places the defendant in technical custody

A person answering bail at court by reporting to the relevant official is technically in custody even though in practice free within the precincts, and is under an implied obligation not to leave without consent; an arrest warrant may be issued against any such person whose case is called but who has left the court building beforehand: *DPP* v *Richards* (above). Section 7(2) of the 1976 Act makes specific provision for this:

> (2)   If a person who has been released on bail in criminal proceedings absents himself from the court at any time after he has surrendered into the custody of the court and before the court is ready to begin or to resume the hearing of the proceedings, the court may issue a warrant for his arrest; but no warrant shall be issued under this subsection where that person is absent in accordance with leave given to him by or on behalf of the court.

It has been suggested that courts might have to consider making it clear to persons who have reported to the appropriate officer that thereafter they were in custody and that, even if they were allowed to sit in the concourse, they were not permitted to leave the building without consent: see *Archbold*, para. 3-30.

4.2   ARREST

4.2.1   Arrest for failing to surrender to a constable

4.2.1.1   Power of arrest without warrant   A constable may arrest without warrant any person who, having been released on bail under Part IV of PACE 1984 subject to a duty to attend at a police station, fails to attend at that police station at the appointed time: PACE 1984, s. 46A(1). (Section 46A was inserted by s. 29(1) of the CJPOA 1994; see also Chapter 6, para. 6.2.3.2.)

4.2.1.2 Duty to take arrested person to the police station A person so arrested must be taken to the appointed police station as soon as practicable: PACE 1984, s. 46A(2).

4.2.1.3 Arrest is an arrest for an offence An arrest for failure to surrender to a constable is an arrest for an offence which triggers the general detention provisions of Part IV of the 1984 Act: PACE 1984, s. 46A(3). It follows that the person so arrested may be detained under Part IV with a view to being investigated for the offence of failing to surrender. The arrested person may be charged and released on bail to appear in court.

4.2.2   Arrest on a warrant issued upon failure to surrender to a court

4.2.2.1 Discretionary nature of the general court power to issue a warrant
Where a person has been released on bail under a duty to surrender to the custody of a court and fails to do so, the court may issue a warrant under s. 7(1) of the BA 1976. The power is discretionary. It will clearly be inappropriate to issue a warrant when the failure to surrender is due to no fault on the part of the defendant, e.g., where inquiries show that the defendant is in custody to another court or is in hospital.

4.2.2.2 Magistrates' statutory discretion to grant further remand in absence of a defendant who has not surrendered to custody Where in the case of a magistrates' court, the court is satisfied that a person is unable to appear or be brought before the court by reason of illness, accident or through detention in custody on another matter, the court may permit a further remand and enlarge any recognizances: MCA 1980, s. 129(1) and (3) (see further Chapter 7, para. 7.3). Even in cases where illness or accident cannot be put forward, the court may appoint a later date for the accused to appear: MCA 1980, s. 129(2). A magistrates' court which enlarges the recognizance of a surety to a later date must give notice to the accused and to the surety: MCR 1981, r. 84 and BA 1976, s. 5(1). If the accused is on police bail to appear at court, the court may appoint a later date and enlarge any recognizance: MCA 1980, s. 43 (see also para. 6.4.2).

4.2.2.3 Magistrates' court warrant endorsed for bail A magistrate, on issuing a warrant for the arrest of any person, may grant bail by endorsing the warrant for bail, that is to say, by endorsing the warrant with a direction that the person arrested is to be released on bail subject to a duty to appear before such magistrates' court and at such time as may be specified in the endorsement: MCA 1980, s. 117. The endorsement must fix the amounts in which any sureties are to be bound: *ibid.*. The power to endorse – or 'back' – a warrant for bail provides a means by which the absent person can be released by the police to attend court at a later date. The power is most likely to be used where the defendant has failed to appear for a non-imprisonable offence, in particular where road traffic offences have been proved in absence and the court requires the attendance of the defendant in order to consider disqualification.

4.2.2.4 Crown Court warrant endorsed for bail The Crown Court, on issuing a warrant for the arrest of any person, may endorse the warrant for bail, and in any such case:

(a) the person arrested under the warrant must, unless the Crown Court otherwise directs, be taken to a police station; and
(b) the officer in charge of the station must release the person from custody if any sureties required by the endorsement and approved by the officer enter into recognizances of such amount as may be fixed by the endorsement: SCA 1981, s. 81(4).

4.2.2.5 Copy of bail decision record to be sent to Crown Court upon release on bail of person arrested on warrant endorsed for bail Where the officer in charge of a police station releases on bail a person who has been arrested in pursuance of a warrant issued by the Crown Court under s. 81(4) of the SCA 1981, the officer must forthwith notify the appropriate officer of the Crown Court of the action which has been taken and must transmit to the appropriate officer of the Crown Court as soon as practicable a copy of the record made in pursuance of s. 5 of the BA 1976 relating to such bail: MCR 1981, r. 89, as construed in the light of the repeal by the SCA 1981 of s. 13 of the Courts Act 1971.

4.2.2.6 Magistrates' warrant not endorsed for bail Where a non-appearance warrant issued by the magistrates' court is not endorsed for bail, the person arrested on the warrant must be produced before the magistrates' court. The court will then review the question of bail afresh.

4.2.2.7 Crown Court warrant not endorsed for bail A person in custody in pursuance of a warrant issued by the Crown Court with a view to being produced before that court (that is, a warrant not endorsed for bail) must be brought forthwith before either the Crown Court or a magistrates' court: SCA 1981, s. 81(5).

4.2.2.8 Options open to magistrates' court upon production of person arrested on a Crown Court non-appearance warrant Section 43A of the MCA 1980 (inserted by the SCA 1981, sch. 5) provides that where a person in custody in pursuance of a warrant issued by the Crown Court for the person's appearance before that court is brought before a magistrates' court in pursuance of s. 81(5) of the SCA 1981:

(a)   the magistrates' court must order the person either to be committed in custody or released on bail pending appearance before the Crown Court at the time and place appointed by the Crown Court;

(b)   if the warrant is endorsed for bail but the conditions endorsed cannot be satisfied, the magistrates' court may vary those conditions, if satisfied that it is proper to do so.

A magistrates' court has jurisdiction under s. 43A(1) whether or not the offence was committed, or the arrest was made, within the court's area: MCA 1980, s. 43A(2).

4.2.2.9   Copy of magistrates' court bail decision record to be sent to Crown Court upon committal to custody or release on bail of a person arrested on a Crown Court non-appearance warrant   Where under the MCA 1980, s. 43A a magistrates' court commits to custody or releases on bail a person who has been arrested in pursuance of a warrant issued by the Crown Court, the clerk of the magistrates' court shall forthwith notify the appropriate officer of the Crown Court of the action which has been taken and, if that person has been released, must transmit to the appropriate officer of the Crown Court as soon as practicable a copy of the record made in pursuance of s. 5 of the BA 1976 relating to such bail: MCR 1981, r. 89, as construed in the light of the repeal by the SCA 1981 of s. 13 of the Courts Act 1971.

4.2.3   Police power to arrest potential absconders without warrant

4.2.3.1   Statutory power   Section 7(3) of the BA 1976 empowers a constable to arrest without warrant a person who has been released on bail in criminal proceedings and is under a duty to surrender to the custody of a court:

(a)   if the constable has reasonable grounds for believing that the person is not likely to surrender to custody; or

(b)   in a case where that person was released on bail with a surety or sureties, if a surety notifies a constable in writing that the bailed person is unlikely to surrender to custody and that for that reason the surety wishes to be relieved of the obligation of remaining a surety.

It is to be noted that the power of arrest is contingent on the duty of the person bailed to surrender to a court and not at a police station. (There is also a power of arrest without warrant under the subsection where a constable has reasonable grounds for believing that the person is likely to break any of the conditions of bail, or has reasonable grounds for suspecting that that person has broken any of those conditions: see Chapter 3, para. 3.2.9.1.) The constable's power is discretionary and it has been pointed out that a constable will wish to see some basis for the claim that the person on bail is unlikely to surrender (see Chatterton, *Bail: Law and Practice*, London: Butterworths, 1986, p. 190, note 4). As to the question of the surety's desire to withdraw, see Chapter 2, para. 2.1.13.

4.2.3.2 Duties of police following arrest A person arrested under s. 7(3) of the 1976 Act must be brought as soon as practicable, and in any event within 24 hours, before a magistrate in the petty sessional area in which the arrest was effected: BA 1976, s. 7(4)(a). If arrested within 24 hours of the time originally appointed for surrendering to custody, the person must be taken to the court at which the surrender was to be made: s. 7(4)(b). In reckoning any period of 24 hours, no account is to be taken of Christmas Day, Good Friday or any Sunday: s. 7(4). A person who is arrested in pursuance of s. 7(3) must be released if not brought before the justices within 24 hours of arrest, and it is insufficient to bring the person merely within the precincts of the magistrates' court within 24 hours: *R* v *Governor of Glen Parva Young Offenders Institution, ex parte G, The Times*, 24 January 1998, DC.

4.2.3.3 Powers of the court If the magistrate is of opinion that the person brought before the court under the BA 1976, s. 7:

(a) is not likely to surrender to custody; or
(b) has broken or is likely to break a bail condition,

bail may be refused, or, granted subject to the same or to different conditions: s. 7(5). If the magistrate is not of that opinion, bail must be granted subject to the same conditions (if any) as were originally imposed: *ibid*. Apart from any admissions by the defendant, the court's opinion will be a judgment based on the representations of both sides. The statutory right to bail does not apply: see BA 1976, sch. 1, Part I, para. 6, and Part II, para. 5. (See Chapter 11 for disposal in the case of children or young persons.) It is suggested that where any conditions are varied courts ought to consider advising any surety who is not present of the variation: see *R* v *Wells Street Magistrates' Court, ex parte Albanese* [1982] QB 333.

4.2.3.4 Copy record of a magistrate's bail decision following arrest in anticipation of breach of bail to be sent to court to which bailed person was under a duty to surrender Where a person who has been released on bail and is under a duty to surrender into the custody of a court is brought under BA 1976, s. 7(4)(a) before a justice of the peace, the justice must cause a copy of the record made in pursuance of s. 5 of the Act relating to the decision under s. 7(5) to be sent:

(a) in the case of a magistrates' court, to the clerk; or
(b) in the case of any other court, to the appropriate officer: MCR 1981, r. 92.

This rule does not apply where the court is a magistrates' court acting for the same petty sessions area as that for which the justice acts.

4.2.3.5 Decision must be made without adjournment The determination under BA 1976, s. 7(5) must be made there and then. In *R* v *Liverpool City Justices, ex parte DPP* [1992] 3 All ER 249, it was held that the s. 7(5) procedure is not a trial or a hearing governed by s. 121 of the MCA 1980 requiring at least two justices, and there is no power to adjourn the hearing. A single justice may preside and must reach a decision virtually on the spot. This is liable to raise difficulties. While a good starting point for the formation of the justice's opinion will be the arresting constable's 'reasonable grounds' (see *Stone's Justices' Manual*, 1990 ed., para. 1–476, footnote (e)), there may be no option but to base that judgment on evidential grounds. In a case, for example, where the defendant is denying an allegation of breaking a condition of bail the issue can be fairly resolved only by hearing evidence on the point. Alternatively, only the arresting officer may possess sufficient knowledge of the circumstances and of the accused to give the court a full account of the basis of any risks involved if the defendant is to be again released. That evidence must be available at the hearing, because no adjournment is allowed, but circumstances will frequently preclude this. Often, the arresting constable will have been on night duty and will have signed off in order to go home to sleep. The only witness to a breach of a condition may be a private individual who is not in court. If a decision denying bail cannot fairly be made without hearing the evidence of the constable or the witness, there being no power to adjourn so that the evidence can be called to court, the justice will be in no position to form a valid opinion that the case falls within either s. 7(5)(a) or (b) unless 'section 9' statements are available (s. 9, CJA 1967). In such a case it will follow that the court will have no choice but to order the defendant's release on the same conditions as before.

4.2.4 Customs and Excise power of arrest

4.2.4.1 Arrest without warrant Section 151(1), (4) and (5) of the CJA 1988 make provision for the arrest without warrant of a person who, having been released on bail in criminal proceedings for an offence under s. 5(2) of the Misuse of Drugs Act 1971 (possession of controlled drugs) or for a drugs trafficking offence as defined by s. 1(3) of the Drug Trafficking Act 1994, other than an offence under s. 50 of that Act (assisting another to retain the benefit of drug trafficking), is under a duty to surrender into customs detention but is believed by an officer of Customs and Excise on reasonable grounds to be not likely to surrender to custody. In such a case the person may be arrested without warrant by an officer of Customs and Excise.

4.2.4.2 Requirement to bring an arrested person before a magistrate A person arrested under s. 151 of the CJA 1988 must be brought as soon as practicable, and in any event within 24 hours after arrest, before a justice of the peace for the petty sessions area in which the arrest was made: s. 151(2). In reckoning any period of 24 hours, no account is taken of Christmas Day, Good Friday, or any Sunday: s. 151(3).

4.3 THE BAIL ACT OFFENCE OF FAILING TO SURRENDER

4.3.1 Introduction of the offence by the Bail Act

Before the Bail Act 1976 it was not an offence to fail to surrender, although absconders were liable to forfeit any personal recognizance and to be dealt with for what was known as 'estreating' bail. Section 3(2) of the 1976 Act abolished personal recognizances and s. 6 made failure to surrender a criminal offence.

4.3.2 Two offences

The 1976 Act actually creates two distinct offences (s. 6(1) and (2)), either of which may be tried summarily or as if they constituted a criminal contempt of court (s. 6(5)).

4.3.2.1 Failure to surrender without reasonable cause

Section 6(1) of the BA 1976 makes it an offence for a person who has been released on bail in criminal proceedings to fail without reasonable cause to surrender to custody.

4.3.2.2 Failure to surrender as soon as practicable after appointed time at which defendant failed to surrender with reasonable cause

It is also an offence, contrary to s. 6(2) of the 1976 Act, if a person who has been released on bail in criminal proceedings, and having reasonable cause for failing to surrender to custody, fails to surrender to custody at the appointed place as soon after the appointed time as is reasonably practicable.

4.3.2.3 Offence committed by late arrival

Since surrender to custody means at the time, as well as the place, appointed, the offence is also committed if the defendant is late. A literal interpretation will mean that the offence is committed if the defendant is only marginally late in appearing, that is, even by as little as a minute or a few minutes after the appointed time. However, in *R v Gateshead Justices, ex parte Usher and Another* [1981] Crim LR 491, it was held that to arrive at court seven minutes late could not be said to amount to such an offence. This may be regarded as an application of the *de minimis* principle, although that was not the *ratio* of the decision. Perhaps the underlying reason for the decision is the finding of the Divisional Court that there had been a number of irregularities in the case. The justices had refused to withdraw a warrant issued under s. 7 and so the applicants were required to surrender to a police station. More importantly, at the subsequent trial the clerk gave evidence as to failure to surrender and then returned to his seat and conducted legal argument with the applicants. The Divisional Court held that the clerk was not a person who was authorised to lay the information. This latter point must now be seen in the light of *Schiavo v Anderton* [1986] 3 WLR 176, and *Practice Direction (Bail: Failure to Surrender)* [1987] 1 WLR 79, which are discussed below. It has been argued by Professor Sir

John Smith QC that a difficult question of degree arises once the court departs from the literal meaning of the words 'at the time and place for the time being appointed'; does the defendant commit the offence if he is eight minutes late, 30 minutes late, or one hour late? (See commentary on *Ex parte Usher*, above).

4.3.3 'Reasonable cause'

4.3.3.1 Requirement is 'cause' not 'excuse' Unlike certain other criminal offences, such as possession of an offensive weapon or failing to provide a specimen, the defence is not reasonable *excuse* but reasonable *cause*. 'Cause' has a narrower meaning than 'excuse'. The failure to surrender must be the effect or the result of the cause so that there is a direct relationship between the two. The defence is not established by pointing to something that merely exonerates the defendant. Exoneration does not amount to exculpation in this context.

4.3.3.2 Question of fact for the judge Reasonable cause is a question of fact for the judge. Whether a mistake by a solicitor, in giving the defendant the wrong date, amounts to a reasonable cause is a question of fact to be decided in all the circumstances of the particular case: *R v Liverpool City JJ, ex parte Santos*, *The Times*, 23 January 1997, DC. The Court of Appeal will not interfere with the judge's finding unless he errs in law or goes wholly wrong on the facts: *R v Jordan* (unreported), 4 October 1988, CA transcript No. 2310A388, *per* Macpherson J.

4.3.3.3 Failure to serve copy of bail notice is not a reasonable cause A failure to hand the person granted bail in criminal proceedings a copy of the bail notice, that is the record of the decision, does not constitute a reasonable cause for that person's failure to surrender to custody: BA 1976, s. 6(4).

4.3.3.4 Mistaking the date is not a reasonable cause In *Laidlaw v Atkinson*, *The Times*, 2 August 1988, DC, it was held that it was not a reasonable cause if a defendant makes a mistake about the due date for surrender. In that case the defendant had given his charge sheet, which contained details of the correct date, to his solicitor. The court held that this was his responsibility and he should have made a note of the date. Where a solicitor has allegedly given the defendant the wrong date, this could constitute reasonable cause for failing to appear, depending on all the circumstances: *R v Liverpool City JJ, ex parte Santos*, above.

4.3.4 Definition of 'court'

The BA 1976, s. 2(2) defines 'court' to include a judge of the court and a justice of the peace. Notwithstanding these definitions, it was held in *DPP v Richards* [1988] Crim LR 606, DC, that surrender to custody was achieved where the person released on bail reported at the appointed time and place to the appointed official deputed by the court for this purpose. Section 47A PACE 1984, as inserted by sch. 8, para. 62, CDA 1998, provides that any requirement of a person who has been charged with an offence at a police station to appear or be brought before a magistrates' court shall be taken to be satisfied if the person appears or is brought before the clerk to the justices in order for the clerk to conduct an early administrative hearing under s. 50, CDA 1998.

4.3.5 Proof

4.3.5.1 Evidence of time and place appointed for surrender In any proceedings for an offence under the BA 1976, s. 6(1) or (2), a document purporting to be a copy of the part of the prescribed record which relates to the time and place appointed for the person specified in the record to surrender to custody, and duly certified to be a true copy of that part of the record, is evidence of the time and place appointed for that person to surrender to custody: BA 1976, s. 6(8).

4.3.5.2 Onus on the defendant Once it is established that the defendant failed to surrender (and this is usually achieved by virtue of s. 6(8) above) he must prove that he had reasonable cause for his failure to surrender to custody: BA 1976, s. 6(3). As in all cases in which a defendant in criminal proceedings bears the burden of proof, the burden is discharged on the balance of probabilities. The question for the court will therefore be, has the defendant proved that it is more likely than not that he had reasonable cause for failing to surrender? (See *R v Carr-Briant* [1943] 2 All ER 156.)

4.3.6 Basic statutory provisions on jurisdiction and penalties

4.3.6.1 Provision for summary trial or punishment as a criminal contempt An offence under the BA 1976, s. 6(1) or (2) is punishable either on summary conviction or as if it were a criminal contempt of court: s. 6(5). In *Schiavo* v *Anderton*, [1986] 3 WLR 176, it was held that both the Crown Court and the magistrates' court each have a separate power to punish the offence of absconding. It was observed that the offence is not in fact a contempt of court, although it may be said to bear some relationship to it in the sense that failure to appear amounts to defiance of an essential condition of bail.

4.3.6.2 Penalty in the magistrates' court A person who is convicted summarily of an offence under s. 6(1) or (2) of the 1976 Act and is not committed to the Crown Court for sentence is liable to imprisonment for a term not exceeding three months or to a fine not exceeding level 5 on the standard scale or to both: BA 1976, s. 6(7).

4.3.6.3 Committal for sentence A magistrates' court may commit a defendant to the Crown Court for sentence if it thinks:

(a)   that the circumstances of the offence are such that a greater punishment should be inflicted for the offence than the court has power to inflict; or

(b)   where the defendant is committed for trial for another offence, that it would be appropriate for the bail offence to be dealt with by the court which is to try the other offence: BA 1976, s. 6(6).

In *Schiavo* v *Anderton*, above, the Divisional Court confirmed that justices have power to commit to the Crown Court for sentence if satisfied that their powers are insufficient. The statutory wording makes it clear that the committal must be on the basis of the circumstances of the offence. This approach to a committal for sentence is in accord with (although it pre-dates) the grounds set out in s. 38 of the MCA 1980, as substituted by s. 25 of, and sch. 8, para. 6(d) to, the CJA 1991, and amended by s. 66(8) of the CJA 1993. At the time the BA 1976 came into force, a committal for sentence was based on the character and antecedents of the offender. The committal may be on bail or in custody: BA 1976, s. 6(7). A person who is committed for sentence is liable to imprisonment for a term not exceeding 12 months or to a fine or to both: s. 6(7).

4.3.6.4   Penalty when dealt with as a criminal contempt   When dealt with as if the offence were a contempt the offender is liable to imprisonment for a term not exceeding 12 months or to a fine or to both: BA 1976, s. 6(7). The maximum of 12 months applies only to the Crown Court; in the magistrates' court the maximum is six months: *Murphy* v *DPP* [1990] Crim LR 395.

4.3.7   Magistrates' courts: summary punishment or process by way of contempt

4.3.7.1   Literal construction of the statutory provisions   On a literal construction of BA 1976, s. 6(5), (6) and (7), there would be an open choice as to whether to proceed in the magistrates' court as if the offence generally were punishable summarily or as if it were a contempt. In *R* v *Tyson* (1978) 68 Cr App R 314, Cantley J assumed this construction to be correct when he stated that the effect of s. 6 was that there were three available procedures:

(a)   summary conviction and sentence by a magistrates' court;

(b)   summary conviction by a magistrates' court followed by committal to the Crown Court for sentence; and

(c)   procedure as if the offence were a criminal contempt of court.

A similar assumption was made by Roskill LJ in *R* v *Harbax Singh* [1979] 1 All ER 524, at p. 527, when he said that:

One must look at the structure and purpose of section 6. It seems clear that it has created a wholly new offence punishable in one of two ways. It can be punished as if it were a summary offence, triable in and only in a magistrates' court with additional power to commit for sentence to the Crown Court . . . [A] court other than a magistrates' court, that is the Crown Court [has] power to deal with [an offender] in whatever way as the Crown Court would do if he were guilty of criminal contempt of court.

4.3.7.2 Former practice and later interpretation of the statute Where a warrant was issued in the magistrates' court under BA 1976, s. 7 for failure to surrender, it was the usual practice for the police to charge an offence contrary to s. 6 once the warrant had been executed. This practice was challenged in *Schiavo* v *Anderton*, [1986] 3 WLR 176, on the ground that where proceedings are before a magistrates' court, the offence is summary and so the information must be laid within six months. The Divisional Court rejected this argument as well as the argument that the information is laid when the warrant is issued, and declared that on a proper construction of s. 6, Parliament intended the following:

(a) both the Crown Court and the magistrates' court should each have a separate power to punish the offence of absconding;

(b) the offence should not be subject to the general rule that trial was to be commenced by the laying of an information;

(c) the only proper way to proceed is for the court to initiate the simple procedure of its own motion;

(d) the offence should not be triable either way or on indictment;

(e) the offence should be triable only by the court in respect of which a failure to surrender had occurred;

(f) the Bail Act offence should be tried immediately following the disposal of the substantive offence in respect of which bail was granted.

The declaration that the offence is not triable either way or on indictment is clearly correct as there is no right of election and no power to commit for trial, although there is a power to commit for sentence. The offence is triable only by the court in respect of which the failure to surrender occurred.

4.3.8 The 1986 Practice Direction

In order to clarify any misunderstandings which might have arisen from the decision in *Schiavo* v *Anderton*, the Court of Appeal issued *Practice Direction (Bail: Failure to Surrender)* [1987] 1 WLR 79, in which Lord Lane CJ laid down principles which distinguished between bail granted by a magistrates' court and that granted by the police.

4.3.8.1 Bail granted by a magistrates' court Where a person has been granted bail by a court and subsequently fails to surrender as contemplated by s. 6(1) or s. 6(2) of the BA 1976, on arrest that person should be brought before the court at which the proceedings in respect of which bail was granted are to be heard. It is neither necessary nor desirable to lay an information in order to commence proceedings for the failure to surrender. Having regard to the nature of the offence, which is tantamount to the defiance of a court order, it is more appropriate that the court itself should initiate the proceedings by its own motion, following an express invitation by the prosecutor. The court will only be invited so to move, if, having considered all the circumstances, the prosecutor considers proceedings are appropriate. Where a court complies with such an invitation, the prosecutor will naturally conduct the proceedings and, where the matter is contested, call the evidence. Any trial should normally take place immediately following the proceedings in respect of which bail was granted.

4.3.8.2 Bail granted by a police officer Where a person has been bailed from a police station subject to a duty to appear before a magistrates' court or to attend a police station on an appointed date or time or both, a failure so to appear or attend cannot be said to be tantamount to the defiance of a court order. There does not exist the same compelling justification for the court to act by its own motion. When bail has been granted by a police officer, any proceedings for a failure to surrender to custody, whether at a court or a police station, should accordingly be initiated by charging the accused or by laying an information. In *R* v *Teeside Magistrates' Court, ex parte Bujinowski* [1997] Crim LR 51, it was held to be a breach of the *Practice Direction* where the court had a policy of putting a Bail Act charge if the defendant was more than 30 minutes late and where the prosecutor took no part in the proceedings.

4.3.9 Problems raised by the 1986 Practice Direction

Lord Lane's direction that the court must initiate the proceedings of its own motion should have been an end of the matter. However, it is submitted that his further direction that the initiation of proceedings ought to follow an express invitation by the prosecutor, who must consider all the circumstances before deciding whether proceedings are appropriate, is both wrong in principle and unworkable in practice. Since the onus is on the accused to show reasonable cause for failing to surrender, a *prima facie* case is raised once it is proved that the accused was released on bail in criminal proceedings and failed to surrender at the time and place appointed.

In requiring the prosecutor to consider all the circumstances, the court is effectively imposing on the prosecution a judicial function. Whether or not the court is invited to initiate proceedings will depend on the individual view of the particular prosecutor. In many cases, this will mean that the prosecutor will have to decide upon the reasonableness of the cause of the defendant's failure to surrender. It is surely arguable that it is the function of the court to decide this, after it has heard the evidence. How is the prosecutor to consider all the circumstances? The instructions received from the police may not contain even any of the circumstances. They may contain a reply to caution, in which a reason is given for the failure to surrender, but this cannot be said to amount to all the circumstances. In any event, it is impossible for the prosecutor to know if the accused has told the truth to the police, and self-serving statements are not evidence of the truth of their contents. Alternatively, defendants may, as is their right, make no reply to caution. Should prosecutors then seek out defendants and ask the reason for the failure to surrender? In busy magistrates' courts they will hardly have the time or inclination. If they were to do so, ought they to administer a caution? Even in the absence of a caution, the defendant will be entitled not to speak to the prosecutor.

If the circumstances are to be obtained from the defence solicitor or counsel, there arises the question of breach of privilege. If privilege is waived and the defence have instructions to reveal their case, it is unlikely that the prosecutor will be able to make an informed decision as a result of a hurried and whispered courtroom conference.

These difficulties are usually resolved in practice by the defendant or defence advocate giving the explanation in open court. In many cases, the court will breach the *Practice Direction* by asking the defendant for an explanation. This is a breach of the *Practice Direction* because it makes no mention of hearing representations from the defendant but only of an invitation by the prosecutor.

After hearing representations from the defence, the court will often announce that it either accepts or rejects the explanation. In either case, the court is making a decision on unsworn assertions and not on admissible evidence. To comply with s. 6(3) of the 1976 Act, the defendant must prove reasonable cause and not merely assert it.

If the court rejects the explanation, it may be argued that the bench is disqualified from hearing the trial since it has formed a view before hearing the evidence. If the court accepts the explanation, the prosecution are precluded from putting the Bail Act charge.

This is precisely the situation that arose in *France* v *Dewsbury Magistrates' Court* [1988] Crim LR 295, a case heard at first instance before the *Practice Direction* was issued. The appellant failed to surrender on the appointed date and a warrant was issued for his arrest. He attended court of his own accord on the following day and explained that he had made a mistake about the date. Notwithstanding the decision in *Laidlaw* v *Atkinson*, which had been reported a month earlier, the justices accepted the explanation given. The appellant was again released on bail and duly attended on the subsequent date, when the court of its own motion initiated a charge contrary to s. 6(1). The appellant gave his explanation on oath and was found not to have had a reasonable cause for his failure to surrender. He appealed by way of case stated. The Divisional Court held that there was no jurisdiction to try him for breach of bail after he had been told that his failure to surrender would be overlooked. It was held that:

> . . . there is no circumstance in which, when consideration is given in a magistrates' court to a possible breach of the Bail Act, the question of

proceedings for the breach will not be dealt with by the Crown Prosecution Service, whose discretion whether or not to invite the court to proceed is unfettered.

It is regrettable that the Divisional Court did not take this opportunity to direct justices not to express a view as to the explanation given by a defendant. It is submitted that the only practicable way forward is for a Bail Act charge to be put every time there are *prima facie* grounds for doing so. If the defendant has a reasonable cause this should be said so on oath. Until the evidence has been heard, justices must remain silent as to their view of the defence case. (See Corre, N., 'Three Frequent Questions on the Bail Act' [1989] Crim LR 493.)

4.3.10   Implications of the Practice Direction on penalties

In the light of *Practice Direction* [1987] 1 WLR 79, the literal construction of the BA 1976, s. 6(5), (6) and (7) was rejected by the Divisional Court in *Murphy* v *DPP* [1990] Crim LR 395.

4.3.10.1   Bail granted by magistrates' court   The court held that in the case of failure to surrender to bail granted by a magistrates' court, the implication of the *Practice Direction* was that because the court will initiate the charge of its own motion, it will be dealing with the offence as if it were contempt of court. The maximum term where the offence is dealt with as if for contempt of court is 12 months' imprisonment, but the magistrates' court will be restricted to six months' imprisonment by virtue of s. 31 of the MCA 1980.

4.3.10.2   Bail granted by the police   As to the summary route to conviction provided for by BA 1976, s. 6 (together with the lighter sentence), it was held in *Murphy* v *DPP* that this was intended to apply only for failure to surrender to bail granted by the police.

4.3.10.3   Difficulties raised by the decision in *Murphy* v *DPP*   It is submitted that the Divisional Court went too far in stating that there was an inference that a court acting of its own motion will be treating the offence as if for contempt. There would have been no incongruity in holding that a magistrates' court may institute proceedings of its own motion and yet still deal with failing to surrender as a summary offence. This would have been in accordance with a literal reading of s. 6 and the *Practice Direction*. Although defiance of a court order is a serious matter, it may be asked whether failure to surrender to bail granted by a court is really deserving of six months' imprisonment when the offence is deserving of three months' imprisonment when bail is granted by the police. It is difficult to see if there is any difference between the two cases in terms of the degree of cost and convenience involved. Moreover, as Professor (as she now is) D.J. Birch pointed out in her commentary at [1990] Crim LR 396, since the case was concerned with failure to surrender to police bail, it was strictly unnecessary to consider the position where bail has been granted by a magistrates' court. She questions whether the *obiter dicta* of Parker LJ were worth voicing 'at a time when a settled (if erroneous) interpretation of the Act ha[d] emerged following the Practice Direction'.

4.3.11   Time limits: *Murphy v DPP*

In *Murphy* v *DPP* [1990] Crim LR 395, Parker LJ laid down the following principles.

4.3.11.1   Failure to surrender to the Crown Court   Where a defendant fails to surrender to the Crown Court, the matter will usually be dealt with as if for contempt and no time limit will apply.

4.3.11.2   Failure to surrender to magistrates' court where bail was granted by that court   Where a defendant fails to surrender to a magistrates' court having been granted bail by that court, the offence will be dealt with as if for contempt and no time limit will apply.

4.3.11.3   Failure to surrender to bail granted by the police   Where a defendant fails to surrender to a police station or a magistrates' court after being granted bail by the police, the matter must be dealt with as a summary offence as provided in the *Practice Direction*. The time limit imposed by s. 127 of the MCA 1980 applies, and information laid more than six months after a failure to surrender will be time-barred. This aspect of the decision in *Murphy* v *DPP* raises practical problems for the CPS. Where a defendant has been granted bail by the police and subsequently fails to surrender to custody, the information must be laid within six months. In the first edition of this work it was suggested that since it is impossible to forecast when such a person will be arrested, the information ought to be laid shortly after the failure to surrender in order to avoid any omissions. It will be too late to start proceedings if the prosecuting authority waits until the defendant is arrested and it turns out that this happens more than six months after the failure to surrender. Whether inspired by Corre's suggestion or otherwise, it is now the practice of the CPS to lay an information at the time a warrant is issued (see Corre, N., 'Three Frequent Questions on the Bail Act' [1989] Crim LR 493).

4.3.12   Sentence

4.3.12.1   Non-attendance of trial in progress through drink   In *R* v *Harbax Singh* [1979] 1 All ER 524, the defendant failed to appear during the course of the trial, as he had been drunk the night before. He was dealt with as if the failure to surrender were a contempt of court and was sentenced to three months' imprisonment. The Court of Appeal reduced the sentence to one month but approved the passing of a custodial sentence.

4.3.12.2   Absconding to country with no extradition treaty   In *R* v *Neve* (1986) 8 Cr App R (S) 270, the appellant had absconded to Spain. He was dealt with as if for contempt and sentenced to six months' imprisonment and ordered to forfeit a deposit of £10,000. The Court of Appeal upheld the sentence and approved the trial judge's observation that others must be deterred from going to countries with no extradition treaty.

4.3.12.3   One failure among a series of attendances   In *R* v *Fielding* (unreported), 30 October 1989, CA transcript No. 4446/W/89, the appellant answered bail on two occasions before failing to surrender. He was again released on bail and appeared on three further occasions. His sentence of 14 days' imprisonment was quashed and a fine of £50 substituted.

4.3.12.4   Suspended sentence breached by a failure to surrender offence   A suspended sentence may be implemented where an offence of failing to surrender is committed during its operational period: *R* v *Tyson* (1978) 68 Cr App R 314.

4.3.12.5   Consecutive custodial sentences   In *R* v *Woods* [1990] Crim LR 275, the Court of Appeal held that it was correct in principle to impose a custodial offence for failure to surrender, consecutive to a sentence for a substantive offence, and that it was desirable if there was no excuse for the failure to attend. However, in *R* v *Gorman* (1992) 14 Cr App R (S) 120, the Court of Appeal said that it would seldom be appropriate to add to a sentence as long as 12 months' imprisonment a short consecutive sentence. Two consecutive sentences of seven days' imprisonment for offences of absconding were, accordingly, ordered to run concurrently with the sentence for the substantive offence. Noting that the report is extremely brief and that it is not apparent whether any earlier authorities were referred to, the editors of *Archbold* submit (at para. 3–35) that the basic principle that sentences for absconding should normally be consecutive should not be regarded as in any way impugned by the decision. In *R* v *Deeley (Andrew)* [1998] 1 Cr App R (S) 113, the defendant was convicted of a Bail Act offence in the Crown Court and sentenced to six months' imprisonment. He had been committed for trial in custody but released on bail because of the expiry of a custody time limit (see Chapter 12). He failed to appear on the date fixed for the plea and directions hearing and was arrested three weeks later on a bench warrant. It was held that the sentence of six months was disproportionate and unjustified. A sentence of three months would be substituted. In *R* v *Cozens* (1996) 2 Cr App R (S) 321, the Court of Appeal stated that the sentencer must consider the effect of a short consecutive sentence imposed for a bail offence on the offender's prospects of release and remission which results in a change of status from short-term prisoner to that of a long-term one. The appellant pleaded guilty to being concerned knowingly in the fraudulent evasion of the prohibition on the importation of cannabis resin. He was granted bail a few weeks after his arrest, absconded to Spain and remained at large for two years. He was sentenced to 42 months' imprisonment for drug offences and 6 months consecutively for the bail offence, making a total of four years. (Persons sentenced to less than four years normally serve only half their sentence.) In giving judgment the court considered *R* v *Waite* (1992) 13 Cr App R (S) 26, the decision in which illustrates the principle that it is wrong to impose a short consecutive sentence if the effect is to place the offender in a different category such that the sentence to be served is out of all proportion to the additional short sentence. The effect of the consecutive sentence for the bail offence was to subject the appellant to the possibility of serving an additional 11 months. If the sentencer's attention had been drawn to *Waite*, he might have taken a different view, even though six months was otherwise an unobjectionable sentence. Sentence for the bail offence was therefore reduced to three months. The difference was between 21 months, if serving less than four years, and 32 months, if serving more than four years. The effect of the original sentence was to make the appellant a long-term prisoner instead of a short-term one (CJA 1991, s. 33(5)).

4.3.12.6 Defence must be afforded an opportunity to give an explanation and make submissions Where the court decides of its own motion to deal with failure to surrender as if it were a contempt of court, the defendant must be afforded an opportunity to give an explanation and counsel must be invited to make submissions: *R* v *Davis (Seaton Roy)* (1986) 8 Cr App R (S) 64, CA. In *R* v *Woods* [1990] Crim LR 275, the appellant was sentenced to 18 months' imprisonment for substantive offences and three months' imprisonment for failing to surrender to bail. The trial judge had failed to follow the procedure laid down in *Davis* and the Court of Appeal quashed the sentence for the bail offence. In *R* v *Boyle* [1993] Crim LR 40, the defendant was charged with a s. 6(1) offence after arriving 50 minutes late. He pleaded not guilty to the Bail Act offence but no evidence was heard before the judge proceeded to sentence him. It was held that as failing to surrender was a criminal offence, it had to be proved properly and in the usual manner. It was held in *R* v *Donnelly* [1998] Crim LR 131, that where a defendant on bail voluntarily fails to appear for trial and the trial takes place in the absence of the defendant, there is no basis for quashing the conviction on the ground that the trial should not have taken place. See also *R* v *Lubega, The Times*, 10 February 1999, CA.

4.3.13 Appeal

A conviction, sentence or a finding of contempt in the magistrates' court may be appealed against in the Crown Court: MCA 1980, s. 108. Application may also be made for a case to be stated for the opinion of the High Court on a point of law or jurisdiction: MCA 1980, s. 113. Appeal lies as of right against a sentence by the Crown Court for a criminal contempt of court under the BA 1976, s. 6(5). This is apparently the effect of the Administration of Justice Act 1960, s. 13(1), (2)(bb) and (5)(a): *R* v *Maguire (Joseph), The Times*, 1 July 1992, CA.

4.3.14 Bail Act proceedings and legal aid

For legal aid orders granted before 1 December 1998. Proceedings under s. 6 of the BA 1976 attract a separate standard fee under the Legal Aid in Criminal and

Care proceedings (Costs) Regulations 1989, SI 1989 No. 343: *R v Legal Aid Board, ex parte Heptonstalls* (unreported 1994), CA transcript No. CO/2545/94. Where a defendant is charged with offences under both ss. 6(1) and 6(2) of the BA 1976, and has legal aid for both charges, the whole matter should be treated as a category 2 mixed plea for standard fee purposes if the defendant pleads guilty to one and not guilty to the other (Legal Aid Board Costs Appeals Committee Reference CRIMLA 69; see *Law Society's Gazette*, 4 February 1998, p. 32). A breach of bail conditions leading to an arrest in pursuance of s. 7, BA 1976, does not constitute a separate case for standard fee purposes when no s. 6 offence is charged. Since s. 7 does not create an offence, work undertaken in relation to a breach of bail is therefore incidental to the main proceedings: CRIMLA 72, *Law Society's Gazette*, 16 September 1998. For legal aid orders made on or after 1 December 1998, the standard fee covers all ancillary proceedings, including proceedings for offences under the BA 1976, provided they are legally aided: Legal Aid in Criminal and Care Proceedings (Costs) (Amendment) (No. 2) Regulations 1998 (SI 1998 No. 2401).

5 Renewed Applications for Bail

5.1 THE FORMER LIBERTY TO RE-APPLY FOR BAIL AT EVERY REMAND HEARING

The general entitlement to bail given by s. 4 of the Bail Act 1976 applies whenever accused persons appear or are brought before a magistrates' court or the Crown Court in the course of or in connection with proceedings for the offence or whenever they apply for bail. At the time of the enactment of the Bail Act 1976 a rule originating in the 19th century precluded magistrates' courts from remanding an unconvicted person in custody for a period exceeding eight clear days: Magistrates' Courts Act 1952, s. 105 (now MCA 1980, s. 128(6)). There was no power to remand in custody for longer than eight days, even with the accused person's consent. There was no pre-committal right of appeal to the Crown Court against the decision of a magistrates' court to refuse bail. The only remedy was to apply to the judge in chambers, but criminal legal aid was not, and is not, available for this purpose. The result was that defendants in custody would often make routine applications for bail every week, a state of affairs that was tolerated for many years.

5.2 THE IMPOSITION OF RESTRICTIONS ON THE RIGHT TO RE-APPLY

5.2.1 Policy of the Nottingham Justices: no more than two successive permitted applications without change of circumstances

The practice of making weekly bail applications provoked the extra-curial declaration by Ackner J (as he then was) that it would be proper, in the interests of both 'comity and common sense', for a bench to honour the bail decision originally made unless circumstances had changed (see *The Magistrate*, March 1980). Inspired by this comment, the justices of Nottingham agreed in March 1980 that they would apply a new policy to repeated bail applications. They decided that, on and after the third successive application, if previous applications had been refused, they would refuse to consider bail unless the defendant could show 'new circumstances'. The policy of allowing two bites at the cherry was devised to deal with the fact that bail applications made on the first appearance of a defendant in custody are usually based on instructions taken at short notice at the police station or at court, with little or no opportunity for the defence legal representative to make full inquiries (for further consideration see para. 5.5.4, below).

5.2.2 Nottingham practice upheld subject to widening of test to new considerations

A challenge to the policy was mounted in *R* v *Nottingham Justices, ex parte Davies* [1980] 2 All ER 775. Charged with rape, Davies had made two applications for bail in successive weeks and was refused leave to make a third application because there had been no change of circumstances. He applied for judicial review by way of an order of *mandamus* directing the justices to hear the full facts supporting the application and to determine the application. Although Davies was the nominal applicant, the case was in effect brought by a group of Nottingham solicitors seeking guidance on renewed applications for bail.

The Divisional Court accepted that the fact that a bench of the same or a different constitution had refused to grant bail on one or more previous remand hearings did not absolve the bench on a subsequent occasion from considering whether the accused was entitled to bail, whether or not an application were made. However, the court held, this did not mean that the justices should ignore their own previous decision or a previous decision of their colleagues. On those previous occasions, the court would have been under an obligation to grant bail unless satisfied that a sch. 1 exception had been made out. That 'satisfaction' was not a personal intellectual conclusion by each justice. It was a finding by the court that sch. 1 circumstances then existed and was to be treated like every other finding of the court. It was *res judicata* or analogous thereto and stood as a finding unless and until overturned on appeal. Appeal was not to the same court, whether or not of the same constitution, on a later occasion, but to the judge in chambers. It followed that on the next occasion when bail was considered the court should treat, as an essential fact, that at the time when the matter of bail was last considered, sch. 1 circumstances did indeed exist.

Strictly speaking, the court held, the justices were bound to investigate only whether that situation had changed since the last remand in custody. There was always a possibility of such a change because of the lapse of time. For example, the ability to interfere with witnesses might have diminished as police inquiries had progressed and statements had been taken. Again, it was well established as a proper exercise of judicial discretion that when the prosecution were unreasonably delaying the case the accused should no longer be held in custody. However, in the view of the court there was one qualification to the general rule that there must be a change of circumstances. The question which the justices ought to ask was slightly wider than whether there had been a *change*. The question which had to be asked was whether there were *any new considerations* which were not before the court when the accused was last remanded in custody. In the first edition of the present work Corre argued that 'new considerations' was a less stringent and more easily identifiable test. It meant that the court might consider matters which, although they existed, were not before the court on the previous occasion. A strictly observed change in circumstances rule would have meant that the court would not consider material which previously existed even though it was not known to the applicant and therefore not put before the court.

The decision was amplified in *Re Moles* [1981] Crim LR 170, in which it was held that magistrates were bound to investigate all alleged circumstances and where they refused to do so a court with appropriate jurisdiction could set aside the subsequent decision.

5.2.3 Nottingham principle applied to Crown Court jurisdiction

In *R v Reading Crown Court, ex parte Malik* (1981) 72 Cr App R 146, the principles in *Nottingham Justices* were held by the Divisional Court to apply to the Crown Court.

5.3 FURTHER DEVELOPMENTS

5.3.1 Amelioration of the rule: general right to re-apply at committal

In an *obiter dictum* in *R v Reading Crown Court, ex parte Malik*, above, Donaldson LJ expressed the view that as a general rule, but subject to exceptional cases, the accused was entitled to have the right to bail fully reviewed at committal. In the view of the Divisional Court, Donaldson LJ observed, the eligibility of the accused for bail in any particular case may not have improved but it was almost inevitable that there would have been a change of circumstances. The committing court would be in a much better position to assess the nature and seriousness of the circumstances of the offence, and the strength of the prosecution case could for the first time be fully assessed. These are factors which would be material in considering the risk that the accused might fail to surrender.

5.3.2 Retrenchment: no leave to be given if only change at committal was the committal itself

Being *obiter*, the declaration by Donaldson LJ in *R v Reading Crown Court, ex parte Malik* of an unqualified right to renew a bail application immediately following committal for trial was fated not to survive intact for very long. In *R v Slough Justices, ex parte Duncan* (1982) 75 Cr App R 384, Ormrod LJ was free to characterise it as no more than a general observation of good sense but not a proposition of law. In his view the mere fact that the committal stage had been reached was not in itself a material change in circumstances. The crucial factor was the existence of substantial grounds for belief, not the belief itself. If, therefore, a court found as a fact that substantial grounds existed, a later court had to accept that finding unless there had been a material change in circumstances.

Otherwise, the second court would be acting as a court of appeal. Justices did not therefore need to hear an application for bail on committal if the only change was the committal itself and there was nothing in the evidence of the committal documents which would affect the merits of the application for bail. In many cases, however, the last bail application would have preceded service of the full committal bundle. (The complete bundle is often only served immediately prior to a short form of committal without consideration of the evidence.) Disclosure in the papers of relevant details not previously known to the defence or the court may give rise to an argument for the existence of 'new considerations'. Conversely, the newly disclosed details may have no bearing on the only ground for refusing bail, for example, the risk of 'further' offences.

5.4   CRITICISM OF THE RESTRICTIVE RULE AND ITS RATIONALE

5.4.1   Future bench ought not to be bound by decision based on limited opportunity for consideration

One commentator characterised as 'truly astonishing, not to say ludicrous' the idea in *Nottingham Justices* that a decision taken 'in the course of a few minutes' hearing in all the bustle of the remands court, should be binding for the future on another court, similarly constituted', and he urged that '[m]agistrates should decide each and every case as it comes before them, on its merits, without regard to the sensitivity, vanity or reaction of colleagues who were involved in the matter previously' (Alec Samuels, 'Bail: Renewal Applications', *New Law Journal*, 1981, vol. 131, pp. 132–133, at p. 132). However, it might be argued that magistrates are required under similar pressure of business to take many decisions affecting the liberty of the subject which have finality. However, the essential difference is that the bail decision is usually made in relation to an unconvicted person.

5.4.2   Criticism of the idea that bail refusal is not the personal intellectual conclusion of each magistrate

The opinion of the Divisional Court in *Nottingham Justices* that a bench's acceptance of one of the exceptions to bail is not a personal intellectual conclusion by each justice has been criticised as 'legal sophistry and not an accurate reflection of the bail decision', because magistrates speak to one another in lay terms and not on the basis of a disciplined analysis of the terms of the Bail Act (Mary Hayes, 'Where Now the Right to Bail?' [1981] Crim LR 21).

5.4.3   Uncertainty in determining what factors amounted to a change of circumstances

Hayes (*op. cit.*, para. 5.4.2) drew attention to the difficulty of determining what factors amounted to a change of circumstances. This point was developed by another commentator, who noted that magistrates' courts had been extremely reluctant to accept that any particular situation amounted to a change in circumstances and observed that factors which might reasonably have been expected to suffice, but which seldom did, included acquiring a job, offering sureties, finding a fixed address or an address well away from the area in which witnesses live, deterioration of health, dependants at home, and completion of police inquiries making interference with witnesses less likely (John Burrows, *New Law Journal*, 29 April 1982). In *R* v *Blyth Juvenile Court, ex parte G* [1991] Crim LR 693, it was held that the change of circumstances which must be demonstrated to justify a further appliction for bail need not be major.

5.4.4 Change of circumstances test wrongly applied instead of new considerations test

It was a point of criticism that practitioners and the courts continued to apply the 'change in circumstances' test when *Nottingham Justices* made it clear that the true test was 'new considerations'. Even Donaldson LJ, who had given the judgment of the court, himself spoke of 'change of circumstances' in *R* v *Reading Crown Court, ex part Malik*, above. It has been suggested that the justices in Nottingham deliberately applied the change in circumstances test because of 'the inability of courts to determine reliably what information was presented to the magistrates during previous bail applications', and that a change of circumstances test overcame this difficulty by 'guaranteeing that the information now before the court was not considered during any previous application' (Brink and Stone, 'Defendants Who Do Not Ask For Bail', [1988] Crim LR 152).

5.4.5 *Res judicata*

The idea that the upholding of a sch. 1 exception is '*res judicata* or analagous thereto' was described by Hayes as 'very strained'. In her view the doctrine could not apply to the bail decision because there was no finding of fact but only a prediction about future behaviour. By way of contrast, E.C.J. McBride assumed that *res judicata* was synonymous with issue estoppel and argued that *Nottingham Justices* was therefore wrongly decided, because in *DPP* v *Humphrys* [1976] 2 All ER 497 the House of Lords held that issue estoppel had no place in English criminal law (letter, [1990] Crim LR 70, responding to Corre, N. 'Three Frequent Questions on the Bail Act' [1989] Crim LR 493). In *Miles* v *Cooper* [1967] 2 All ER 100, it was said that issue estoppel meant in relation to civil proceedings that a party:

> . . . is not entitled to make, as against the other party, an assertion, whether of fact or of the legal consequences of facts, the correctness of which is an essential element in the cause of action or defence, if the same assertion was an essential element in his cause of action or defence in previous civil proceedings and found

by a court of competent jurisdiction in such previous civil proceedings to be incorrect. It was said that issue estoppel is a particular application of the general rule of public policy that there should be finality in litigation. The general rule applies to criminal proceedings in the form of the rule against double jeopardy.

The essential difference between civil and criminal proceedings in this context is that issue estoppel prevents the issue being raised again, whereas the rule against double jeopardy depends not on the issue but on the verdict of the trial. In criminal proceedings the issues are not usually separated or identified; the essential factor is the verdict. In *Sambasivam* v *Public Prosecutor, Federation of Malaya* [1950] AC 458, Lord MacDermott said that 'the maxim *res judicata pro veritae accipitur* is no less applicable to criminal than to civil proceedings'. It must follow that *res judicata* in criminal proceedings applies only to the verdict. The bail decision is self-evidently not a verdict of the court. Indeed, even if the court does find substantial grounds for believing that any of the exceptions to bail applies, it is not obliged to refuse bail, at least in theory. Schedule 1 of the 1976 Act makes it clear that the defendant *need* not be granted bail in such circumstances: it does not state that the defendant *shall* not be granted bail. The conclusion is that, contrary to McBride's contention, the doctrine of *res judicata*, being distinguishable from issue estoppel, applies to criminal proceedings. Since it applies only to verdicts and the bail decision is not a verdict, the argument proposed by Hayes is to be preferred to McBride's.

5.5 MITIGATION BY ENACTMENT OF THE RIGHT TO APPLY FOR BAIL TO THE CROWN COURT BEFORE COMMITTAL

5.5.1 Right to appeal to the Crown Court against refusal of bail by the magistrates' court

The restrictive rule in *Nottingham Justices* was mitigated by the enactment of s. 60 of the CJA 1982, which, for the first time, allowed an application to be made to the Crown Court for bail before committal (see further Chapter 8, para. 8.2.4). The Crown Court will deal with an application only if it is satisfied that the magistrates' court has issued a certificate under s. 5(6A) of the BA 1976 (inserted by s. 60(3) of the 1982 Act) that it has heard full argument on the question of bail before refusing the application.

5.5.2 Full argument certificate

5.5.2.1 Conditions for issuing of certificate   Section 5(6A) of the 1976 Act provides that where, in criminal proceedings:

(a) a magistrates' court remands a person in custody under any of the following provisions of the Magistrates' Courts Act 1980—

    (i)   section 5 (adjournment of inquiry into offence);

    (ii)   section 10 (adjournment of trial);

    (iii)   section 18 (initial procedure on information against adult for offence triable either way); or

    (iv)   section 30 (remand for medical examination),

after hearing full argument on an application for bail from him; and

    (b) either—

    (i)   it has not previously heard such argument on an application for bail from him in those proceedings; or

    (ii)   it has previously heard full argument from him on such an application but it is satisfied that there has been a change in his circumstances or that new considerations have been placed before it,

it shall be the duty of the court to issue a certificate in the prescribed form that they heard full argument on his application for bail before they refused the application.

5.5.2.2 Entries required to be made in the court register Records required by the BA 1976, s. 5 to be made by a magistrates' court, together with notes of reasons required by that section or by sch. 1, Part I, para. 9A, are to be made by way of an entry in the register: MCR 1981, r. 90. Presumably, therefore, the fact that a court has heard full argument should be entered in the register, as well as the reasons for the court's having issued it. Where a magistrates' court hears full argument as to bail, the clerk of the court must take a note thereof: MCR 1981 r. 90A.

5.5.2.3 Form of certificate The full argument certificate shall be in Form 151A, annexed to the MCR 1981.

5.5.2.4 Statement of nature of change of circumstances or new considerations to be included in the certificate where applicable Where, having on a previous occasion heard full argument, the court subsequently finds that there has been a change of circumstances or that new considerations have been presented and hears full argument, and again remands the defendant in custody and issues a certificate of full argument, the certificate must state the nature of the change of circumstances or the new considerations which caused the court to hear a further fully argued bail application: BA 1976, s. 5(6B), inserted by the CJA 1982.

5.5.2.5 Copy of certificate to be given to defendant Where in refusing bail a court issues a full argument certificate, it must give the defendant a copy of the certificate: BA 1976, s. 5(6C), inserted by the CJA 1982.

5.5.2.6 Unrepresented defendants to be informed of their right to appeal Where a magistrates' court withholds bail in criminal proceedings from a defendant who is not represented by counsel or a solicitor, the court must, if it issues a full argument certificate under s. 5(6A) of the BA 1976, inform the defendant of the right to apply to the High Court or to the Crown Court to be granted bail: BA 1976, s. 5(6)(a).

5.5.3 Defendant's legal aid covers appeal

If the defendant is legally aided in the magistrates' court, the legal aid order covers bail appeals to the Crown Court: *Practice Direction (Crown Court–Bail)* (1983) 77 Cr App R 69, para. 5. This important provision enables most defendants to exercise their right of appeal.

5.5.4 The restrictive rule after enactment of the right of appeal

Despite the enactment of s. 60 of the CJA 1982, *Nottingham Justices* continued to have an effect on bail procedure. In Brink and Stone's empirical study (see para. 5.4.4) it was revealed that because of the risk inherent in applying for bail, many defendants simply made no application. The research disclosed that between one-half and three-quarters of defendants remanded in custody at their first appearance had not asked the court for their liberty. The risk inherent in applying for bail was identified as the practice of courts to allow only one application. If that failed, and especially if a full argument certificate was issued, new considerations would have to be shown before a further application could be made. The result was that solicitors advised their clients to delay their applications or to make no application at all. The practice in Nottingham had been to allow a second application, and the Divisional Court had dealt with this:

> [O]n the occasion of the first application, the full facts are not usually available to the duty solicitor and so to the court. Accordingly, on the second application it is almost always possible for an applicant for bail or his advocate to submit correctly that there are matters to be considered by the court which were not considered on the first occasion. Where this is the experience of any particular Bench of magistrates, the Nottingham practice is not only convenient, but right. (*R v Nottingham Justices, ex parte Davies* [1980] 2 All ER 775, at p. 779, *per* Donaldson LJ.)

The question of allowing a second application was therefore left to local policy, and it was this aspect of the decision which caused solicitors to delay or withhold their applications for bail. A significant finding of Brink and Stone was that at Newcastle-upon-Tyne Magistrates' Court, which allowed defendants to make at least two applications for bail, only 16 per cent of those remanded in custody at first appearance had made no application. Brink and Stone concluded their study by recommending a reversion to the original policy of the justices in Nottingham of allowing two full applications for bail.

5.6 SECTION 154 OF THE CRIMINAL JUSTICE ACT 1988

5.6.1 Addition of Part IIA to Bail Act 1976, Schedule 1

Conceivably inspired by Brink and Stone's recommendation in favour of the adoption of the policy originally followed at Nottingham Magistrates' Court of allowing two applications, s. 154 of the CJA 1988 inserted a new part, Part IIA, into sch. 1 to the BA 1976. Under the heading 'Decisions where bail refused on previous hearing', Part IIA provides:

1. If the court decides not to grant the defendant bail, it is the court's duty to consider, at each subsequent hearing while the defendant is a person to whom section 4 above applies and remains in custody, whether he ought to be granted bail.
2. At the first hearing after that at which the court decided not to grant the defendant bail he may support an application for bail with any argument as to fact or law that he desires (whether or not he has advanced that argument previously).
3. At subsequent hearings the court need not hear arguments as to fact or law which it has heard previously.

5.6.2 Effect of Part IIA

Consideration of the effect of Part IIA of sch. 1 to the BA 1976 is conveniently set out under the following heads:

5.6.2.1 General right to bail confirmed It is noteworthy that para. 1 confirms that the general right to bail applies in the circumstances set out in s. 4, a principle which was fully accepted in *Nottingham Justices*.

5.6.2.2 Original hearing At the first hearing of the case of a defendant to whom s. 4 of the 1979 Act applies, the court must consider the question of bail regardless of whether or not any bail application is made. If the defendant applies for bail the application may be supported with any relevant argument as to fact or law. The court must grant bail unless satisfied that one of the exceptions under Parts I or II of sch. 1 is established.

5.6.2.3 Subsequent hearings: general If the defendant is remanded in custody at the first hearing, the case then comes within para. 1 of sch. 1, Part IIA, and at each subsequent hearing, for as long as s. 4 remains applicable, the court is duty bound to consider the question of bail irrespective of whether the defendant makes an application.

5.6.2.4 First hearing after refusal At the first hearing after that at which the court decided not to grant bail the defendant may support an application for bail with any argument as to fact or law, whether or not that argument was previously advanced: sch. 1 Part IIA, para. 2.

5.6.2.5   Relevant hearing is one in the defendant's presence   Applications for further remands in the absence of the defendant under s. 128(3A) of the MCA 1980 are not hearings within para. 1 of sch. 1, Part IIA. At such a hearing s. 4 of the BA 1976 does not apply to the defendant because s. 4(2) confines the application of the section to any person accused of an offence 'who appears or is brought before a magistrates' court or the Crown Court in the course of or in connection with proceedings for the offence, or [who] applies to a court for bail in connection with the proceedings'. (The second limb implies an application made in the defendant's absence.) Although this was not the *ratio decidendi* of *R v Dover and East Kent Justices, ex parte Dean* [1992] Crim LR 33, DC, it was clearly the view taken by the Divisional Court. The effect of this is that the defendant will not forfeit the second opportunity to present argument in support of a bail application by reason of consenting to a remand *in absentia*. The contrary construction would defeat the purpose of the legislation.

5.6.2.6   Right to make two argument-supported applications applies only where the first is made at the original hearing and the second is made at the next relevant hearing   The effect of the foregoing is that defendants who exercise the option of making an argument-supported application at the original hearing enjoy the right to repeat those arguments subsequently. However, they may only do so at the next hearing at which they appear (provided there has been no intervening hearing in the defendant's absence at which a bail application was made on the defendant's behalf). This is because the court is obliged by sch. 1, Part IIA, para. 1 to make a bail decision at every hearing at which the defendant appears or applies for bail and the right to repeat arguments applies only at the first hearing after that at which the court decided not to grant bail (combined effect of paras 2 and 3 of Part IIA; the reference in para. 3 to 'subsequent hearings' must be read *eiusdem generis* with para. 2, that is, it must be taken to mean subsequent hearings after the court has decided not to grant the defendant bail). It is entirely understandable why in order to have the benefit of the right to make two argument-supported applications the first must be made on the first appearance before the court. The rationale, as with the old Nottingham practice, is that first appearance bail applications may be assumed to be perfunctory, being based on very limited facilities for taking instructions. However, it is not at all clear why the second opportunity must be taken at the second hearing or otherwise be forfeited. Why should not the defendant be entitled to defer the occasion for repeating the arguments to a hearing later than the second hearing?

5.6.2.7   No right to defer the option of two attempts to run the same arguments   It follows from the previous statement of principle that defendants enjoy no statutory right to defer the option of an argument-supported application at the first relevant hearing *and* still retain the right to advance the same arguments on a second occasion at some stage in due course. If the option available at the original hearing is waived it is forfeited, and defendants are left with the statutory right to advance a particular argument in support of a subsequent application only once. There is no right to advance the same arguments a second time. But there may be a discretion to allow this (as to which see para. 5.6.2.10 below).

5.6.2.8 Right to make a bail application exists at common law, applies at every stage, and is distinct from the issue of whether arguments in support may be repeated If no application for bail is made at the first hearing after that at which the court decided not to grant bail, sch. 1, Part IIA, para. 2 does not apply so as to confer a right to make an application at any subsequent hearing, whether or not an application was made when bail was originally refused. However, although para. 3 absolves the court from any duty to hear previously heard arguments on subsequent hearings, it does not absolve the court from the duty to consider bail in accordance with s. 4. There is a clear distinction between an application and the advancing of particular arguments. This point was made in the first edition of the present work (at p. 79), from where it was cited in argument in *R v Dover and East Kent Justices, ex parte Dean*, above. The justices had declined to allow the accused to apply for bail on an occasion subsequent to the first hearing after that at which the court had decided not to grant bail and the Divisional Court held that there was always a right to make an application for bail, which existed at common law independently of the statute. Whether, however, the justices were obliged to entertain arguments previously advanced was a separate issue. As Corre observed in the first edition, the result may be that there is nothing left for the applicant to argue, but the principle remains. This may be contrasted with the law as it stood under *Nottingham Justices*. The question of new considerations was then decided as a preliminary issue before deciding whether to allow a further application. If the court found that there were new considerations, the application would include the old as well as the new material.

5.6.2.9 Deferring first occasion for presenting argument If a defendant who waives the entitlement to make an argument-supported application at the original hearing then declines also to make such an application at the next relevant hearing, it appears that sch. 1, Part IIA will not preclude the right to present argument later. Paragraph 3 provides that a court need not hear arguments as to fact or law which it has heard at a previous hearing. If the court has not heard those arguments before there can be no lawful obstacle preventing the defendant from raising arguments for the first time later in support of an application. As the editors of *Archbold* submit, where no application has previously been made, any relevant argument may be placed before the court, and the provisions of sch. 1, Part IIA in no way derogate from this principle.

5.6.2.10 Discretion to allow renewal of arguments at hearings subsequent to the first hearing after that at which the court decided to refuse bail The provision in sch. 1, Part IIA para. 3 that at hearings subsequent to the first hearing after the hearing at which the court decided to refuse bail the court *need not* hear arguments as to fact or law which it has heard previously, implies that it *may do so* in its discretion.

5.6.3   Bail withheld for lack of sufficient information

Where justices decided that a defendant need not be granted bail because it had not been practicable to obtain sufficient information to decide whether or not to grant it (applying para. 5 of sch. 1, Part I, as to which see para. 1.3.1.4, above) that was not a decision not to grant it within para. 1 of sch. 1, Part IIA: *R* v *Calder Justices, ex parte Kennedy* [1992] Crim LR 496, DC.

5.6.4   Application of Part IIA to the prosecution

Part IIA of sch. 1 to the BA 1976 applies only where the court decides not to admit the accused to bail, para. 2 referring to the 'first hearing after that at which the court decided not to grant the defendant bail'. As observed above, para. 3 refers only to 'subsequent hearings' but should be read *eiusdem generis* with para. 2, that is, it refers to subsequent hearings after the court has decided not to grant the defendant bail. The 'argument' test applies only to applications for bail and not to applications for custody. Paragraph 2 referred only to argument as to fact or law in support of an application for bail. Where bail was granted but the prosecution sought to renew their objections to bail at a subsequent hearing, it was submitted in the first edition of the present work that for reasons of parity and fairness the prosecution had to advance fresh argument. This would have needed to take the form of information that was not previously known (analogous to new considerations) or events that had arisen since bail was granted (analogous to a change in circumstances). The argument was adopted by the legislature in s. 5B of the BA 1976, as inserted by CJPOA 1994, s. 30. The new section provides that the prosecution may apply for a reconsideration of the grant of bail, in relation to indictable and either-way offences, if the application is based on information which was not available to the court (or a constable) when the decision was taken.

5.7   TO WHAT EXTENT DO THE PRE-1988 AUTHORITIES REMAIN RELEVANT?

5.7.1   Fresh argument and new considerations

Paragraph 2 of sch. 1, Part IIA departed from *Nottingham Justices* when it abandoned the criteria of 'change in circumstances' and 'new considerations' and introduced instead the idea of 'fresh argument as to fact or law'. In spite of this change the principles in *Nottingham Justices* may still have relevance in determining the criteria which the courts ought to deploy in deciding whether to allow a further argument-supported (as distinct from nominal) application. It is not clear if 'fresh argument' is qualitatively something different from 'new considerations', or whether the distinction between the two concepts is in reality no more than one without a difference. An argument is a contention based on a process of reasoning. While a 'consideration' may include an argument within its meaning, it can also be used to refer, *inter alia*, to a fact, a state of affairs or a legal principle. In other words, 'consideration' subsumes 'argument' but is of wider embrace. A fresh argument (in favour of bail) may be anchored on facts that remain unchanged, or may relate to a legal concept that was previously under examination. However, a new consideration will not necessarily involve a fresh argument. For example, the defence may, at hearing (1), have argued that the more sureties a defendant can produce the less will be the risk of absconding, but as things stand they can offer only two substantial sureties. At hearing (2) they are able to offer two additional substantial sureties and wish to be granted leave to give full details in support of re-opening the bail question. This is a materially new consideration which clearly involves no fresh argument, as such. If sch. 1, Part IIA is applied there will be nothing to add to what was said at hearing (1). But since Part IIA is silent about 'new considerations' there ought to be nothing to prevent citation of *Nottingham Justices* in applying for leave to re-apply for bail on the basis of the availability of the new sureties. Moreover, at common law, the right to present new considerations is not restricted to the second hearing, as appears to be the case under sch. 1, Part IIA.

5.7.2 New considerations warrant full application *de novo*

On the assumption that the existence of new considerations (absent fresh argument) still affords a right under *Nottingham Justices* to present them to the court in support of a renewed application, the question arises as to whether this will warrant a fully argued application *de novo* or whether the renewed application is restricted to the status of a codicil or postscript. In *R v Barking Justices, ex parte Shankshaft* (1983) 147 JP 399, the accused submitted that there were new considerations in the form of suitable sureties and the fact of his mother's illness. The justices agreed to hear his application but formed the view that they could consider only the fresh grounds and not the old ones which had been put at an earlier application. The Divisional Court held that they had misdirected themselves and Comyn J, giving judgment, said:

> You can only make a second application of any value or use to anybody if you take into account the whole circumstances, the old as well as the new. You cannot regard it as a half shut, half open door. That is not doing justice to the individual or justice in the eyes of the public. . . . In these matters one has got to look at the accumulation of facts. One has got to bear wholly in mind the facts of the previous applications, how they were put and what the objections were at that particular time.

5.7.3   Fresh argument under Part IIA warrants a full application *de novo*

There may be a difficulty of approach where the defence, having made a full application previously, wish at a later hearing to advance an argument which was not canvassed earlier. This will mean having to satisfy the court, in the absence of a verbatim record of the previous application, that the fresh argument was not relied on previously and that it is in fact a novel point and not merely another way of repeating submissions already made. Then, if this hurdle is overcome, the question will arise whether it is feasible in practice to advance the argument coherently without combining it with a reiteration of submissions previously made and whether formulation of the fresh argument should warrant the presentation of arguments at large. In this respect the decision in *R v Barking Justices, ex parte Shankshaft*, above, may be applied by analogy.

5.7.4   Court may re-open question of bail of its own motion

A court may re-open the question of bail of its own motion. In *R v Tower Bridge Magistrates' Court, ex parte Gilbert* (1988) 152 JPN 287, the applicant was charged with possession of an offensive weapon. At his first appearance before the court, the justices made no inquiry before granting him unconditional bail. On his next appearance, he was represented by a solicitor who asked for medical reports because the applicant claimed to be the son of Julius Caesar. The stipendiary magistrate asked for the facts of the alleged offence and was told that the applicant had been seen waving a two-bladed knife while uttering threats to kill and had later become violent. The stipendiary magistrate found substantial grounds for believing that the applicant would commit an offence if granted bail and therefore remanded him in custody. The Divisional Court held that the magistrate was entitled to his view on the information he had heard and that he was unfettered by the earlier decision of the justices. The decision remains good authority for cases in which the issue is new considerations or change of circumstances and was not affected by the commencement of s. 154 of the CJA 1988. The question of fresh argument on the part of the prosecution could not have arisen since there were no objections to bail. Similarly, the defence could not have relied on previously-heard argument in support of an application for bail since no arguments were previously heard, and in any case, the court had not previously decided not to grant bail. The new considerations arose quite neutrally in support of an ancillary application for medical reports. The case serves as a useful reminder that new considerations may arise independently of any bail-specific application from either party to the proceedings.

5.7.5   Question whether *res judicata* remains applicable

It is arguable that the bail decision cannot be considered *res judicata* if the same argument may be advanced as previously. If this is right, does the decision become *res judicata* after the second hearing at which the court decided not to grant bail? The finding of *Nottingham Justices* was that a court of first instance may not be used as a court of appeal against the decision of a court of first instance because the decision is *res judicata*. It is arguable that sch. 1, Part IIA does allow a court of first instance to be used as a court of appeal against the decision of a court of first instance, notwithstanding that the decision is *res judicata*. If you may rely on the same argument as before then you are making an appeal by way of a re-hearing. This is supported by use of the word 'argument' rather than 'considerations', which in any event was *per curiam* and lacking statutory authority.

Whatever may be the legal rationale of the *Nottingham Justices* rule and of sch. 1, Part IIA, there is no doubting that the real objective involved is simple expedience, and there is perhaps no more apposite a comment than that uttered in a different context by Lord Atkin in *Ras Behari Lal* v *King-Emperor* (1933) 50 TLR 1, when he said: 'Finality is a good thing: but justice is a better. '

6 Police Bail

6.1 INTRODUCTION

Statute has vested the police with the power to release on bail persons who have been arrested and charged with an offence, pending their appearance in court. It has also empowered the police to release on bail persons who have been arrested but not charged, to return to the police station at a later date for questioning or further questioning or to be charged. The police may also release on bail a person arrested in pursuance of a warrant backed for bail. There is a substantial interplay between the police power to grant bail and the regulatory function of magistrates over that power, a relationship which perhaps reflects the fact that, historically, police powers derive from those of the justices of the peace who for many centuries were the officials responsible for investigating and prosecuting crime. However, it is convenient to cover the topic of police bail in a dedicated chapter.

6.2 POLICE POWER TO RELEASE ARRESTED PERSONS

6.2.1 General scheme

Where a person has been arrested for an offence and detained under Part IV of PACE 1984 for inquiries in relation to the offence, Part IV makes provision for the police to release the person on bail or without bail, whether or not the person has been charged. The term 'bail' in Part IV of the 1984 Act means bail subject to a duty:

 (a) to appear before a magistrates' court at such time and such place; or
 (b) to attend at such police station at such time;
as the custody officer may appoint: PACE 1984, s. 47(3).

Normally where a person who has been charged is bailed by the police the requirement will be to surrender at a magistrates' court on a given date. Conversely, where a person who has not been charged is bailed the requirement will normally be to return to the police station for further inquiries (or for the person to be charged). However, there is nothing in the legislative scheme which compartmentalises the contingencies in this way. For example, a person who has been charged, instead of being bailed to attend court, could theoretically be bailed to attend the police station for inquiries to continue in relation to other matters, with a view to the charge being proceeded with in court only when the other inquiries are complete. Similarly, without being charged a person could be bailed to appear at a magistrates' court with a view to an information being laid there if sufficient evidence in the meantime comes to light. In that way the case could be commenced forthwith by avoiding the delay involved in requiring the defendant's return to the police station and subsequent attendance at court. Although these theoretical 'scenarios' are not precluded by statute, in practice they are virtually unknown.

6.2.2 Release without charge

6.2.2.1 Immediate release Section 34(2) of the 1984 Act provides that if at any time a custody officer:

(a) becomes aware, in relation to any person in police detention under the provisions of Part IV, that the grounds for the detention of the person have ceased to apply; and
(b) is not aware of any other grounds on which the continued detention of the person could be justified;
the custody officer's duty is to order the immediate release of the detained person from custody.

6.2.2.2 Persons unlawfully at large A person who appears to the custody officer to have been unlawfully at large when arrested is not to be released under s. 34(2): PACE 1984, s. 34(4).

6.2.2.3 Circumstances when release must be on bail A person whose release is ordered under s. 34(2) of the 1984 Act must be released without bail unless it appears to the custody officer:

(a) that there is need for further investigation of any matter in connection with which the person was detained at any time during the period of detention; or
(b) that proceedings may be taken against the person in respect of any such matter;
and if it so appears, the detained person must be released on bail: PACE 1984, s. 34(5).

6.2.2.4 Bailed suspects: written notice that attendance no longer required
Where a person is bailed to appear at a police station the custody officer may notify the person in writing that attendance is not after all required: PACE 1984, s. 47(4).

6.2.2.5 Grant of bail by police does not preclude re-arrest Section 47(2) of PACE 1984 provides that nothing in the BA 1976 prevents the re-arrest without warrant of a person released on bail subject to a duty to attend at a police station, if new evidence justifying a further arrest has come to light since the person was released.

6.2.3 Re-arrest of suspect bailed to return to the police station

6.2.3.1 Background of PACE scheme As originally enacted PACE 1984 provided in s. 47(5) that where a person who was arrested for an offence was released on bail subject to a duty to attend at a police station and so attended, that person might be detained without charge in connection with that offence only if the custody officer at the police station had reasonable grounds for believing that detention was necessary to secure or preserve evidence relating to the offence, or to obtain such evidence by questioning the person. Further, in its original form s. 47(7) provided that where a person who was released on bail subject to a duty to attend at a police station was re-arrested, the provisions of Part IV of PACE 1984 applied as if the person had been arrested for the first time. The two provisions were complementary. The person might be re-arrested on returning to the police station, or might be arrested for failing to return to the police station. Section 29 of the CJPOA 1994 modified the law relating to re-arrest of a person who had been bailed by police without charge subject to a duty to return to the police station. The section *inter alia*:

(a)   repealed s. 47(5);
(b)   inserted new s. 46A dealing with arrest for failing to return to the police station;
(c)   inserted a new subsection in s. 34 (s. 34(7)); and
(d)   amended s. 47(7).

Section 34(7) provides that for the purposes of Part IV of PACE 1984, a person who returns to the police station to answer to bail or is arrested under s. 46A for failing to do so is to be treated as arrested for an offence, and the offence in connection with which bail was granted is deemed to be that offence. The amendment to s. 47(7) is an addition which provides that the subsection is not to apply to a person who has been arrested under s. 46A or has attended a police station in accordance with the grant of bail (and who is accordingly deemed by s. 34(7) to have been arrested for an offence). This means that the 're-arrest' of a person under s. 47(7) which does cause the provisions of Part IV to apply as if the person had been arrested for the first time can only be in relation to a further or different offence, not one for which the person had previously been in custody. The combined effect of these provisions was that the re-detention of the bailed person who returned voluntarily in connection with the original offence under investigation was no longer to be dependent on the custody officer having reasonable grounds for believing that detention was necessary to secure or preserve evidence relating to the offence or to obtain such evidence by questioning the person. The re-arrested person is detained as if never released; there is no requirement there and then to consider grounds for detention as if the person was being detained for the first time (although, of course, the requirements of periodic review remain applicable). There is a potential difficulty, however, regarding the position of a bailed person arrested for having failed to return to the police station. This is considered under the next immediate heading.

6.2.3.2 Arrest for failing to return to the police station Section 46A(1) of the 1984 Act provides that a constable may arrest without warrant any person who, having been released on bail under Part IV of PACE 1984 subject to a duty to attend at a police station, fails to attend at that police station at the appointed time. A person so arrested must be taken to the appointed police station as soon as practicable: s. 46A(2). Section 46A(3) provides that for the purpose of the provisions of Part IV concerning initial detention for an offence (ss. 30 and 31), an arrest for failure to surrender under s. 46A is an arrest for an offence. It is evident that the arrest in question is not an arrest for the Bail Act offence of failing to surrender but an arrest for the original offence for which the person was bailed to return. So much is clear from s. 34(7), which provides that the offence for which the person is arrested is the offence for which bail was granted in the first place. Thus, arrest for failing to return is not an arrest for the fresh offence of failing to surrender but arrest for the original offence. This saves the custody officer from having to conduct a fresh assessment as to whether there are grounds for detention. It also means that there is no contradiction with s. 47(7), which, as we have seen, states that a person arrested under s. 46A is not to be treated as if arrested for the first time.

6.2.4 Time in detention before grant of bail counts towards detention after return to the police station or arrest for failing to do so

Section 47(6) of PACE 1984 makes provision for the inclusion of any time spent in detention before police bail was granted in the computation of the total allowable detention time following return to the police station or arrest under s. 46A for failing to return.

6.3 RELEASE OF PERSONS AFTER CHARGE

6.3.1 Adults: release compulsory unless certain exceptions apply

Where a person who is not a juvenile is arrested for an offence otherwise than under a warrant endorsed for bail and is charged with an offence, the custody officer must (subject to s. 25 of the CJPOA 1994) order the person's release from police detention, either on bail or without bail, unless one or more of the exceptions which follow apply: PACE 1984, s. 38(1). If the release of a person is not required by s. 38(1), the custody officer may authorise the person to be kept in police detention: s. 38(2). The exceptions specified by s. 38(1) are as follows.

6.3.1.1   Name and address not ascertained   Release is not compulsory if the arrested person's name and address cannot be ascertained or the custody officer has reasonable grounds for doubting whether a name and address furnished is the person's real name and address.

6.3.1.2   Likelihood of failure to appear in court   Release is not compulsory if the custody officer has reasonable grounds for believing that the arrested person will fail to appear in court to answer to bail.

6.3.1.3   Arrest for imprisonable offence: commission of offence likely   In the case of a person arrested for an imprisonable offence, release is not compulsory if the custody officer has reasonable grounds for believing that detention is necessary to prevent the person committing an offence.

6.3.1.4   Arrest for non-imprisonable offence: risk of injury to another or of loss or damage to property   In the case of a person arrested for an offence which is not an imprisonable offence, release is not compulsory if the custody officer has reasonable grounds for believing that detention is necessary to prevent the person arrested from causing physical injury to any other person, or from causing loss of or damage to property.

6.3.1.5   Risk of interference with the administration of justice or the investigation of offences or of a particular offence   Release is not compulsory if the custody officer has reasonable grounds for believing that detention is necessary to prevent the person arrested from interfering with the administration of justice, or with the investigation of offences or of a particular offence.

6.3.1.6   Own protection   Release is not compulsory if the custody officer has reasonable grounds for believing that detention is necessary for the arrested person's own protection.

6.3.2   Juveniles

Where the arrested person who has been charged is a juvenile, the custody officer is not bound to order the person's release under s. 38(1) of PACE 1984:

(a)   if any of the reasons set out in paras 6.3.1.1 to 6.3.1.6 above apply; or
(b)   if the custody officer has reasonable grounds for believing that detention is in the arrested juvenile's own interest.

(For special requirements in relation to juveniles see Chapter 11, para. 11.1.5.)

6.3.3 Custody officer to consider same factors as the courts under the Bail Act 1976

Where exceptions listed in paras 6.3.1.2, 6.3.1.3, 6.3.1.4 and 6.3.1.5, above, apply, the custody officer must have regard to the same considerations as those to which a court is required to have regard in taking the corresponding decisions under the BA 1976, sch. 1, Part I, para. 2: PACE 1984, s. 38(2A), inserted by s. 24 of the CJPOA 1994. The corresponding conditions when bail need not be granted in the case of imprisonable offences are where a court is satisfied that there are substantial grounds for believing that if released on bail the defendant would:

(a)   fail to surrender to custody;
(b)   commit an offence; or
(c)   interfere with witnesses or otherwise obstruct the course of justice, whether in relation to the defendant or any other person: see Chapter 1, para. 1.3.1.1.

However, as Corre has pointed out, '[p]roblems may arise because the CJPOA 1994 retains the wording of s. 38 of PACE 1984, in that the custody officer must have *reasonable* grounds, whereas sch. 1, Part I, para. 2 of the Bail Act 1976 requires the court to have *substantial* grounds': Corre, N., *A Guide to the 1995 Revisions to the PACE Codes of Practice* London: Callow Publishing, 1995, p. 25.

6.3.4 Record of grounds for detention

A custody officer who authorises the keeping of a person in police detention must as soon as practicable make a written record of the grounds for the detention: PACE 1984, s. 38(3).

6.3.5 Incidence of the grant or refusal of bail after charge

6.3.5.1 Bail or custody after charge   Home Office sponsored research has disclosed that 63 per cent of a sample of defendants were granted unconditional bail, 17 per cent were bailed with conditions and 20 per cent were detained in police custody to be brought before the court: Bucke, T., and Brown, D., *In Police Custody: Police Powers and Suspects' Rights under the Revised PACE Codes of Practice*, Home Office Research Study No. 174, London: Home Office, 1997, p. 61.

6.3.5.2 Reasons for refusing police bail   The same research study found that the most common reason for refusing bail after charge is to prevent further offences (32 per cent), followed by risk of failing to surrender (31 per cent) and risk of interfering with the administration of justice (13 per cent): *op. cit.*, p. 62.

6.4   BAIL BY POLICE FOR APPEARANCE AT COURT

6.4.1   New requirement for appearance at next court sitting after charge

Where a person was charged and released by the police on bail under
s. 38(1) of PACE 1984 subject to a duty to appear before a magistrates' court, there
was until very recently no time limit before the latest date which the police were
required to set for the defendant's first court appearance after charge. This could
be, and often was, the cause of considerable delay before court process began and
was liable to undermine the maxim 'justice delayed is justice denied'. In many
cases a first court date might be many weeks or even months hence. Accordingly, s.
46(2) of the CDA 1998 inserts in s. 47 of PACE 1984 a new subsection, s. 47(3A),
which provides that where a custody officer grants bail to a person subject to a duty
to appear before a magistrates' court, the officer must appoint for the appearance:

(a)   a date which is not later than the first sitting of the court after the person
is charged with the offence; or
(b)   where the custody officer is informed by the clerk to the justices for the
relevant petty sessions area that the appearance cannot be accommodated until a
later date, that later date.

While para. (b) permits some leeway where pressure of court business is for the
time being so intense that listing in accordance with (a) would be likely to involve
an intolerable administrative burden, it is clear that the purpose of the new
provision is to ensure that defendants released by the police on bail to appear at
court are required to do so much more quickly than hitherto has been the case. The
section is consistent with a number of other provisions designed to expedite
criminal justice. No doubt arrangements will be made for court clerks to give
regular information to custody officers about court availability.

6.4.2   Postponement of due date and enlargement of sureties

Where having been charged a person is released on bail under s. 38(1) of PACE
1984 subject to a duty to appear before a magistrates' court at a time and date
specified, s. 43(1) of the MCA 1980 provides that the court before which the
accused is to appear may appoint a later time for that appearance and may
accordingly enlarge the recognizances of any sureties taken by the police, to that
later time. Section 43(1) is not incompatible with s. 47(3A) of PACE 1984. Where
a defendant granted police bail after charge subject to a duty to appear in court is
required to appear at the next court sitting, this will not preclude the court from
appointing a later date and enlarging the recognizances. This may be done before
the sitting, e.g. where the court receives notice that the defendant is unwell and
will not be attending, or the court may appoint the later date when the defendant
fails to appear and is then discovered to be indisposed.

6.5   IMPOSITION OF CONDITIONS IN ADDITION TO SURETY

6.5.1   Conditions additional to surety now permissible where arrested person has been charged

Originally, the police had no power to impose conditions of bail in relation to persons arrested and detained under Part IV of PACE 1984, save that of requiring sureties. Section 3(6) of the BA 1976, which provided for the imposing of other conditions, expressly restricted its application to bail granted by the court (and therefore excluded its application to bail granted by the police). This was altered in part by the CJPOA 1994, which in the case of persons released by the police on bail *following charge*, gave custody officers the power to impose the full range of conditions normally available under s. 3(6) of the 1976 Act, except a condition of residence at a bail hostel (s. 3A(2), BA 1976), conditions to enable a report to be prepared (s. 3(6)(d), BA 1976) and conditions with regard to medical reports on a charge of murder (s. 3(6A), BA 1976). Section 27(1) of the 1994 Act inserts in s. 47 of PACE 1984 a new subsection, s. 47(1A), which enacts that the normal powers to impose conditions of bail are available to a custody officer releasing a person on bail following charge under s. 38(1) of PACE 1984, but 'not in any other cases'. The expression 'normal powers to impose conditions of bail' has the meaning given in s. 3(6) of the BA 1976. There remains no power, beyond that of requiring sureties, to impose conditions under s. 3(6) in the case of persons released on bail without charge.

6.5.2   Statistical findings

6.5.2.1   General use of conditions   The power to impose conditions under s. 27 of the CJPOA 1994 is used in 17 per cent of cases: Bucke, T., and Brown D., *In Police Custody: Police Powers and Suspects' Rights under the Revised PACE Codes of Practice*, Home Office Research Study No. 174, London: Home Office, 1997, p. 61. The proportion of persons detained after charge has not been substantially affected by the power of the police to impose conditions. The proportion after implementation of s. 27 was 20 per cent (*op. cit.*, p. 64), as against 22 per cent before implementation (Phillips, C., and Brown, D., with the assistance of Goodrich, P., and James, Z., *Entry into the Criminal Justice System: a survey of police arrests and their outcomes*, Home Office Research and Statistics Directorate study, London: HMSO (forthcoming).

6.5.2.2   Common conditions   The conditions most commonly imposed by the police were found by Bucke and Brown (*op. cit.*, p. 66) to be as follows:

- not to contact victims/witnesses (67 per cent)
- to keep away from named places (61 per cent)
- curfew (33 per cent)

- report to the police (16 per cent)
- residence (7 per cent).

6.5.2.3 Reasons for conditions Bucke and Brown (*op. cit.*, p. 67) found that the most commonly cited reason for imposing conditions is to prevent offences (67 per cent). The comparable figures for ensuring attendance and prevention of interference with justice are 13 per cent and 54 per cent, respectively.

6.5.2.4 The police view Research conducted for the Home Office by Henderson found that 69 per cent of custody officer respondents reported that conditions were being imposed regularly in their division, and 23 per cent reported that conditions were being used occasionally (Henderson, P., *A Survey of Custody Officers' Views on New Provisions of the Criminal Justice and Public Order Act 1994*, Home Office Research and Statistics Directorate unpublished paper, p. 5; study cited in Morgan, P., and Henderson, P., *Remand Decisions and Offending on Bail: Evaluation of the Bail Process Project*, Home Office Research and Statistics Directorate Research Findings No. 184, London: Home Office, 1998; the full text of Henderson's study has been perused by the authors with the kind permission of the Home Office). Difficulties with the use and operation of conditional bail, mostly in relation to ensuring that officers were made aware of conditions imposed, were mentioned by 23 per cent of the custody officers canvassed (Henderson, *op. cit.*, p. 7). Benefits from the power to impose conditions were reported by 53 per cent (*ibid.*). The benefits mentioned were mostly in relation to the fact that fewer persons were kept in custody overnight, a saving of court time, and the belief in the ability of the police to choose more appropriate conditions than the courts.

6.5.2.5 Police-imposed conditions and the court In a substantial minority of cases the police decision to grant conditional bail is varied by the courts. A study at Leicester Magistrates' Court found that the police decision to grant conditional bail was upheld in 57 per cent of cases, but varied to unconditional bail in 23 per cent of cases, and to a remand in custody in 17 per cent of cases (Hucklesby, A., and Marshall, E., *Tackling Offending on Bail: the impact of section 26 of the Criminal Justice and Public Order Act 1994*, unpublished Home Office paper 1996, cited in Morgan and Henderson, *Remand Decisions, etc*; the authors have perused the full text of the study, with the kind permission of the Home Office).

6.5.2.6 Conclusion It has been observed that the police are cautious about taking on the extra responsibility of granting bail where there are doubts: Raine, J., and Willson, M., *Police Bail With Conditions – The cost/savings effect of the new power*, unpublished report to the Home Office, 1996, p. 12, *sub nom*, Birmingham University School of Public Policy. The introduction of police bail with conditions has had only a limited impact on detention after charge. Instead, conditions appeared to be placed on those people who would in the past have been bailed unconditionally: see Bucke, T., and Brown, D., *In Police Custody: Police*

Powers and Suspects' Rights under the Revised PACE Codes of Practice, Home Office Research Study No. 174, London: Home Office, 1997, p. 67. Dr Anthea Hucklesby has raised three issues in relation to the police power to grant conditional bail ('Remand Decision Makers' [1998] Crim LR 269, at p. 274). First, she argues, research suggests that officers have only limited training on bail decision-making and would welcome further training. Secondly, she suggests that the police decision is taken on limited and sometimes incomplete information. Thirdly, she submits that custody officers 'may be too readily swayed by the recommendations of investigating officers'.

6.5.3 Reasons for imposing or varying conditions to be given

Where a custody officer:

(a) imposes conditions in granting bail in criminal proceedings; or

(b) varies any conditions of bail or imposes conditions in respect of bail in criminal proceedings;
the custody officer must, with a view to enabling the person concerned to consider requesting that or another custody officer, or making an application to a magistrates' court to vary the conditions, give reasons for imposing or varying the conditions: BA 1976, s. 5A(2), inserted by CJPOA 1994, s. 27(4) and sch. 3, para. 2, modifying s. 5(3) as applied to bail granted by the police.

6.5.4 Reasons to be noted in the custody record and copy of the note to be served on the person concerned

A custody officer who by virtue of the measure set out in the last preceding paragraph is required to give reasons for the decision must include a note of those reasons in the custody record and must give a copy to the person concerned: BA 1976, s. 5A(3), inserted by CJPOA 1994, s. 27(4) and sch. 3, para. 2, modifying s. 5(3) as applied to bail granted by the police.

6.5.5 Impact of the Crime and Disorder Act 1998

As has been seen, new s. 47(3A) of PACE 1984, inserted by s. 43(2) of the CDA 1998, requires the custody officer in granting bail to a person charged with an offence and subject to a duty to appear in court to appoint the next sitting of the court after charge for the due appearance. The obligation is subject to representations from the court clerk as to court availability. Since under the new provision bail is unlikely to be longer than overnight, or at most over a weekend or a public holiday, the power to impose conditions is likely to be restricted in practice to those of residence, not to contact witnesses or victims, and not to go to a specified location.

6.6   CHARGED PERSON'S RIGHT TO APPLY TO MAGISTRATES' COURT FOR VARIATION OF CONDITIONS

6.6.1   The basic provision

The CJPOA 1994 (s. 27(4) and sch. 3, para. 3) inserted in the MCA 1980 a new section, s. 43B, which entitles persons granted conditional bail by the police to apply to the magistrates' court for a variation in the terms of such bail. Section 43B(1) provides that where a custody officer:

(a)   grants bail to any person under Part IV of PACE 1984 in criminal proceedings and imposes conditions; or
(b)   varies, in relation to any person, conditions of bail in criminal proceedings;

a magistrates' court may, on application by or on behalf of that person, *grant bail or vary the conditions*. The words emphasised, which are directly quoted from the section, clearly have the meaning that the court may grant bail by virtue of removing the conditions imposed by the police, either in their entirety or only those which the applicant was unable to meet. (Otherwise the words 'grant bail' would be redundant since the section confers an entitlement to apply only for a variation in the terms of bail already granted in principle.)

The right to apply to a court for a variation of conditions imposed by the police may have been rendered largely redundant by the new rule that when a person is bailed after charge to surrender to a court the police must appoint the next court sitting after charge as the date for such surrender (unless the custody officer is informed by the court clerk that the court cannot accommodate the matter until a later date). This is because the police may impose conditions apart from surety as a condition of bail only after charge. In the normal case the defendant granted police bail after charge with a duty to appear at court (which is the general practice after charge) will be required to appear the next day or the day after that. There will be little opportunity therefore to apply to the court for variation of conditions pending the point at which the court assumes exclusive jurisdiction over bail in any event. Section 43B will presumably continue to be available in those rare cases when the first appearance on bail after charge is delayed for a matter of weeks under s. 47(3A) of PACE 1984 because of pressure of court business. In the theoretically permissible circumstances of the person being bailed after charge with a requirement to return to the police station instead of appearing in court, an application for variation of conditions other than surety might be made to the court.

6.6.2   Question whether right of application applies in the case of persons released on bail without charge

Section 43B(1) of the MCA 1980 refers to *any* person, and presumably therefore applies to persons who have not been charged, as well as to those who have been charged. Although the normal powers to impose conditions of bail under s. 3(6) of the BA 1976 are applicable under s. 47(1A) of PACE 1984 only to persons who have been charged under s. 38 of the Act, the imposition of a surety is also a condition of bail and under PACE 1984 the police have always been empowered to impose a requirement for a surety as a condition of police bail in relation both to persons who have been charged and to those who have not been charged. Presumably, therefore, a person who has been granted bail by a custody officer without being charged may apply to the magistrates' court under s. 43B for a variation of a condition relating to the requirement of a surety. There should be no difficulty presented by r. 84A(1) of the MCR 1981 (which was inserted by the Magistrates' Courts (Amendment) Rules 1995 (SI 1995 No. 585). The rule states that an application under s. 43B must, *inter alia*, 'specify the offence with which the applicant was charged before his release on bail'. This is neither inconsistent with the section nor does it reflect a legislative intent to restrict its ambit to applications only by persons who had been charged. Clearly, the requirement of the rule is to specify the offence charged *if any*. If no charge has been made, there will be none to specify.

6.6.3 Power of court to impose more stringent conditions

On an application under the MCA 1980, s. 43B(1), if the court grants bail and imposes conditions or if it varies the conditions, it may impose more onerous conditions: s. 43B(2).

6.6.4 Duty of the court to remand the applicant

On determining an application under the MCA 1980, s. 43B(1), it is the duty of the court to remand the applicant, in custody or on bail in accordance with the determination, and where the court withholds bail or grants bail the grant of bail made by the custody officer lapses: s. 43B(3). If the remand is on bail it will presumably be to the date and police station set by the custody officer in the case of a suspect who has not been charged, or to the date and court set by the custody officer in a case where the person was charged. The section appears to make no provision for a court to withdraw bail in principle where it has been granted by the custody officer, although by empowering the court to fix more onerous conditions the court may effectively be withholding bail from a person granted it by the police. Thus a person who is at liberty on police bail may have gone to court with a view to easing conditions of police bail only to find the court imposing conditions which, because they cannot be met, result in the person being placed in custody.

6.6.5 General procedural requirements for an application to the court for variation of police imposed conditions

Rule 84A(1) of the MCR 1981 provides that an application under the MCA 1980, s. 43B must:

(a) be made in writing;

(b) contain a statement of the grounds upon which it is made;

(c) specify the offence with which the applicant was charged before being released on bail;

(d) specify, or be accompanied by a copy of the note of, the reasons given by the custody officer for imposing or varying the conditions of bail; and

(e) specify the name and address of any surety provided by the applicant before being released on bail to secure the applicant's surrender to custody.

6.6.6 Notices to be sent by the applicant

An application must be sent to the clerk of the magistrates' court (if any) appointed by the custody officer as the court before which the applicant has a duty to appear, or, if no such court has been appointed, a magistrates' court acting for the petty sessions area in which the police station at which the applicant was granted bail, or at which the conditions of bail were varied, is situated: MCR 1981, r. 84A(2). In either case a copy must be sent to a custody officer appointed for that police station: *ibid*. The notice of application must either be delivered to the clerk or sent by post in a letter: MCR 1981, r. 84A(5).

6.6.7 Notices to be sent by the court

The clerk of the court to whom an application is sent must send a notice in writing of the day, time and place fixed for the hearing of the application to the applicant, the prosecutor and any surety in connection with bail granted to, or the conditions of which were varied by the custody officer in relation to, the applicant: MCR 1981, r. 84A(3). Any notice must either be delivered, or sent by post in a letter, to the recipient and, if sent by post to the applicant or a surety, must be addressed to the recipient's last known or usual place of abode: MCR 1981, r. 84A(5).

6.6.8 Time for the hearing

The time fixed for the hearing must be not later than 72 hours after receipt of the application; and in reckoning any period of 72 hours no account is to be taken of Christmas Day, Good Friday, any bank holiday, or any Saturday or Sunday: MCR 1981, r. 84(4).

6.6.9 Discharge or enlargement of recognizances

If the magistrates' court hearing an application under s. 43B(1) of the MCA 1980 discharges or enlarges any recognizance entered into by any surety, or increases or reduces the amount in which that person is bound, the clerk of the court must forthwith give notice to the applicant and to any such surety. The requirements for notice contained in MCR 1981, r. 84A(5), as to which see para. 6.6.6, apply.

6.7 RIGHT OF PROSECUTOR TO APPLY TO COURT FOR RE-CONSIDERATION OF BAIL GRANTED BY THE POLICE

6.7.1 The basic provision

Section 5B(1) and (2) of the BA 1976 (as inserted by the CJPOA 1994, s. 30) provide that where a constable has granted bail in criminal proceedings in connection with proceedings for an offence which is triable on indictment or either way, the appropriate court in relation to the constable may, on application by the prosecutor for the decision to be reconsidered:

(a) vary the conditions of bail;
(b) impose conditions in respect of bail which has been granted uncondi-tionally; or
(c) withhold bail.

The right of the prosecutor to request a court to revoke bail granted by a constable contrasts with the fact that the arrested person has no *immediate* right to ask a court to grant bail refused by a constable. (However, the time during which a person can continue to be detained under Part IV of PACE 1984, having been refused bail by a custody officer, can be measured in hours rather than days so that before very long such a person would have to be produced before a court in any event: see para. 6.8.)

6.7.2 Appropriate court

The appropriate court is:

(a) the magistrates' court (if any) appointed by the custody officer as the court before which the person to whom bail was granted has a duty to appear; or
(b) if no such court has been appointed, a magistrates' court acting for the petty sessions area in which the police station at which bail was granted is situated: MCR 1981 r. 93B(1), inserted by Magistrates' Courts (Amendment) Rules 1995 (SI 1995 No. 585) made in pursuance of s. 5B(9) of the BA 1976.

6.7.3 Application must be based on newly available information

No application by the prosecutor for the reconsideration of a decision by a constable to grant bail may be made unless it is based on information which was not available to the court or constable when the decision was taken: BA 1976, s. 5B(3).

6.7.4 Presumption in favour of bail applies

Whether or not the person to whom the application relates appears before the magistrates' court, the right to bail enacted by BA 1976, s. 4 and sch. 1, must be applied in taking the decision: BA 1976, s. 5B(4).

6.7.5   Particulars to be specified in the application

Rule 93B(2) of the MCR 1981, inserted by Magistrates' Courts (Amendment) Rules 1995 (SI 1995 No. 585) made in pursuance of s. 5B(9) of the BA 1976, lays down a number of procedural requirements for an application under s. 5B. Such an application must:

(a)   be made in writing;

(b)   contain a statement of the grounds on which it is made;

(c)   specify the offence with which the proceedings in which bail was granted were connected, or those for which bail was granted;

(d)   specify the decision to be reconsidered (including any conditions of bail which have been imposed and why they have been imposed); and

(e)   specify the name and address of any surety provided by the person to whom the application relates to secure the person's surrender to custody.

6.7.6   Clerk's duty over listing

The clerk of a magistrates' court to which an application under BA 1976, s. 5B has been made must fix a date, time and place for the hearing of the application and must give a notice of the application and of the date, time and place so fixed in the prescribed form to the person affected, and send a copy of the notice to the prosecutor who made the application and to any surety specified in the application: MCR 1981, r. 93B(5).

6.7.7   Time for the hearing

The time for the hearing must be no later than 72 hours after receipt of the application. In reckoning any period of 72 hours, no account is to be taken of Christmas Day, Good Friday, any bank holiday, or any Saturday or Sunday: MCR 1981, r. 93B(4).

6.7.8   Service of notice of hearing

Service of a notice of the fixing of the hearing may be effected by delivering it to the person affected: MCR 1981, r. 93B(5).

6.7.9   Requirement to consider representations by the person affected

At the hearing of an application under BA 1976, s. 5B, the court must consider any representations made by the person affected (whether in writing or orally) before taking any decision under the section with respect to the person: MCR 1981, r. 93B(6). Where the person affected does not appear before the court, the court must not take such a decision unless it is proved to the satisfaction of the court, on oath, that the notice required to be given under r. 93B(3) was served on the person before the hearing: MCR 1981, r. 93B(6). 'Oath' includes affirmation: Interpretation Act 1978, sch. 1.

6.7.10 Decision to vary or impose conditions taken in the absence of the person affected

Where the court proceeds in the absence of the person affected to vary the conditions of bail or impose conditions in respect of bail which has been granted unconditionally, the clerk of the court must notify the person affected in the prescribed form: MCR 1981, r. 93B(7).

6.7.11 Decision to withhold bail taken in the affected person's absence

Where in the absence of the affected person the court decides to withhold bail, the order of the court requiring the person to surrender to custody must be signed by the justice issuing it, or must state the name of the justice and must be authenticated by the signature of the clerk of the court and must be in prescribed form: MCR 1981, r. 93B(7).

6.7.12 Service of notice of decision taken in the affected person's absence

Service of the necessary notice of a decision taken in the absence of the affected person may be effected by delivering it to the person to whom it is directed, or by leaving if with some person at the affected person's last known or usual place of abode: MCR 1981 r. 93B(8).

6.7.13 Court's action in relation to persons withheld bail after prosecution apply for reconsideration

Where the decision of the court on a reconsideration under BA 1976, s. 5B is to withhold bail from the person to whom it was originally granted, the court must:

   (a)   remand in custody a person who is before the court; or
   (b)   order a person who is not before the court to surrender forthwith into the custody of the court: BA 1976, s. 5B(5).

A person who surrenders to the custody of the court in compliance with an order to surrender must be remanded in custody: BA 1976, s. 5B(6).

6.7.14 Failure to surrender where person is ordered to do so by a court after deciding to withhold bail upon application for reconsideration

A person who has been ordered to surrender to custody by a court following a decision to withhold bail and has failed without reasonable cause to do so in accordance with the order, may be arrested without warrant by a constable: BA 1976, s. 5B(7). A person so arrested must be brought as soon as practicable, and in any event within 24 hours after being arrested, before a justice of the peace in the petty sessions area where the arrest was made and the justice must remand the person in custody: BA 1976, s. 5B(8). In reckoning any period of 24 hours, no account may be taken of Christmas Day, Good Friday, or any Sunday: *ibid.*

6.8   REFUSAL BY THE POLICE OF BAIL IN PRINCIPLE

6.8.1   Charged persons refused police bail

A person charged with an offence may be granted bail by the police under PACE 1984 to appear at a magistrates' court on a particular date. Conversely, any person charged with an offence but refused bail by the police must be brought before a magistrates' court as soon as is practicable in accordance with the provisions of s. 46 of the 1984 Act. Jurisdiction over the issue of bail will then proceed in the normal way.

6.8.2   The refusal of bail to persons who have not been charged: section 43 procedure

A person who has been arrested but not charged and who is refused bail, or denied unconditional release, pending a requirement to return to the police station for further inquiries in due course, and who therefore remains in police detention, has no immediate right to apply to the magistrates' court for a review of that detention. The detention provisions of Part IV of PACE 1984 will apply with all the requirements for regular review and eventual production before the magistrates' court under s. 43 of the Act if that stage is reached (see below), but with the magistrates having no immediate power to grant bail against the decision of the police to refuse it in principle. In the case of persons who have not been charged the court only enjoys immediate jurisdiction over bail matters as an arbiter of conditions imposed by police where bail has been granted in principle in accordance with the provisions of s. 47 of PACE 1984.

6.8.3   Bail granted to a person who has not been charged, on terms which cannot be met

The ordinary detention provisions of Part IV will apply also where, under s. 47 of PACE 1984, a person not charged following arrest is granted bail by the police to return at some future date to the police station for further inquiries, and the bail is on terms which the person is unable to meet. The effect of the person remaining in custody, or of being remanded back into police custody by a court which refuses an application under s. 43B of the MCA 1980 (see para. 6.6.1.) will mean that all the detention provisions of PACE 1984 will continue to apply. The options open to the police would then be:

(a) to reduce the amount of surety;

(b) to relent and forgo a surety requirement altogether;

(c) to charge the suspect; or

(d) to grant release without bail if there be insufficient evidence to charge and no grounds justifying continued detention (this would not preclude re-arrest if the evidence materialised later).

If, however, they wish to detain the suspect further and believe they can justify doing so, the police would eventually face the stage 36 hours after arrest when their power of detention ceases. At that stage they would have to bring the suspect before the magistrates' court under s. 43 of PACE 1984 and apply for a warrant empowering them to continue with detention for inquiries for the further period limited by the Act. If the magistrates dismiss the application for the warrant the detainee must be released unconditionally; there is no power to grant bail in such circumstances. Although the s. 43 procedure is strictly speaking not a bail overseeing function, it may indirectly serve that purpose in the example conjectured here because it will be the inability of the detainee to comply with conditions of bail set by the police which will ultimately oblige the police to produce the detained suspect before the court.

6.8.4 Significance of section 43 procedure

While imposing no duty directly relevant to bail, the PACE 1984, s. 43 procedure does nevertheless underwrite the liberty of the subject in a most significant way. In furnishing a check on the power of the police to detain for inquiries it is probably superior in practical terms to the right to apply for a writ of habeas corpus or other prerogative remedy (a right explicitly preserved by s. 51 of PACE 1984). Whereas s. 43 imposes a strict limit on the running of the clock, habeas corpus always allowed the police an imprecise leeway in the past which often extended to several days.

6.9 PERSONS IN CUSTOMS DETENTION

Section 150 of the CJA 1988 amends s. 114(2) of PACE 1984 by inserting new para. (c) empowering the Treasury by order to direct that in relation to customs detention the BA 1976 shall have effect as if references in it to a constable were references to an officer of Customs and Excise of such grade as may be specified in the order. The section has not yet been brought into effect. Officers of Customs and Excise means officers commissioned by the Commissioners of Customs and Excise under s. 6(3) of the Customs and Excise Management Act 1979: PACE 1984, s. 114(4).

7 The Jurisdiction of the Magistrates' Court

7.1 THE POWER OF REMAND BEFORE CONVICTION OR COMMITTAL FOR TRIAL

7.1.1 Adjournment and remand

7.1.1.1 Relationship between adjournment and remand To *remand* a defendant means that when a case is *adjourned* to a future date the defendant is ordered to appear at court on that date and in the meantime to be committed to custody or to be admitted to bail. Adjournment and remand are therefore not synonymous.

7.1.1.2 Adjournment and remand in the initial phase of dealing with indictable and either way offences Where a defendant appears before a magistrates' court charged with an indictable offence or an offence triable 'either way', the court may adjourn the matter. The new rule under s. 51 of the CDA 1998, whereby an adult (i.e. a person aged 18 or over) who is charged with an offence which may only be tried on indictment must be sent by a magistrates' court forthwith to the Crown Court for trial (see para. 7.5), is subject to the discretion of the magistrates' court to adjourn such proceedings and to the requirement that upon such an adjournment the defendant must be remanded: CDA 1998, s. 52(5). In the case of an offence which may be tried 'either way', the magistrates' court may adjourn the hearing before beginning to inquire into the offence as examining justices, and if it does so it must remand the accused: MCA 1980, s. 5. This includes the stage prior to determination of mode of trial. Further, the court may at any time during the inquiry adjourn the hearing and, if it does so, it must remand the accused.

7.1.1.3 Remand to police detention A magistrates' court having power to remand a person in custody may commit the person to detention at a police station for a limited period. The power has only ever been and can only be used where inquiries are continuing into other offences and the police wish to have the defendant available at hand for questioning. The power is discussed further below.

7.1.1.4 Adjournment before or during a summary trial Section 10 of the MCA 1980 makes provision for a magistrates' court to adjourn a trial at any time before or after starting it. If the court does adjourn the trial and the offence is summary only it need not remand the defendant, but it must remand the defendant if:

(a) the offence is an either-way matter; and
(b) the defendant is aged 18 or over; and
(c) the defendant was in custody on first appearing, or, having been released on bail, surrendered to custody; or
(d) the defendant has been remanded at any time in the course of the proceedings.

The court is not obliged to remand a defendant who appears in answer to a summons if the hearing is adjourned. It may simply adjourn the hearing without remanding the defendant. The discretion to adjourn is unfettered. In certain instances it may be exercised by a justices' clerk: Justices Clerks Rules 1970, r. 4.

7.1.1.5 Remand on changing from summary trial to committal proceedings
Where a magistrates' court has begun to try summarily an accused charged with an offence triable either way and the court decides to discontinue summary trial and proceed to inquire as examining justices, it must adjourn the hearing: MCA 1980, s. 25(2), as amended by CPIA 1996, s. 47 and sch. 1, para. 5.

7.1.1.6 Restriction on justices sitting after dealing with bail Section 42 of the MCA 1980 prohibits a magistrate from taking part in the trial of the issue of an accused's guilt on the summary trial of an information if in the course of the *same* proceedings the magistrate has been informed, for the purpose of determining whether the accused is to be granted bail, that the accused has one or more previous convictions. In *R* v *McElligott, ex parte Gallagher and Seal* [1972] Crim LR 332, the applicants applied for an order of *prohibition* against the respondent stipendiary magistrate from personally presiding over the trial, since he had tried and convicted them on previous occasions. In refusing their application, the Divisional Court held that there was no proposition of law that a defendant should not be tried by a magistrate to whom the defendant's past record was well known. Although it was desirable that magistrates who knew of a defendant's record should not hear the case, this statement could not be elevated to a point of law. However, the Divisional Court went on to say that consideration should be given for the case to be tried by another magistrate. A more robust view was taken by the Divisional Court in *R* v *Downham Market Magistrates' Court, ex parte Nudd* [1989] Crim LR 147. The applicant was convicted of a number of motoring offences, including failing to provide a specimen of breath. The chairman of the bench which convicted him had a month earlier imposed on him a suspended sentence for another offence and had seen his criminal record which included a conviction for driving while unfit. The chairman had also sentenced the applicant in the previous year for other offences. The Divisional Court quashed the convictions on the ground that there had been ostensible bias. Justice had to be seen to be done. The public could not have come to any conclusion other than that the chairman might not have been able to put out of his mind what he knew about the applicant when it came to the issue of credit. The decision imposes serious practical difficulties in districts where there are only a small number of justices. A frequent offender may become known to every member of the bench. At the time of *ex parte Nudd* there were only 11 members of the Downham Market bench. The principle that 'justice should not only be done, but should manifestly and undoubtedly be seen to be done' (*R* v *Sussex Justices, ex parte McCarthy* [1924] KB 256, at p. 259 per Hewart LJ) is not confined to the financial interests of a member of a tribunal (in *Re Pinochet Ugarte, The Times*, 18 January 1999, HL).

7.1.2   Remand in custody

7.1.2.1   Bail disallowed in principle   Section 128(1)(a) of the MCA 1980 provides that where a magistrates' court has power to remand any person then, subject to s. 4 of the Bail Act 1976 and to any other enactment modifying that power, the court may remand the defendant in custody, that is to say, commit the defendant to custody to be brought before the court at the end of the period of remand or such earlier time as the court may require, unless remanded to a date when the defendant may be further remanded without being brought before the court, in accordance with the power conferred by s. 128(3A) (as to which see para. 7.1.4.6. below).

7.1.2.2   Bail allowed but defendant remanded in custody pending the taking of a surety's recognizance   Where an accused is remanded on bail and the court fixes the amount of a recognizance by way of surety under s. 128(1) and (4) of the MCA 1980 or under s. 8(3) of the BA 1976 with a view to its being taken subsequently, the court must in the meantime commit the accused so remanded to custody in accordance with s. 128(1)(a).

7.1.2.3   Transfer of remand hearings when accused is in custody   A magistrates' court adjourning a summary trial under s. 10 of the MCA 1980, an inquiry under s. 5, before determining mode of trial for an either-way offence under s. 18(4), or indication of plea proceedings under s. 17C (as inserted by s. 49 of the CPIA 1996) and remanding the defendant in custody, may, if the defendant has attained the age of 17, order that the defendant be brought up for any subsequent remands before an alternate magistrates' court nearer to the prison where the defendant is confined while on remand: MCA 1980, s. 130(1). The order must require the defendant to be brought before the alternate court at the end of the period of remand or at such earlier time as the alternate court may require: s. 130(2). While the order is in force, the alternate court possesses, to the exclusion of the court which made the order, all the powers in relation to further remand (whether in custody or on bail) and the grant of legal aid which that court would have had but for the order: s. 130(3). Details of the case must be sent to the alternate court by the original court: MCR 1981, r. 25. The alternate court may, on remanding the defendant in custody, require the defendant to be brought before the court which made the order at the end of the period of remand or at such earlier time as the court may require; and if the alternate court does so, or the defendant is released on bail, the order under s. 130(1) ceases to be in force: MCA 1980, s. 130(4). Bail will be conditional on the defendant's appearance before the original court, but a defendant who remains in custody having failed to comply with pre-release conditions will be brought before the alternate court after the period of remand: MCA 1980, sch. 5, para. 5. By s. 130(4A) of the 1980 Act a transfer order may also apply, *mutatis mutandis*, where an extended order of remand is made under s. 128(3A), as to which see para. 7.1.4.6. The provisions therefore apply not where the court orders the defendant to be brought before the alternate court, but where it orders *applications for subsequent remands to be made* to the alternate court.

A Home Office circular issued on 10 July 1978, advised courts that cases in which transfer seems likely to provide positive advantages are those where:

(a)   bail is not likely to be granted; and
(b)   several remands in custody are likely to be necessary before trial or committal;

and those where:

(c)   transport to and from prison is likely to involve a significant risk; or
(d)   the journey between the original magistrates' court and the prison or remand centre is particularly lengthy or in some way inconvenient.

It was pointed out in the circular that in the main (c) is likely to involve a prisoner who is provisionally in category A (i.e., a prisoner whose escape would be highly dangerous to the public, the police or the security of the state). Consideration (d) is less likely to apply when the original magistrates' court is on or close to the route of a daily prison van to a Crown Court centre.

7.1.2.4   Power of remand for up to three days in police detention   A magistrates' court having power to remand an accused in custody may, if the remand is for a period not exceeding three clear days, commit the accused to detention at a police station: MCA 1980, s. 128(7). The accused must not be kept in detention unless there is a need for such detention for the purposes of inquiries into other offences: s. 128(8)(a). If kept in such detention the accused must be brought back before the same court as soon as that need ceases: s. 128(8)(b). The accused must be treated as a person in police detention to whom the responsibilities in relation to persons detained under PACE 1984 apply: s. 128(8)(c). The detention must be subject to periodic review in accordance with the 1984 Act: s. 128(8)(d).

The use of s. 48 of PACE 1984 sometimes causes conflict between custody officers and investigating officers. Custody officers are sometimes of the view that the provision is used by the CID in order to avoid having to travel to prisons in order to question suspects, and as a way of avoiding active inquiries (*The Impact of Aspects of the Police and Criminal Evidence Act 1984 on Policing in a Force in the North of England*, Final Report to ESRC, unpublished, cited in Brown, D., *PACE ten years on: a review of the research*, Home Office Research and Statistics Directorate Research Findings No. 155, London: HMSO, 1997, p. 68). The maximum period of three days' detention is rarely used (Brown, D., *Investigating burglars; the effects of PACE*, HORS Directorate Research Findings No. 123, London: HMSO, 1991, cited in *ibid.*).

7.1.2.5 Remand to customs detention   Section 152 of the CJA 1988 provides that where a person aged 17 or over is brought before a magistrates' court on a charge of an offence against s. 5(2) of the Misuse of Drugs Act 1971 (possession of controlled drugs) or a drug trafficking offence (as defined by s. 1(3) of the Drug Trafficking Act 1994, but not an offence under s. 50 of that Act, i.e. assisting another to retain the benefit of drug trafficking) and the court has power to remand that person then, subject to s. 4 of the BA 1976, it shall have power, if it considers it appropriate to do so, to remand the person to customs detention, that it is to say, to the custody of a customs officer for a period not exceeding 192 hours.

7.1.2.6 Duty to notify unrepresented defendants of their right to apply for bail to a higher court   Section 5(6) of the BA 1976 provides that where a magistrates' court withholds bail in criminal proceedings from a defendant who is not represented by counsel or a solicitor, it must:

(a)   if it issues a full argument certificate under s. 5(6A) of the BA 1976 (see Chapter 5) inform the defendant of the right to apply for bail to the Crown Court or to the High Court; or
(b)   in any other case, inform the defendant of the right to apply for bail to the High Court.

The provision in (b) clearly applies where the defendant either makes no application for bail or else makes a perfunctory first appearance application which the court agrees not to treat as involving full argument. In either case there is no right to apply to the Crown Court. The application to the High Court is to a High Court judge in chambers, and in practice magistrates' courts almost invariably makes this clear in the formal notification.

7.1.2.7 Defendants previously remanded in custody and liable to be remanded in custody again: right to legal aid for bail application   Subject to financial eligibility, representation under legal aid must be granted for so much of the proceedings as relates to the grant of bail where a person charged with an offence before a magistrates' court is brought before the court in pursuance of a remand in custody when the person may again be remanded or committed in custody and is not, but wishes to be, legally represented: Legal Aid Act 1988, s. 21(3)(c) and (5).

7.1.3   Remands on bail

Where the court has power to remand any defendant then, subject to s. 4 of the BA 1976 and to any other enactment modifying that power, it may remand the defendant on bail in accordance with the BA 1976: MCA 1980, s. 128(1) and (4). The structure, interrelation and effect of these subsections are particularly convoluted.

7.1.3.1   Unconditional bail or conditional bail without surety   Where the court is inquiring into or trying an offence alleged to have been committed by the defendant, or has convicted the defendant of an offence, the defendant may be remanded on bail unconditionally or conditionally but without a surety, to appear before that court at the end of the period of remand.

7.1.3.2   Bail with a surety: provision for continuous bail   Where the court is inquiring into or trying an offence alleged to have been committed by the defendant, or has convicted the defendant of an offence, the defendant may be remanded on bail with a surety, either to appear:

(a)   before that court at the end of the period of remand; or
(b)   at every time and place to which during the course of the proceedings the hearing may be from time to time adjourned.

The court may fix the amount of the recognizance of a surety with a view to its being taken subsequently under s. 119 of the 1980 Act: MCA 1980, s. 128(1). The effect of (b) is to make the surety 'continuous'. The defendant is described as being on 'continuous bail'. It is for the sureties themselves to keep abreast of any bail conditions, and it has been said that they can help themselves, if they wish, by entering into recognizances only from one remand to the next and thereby learn of any variations of bail which may be ordered: see *R* v *Wells Street Magistrates' Court, ex parte Albanese* [1982] QB 333.

7.1.3.3   Bail with surety where court is inquiring into an offence   Section 128(4)(c) of the MCA 1980 provides that where during an inquiry into an offence a defendant is remanded on bail conditionally on the provision of a surety, the court:

. . . may direct that the recognizance of the surety be conditioned to secure that the person so bailed appears . . . at every time and place to which during the course of the proceedings the hearing may be from time to time adjourned and also before the Crown Court in the event of the person so bailed being committed for trial there.

This provision allows the court to make a surety continuous to the defendant's appearance for trial at the Crown Court. In either-way offences the magistrates will enjoy the power to make a surety continuous to the Crown Court only from the stage at which they become examining justices, that is, when, following 'plea before venue' under CPIA 1996, s. 49(2), they decline summary jurisdiction or the defendant elects trial on indictment. In the case of indictable only offences the magistrates assume the rôle of examining justices on the first appearance of the accused.

7.1.3.4   Enlargement of recognizance at committal or transfer when surety not continuous to trial   Where a magistrates' court has remanded the accused in accordance with MCA 1980, s. 128(4)(a) (recognizance conditioned for appearance before the court at the end of the period of remand), if the accused is then committed for trial, or proceedings are transferred to the Crown Court, the court may, in the absence of the surety, enlarge the surety's recognizance so binding the surety to secure that the defendant appears at the Crown Court: MCA 1980, 129(4). The surety must be given notice of any such enlargement of recognizance: MCR 1981, r. 84(1).

7.1.3.5   Overriding power of the court to remand the accused afresh   Where a defendant is directed to appear or a recognizance is conditioned for the defendant's appearance at every time and place to which during the course of the proceedings the hearing may be from time to time adjourned (continuous bail), the fixing at any time of the time for the accused next to appear is deemed to be a remand, but nothing shall deprive the court of the power at any subsequent hearing to remand the defendant afresh: MCA 1980, s. 128(5).

7.1.3.6   Defendant on bail remanded in custody on other matters   In *Walsh* v *Governor of Brixton Prison* [1985] AC 154, HL, the appellant was granted bail by one magistrates' court but subsequently remanded in custody by another magistrates' court on separate charges. On several occasions he was not produced before the magistrates' court which had granted him bail. The prison governor stated that he was unable to produce the appellant because, owing to staff shortages, he was unable to provide an escort. The Divisional Court dismissed the appellant's application for an order that the prison governor and the Home Secretary produce him before the court. Dismissing his appeal, the House of Lords held that neither was under an unconditional duty to produce prisoners at court. Their duty was to consider, in accordance with s. 29(1) of the CJA 1961, whether they were satisfied that it was desirable in the interests of justice that such prisoners should be produced, and if they were so satisfied, not unreasonably to refuse to produce them.

It should be noted that s. 29(1) refers to 'the responsible Minister' and makes no reference to a prison governor.

7.1.3.7 Variation of conditions of bail Where a court has granted bail in criminal proceedings, that court may on application by or on behalf of the person to whom bail was granted, or by the prosecutor or a constable vary the conditions of bail or impose conditions in respect of bail which has been granted unconditionally: BA 1976, s. 3(8).

7.1.4 Permissible periods of remand

7.1.4.1 Maximum of eight clear days without consent of the parties The basic rule is that prior to summary conviction or committal for trial a magistrates' court may not remand a defendant, whether in custody or on bail, for a period exceeding eight clear days: MCA 1980, s. 128(6). The rule is subject to various exceptions. For the sake of completeness it is necessary to state that repeated remands are permissible in that where a defendant is brought before a court after remand, the court may order a further remand: s. 128(3). (Reference has already been made, at para. 7.1.2.4 to the power of remand for up to three days in police detention.)

7.1.4.2 Meaning of 'clear' days Clear days mean that the days on which the defendant respectively was remanded and was due to appear at the end of the remand are not counted.

7.1.4.3 Exception for defendants on bail If the defendant is remanded on bail, the period of remand may be longer than eight days if the prosecution and the defendant consent: MCA 1980, s. 128(6)(a).

7.1.4.4 Court not presently constituted or located to enable it to try either-way offence summarily Where a defendant is charged with an offence triable either way, if it falls to the court to try the case summarily but the court is not at the time so constituted, and sitting in such a place, as will enable it to proceed with the trial, the court may remand the defendant until the next occasion on which it will be practicable for the court to be so constituted, and to sit in such a place, notwithstanding that the remand is for a period exceeding eight clear days: MCA 1980, s. 128(6)(c). If the remand hearing is at an 'occasional court', that court may not try an information summarily: MCA 1980, s. 121.

7.1.4.5 Sureties not taken Where a magistrates' court has granted bail with a surety or sureties and has adjourned the case for longer than eight clear days, but the surety or sureties have not been taken, the defendant, who in consequence remains in custody, must be brought before the court at the end of eight clear days or such earlier time as may be specified: MCR 1981, r. 23.

7.1.4.6   Consent to custodial remand in absence   Section 128(3A) of the MCA 1980 (inserted by the CJA 1982, sch. 9, and amended by the CJA 1988, sch. 15, para. 69, and by the Criminal Procedure and Investigations Act 1996 (CPIA 1996), s. 52(1)) makes provision on certain conditions for what is generally known as a 'consent to remand in absence' where the defendant has previously been remanded in custody otherwise than for more than eight clear days in the exercise of the more recently enacted power conferred by s. 128A (see para. 7.1.4.9, below). As originally enacted, the provision applied only to adults. This restriction was removed by the CPIA 1996, s. 52(1), which allowed persons under the age of 17 years to consent to remand in absence. In an applicable case, on an adjournment of a preliminary inquiry (s. 5) or of a summary trial (s. 10(1)), or on an adjournment prior to the determination of mode of trial on an information for an offence triable either way (s. 18(4)), a defendant who is not brought before the court may be further remanded in custody (otherwise than under s. 128A) provided the following conditions are satisfied:

(a)   that the defendant has not by virtue of the subsection been remanded without being brought before the court on more than two successive applications for such a remand immediately preceding the application which the court is hearing;

(b)   that the defendant has a legal representative acting in the case, whether actually present in court or not: MCA 1980, s. 128(3B) (inserted by the 1982 Act);

(c)   that when previously before the court the defendant consented to the subsequent applications being heard *in absentia*, such consent having been obtained in response to a question required by s. 128(1C) of the 1980 Act (as to which see para. 7.1.4.7, below), or otherwise;

(d)   and that such consent has not been withdrawn.

The effect of (a) is that a defendant must be brought before the court at least every fourth application for a remand. Up to 32 clear days may therefore accrue between appearances. Although the legal representative need not actually be present at the remand hearing when the defendant is absent, the requirement that the defendant be represented in the case is a reflection of the principle that no unconvicted defendant should be held in custody without the right to appear on a regular and frequent basis before an overseeing court conducting its business in public. The involvement of a solicitor will facilitate arrangements where a defendant wishes after all to be brought before the court. It has already been mentioned (at para. 7.1.2.3) that MCA 1980, s. 130(4A) makes provision for an order transferring remands to a more convenient court to apply, *mutatis mutandis*, to extended orders of remand.

7.1.4.7   Obtaining the necessary consent   The consent necessary for a remand in the absence of the defendant under MCA 1980, s. 128(3A) can only be obtained by complying with the procedure required by s. 128(1A) (inserted by the 1982 Act, sch. 9). This provides that where:

(a)   on an adjournment of a preliminary inquiry (s. 5), or of summary trial (s. 10(1)), or on an adjournment prior to the determination of mode of trial on an information for an offence triable either way (s. 18(4)), or 'plea before venue' under s. 17C, the court proposes to remand or further remand a defendant in custody; and

(b)   the defendant is before the court; and

(c)   is legally represented in that court,

the court must:

(i)   explain the effect of s. 128(3A) and (3B) in ordinary language; and

(ii)   inform the defendant in ordinary language that, notwithstanding the procedure for a remand without bringing an accused before the court, the defendant would be brought before a court for the hearing and determination of at least every fourth application for a remand heard at a time when it appeared to the court that a legal representative was acting for the defendant in the case.

After giving this explanation the court must ask whether the defendant consents to a hearing without being brought before the court: MCA 1980, s. 128(1C). For the purposes of s. 128(1A) defendants are to be treated as legally represented in a court if, but only if, they have the assistance of a legal representative to represent them in the proceedings in that court: s. 128(1B).

7.1.4.8   Conditions for a further custodial remand in absentia not satisfied: defendant to be brought before the court as soon as possible   Section 128(3C) and (3D) of the MCA 1980, as inserted by the 1982 Act, provide for the position where a defendant who was remanded in custody on an adjournment under s. 5, s. 10(1) or s. 18(4), is not subsequently brought before the court and an application is made for a further remanded in custody on such an adjournment, but the court is not satisfied that the conditions required by s. 128(3A) and (3B) for a further remand in absence have been met. For example, the defendant may have withdrawn consent to being further remand without being produced. In such circumstances, the court must remand the defendant in custody but for no longer than the shortest period that appears to the court to make it possible for the accused to be brought before it. Similarly, where there was a remand in custody under s. 130 of the Act to an alternate magistrates' court in accordance with the procedure considered above for hearings in the absence of defendants, and it appears that no such remand ought to have been so ordered, the court must require the defendant to be brought before it at the earliest time that appears to it to be possible: MCA 1980, s. 128(3E).

7.1.4.9   Remand in custody exceeding eight clear days   A more streamlined procedure than the 1982 innovation of consent remands in absence was the introduction by the CJA 1988 of longer remands in custody *without an interim* *hearing* in the absence of the defendant. The 1988 Act inserted s. 128A into the MCA 1980, subs. (2) of which makes provision for remands in custody to exceed eight clear days. The accused must be before the magistrates' court and must previously have been remanded in custody for the same offence. Further, an opportunity must be afforded to the parties to make representations and the court must then set a date on which it expects that it will be possible to continue with the next stage in the proceedings, other than a hearing relating to a further remand in custody or on bail. Provided these conditions are met, the defendant may be remanded in custody for a period ending not later than that date or for a period of 28 clear days whichever is the less. Section 128A(3) provides that nothing in the section affects the right of the accused to apply for bail during the period of remand.

The section was inserted by the CJA 1988, s. 155(1), and its implementation originally started at four courts (Manchester, Nottingham, Croydon and Highbury Corner, London) on an experimental basis in 1988. It was extended nationally by the Magistrates' Courts (Remands in Custody) Orders 1989 (SI 1989 No. 970) and 1991 (SI 1991 No. 2667). Both were amended by the Magistrates' Courts (Remands in Custody (Amendment Order) 1997 (SI 1987 No. 35). As originally enacted, the provision applied only to adults. This restriction was removed by the CPIA 1996, s. 52(2), which, together with s. 52(1), brings the remand arrangements for persons under the age of 17 years into line with those relating to adults (see para. 7.1.4.6). These changes will be welcomed by many practitioners and social workers. They will put an end to unproductive weekly appearances of juveniles, who sometimes have to travel long distances from local authority accommodation (see Corre, N., *A Practical Guide to the Criminal Procedure and Investigations Act 1996*, London: Callow Publishing, 1996, p. 55).

7.1.4.10   Remand of an accused already serving a custodial sentence   When a magistrates' court remands in custody an accused who is already detained under a custodial sentence, the remand period may be up to 28 clear days: MCA 1980, s. 131(1). However, the court is under a duty to 'inquire as to the expected date of his release from that detention; and if it appears that it will be before 28 clear days have expired, he shall not be remanded in custody for more than eight clear days or (if longer) a period ending with that date': s. 131(2). The effect of the parenthesis is less clear than it perhaps might be. The obvious intent of the provision is to avoid a defendant being kept in custody after the end of the custodial sentence. The language appears to mean that there is an absolute limit of 28 clear days but that if the estimated date of release is less than eight days away then the remand should not exceed eight days. If the date of release lies between eight and 28 clear days away the remand period must expire not later than the date of release. The bracketed words 'if longer' would appear to be a reference to the release date, i.e., if it – the date of release – is more than eight days away, the remand should be to that date. 'Custodial sentence' includes imprisonment and detention in a young offenders institution, but does not include a committal in default of payment of any sum of money or for want of sufficient distress, to satisfy

any sum of money or for failure to do or abstain from doing anything required to be done or left undone: MCA 1980, s. 150.

7.2 REMAND FOLLOWING CONVICTION

7.2.1 Remand for inquiries and reports

A magistrates' court may remand an accused following conviction for the purpose of enabling inquiries to be made or determining the most suitable method of dealing with the case: MCA 1980, s. 10(3). The convicted defendant may be remanded in custody or on bail: MCA 1980, s. 128(1). The power to adjourn after conviction must be exercised judicially, and for a proper purpose, that is for inquiries or reports. It is a truism that it ought not to be used as a disguised additional means of punishing the accused. Where a defendant is remanded on bail the court may, on the application of the defendant or the prosecutor or a constable, vary the conditions of bail or impose conditions in respect of bail granted unconditionally: BA 1976, s. 3(8).

7.2.2 Remand for medical report

Section 30(1) of the MCA 1980 provides that if on the trial by a magistrates' court of an offence punishable on summary conviction with imprisonment, the court is satisfied that the accused 'did the act or made the omission charged' but is of the opinion that an inquiry ought to be made into the physical or mental condition of the accused before the method of dealing with the accused is determined, the court must adjourn the case and remand the accused to enable such a report to be prepared. The statutory right to bail applies. If the offence charged is not punishable by imprisonment, there will be no power of remand under the section, but the power to remand for inquiries and reports under s. 10 is wide enough to permit a remand for medical reports in such a case: *Boaks* v *Reece* [1957] 1 QB 219.

7.2.3 Remand to hospital for a report

7.2.3.1 Remand in the first instance Section 35 of the MHA 1983 empowers a magistrates' court to remand an accused person to a hospital specified by the court for a report on that person's mental condition. The power applies in the case of any defendant convicted by the court of an offence punishable on summary conviction with imprisonment and any defendant charged with such an offence if the court is satisfied that the defendant did the act or made the omission charged, or any person who has consented to the exercise by the court of the powers conferred by the section. The topic is considered in Chapter 11.

7.2.3.2 Further remand Section 35 of the 1983 Act also provides that an accused may be further remanded if it appears to the court, on the written or oral evidence of the registered medical practitioner responsible for making the report, that a further remand is necessary for completing the assessment of the accused's medical condition. A further such remand may take place in the absence of an accused represented by counsel or a solicitor who is given the opportunity of being heard.

7.2.3.3 Defendant absconding from hospital

An accused who absconds from a hospital while on remand for reports under the MHA 1983, s. 35, or absconds while being conveyed to or from that hospital, may be arrested without warrant by a constable and must then be brought, as soon as practicable, before the court that ordered the remand.

7.2.4 Remittal to another magistrates' court for sentence

Section 39 of the MCA 1980 makes provision for an accused of at least 18 years of age who is convicted of an offence to be remitted to another magistrates' court for sentence. The meaning of 'convicted' includes a finding that the accused did the act or made the omission charged: s. 30(1). The circumstances in which this may be ordered are where:

(a) the offence is punishable by imprisonment; or
(b) the offence is one for which the court has a power or duty to order the offender to be disqualified from driving; and
(c) it appears to the convicting court that another magistrates' court has convicted the accused of another such offence, which has not yet been dealt with; and
(d) the other court consents to the accused being remitted to it for sentence.

Where a person who appears or is brought before a youth court charged with an offence subsequently attains the age of 18, the youth court may remit that person to a magistrates' court acting for the same petty sessions area as the youth court; the remittal may be for trial or sentence: CDA 1998, s. 47. Section 47(3) provides that s. 128, MCA 1980, and 'all other enactments (whenever passed) relating to remand or the granting of bail in criminal proceedings, shall have effect in relation to the remitting court's power or duty to remand the person on the adjournment as if any reference to the court to or before which the person remanded is to be brought or appear after remand were a reference to the court to which he is being remitted ('the other court'). Section 39(3), MCA 1980, provides: 'Where the convicting court remits the offender to the other court under this section, it shall adjourn the trial of the information charging him with the instant offence, and . . . section 128 below and all other enactments (whenever passed) relating to remand or the granting of bail in criminal proceedings shall have effect in relation to the convicting court's power to remand the offender on that adjournment as if any reference to the court to or before which the person remanded is to be brought or appear after remand were a reference to the court to which he is being remitted.'

7.2.5 Deferred sentence

Section 1(6A) of the PCCA 1973 provides: 'Notwithstanding any enactment, a court which under this section defers passing sentence on an offender shall not on the same occasion remand him.' Accordingly, a defendant whose sentence is deferred may not be remanded in custody or on bail on the same occasion: see *R* v *Ross* (1988) 86 Cr App R 337.

7.2.6 Permissible periods of remand

7.2.6.1 Remands on bail   Where a defendant is remanded on bail for inquiry or reports under s. 10(4) of the MCA 1980, or for a medical report under s. 30, the maximum permitted period is 28 days. It has been held that this requirement is directory not mandatory, and although it should not be exceeded it does not nullify the court's action when a breach of the rule occurs: *R* v *Manchester City Justices, ex parte Miley and Dynan* (unreported), 16 February 1977 cited in 141 JP Jo 248, 276.

7.2.6.2 Remands in custody   Where a defendant is remanded in custody for inquiry or reports, or for a medical report where applicable, the maximum permitted period of remand is 21 days: MCA 1980, s. 10(4) and s. 30(1), as the case may be.

7.2.6.3 Defendant currently serving a sentence   Where the accused is already serving a custodial sentence, the period of remand in custody is 28 days: MCA 1980, s. 131. This is subject to the same proviso as applies in relation to the remand in custody of an unconvicted defendant (see para. 7.1.4.10, above).

7.2.6.4 Remands to hospital for report   A defendant must not be remanded or further remanded to a hospital for the preparation of a report under s. 35 of the MHA 1983 (see para. 7.2.3.1, above) for more than 28 days at a time or for more than 12 weeks in all. The court may at any time terminate the remand if it appears to that court that it is appropriate to do so.

7.2.7 Duty to notify unrepresented defendants who are denied bail of their right to apply for bail to a higher court

Where a magistrates' court remands a defendant, not represented by counsel or a solicitor, in custody for a medical report under s. 30(1) of the MCA 1980 and issues a full argument certificate under s. 5(6A) of the BA 1976 (see Chapter 5), it must inform the defendant of the right to apply for bail to the Crown Court or to the High Court: BA 1976, s. 5(6)(a). In any other case where it remands a defendant, not represented by counsel or solicitor, in custody it must inform the defendant of the right to apply for bail to the High Court: s. 5(6)(b). This is consistent with the fact that the Crown Court has no jurisdiction to entertain an application for bail by a defendant waiting to be sentenced by a magistrates' court.

The application to the High Court is to a judge in chambers and magistrates customarily make this clear in the formal notification.

7.3 POWERS OF FURTHER REMAND ON FAILURE BY DEFENDANTS IN CUSTODY OR ON BAIL TO APPEAR ON DUE DATE

7.3.1 Illness or accident

If a magistrates' court is satisfied that a defendant who has been remanded (whether on bail or in custody) is unable by reason of illness or accident to appear or be brought before the court on the due date, the court may remand the absent defendant for a further time: MCA 1980, s. 129(1). In such a case the period of the remand may exceed eight clear days. An 'accident' includes the situation where prison authorities cannot produce a defendant because he has been remanded in custody on the same day by another court in respect of other charges: *Re Jenkins* [1997] COD 38, DC. A remand in absence is permissible only if there are solid grounds on which justices can form a reliable opinion that the defendant is unable to attend by reason of accident or illness: (*R v Liverpool City Justices, ex parte Grogan* [1991] JPR 450.

7.3.2 Failure of defendant on bail to appear other than by reason of illness or accident

Where a defendant remanded on bail is unable to appear, but that failure is not by reason of illness or accident, the court may still appoint a later date for an appearance and this will be deemed to be a further remand: MCA 1980, s. 129(3).

7.3.3 Enlargement of surety when defendant on bail fails to appear

Where a defendant is on bail at the time of being precluded from attendance by illness or accident, or for some other reason, the magistrates in appointing a later time for the defendant to appear may enlarge the recognizance of any surety to the later date: MCA 1980, s. 129(2) and (3). If a magistrates' court before which any person is bound by a recognizance to appear enlarges the recognizance to a later time under s. 129 in the person's absence, the court must give the person and any sureties notice thereof: MCR 1981, r. 84(1).

7.4 COMMITTAL TO THE CROWN COURT FOR SENTENCE

7.4.1 The general power to commit for sentence when magistrates' powers are inadequate

7.4.1.1 The basic principle: adults Where a person who is not less than 18 years old is convicted on summary trial of an either-way offence (except for those

either-way offences which must be tried summarily if the value is low (MCA 1980, s. 22) and which are thereby excluded by s. 33) the court may, in accordance with the CJA 1967, s. 56, commit the offender in custody or on bail to the Crown Court for sentence in accordance with the provisions of PCCA 1973, s. 42, and MCA 1980, s. 38(1).

7.4.1.2   Circumstances in which the power may be exercised   Section 38(2) of the MCA 1980 provides that the power may only be exercised if the court is of the opinion:

(a)   that the offence or the combination of the offence and one or more offences associated with it was so serious that greater punishment should be inflicted for the offence than the court has power to impose; or

(b)   in the case of a violent or sexual offence committed by a person who is not less than 21 years old, that a sentence of imprisonment for a term longer than the court has power to impose is necessary to protect the public from serious harm.

(For further consideration see *R* v *Warley Magistrates' Court, ex parte DPP, The Times*, 18 May 1998; see para. 7.4.3.)

7.4.2   General principles on bail or custody on committal

Section 4(2) of the BA 1976 makes it clear that the general right to bail does not apply after conviction: 'This subsection does not apply as respects proceedings on or after a person's conviction of the offence . . .' Whether to commit in custody or on bail is a matter of judicial discretion, but since the exercise of the power of committal is based on the opinion that greater punishment should be imposed than the magistrates have power to inflict it follows that committal for sentence will usually be in custody. In *R* v *Coe* (1969) 53 Cr App R 66, at p. 68, Lord Parker CJ observed: '. . . in the opinion of this court the cases must be rare when justices can properly commit [for sentence] on bail because the whole purpose of committal is to have the accused sent to prison for a longer period than the justices could impose.'

7.4.3   Effect of section 49 of the Criminal Procedure and Investigations Act 1996 and section 51 of the Crime (Sentences) Act 1997

Section 17A of the MCA 1980 (inserted by s. 49 of the CPIA 1996 – plea before venue) and s. 38A of the MCA 1980 (inserted by s. 51 of the Crime (Sentences) Act 1997 – committal for sentence on indication of guilty plea to offence triable either way) provide that a committal for sentence may be in custody or on bail. The sections do not change the general principles set out in para. 7.4.2, above. However, the Justices' Clerks Society sought guidance from Lord Bingham of Cornhill CJ, on:

. . . the criteria governing the decision whether to commit in custody or on bail a defendant committed for sentence and the effect of an indication of guilty plea before the magistrates' court on the extent of credit given, compared with the situation where the guilty plea is not indicated until after committal for trial has taken place. (*Justices' Clerks Society Newsletter*, No. 97/63, 23 December 1997)

In response, Lord Bingham endorsed the following advice:

It is the view of the Council of the Society that the determining criteria should be the defendant's status before committal. Council considers that the authorities usually relied upon are largely based on the need to prevent a defendant going in and out of custody throughout the course of proceedings and that there is no need for a defendant on bail up to committal to be committed in custody unless the court has substantial grounds for believing that the defendant will fail to surrender to the court or will commit further offences (*ibid.*)

The Lord Chief Justice had the opportunity to apply this advice in *R v Rafferty*, *The Times*, 9 April 1998 (judgment given 30 March), in which Thomas J (sitting with Lord Bingham and Smedley J) held:

(a)   that under the procedure introduced by the CPIA 1996, s. 49, a defendant who pleads guilty to an either-way offence before the magistrates' court and is committed to the Crown Court for sentence should normally be entitled to a greater discount on sentence than a defendant who delayed making such a plea until appearing on indictment in the Crown Court; and

(b)   that such a guilty plea did not normally alter the position as to the defendant's bail or remand in custody. In the usual case, when a person who had been on bail entered a guilty plea at that stage, the usual practice should be to continue the bail, even if it were anticipated that a custodial sentence would be imposed by the Crown Court, unless there was good reason for remanding the defendant in custody.

Section 48(1) of the CJPOA 1994 provides:

In determining what sentence to pass on an offender who has pleaded guilty to an offence in proceedings before that or another court a court shall take into account—

(a)   the stage in the proceedings for the offence at which the offender indicated his intention to plead guilty, and

(b)   the circumstances in which this indication was given.

It was observed in a critique of the Act that, having regard to s. 48(1):

An early indication of a guilty plea will count in favour of the defendant . . . The reference to 'that or another court' clearly contemplates that credit should be given to a defendant who is committed to the Crown Court for sentence after pleading guilty in the magistrates' court. The disadvantage of a guilty plea in the magistrates' court will be the consequent loss of unconvicted remand privileges for persons in custody and the loss of the general right to bail (BA 1976, s. 4) for others. (Corre, N., *A Practical Guide to the Criminal Procedure and Investigations Act 1996*, London: Callow Publishing, 1996, p. 55)

Another commentator has criticised *R* v *Rafferty* as without legal justification (James Richardson, *Criminal Law Week*, 1998, 98/14/32).

In *R* v *Warley Magistrates' Court, ex parte DPP*; *R* v *Staines Magistrates' Court, ex parte DPP*; *R* v *North East Suffolk Magistrates' Court, ex parte DPP*, *The Times*, 18 May 1998, the Divisional Court considered the new mode of trial procedure in relation to committal for sentence and gave approval to the following propositions:

(a)   Where magistrates considered their own sentencing powers to be adequate it was not appropriate for them to commit for sentence simply because the case was of a type which they considered ought to be dealt with at a higher level. A magistrates' court had power to commit for sentence only if it was of the opinion that the sentence should be greater than it had power to impose.

(b)   Where the decision whether or not to commit for sentence required the resolution of a dispute as to facts, the magistrates should conduct a hearing to resolve the dispute before sentencing or committing for sentence.

(c)   Where the magistrates were minded to commit for sentence, the defendant should be invited to make representations against that decision and if the court was minded to change its decision the prosecution should be invited to reply.

(d)   Magistrates were entitled to take into consideration all aspects of the defendant's character and antecedents before deciding whether to commit for sentence.

Point (d) was foreshadowed by the following observation by Corre: 'A more principled approach might have been to revert to the conditions which existed before s. 25 of the CJA 1991: a committal for sentence based on the character and antecedents of the offender' (*A Practical Guide to the Criminal Procedure and Investigations Act 1996, loc. cit.*).

In *R* v *Southampton Magistrates' Court, ex parte Sansome* (*sub nom R* v *Eastleigh Magistrates' Court ex parte Sansome*) [1998] Crim LR 595, DC, it was held that:

(a)   magistrates have an unfettered discretion to commit for sentence under s. 38 of the MCA 1980;

(b)   it is immaterial that no new information relating to the offence has been disclosed since their decision to accept jurisdiction; and

(c)   their option to commit for sentence is not restrained by adjourning for a pre-sentence report.

7.4.4   Other powers of committal for sentence

7.4.4.1   Committal for sentence on indicating a guilty plea to an offence triable either way where the defendant has been committed to the Crown Court for trial on a related offence   Section 51 of the Crime (Sentences) Act 1997 has inserted a new section, s. 38A, into the MCA 1980, which empowers a magistrates' court to commit an offender to the Crown Court for sentence following the indication of a guilty plea to an either-way offence, if the court has committed the offender to the Crown Court for trial for one or more related offences. Such a committal may be on bail or in custody.

7.4.4.2   Breach of Crown Court imposed suspended sentence   A magistrates' court *may* commit an offender to be dealt with in respect of breach of a suspended sentence of imprisonment imposed by the Crown Court: PCCA 1973, s. 24(2). The court may, if it thinks fit, commit the offender to the Crown Court in custody or on bail: s. 24(2)(a).

7.4.4.3   Breach of the requirements of a community order imposed by the Crown Court   Schedule 2, Part II, para. 3, to the CJA 1991 provides that where a relevant order (i.e. a probation order, community service order or a curfew order: sch. 2, Part I, para. 1(i)) was made by the Crown Court and a magistrates' court has power to deal with the offender for breach of the order by way of imposing a fine not exceeding £1,000 (sch. 2, Part II, para. 3(1)(a)), or by way of making a community service order (para. 3(1)(b)), or, where the relevant order is a probation order and the case is one to which s. 17 of the CJA 1982 applies, by ordering an offender under the age of 21 who is in breach of a probation order to attend at an attendance centre (para. 3(1)(c)), the offender may instead be committed to custody or released on bail pending appearance before the Crown Court. A young offender who is in breach of the requirements of a supervision order made by the Crown Court may be committed on bail or in custody to the Crown Court: s. 15(3)(c), CYPA 1969, as amended by s. 72, CDA 1998.

7.4.4.4   Power to commit to the Crown Court for breach of a Crown Court conditional discharge   Section 1B(5) of the PCCA 1973 provides that an offender who is subject to a conditional discharge made by the Crown Court and is convicted by a magistrates' court of an offence committed during the period of the conditional discharge may be committed by the magistrates' court to custody or released on bail pending production or appearance before the Crown Court. Where this action is taken the magistrates' court must send the Crown Court a copy of the minute or memorandum of the conviction entered in the register, signed by the clerk of the court by whom the register is kept.

7.4.4.5   Power to commit offender convicted of an offence between release and expiry of a sentence   Subject to s. 25 of the CJPOA 1994, s. 40(3)(b) of the CJA 1991 empowers the magistrates' court to commit an offender convicted of an imprisonable offence committed between the date of release and the expiry of the full term of sentence to the Crown Court in custody or on bail for sentence.

7.4.4.6 Committal under section 56 of the Criminal Justice Act 1967 Where a magistrates' court commits a person in custody or on bail to the Crown Court under any enactment (see below) to which s. 56 of the CJA 1967 applies to be sentenced or otherwise dealt with in respect of an offence, the committing court may:

(a) if the relevant offence is indictable, also commit the offender in custody or on bail as the case may require, to the Crown Court to be dealt with in respect of any other offence whatsoever in respect of which the committing court has power to deal with him (being an offence of which the offender has been convicted by that or any other court); or

(b) if the relevant offence is a summary offence, commit the offender in custody or on bail as the case may require, being either an imprisonable offence or one in respect of which the committing court has a mandatory or discretionary power of disqualification from driving; or

(c) any suspended sentence in respect of which the committing court has power under s. 24(1) of the PCCA 1973 to deal with (see above).

The enactments to which s. 56 of the 1967 Act applies are:

(a) Vagrancy Act 1824 (incorrigible rogues);

(b) MCA 1980, s. 38 (committal for sentence of adults);

(c) PCCA 1973, s. 24(2) (conviction in a magistrates' court of imprisonable offence committed by a person subject to a suspended sentence passed by the Crown Court.

7.4.5 Duty to notify unrepresented defendants of the right to apply to the High Court for bail

Where a defendant who is not represented by counsel or a solicitor is committed to the Crown Court for sentence and the magistrates' court withholds bail, it must inform the defendant of the right to apply for bail to the High Court: BA 1976, s. 5(6)(b). It is not clear why there is no duty to inform such defendants of the right to apply to the Crown Court for bail, since the Crown Court certainly enjoys jurisdiction, under s. 81(1) of the SCA 1981 (see Chapter 8), to grant bail pending sentence to defendants who have been committed for sentence to the Crown Court.

7.5 SENDING DEFENDANTS FOR TRIAL

7.5.1 Committals for trial

Traditionally, examining magistrates inquiring into offences which either were to be tried before the Assizes or could be tried at quarter sessions were required to examine witnesses and record their depositions. If these disclosed a case to answer the defendant would be committed for trial by jury. This basic system remained virtually unchanged for centuries. As an alternative to the taking of live evidence in the compilation of depositions, the CJA 1967 allowed committals to proceed for the first time on the basis of the reading of statements previously taken by the police or other investigators. More radically, defendants could consent to committal without consideration of the written statements. However, defendants remained entitled to a full committal by way of live evidence. The CJAs of 1987 and 1991 introduced schemes for the compulsory transferring of certain classes of case from the magistrates' court to the Crown Court for trial without committal proceedings and without consideration of the evidence. The classes of case in question were serious and complex fraud and those involving child victims or witnesses of certain sex offences or offences of violence (see para. 7.6). At the Crown Court the judge may be invited to consider the evidence before trial and to decide whether there is a case to put the defendant on trial. The next development was the CJPOA 1994, which contained provisions abolishing committal for trial generally and extending the transfer system to all indictable and either-way offences. Because of deficiencies in the provisions and general dissatisfaction with their structure they were never brought into effect, and instead, new measures were introduced by the CPIA 1996, which streamlined the committal process. Henceforth there was no general procedure for the taking of live evidence from witnesses in an adversarial setting. Magistrates could be asked to examine the written evidence and to determine whether the statements disclosed a case to go for trial and the defence could make a 'no case' submission on the strength of the statements. Witnesses who had not given statements to the police could be summoned to appear before the court and could be examined in private without the parties being present. This system has now been further streamlined by the CDA 1998, which in the case of indictable offences now abolishes even the limited rights afforded by the 1996 Act (see para. 7.5.5, below).

7.5.2   Committal for trial in custody or on bail

Section 6(3) of the MCA 1980 provides that except where a person is charged with treason, a magistrates' court may, subject to s. 4 of the BA 1976, commit a defendant for trial:

(a)   in custody, that is to say, by committing the defendant to custody there to be safely kept until delivered in due course of law; or
(b)   on bail in accordance with the BA 1976, to surrender for trial before the Crown Court.

(See *R* v *Lincoln Magistrates' Court, ex parte Mawer* [1995] Crim LR 878.) A warrant of commitment directing a prisoner governor to detain a person until 'delivered in due course of law' is understood to refer to delivery to the Crown Court (*Olutu* v *Home Office and another*, *The Times*, 11 December 1996).

7.5.3 Duty to notify unrepresented defendants of their right to apply for bail to the Crown Court or the High Court

Defendants who without being represented by counsel or a solicitor are committed for trial in custody must be informed by the magistrates' court that they may apply to the High Court or the Crown Court for bail: BA 1976, s. 5(6)(b), Bail Act 1976. The application to the High Court is to a judge in chambers and this is customarily made clear.

7.5.4 Power to vary conditions on application after committal at any time before surrender to the Crown Court

Section 3(8) of the BA 1976, as amended by sch. 12 to the CLA 1977, provides that where a magistrates' court has committed a person on bail to the Crown Court for trial, it may on application:

(a)   by or on behalf of the person granted bail; or
(b)   by the prosecutor or a constable;

vary the conditions of bail or impose conditions in respect of bail which has been granted unconditionally. The effect of this provision is that following committal for trial, when in all other respects the magistrates' court has become *functus officio*, the court retains a jurisdiction to entertain applications, made by both defence and prosecution, to vary bail conditions. The limits of that jurisdiction were considered by the Divisional Court in *R* v *Lincoln Magistrates' Court, ex parte Mawer* [1995] Crim LR 878. The applicant sought judicial review of the magistrates' decision that they had no jurisdiction to vary conditions for bail under s. 3(8) of the 1976 Act where a defendant who had been committed for trial on bail had been readmitted to bail by the Crown Court on the same terms as those imposed by the magistrates. It was held that between committal for trial on bail and surrender to custody at the Crown Court in compliance with the terms of that bail, s. 3(8) conferred a concurrent jurisdiction on both the magistrates' court and the Crown Court to vary conditions. However, once the defendant surrenders to the Crown Court and is again released on bail the jurisdiction of the magistrates' court ceases and only the Crown Court enjoys jurisdiction to vary conditions.

7.5.5 Sending defendants charged with indictable offences forthwith to the Crown Court for trial (Crime and Disorder Act 1998)

7.5.5.1 Automatic sending of defendants for trial without possession or disclosure of sufficient evidence   Under s. 51(1) and (11) of the CDA 1998, where an adult (i.e. a person aged 18 or over: s. 51(12)) appears or is brought before a magistrates' court charged with an indictable only offence, the court must send that defendant forthwith to the Crown Court for trial:

(a) for that offence; and

(b) for an either-way offence, or a summary offence punishable with imprisonment or by obligatory or discretionary disqualification, where the offence appears to the court to be related to the indictable-only offence.

In contrast with traditional committal for trial, the prosecution need not serve on the court or the defence, nor need they even be in possession of, statements disclosing sufficient evidence to put the adult defendant on trial for an indictable offence, if the magistrates are to send the defendant forthwith to the Crown Court for trial under s. 48 of the CDA 1998. That the defendant is charged with an indictable offence and is brought or appears before the magistrates' court is now enough to require the court to send the case to the Crown Court for trial. Thus, although the defendant will have been charged on the basis that the police assembled, or purport to have assembled, sufficient material for that purpose and the case papers will have been reviewed by the CPS, the case can be sent to the Crown Court without any of that material being served on the defence or produced before the court. The Crime and Disorder Act 1998 (Service of Prosecution Evidence) Regulations 1998 (SI 1998 No. 3115) provides that copies of the documents containing the evidence shall be served on the defendant and given to the Crown Court within one year after the date that the defendant was sent for trial. It is difficult to see how this regulation will achieve the purported aim of s. 51, which is to expedite the administration of justice. The latest date for which the first Crown Court appearance of a person sent for trial shall be listed is, for defendants on bail, not later than 28 days after the Crown Court received the notice specifying the offence or offences required to be sent to it under s. 51(7), and 8 days for those in custody: r. 24ZA, CCR 1982, as inserted by Crown Court (Modification) Rules 1998 (SI 1998 No. 3047).

Crown Court judges may be required to consider whether the written statements produced before the court disclose a case warranting the defendant being put on trial. This duty will therefore join that of presiding over pleas and directions hearings, and will increase still further, and significantly, all that is involved in preparing for these duties. In the House of Lords, Baroness Anelay of St Johns pointed out (HL Deb, vol. 586, coll. 551–552) that the problem with s. 51 of the CDA 1998 is that senior judges will have less time to spend on trials if they are to undertake such case management. This will cause delay in the disposal of cases and a tendency to allocate trials to recorders and assistant recorders. Further, the critical commentator might be minded to observe that there seems little reason now not to 'streamline' the whole process even further, simply by requiring custody officers before whom a defendant is charged with an indictable offence to send that defendant 'forthwith' to the Crown Court for trial.

7.5.5.2 Provision for sending to the Crown Court in custody or on bail Section 49(1) of the CDA 1998 provides that subject to the BA 1976, s. 4, the MCA 1980, s. 41, regulations made under the Prosecution of Offences Act

1985, s. 22, and CJPOA 1994, s. 25, the court may send a person for trial under s. 51:

(a)   in custody, that is to say, by committing the person to custody to be safely kept until delivered in due course of law; or

(b)   on bail in accordance with the BA 1976, that is to say, by directing the person to appear before the Crown Court for trial.

7.5.5.3   Provision for postponed taking of recognizance   Section 52(2)(a) of the 1998 Act provides that where the person's release on bail is conditional on his providing one or more sureties and in accordance with the BA 1976, s. 8(3) the court fixes the amount in which a surety is to be bound with a view to entering into a recognizance subsequently in accordance with s. 8(4), (5) or (6), the court must in the meantime make an order committing the person to custody.

7.5.5.4   Defendants jointly charged with an either way offence related to an indictable offence charged against one of them   Section 52(3) of the CDA 1998 provides that where an adult charged with an indictable offence is sent forthwith to the Crown Court for trial and is charged jointly with a second adult with an either-way offence related to the indictable offence for which the first adult was sent to the Crown Court, the second adult may also be sent forthwith to the Crown Court for trial.

7.5.5.5   Child jointly charged with an adult sent forthwith to the Crown Court for trial   Section 52(5) of the 1998 Act enacts the power to send forthwith to the Crown Court for trial a child or young person jointly charged with an adult sent forthwith to the Crown Court for an indictable only offence.

7.6   TRANSFER FOR TRIAL

The CJA 1987 replaced committal for trial by the procedure of transfer to the Crown Court for trial in cases of serious or complex fraud. In cases involving child victims or witnesses of certain sex offences or offences of violence, transfer replaced committal by virtue of the CJA 1991 s. 53. Since many offences amounting to 'serious' fraud and many sexual offences are not of their nature indictable only they will not come within the new provisions for 'sending forthwith' under the CDA 1998 and so the transfer provisions will continue to apply to them.

7.6.1   Serious Fraud

7.6.1.1   Notice of transfer   Section 4(1) of the 1987 Act provides that where a person has been charged with an indictable offence and, before the magistrates' court in whose jurisdiction the offence has been charged begins to inquire into the case as examining justices, an authority designated by s. 4(2), or an officer of any such authority acting on behalf of that authority, gives the court a notice of transfer certifying that, in the opinion of the authority, or an officer of the authority acting on the authority's behalf, the evidence of the offence:

    (a)   would be sufficient for the person charged to be committed for trial; and
    (b)   reveals a case of fraud of such seriousness or complexity that it is appropriate that the management of the case should without delay be taken over by the Crown Court,

the functions of the magistrates' court shall cease in relation to the case, except as otherwise provided by s. 5 of the Act. The authorities referred to as 'designated authorities' in s. 4(1) are the Director of Public Prosecutions, the Director of the Serious Fraud Office, the Commissioners of Inland Revenue, the Commissioners of Customs and Excise and the Secretary of State: CJA 1987, s. 4(2). The notice of transfer must specify the proposed place of trial, and in selecting that place the designated authority must have regard to the considerations to which s. 7 of the MCA 1980 requires a magistrates' court committing a person for trial to have regard when selecting the place at which the person is to be tried: CJA 1987, s. 5(1).

7.6.1.2   Continuation of existing custody order, or release on bail, following notice of transfer   If a magistrates' court has previously remanded in custody a person to whom a notice of transfer relates, then, subject to s. 4 of the BA 1976 and regulations relating to the prosecution of offences made under s. 22 of the Prosecution of Offences Act 1985, s. 5(3) of the CJA 1987 empowers the court:

    (a)   to order that the accused must be safely kept in custody until delivered in due course of law; or
    (b)   to release the accused on bail in accordance with the BA 1976, that is by directing the accused to appear before the Crown Court for trial.

Where a person in respect of whom notice of transfer has been given is granted bail under s. 5(3) by the magistrates' court to which notice of transfer was given, the clerk of the court must give notice thereof in writing to the governor of the prison or remand centre to which the said person would have been committed by that court if there had been a committal in custody for trial: r. 3(1), Magistrates' Courts (Notice of Transfer) Rules 1988 (SI 1988 No. 1701), made in exercise of powers conferred by ss. 144 and 145 of the MCA 1980. Rather bafflingly, r. 3(1) also provides that where notice of transfer is given in respect of a *corporation,* the clerk of the court to which notice of transfer was given shall give notice thereof to the governor of the prison to which would be committed a male over 21 by that court in custody for trial. The relevance to corporations of a procedural provision relating to bail seems obscure, to say the least.

7.6.1.3 Release on bail subject to the subsequent provision of sureties
Where the accused to whom a notice of transfer relates is to be released on bail
conditionally on the provision of one or more surety or sureties and, in accordance
with s. 8(3) of the BA 1976, the court fixes the amount in which the surety is to
be bound with a view to entering into a recognizance subsequently in accordance
with s. 8(4), (5) or (6), the court shall in the meantime make an order for the
accused's safe keeping in custody until delivery in due course of law: s. 5(3).

**7.6.1.4 Order made in the absence of the accused for continuation of
previous custody order or admission to bail following notice of transfer**
Where an accused is in custody and a notice of transfer is given, the magistrates'
court may order the accused to be kept in custody or released on bail in accordance
with the CJA 1987 s. 5(3) without the accused being brought before the court in
any case in which by virtue of s. 128(3A) of the MCA 1980 it would have power
further to order a remand on an adjournment under that provision (see para. 7.1.4.6,
above): CJA 1987, s. 5(4). However, this is permitted only where the person
charged has given written consent and where the court is satisfied that, when the
consent was given, the accused knew that the notice of transfer had been issued:
CJA 1987, s. 5(5).

**7.6.1.5 Notice of transfer following remand on bail: duty to appear at the
Crown Court replaces duty to appear at the magistrates' court unless
otherwise stated in the notice**   Where a notice of transfer is given after a person
to whom it relates has been remanded on bail to appear before a magistrates' court
on an appointed day, the requirement for appearance ceases on the giving of the
notice, unless the notice states that it is to continue: CJA 1987, s. 5(6). A person
no longer so required to appear before a magistrates' court must appear before the
Crown Court at the place specified by the notice of transfer as the proposed place
of trial, or at any place substituted for it under s. 76 of the SCA 1981: CJA 1987,
s. 5(7).

**7.6.1.6 Notice of transfer following remand on bail: powers and duties of the
magistrates' court**   If the accused is already on bail when a notice of transfer is
given and the notice states that the requirement in s. 5(6) of the 1987 Act for the
accused to appear is to continue (see para. 7.6.1.5) then, when the accused appears
before the magistrates' court, the court has the powers and duty conferred on it by
s. 5(3), subject as there provided: CJA 1987, s. 5(7A)(a), inserted by the CJA 1988.
The court also has the power to enlarge, in the surety's absence, a recognizance
conditioned in accordance with s. 128(4)(a) of the MCA 1980 so that the surety is
bound to secure that the person charged appears also before the Crown Court: CJA
1987, s. 5(7A)(b). Where a person in respect of whom a transfer has been given
is granted bail under s. 5(3) or (7A) of the 1987 Act by the magistrates' court to
which notice of transfer was given, the clerk of the court must give notice thereof
in writing to the governor of the prison or remand centre to which the said person

would have been committed by that court if he had been committed in custody for trial: r. 3(1), Magistrates' Courts (Notice of Transfer) Rules 1988.

7.6.1.7   Notice to prison governor, etc   Where a notice of transfer is given by or on behalf of a designated authority, a copy of the notice must be given by or on behalf of the authority to any person who has custody of any person to whom the notice of transfer relates: Criminal Justice Act 1987 (Notice of Transfer) Regulations 1988 (SI 1988 No. 1691) reg. 6. A copy of the notice in Form 2 in the Schedule to the Regulations must also be served on the custodian: *ibid.*

7.6.1.8   Notice where person removed to hospital   Where a transfer direction has been given by the Secretary of State under s. 47 or s. 48 of the MHA 1983 in respect of a person remanded in custody by a magistrates' court and, before the direction ceases to have effect, notice of transfer is given in respect of that person, the clerk of the court to which notice of transfer was given shall give notice thereof in writing:

(a)   to the governor of the prison to which that person would have been committed by that court if the person had been committed for trial in custody; and
(b)   to the managers of the hospital where the person is detained: r. 4, Magistrates' Courts (Notice of Transfer) Rules 1988.

(See Chapter 11, para. 11.2.4.)

7.6.1.9   Application to the Crown Court to vary or impose conditions of bail   Where a magistrates' court has granted bail in criminal proceedings and a notice of transfer is given under s. 4 of the Act of 1987, the magistrates' court may, on application by or on behalf of the person to whom bail was granted, or by the prosecutor or a constable, vary the conditions of bail or impose conditions in respect of bail previously granted unconditionally: BA 1976, s. 3(8) and (8A) BA 1976 (latter subsection inserted by the CJA 1987). A person who intends to make such an application to a magistrates' court must give notice thereof in writing to the clerk of the court to which the application is to be made, and to the designated authority or the defendant, as the case may be, and to any sureties concerned: r. 5(1), 1988 Rules. Where on such an application a magistrates' court varies or imposes any conditions of bail, the clerk of the court must send to the appropriate officer of the Crown Court a copy of the record made in pursuance of s. 5 of the BA 1976 relating to such variation or imposition of conditions: r. 5(2). It is assumed, as in the case of committal for trial, that the jurisdiction of the magistrates' court following notice of transfer to entertain applications for variation or imposition of conditions exists concurrently with that of the Crown Court but lasts only until surrender by the defendant to bail at the Crown Court (see para. 7.5.4 above).

7.6.1.10 Relevant documents to be sent to the Crown Court As soon as practicable after a magistrates' court to which notice of transfer has been given has discharged the functions reserved to it under s. 4(1) of the 1987 Act, the clerk of the magistrates' court shall send to the appropriate officer of the Crown Court a copy of the record made in pursuance of s. 5 of the BA 1976 relating to the grant or withholding of bail in respect of the accused and any recognizance entered into by any person as surety for the accused together with a statement of any enlargement thereof: r. 7, 1988 Rules.

7.6.2 Cases involving children

7.6.2.1 Notice of transfer If a person has been charged with an offence to which s. 32(2) of the CJA 1988 applies (sexual offences and offences involving violence or cruelty) and the Director of Public Prosecutions is of the opinion:

(a) that the evidence of the offence would be sufficient for the person charged to be committed for trial;
(b) that a child who is alleged:

(i) to be a person against whom the offence was committed, or
(ii) to have witnessed the commission of the offence,
will be called as a witness at the trial; and

(c) that, for the purpose of avoiding any prejudice to the welfare of the child, the case should be taken over and proceeded with without delay by the Crown Court;

a notice of transfer certifying that opinion may be given by or on behalf of the Director to the magistrates' court in whose jurisdiction the offence has been charged: CJA 1991, s. 53(1). On the giving of a notice of transfer the functions of the magistrates' court cease in relation to the case except as provided, *inter alia*, by paras 2 and 3 of sch. 6 to the Act: CJA 1991, s. 53(3). The meaning of the term 'child' is given in s. 53(6).

7.6.2.2 Time for the giving of the notice of transfer The notice of transfer must be given before the magistrates' court begins to inquire into the case as examining justices: CJA 1991, s. 53(2).

7.6.2.3 Continuation of existing custody order, or release on bail, following notice of transfer If a magistrates' court has remanded in custody a defendant to whom a notice of transfer relates, sch. 6, para. 2(1), to the 1991 Act provides that the court shall have power, subject to s. 4 of the BA 1976, s. 25 of the CJPOA 1994, and regulations under s. 22 of the Prosecution of Offences Act 1985:

(a)   to order that the defendant shall be safely kept in custody until delivered in due course of law; or

(b)   to release the defendant on bail in accordance with the BA 1976, that is to say, by directing the defendant to appear before the Crown Court for trial.

7.6.2.4   Release on bail subject to the subsequent provision of sureties
Where under CJA 1991, sch. 6, para. 2(1)(b) the accused to whom a notice of transfer relates is to be released on bail conditionally on the provision of one or more surety or sureties and, in accordance with s. 8(3) of the BA 1976, the court fixes the amount in which the surety is to be bound with a view to entering into a recognizance subsequently in accordance with s. 8(4), (5) or (6), the court shall in the meantime make an order under sch. 6, para. 2(1)(a) for the accused's safe keeping in custody until delivery in due course of law: CJA 1991, sch. 6, para. 2(2).

7.6.2.5   Order made in the absence of the accused for continuation of previous custody order or admission to bail following notice of transfer
Where an accused is in custody and a notice of transfer is given, the magistrates' court may order the accused to be kept in custody or released on bail in accordance with the CJA 1991, sch. 6, para. 2(1) without the accused being brought before the court in any case in which by virtue of s. 128(3A) of the MCA 1980 it would have power further to order a remand on an adjournment under that provision (see para. 7.1.4.6, above): sch. 6, para. 2(3). However, this is permitted only where the person charged has given written consent and where the court is satisfied that, when the consent was given, the accused knew that the notice of transfer had been issued: sch. 6, para. 2(4).

7.6.2.6   Notice of transfer following remand on bail: duty to appear at the Crown Court replaces duty to appear at the magistrates' court unless otherwise stated in the notice   Where a notice of transfer is given after a person to whom it relates has been remanded on bail to appear before a magistrates' court on an appointed day, the requirement for appearance ceases on the giving of the notice, unless the notice states that it is to continue: CJA 1991, sch. 6, para. 2(5). A person no longer so required to appear before a magistrates' court must appear before the Crown Court at the place specified by the notice of transfer as the proposed place of trial or at any place substituted for it under s. 76 of the SCA 1981: CJA 1991, sch. 6, para. 2(6).

7.6.2.7   Notice of transfer following remand on bail: powers and duties of the magistrates' court   If the accused is already on bail when a notice of transfer is given and the notice states that the requirement in sch. 6, para. 2(5) for the accused to appear is to continue (see para. 7.6.2.7) then, when the accused appears before the magistrates' court, the court has the powers and duty conferred on it by sch. 6, para. 2(1), subject as there provided: CJA 1991, sch. 6, para. 2(7)(a). The court also has the power to enlarge, in the surety's absence, a recognizance conditioned in accordance with s. 128(4)(a) of the MCA 1980 so that the surety is bound to secure that the person charged appears also before the Crown Court: sch. 6, para. 2(7)(b). Where a person in respect of whom a transfer has been given is granted bail under para. 2(1) or 2(7) of sch. 6 to the Act of 1991 by the magistrates' court to which notice of transfer was given, the clerk of the court must give notice thereof in writing to the governor of the prison or remand centre to which the said person would have been committed by that court if he had been committed in custody for trial: r. 3, Magistrates' Courts (Notice of Transfer) (Children's Evidence) Rules 1992 (SI 1992 No. 2070), made under s. 144 of the MCA 1980.

7.6.2.8 Notice to prison governor, etc Where a notice of transfer is served by or on behalf of the Director, a copy of the notice must be given by or on behalf of the Director to any person who has custody of any person to whom the notice of transfer relates: reg. 5, Criminal Justice Act 1991 (Notice of Transfer) Regulations 1992 (SI 1992 No. 1670), made by the Attorney-General in exercise of powers conferred by the 1991 Act, s. 53(5) and sch. 6, para. 4. A copy of the notice in Form 2 in the Schedule to the Regulations must also be served on the custodian: reg. 5.

7.6.2.9 Notice where person removed to hospital Where a transfer direction has been given by the Secretary of State under s. 47 or 48 of the MHA 1983 in respect of a person remanded in custody by a magistrates' court and, before the direction ceases to have effect, notice of transfer is given in respect of that person, the clerk of the court to which notice of transfer was given shall give notice thereof in writing:

(a) to the governor of the prison to which that person would have been committed by that court if the person had been committed for trial in custody; and
(b) to the managers of the hospital where the person is detained: r. 4, Magistrates' Courts (Notice of Transfer) (Children's Evidence) Rules 1992.

(See Chapter 11, para. 11.2.4.)

7.6.2.10 Relevant documents to be sent to the Crown Court As soon as practicable after a magistrates' court to which notice of transfer has been given has discharged the functions reserved to it under s. 53(1) of the CJA 1991, the clerk of the magistrates' court shall send to the appropriate officer of the Crown Court a copy of the record made in pursuance of s. 5 of the BA 1976 relating to the grant or withholding of bail in respect of the accused and any recognizance entered into by any person as surety for the accused together with a statement of any enlargement thereof: r. 7, Magistrates' Courts (Notice of Transfer) Rules 1988.

7.6.2.11 Variation of conditions of bail Although it will have been noticed that the provisions for transfer in relation to cases involving children follow closely those relating to the transfer of serious fraud cases, there is no provision in relation to children for the variation of arrangements for bail conditions as there is for serious fraud set out in r. 5 of the 1988 Rules (see para. 7.6.1.9). The reasons for this hiatus are unclear. However, there is no doubt that, as in the case of serious fraud, the magistrates' court does have jurisdiction to vary bail on an application made by the defendant or the prosecution following notice of transfer. Section 3(8A) of the BA 1976 provides that '[w]here a notice of transfer is given under a relevant transfer provision, subsection (8) above shall have effect in relation to a person in relation to whose case the notice is given as if he had been committed on bail to the Crown Court for trial'. The 'relevant transfer provision' includes s. 53 of the CJA 1991: BA 1976, s. 3, 2nd subs. (10).

7.7 POWERS RELATING TO BAIL WHICH MAY BE EXERCISED BY A SINGLE JUSTICE OR A JUSTICES' CLERK

7.7.1 The single justice

Section 49(1) of the CDA 1998 enables a single justice to exercise the following powers relating to bail:

(a) to extend bail, or to impose or vary conditions of bail (s. 49(1)(a));

(b) to request a medical report and, for that purpose, to remand the accused in custody or on bail (s. 49(1)(f));

(c) where a person has been granted police bail to appear at a magistrates' court, to appoint an earlier time for appearance (s. 49(1)(i));

(d) to extend, with the consent of the accused, a custody time limit or an overall time limit (s. 49(1)(j)).

Paragraph (d) must now be considered in the light of *R* v *Manchester Crown Court, ex parte McDonald*; *R* v *Leeds Crown Court, ex parte Hunt*; *R* v *Winchester Crown Court, ex parte Wilson and Mason, The Times*, 19 November 1998, CA (see generally Chapter 12).

7.7.2 The justices' clerk

Section 49(2)(a) CDA 1998 provides that rules made under s. 144 of the MCA 1980 may provide that any of the powers above which may be exercised by a single justice may, subject to any specified restrictions or conditions, be done by a justices' clerk.

Section 49(3) makes it clear that such rules shall not authorise a justices' clerk:

(a) without the consent of the prosecutor and the accused, to extend bail on conditions other than those (if any) previously imposed, or to impose or vary conditions of bail (s. 49(3)(a)); or

(b)   to remand the accused in custody for the purposes of a medical report, or without the consent of the prosecutor and the accused, to remand the accused on bail for those purposes on conditions other than those (if any) previously imposed (s. 49(3)(c)).

Although s. 49(3) is prohibitive in terms justices' clerks in a limited number of petty sessions areas and petty sessional divisions now enjoy certain limited powers of a quasi-judicial nature. The Magistrates' Courts (Miscellaneous Amendments) Rules 1998 (SI 1998 No. 2167) amend the Justices' Clerks Rules 1970 (SI 1970 No. 231) so that at an early administrative hearing a justices' clerk is empowered under s. 50, CDA 1998—

(a)   to extend bail on the same conditions as those (if any) previously imposed, or, with the consent of the prosecutor and the accused, to impose or vary conditions of bail (para. 19);
(b)   to request a medical report and, for that purpose, to remand the accused on bail on the same conditions as those (if any) previously imposed, or, with the consent of the prosecutor and the accused, on other conditions (para. 24);
(c)   to remit an offender to another court for sentence (para. 25);
(d)   where a person has been granted police bail to appear at a magistrates' court, to appoint an earlier time for the person's appearance (para. 26).

The Government originally proposed wider powers than these but in the face of opposition for the time being opted for a narrower scope of regime. However, it is clear that they remain committed to bestowing on justices' clerks a more ambitious range of powers in accordance with their original proposal, as is evident from the following statement:

[M]agistrates have neither the detailed background knowledge of law and procedure, nor the confidence, which enables stipendiaries or professionally qualified clerks to take the type of robust decision necessary to drive the case forward. (*The Review of Delay in the Criminal Justice System*, London: Home Office, 1997, p. 24)

In particular it is likely that they will grant powers enabling clerks to extend custody and overall time limits with the consent of the accused (although any such proposal would have to be considered in the light of *Ex parte McDonald, supra*). A significant factor in implementing such a scheme may be the fact that Lord Bingham of Cornhill, the Lord Chief Justice, during the second reading of the Crime and Disorder Bill in the House of Lords, described this as 'probably . . . [a power] which can quite unobjectionably be exercised by a justices' clerk' (HL Deb, vol. 584, cols 561–562, 16 December 1997). Whether this opinion coheres with the relevant part of Lord Bingham's judgment in *Ex parte McDonald* is perhaps debatable (see para 12.5.7).

7.8   USE OF LIVE TELEVISION LINKS AT PRELIMINARY HEARINGS

Section 57(1) of the CDA 1998 provides that in any proceedings for an offence, a court may, after hearing representations from the parties, direct that the accused shall be treated as being present in the court for any particular hearing before the start of the trial if held in custody in a prison or other institution during that hearing and whether by means of a live television link or otherwise able to see and hear the court and to be seen and be heard by it. The section follows a recommendation in the *Review of Prison Service Security in England and Wales and the Escape from Parkhurst Prison on Tuesday 3rd January 1995*, Cm 3020, London: HMSO, 1995, paras 4–36 to 4–38, and in *Reducing Remand Delays*, London: Home Office, 1997, paras. 34–35.

7.9   RESEARCH FINDINGS ON DECISION-MAKING IN THE MAGISTRATES' COURT

7.9.1   Introduction

In 'An Essay on the Importance and Neglect of the Magistracy' [1997] Crim LR 627, Penny Darbyshire argues that the jury romantics, notably the Bar, who in Blackstonian rhetoric, hail the jury as guardian of civil liberties, are uttering dangerous, deceptive, distracting nonsense. The magistrates' court is the central criminal forum, dealing with at least 95 per cent of criminal cases, yet it is neglected by judges, law makers, lawyers, academics and journalists. As Lord Bingham of Cornhill, the Lord Chief Justice, has stated: '[T]he magistrates' courts are the work-horses of the criminal justice system' (*R v Hereford Magistrates' Court, ex parte Rowlands* [1997] 2 WLR 854). These 'work-horses' have to make important and difficult decisions about the liberty of unconvicted persons. The bail decision has been described as 'an exercise in risk assessment' (Burrows, J., *et al.*, 'Improving Bail Decisions: The Bail Process Project, Phase I,' Research and Planning Unit Paper 90, London: Home Office, 1994, p. 13).

7.9.2   Information identified as important in remand decisions

In research by Morgan and Henderson for the Home Office, magistrates and others involved in pre-trial, namely custody officers, CPS prosecutors, defence solicitors, court clerks and probation officers, were asked in hypothetical cases to identify the most important information in remand decisions: Morgan, P., and Henderson, P., *Remand Decisions and Offending on Bail: Evaluation of the Bail Process Project*, Home Office Research and Statistics Directorate Research Study No. 184, London: Home Office, 1998, pp. 27–28.) The results were as follows:

(a)   *Information regarding risk of further offences.* In order of importance the most important information was considered to be:

- the defendant's criminal record
- current offence and the harm inflicted
- housing situation
- likely sentence if convicted
- substance abuse
- previous record while on bail
- employment status
- family ties
- community ties or criminal associations.

(b) Information regarding risk of failing to surrender. In order of importance the most important information was considered to be:

- likely sentence if convicted
- current offence and the harm inflicted
- housing situation
- family ties
- criminal record (related to likely sentence)
- previous record while on bail
- employment status
- substance abuse.

7.9.3   Factors associated with the bail/custody decision

An analysis of nearly 4,000 court remand decisions shows the following to be the most important factors in the decision whether or not to grant bail (in order of importance):

- address status (whether the defendant was homeless or not)
- type of offence currently charged
- bail history
- whether the defendant had served a custodial offence
- gender (a marginal consideration only).

(Morgan and Henderson, *op. cit.*, p. 38.)

7.9.4   The influence of other agencies on court decisions

7.9.4.1   Police   Morgan and Henderson (*op. cit.*, p. 38) observe that the police bail/custody decision clearly influences the later decision made by the court. One study found that 81 per cent of those granted bail by the police were granted unconditional bail: Hucklesby, A., 'Remand Decision Makers,' [1997] Crim LR 269, at p. 273. The author of the study concludes that 'neither the magistrates nor the CPS appear to question police decisions to release defendants on bail'. The same study found that of those detained in police custody, 36 per cent were remanded in custody, 53 per cent were granted conditional bail, and only 7 per cent were granted unconditional bail. Another study found that of those granted bail by the police, the CPS had no objection to unconditional bail in 92 per cent of cases, 7 per cent were granted conditional bail and 1 per cent were remanded in custody: Morgan and Henderson, *op. cit.*, p. 35. The same study found that of those detained in police custody, the CPS recommended conditional bail in 46 per cent of such cases, a remand in custody in 48 per cent of such cases, and unconditional bail in 6 per cent of such cases (*op. cit.*, p. 75).

7.9.4.2 Crown Prosecution Service Hucklesby observed that the CPS were one of the most influential decision makers in the remand process (*op. cit.*, p. 277). She found that in 95 per cent of cases mentioned in para. 7.9.4.1 which the CPS made a remand request where the defendant was present in court, the magistrates acceded to that request (*op. cit.*, p. 275). Another study found that when the CPS had no objection to bail, the court granted it in 99 per cent of cases (Morgan and Henderson, *op. cit.*, p. 36). When the CPS recommended conditional bail, the court agreed in 89 per cent of cases. The study found that there was least agreement when the CPS recommended a remand in custody. The court agreed in 75 per cent of cases but granted bail, usually with conditions, in 25 per cent of cases.

7.9.4.3 Defence advocates Hucklesby suggests that '[t]he defence also plays an important rôle in the decision making' (*op. cit.*, at p. 278). This rôle takes several forms:

(a) It may take the form of not contesting remand hearings, either by not applying for bail or by pre-hearing negotiation resulting in the CPS not objecting to bail. In only 9 per cent of cases observed by Hucklesby was the outcome of the hearing contested in court (*op. cit.*, p. 271). An important part of these negotiations was the use of conditions as a bargaining tool to prevent a CPS application for a custodial remand: Hucklesby, A., 'Bail or Jail? The Practical Operation of the Bail Act 1976' (1996) 23(2) J Law Soc 213, at p. 228.

(b) It may take the form of making a bail application. Hucklesby found that in 30 per cent of such cases bail was granted ('Remand Decision Makers', p. 279). Such applications were more likely to be made on the defendant's first appearance. Hucklesby suggests that the reason why an application was made in only just over half of cases where the CPS recommended a remand in custody is because the defendant had already used two statutory bail applications and there had been no change in circumstances ('Remand Decision Makers', p. 278).

7.9.4.4 Court clerks There is no evidence to suggest that court clerks directly assist remand decisions but they indirectly affect the practical operation of the remand process by the way they conduct themselves in and out of court: Hucklesby, A., 'Bail or Jail? The Magistrates' Decision,' unpublished PhD thesis,

University of Glamorgan, 1994, p. 156. They may do this by, for example, their selection of the composition of the bench and the way in which they train magistrates (*ibid.*).

7.9.4.5 Bail information schemes The purpose of bail information schemes is to provide:

> . . . the CPS with the information that will aid them in their remand request to the court. Brief, factual details, usually consisting of a statement verifying that the defendant has an address s/he can stay at if given bail, are provided to the CPS as well as defence solicitors who, it is hoped, take this information into account in making their recommendations and applications to the court. Ultimately, by affecting remand decisions, bail information schemes aim to reduce unnecessary remands in custody. (Lloyd, C., *Bail Information Schemes: practice and effect*, Home Office Research and Planning Unit Paper No. 69, London: Home Office, 1992, cited in Hucklesby, op cit, para. 7.9.4.4, p. 336)

Bail information schemes appear to affect the remand decision in two ways:

(a)   The independently verified information obtained by the schemes influences CPS decision-making: Godson, D., and Mitchell, C., *Bail Information Schemes in English Magistrates' Courts: A Review of the Data*, London: Inner London Probation Service, 1991, cited in Hucklesby, *op. cit.*, p. 337.

(b)   They have an effect on the success of a defence application for bail: Godson and Mitchell, *op. cit.*, cited in *ibid.*)

Hucklesby found that, although 'a relatively large number of professionals involved in the remand process have little, if any, knowledge of the existence or objectives of the BISs', respondents perceived the scheme which was operating in one of the courts she monitored to be reducing the numbers remanded in custody as well as saving court time by decreasing the number of contested bail applications (*op. cit.*, pp. 341–342). A difficulty identified by Morgan and Henderson is whether negative information, or information which would not support the defendant in seeking bail, should be revealed (*op. cit.*, p. 78). The police were concerned that, if the bail information officer obtained such information, it should be made available to the CPS or the court. The research found that information that would not favour bail came to light in 12 per cent of cases (*ibid.*). Lloyd suggested that if negative information were passed on to the court through the CPS, this would increase the confidence of the CPS in the scheme (*op. cit.*, cited in Hucklesby, PhD thesis, p. 340). A Bail Information Officer interviewed by the Home Office thought 'that enough negative information was provided by the police', but stated that she would provide negative information to the court if there was a serious risk to the public (Lloyd, p. 27, cited *ibid.*). The most common type of information provided by Bail Information Officers is details of alternative accommodation (46 per cent) and details of home circumstances and family (32 per cent): Morgan and Henderson, *op. cit.*, p. 78. Hucklesby argues that the fact that the information gathered by bail information schemes goes to the CPS rather than to the court 'provides evidence for both the importance of the CPS decision in the remand process and a move towards informal executive decision making' ('Remand Decision Makers' [1997] Crim LR 269, at p. 277). A further move in this direction is illustrated by the decision in *R* v *Rafferty*, *The Times*, 9 April 1998, in which it was held that the defendant's bail status after committal for sentence should generally be the same as that before committal. This means that defendants who are committed for sentence following the indication of a plea of guilty on their first appearance before the court will never have their bail status considered by the magistrates. The effective decision-maker in such cases will be the police.

8 The Jurisdiction of the Crown Court

8.1 CATEGORIES OF PERSON TO WHOM THE CROWN COURT MAY GRANT BAIL

Section 81(1) of the SCA 1981 (as amended) empowers the Crown Court, subject to s. 25 of the CJPOA 1994, to grant bail to any person in the categories listed immediately below. These are defendants:

(a) sent to the Crown Court in custody, i.e., persons who have been committed in custody to appear before the Crown Court or in relation to whose case a notice of transfer has been given under a relevant transfer provision, i.e., CJA 1987, s. 4 (serious or complex fraud) and CJA 1991, s. 53 (offences of a sexual, violent or cruel nature involving a child witness or child victim) or who have been sent in custody to the Crown Court for trial under s. 51 of the CDA 1998 (as inserted by sch. 8, para. 48, to the CDA 1998);

(b) appealing against a magistrates' court custodial sentence, i.e., persons who have been given a custodial sentence by a magistrates' court, and who have appealed to the Crown Court against conviction or sentence;

(c) in Crown Court custody waiting to be dealt with by that court;

(d) seeking a case stated from the Crown Court, i.e., persons who, after the decision on their case by the Crown Court, have applied to that court for the statement of a case for the High Court on that decision;

(e) who have applied for *certiorari*, i.e., persons who have applied to the High Court for an order of *certiorari* to remove proceedings in the Crown Court in their case into the High Court, or who have applied to the High Court for leave to make such an application;

(f) granted a certificate for appeal by the Crown Court, i.e., persons to whom the Crown Court has granted a certificate under ss. 1(2) or 11(1A) or 11(1B) of the Criminal Appeal Act 1968 (CAA 1968);

(g) remanded in custody by a magistrates' court on adjourning a case under the following sections of the MCA 1980:

   (i)   s. 5 (adjournment of inquiry into offence);

(ii)   s. 10 (adjournment of trial);

(iii)   s. 18 (initial procedure on information against an adult for offence triable either way); or

(iv)   s. 30 (remand for medical examination).

Crown Court jurisdiction on appeal from a magistrates' court applies only to persons who have been committed *in custody*, not to persons who have been granted bail and wish to challenge or vary conditions imposed. Such applications must be made to the High Court (see Chapter 10).

8.2   APPLICATIONS BY THE DEFENDANT

8.2.1   Applications for bail made otherwise than during the hearing of proceedings in the Crown Court

Applications to the Crown Court relating to bail made otherwise than during the hearing of proceedings in the Crown Court are regulated by rr. 19 and 20 of the CCR 1982 (SI 1982 No. 1109): r. 19(1).

8.2.1.1   Ambit of 'hearing of proceedings'   Rules 19 and 20 of the CCR 1982 regulate applications in all cases over which the Crown Court has jurisdiction to grant bail by virtue of s. 81(1) of the SCA 1981, save those made during the hearing of Crown Court proceedings. The ambit of the phrase 'during the hearing of proceedings in the Crown Court' requires scrutiny. Clearly it embraces trial, and this will include the adjourning of the case in respite of sentence following conviction by the jury. It also includes hearings at which defendants plead guilty, immediately following which their cases are respited for sentence at a later date. Defendants on trial or those whose cases, on their being convicted, or otherwise on their pleading guilty, are adjourned for sentence at a later date, are entitled to apply for bail without being required to comply with any of the provisions for notice laid down in r. 19. Conversely, when cases are listed for mention or for plea and directions and no plea is taken or a plea of 'not guilty' is tendered, the defendant is not entitled to apply for bail unless the procedural requirements set out in r. 19 have been met.

8.2.1.2   Requirement for written notice of application by defendants   Notice of a defendant's intention to make such an application must normally be given in writing to the prosecutor, and if the prosecution is being carried on by the CPS, to the appropriate Crown Prosecutor: CCR 1982, r. 19(2).

8.2.1.3   Application by prosecution for variation or imposition of conditions of bail   Where a person has been committed on bail to the Crown Court for trial or sentence or otherwise to be dealt with, the Crown Court may on an application by the prosecutor or a constable vary the conditions of bail or impose conditions in respect of bail which has been granted unconditionally: BA 1976, s. 3(8). Notice of an intention to make such an application must be given in writing to the person

to whom bail was granted: CCR 1982, r. 19(2). (See Chapters 3 and 7.) Where a notice of transfer is given under a relevant transfer provision, s. 3(8) has effect as if the defendant had been committed for trial: BA 1976, s. 3(8A).

8.2.1.4 When notice of application must be served The written notice of an intention to make an application under CCR 1982, r. 19 (whether by the defendant, or by the prosecutor or a constable) must be served at least 24 hours before the application is made.

8.2.1.5 Notices must be in prescribed form Notices required to be given under r. 19(2) must be in a form prescribed in sch. 4 to the Rules or in a form to the like effect: CCR 1982, r. 19(4).

8.2.1.6 Copy of notice to be served on appropriate Crown Court officer A copy of the notice under r. 19(2) must be served on the appropriate officer of the Crown Court: CCR 1982, r. 19(4).

8.2.1.7 Duty of person receiving the written notice of application Rule 19(3) of the CCR 1982 provides that on receiving a notice under r. 19, prosecutors, appropriate Crown Prosecutors or, as the case may be, persons to whom bail was granted must:

(a) notify the appropriate officer of the Crown Court and the applicant that they wish to be represented at the hearing of the application; or
(b) notify the appropriate officer and the applicant that the application is unopposed; or
(c) give the appropriate officer (for the consideration of the Crown Court) and the other party a written statement of the reasons for opposing the application.

8.2.1.8 Defendant making an application relating to bail not entitled to be present Defendants making an application relating to bail under r. 19 of the 1982 Rules, are not entitled to be present at the hearing of the application unless the Crown Court gives leave: CCR 1982 r. 19(5).

8.2.1.9 Applications to be in chambers The CCR 1982 provide that the jurisdiction of the Crown Court relating to the hearing of bail applications may be exercised by a judge in chambers: r. 27(1) and (2)(a). Applications otherwise than in the course of proceedings are always in chambers. Practice varies as to the location of applications in the court building. They are heard in the courtroom, in closed session, or in the judge's private room.

8.2.1.10 Presence of prosecutor or constable A prosecutor or constable making an application under s. 3(8) of the BA 1976 for variation or imposition of conditions of a defendant's bail is entitled to be present at the hearing of the application: CCR 1982, r. 19(5).

8.2.1.11   Representation by the Official Solicitor   Persons in custody or on bail who wish to make an application relating to bail and who have not been able to instruct a solicitor to apply on their behalf under r. 19, may give notice in writing to the Crown Court of their desire to make an application, and the court may, if it thinks fit, assign the Official Solicitor to act accordingly: CCR 1982, r. 19(6). Where the Official Solicitor has been so assigned the Crown Court may, if it thinks fit, dispense with the requirements of r. 19(2) for a written notice and deal with the application in a summary manner: CCR 1982, r. 19(7).

8.2.1.12   Requirement for record of decision to be filed   Rule 19(8) of the CCR 1982 provides that any record required by the BA 1976, s. 5 (together with any note of reasons required by s. 5(4) to be included) must be made by way of an entry in the file relating to the case in question and the record must include the following particulars, namely:

(a)   the effect of the decision;
(b)   a statement of any condition imposed in respect of bail, indicating whether it is to be complied with before or after release;
(c)   where conditions of bail are varied, a statement of the conditions as varied;
(d)   where bail is withheld, a statement of the relevant exception to the right to bail (as provided in the BA 1976, sch. 1) on which the decision is based.

8.2.1.13   Duty to inform the court of earlier application to Crown Court or High Court   Every person who makes an application to the Crown Court relating to bail must inform the court of any earlier application to the High Court or the Crown Court relating to bail in the course of the same proceedings: CCR 1982, r. 20(1).

8.2.1.14   Listing of bail applications before the trial judge   Applications for bail should be listed where possible before the judge by whom the case is expected to be tried: see *Practice Direction* [1995] 1 WLR 1083, para. 6, which also prescribes listing arrangements if the trial judge is unavailable.

8.2.1.15   Prosecution right of reply   The prosecution should be allowed to reply on bail applications in the Crown Court, particularly where there are, in the view of the prosecution, misstatements of fact in the application which require correction: *R v Isleworth Crown Court and D, ex parte Commissioners of Customs and Excise* [1991] COD 1, DC.

8.2.2   Applications where the Crown Court is seized of the case

Not all of the heads under s. 81(1) of the SCA 1981 giving the Crown Court jurisdiction over bail (see para. 8.1) relate to cases in which the Crown Court is seized of the case. Head (g) lies outside this embrace, but *quaere* whether heads

(e) and (f) are also outside. In any event, the procedure for applications where the Crown Court is seized of the case is dealt with in *Practice Direction (Distribution of Crown Court Business)* (1981) 73 Cr App R 370. The provisions of the *Practice Direction* are set out under the following heads; they appear to be additional to the requirements of r. 19 of the CCR 1982.

8.2.2.1 Service of notice of intent to apply for bail   Notice of intention to apply for bail must be given to the appropriate officer at the location of the Crown Court where the proceedings in which the application for bail arises, took place, or are pending: para. 1(a).

8.2.2.2 Official Solicitor cases to be heard in London   Where a person gives notice in writing of a wish to apply for bail and makes a request to be represented by the Official Solicitor in the application, it must be heard by a Crown Court judge in London: para. 1(b).

8.2.2.3 Other cases   In any other case, the application must be heard at the location of the Crown Court where the proceedings in respect of which it arises took place or are pending, or at any other location which the court may direct: para. 1(c).

8.2.2.4 Designation of jurisdiction for Class 1, Class 2 and other offences
Subject to such directions as may be given in any case by or on behalf of the Lord Chief Justice with the concurrence of the Lord Chancellor, any application for bail:

   (a)   by a person charged with a Class 1 offence, or in any case where a presiding judge so directs, must be dealt with by a High Court judge or by a circuit judge nominated by a presiding judge for this purpose;
   (b)   by a person charged with a Class 2 offence may be heard by a High Court judge or by a circuit judge or (on the authority of a presiding judge) by a recorder;
   (c)   in any other case may be heard: para. 2.

8.2.3 Bail during the course of a Crown Court trial

Practice Direction (Bail – Bail During Trial) 59 Cr App R 159, issued 4 June 1974, gives guidance on the issue of bail during the course of a Crown Court trial. As it pre-dates the BA 1976 it must be read subject to the general right to bail contained in s. 4 of that Act. The elements of the *Practice Direction* are as follows:

8.2.3.1 Bail during the trial in the judge's discretion   Once a trial has begun, the further grant of bail, whether during the short adjournment or overnight, is in the discretion of the trial judge. (That the withdrawal of bail may sometimes have unfortunate consequences was demonstrated by the facts in *R v Osborne-Odelli* [1998] Crim LR 902, CA. The judge had revoked the appellant's bail two days before he gave evidence and, on the next day (when the court was not sitting) a judge in chambers re-admitted him to bail. The episode was referred to in an outburst by the appellant during the course of his evidence and counsel then elicited the basic facts. It was held that counsel should have been allowed to address the jury to the effect that a possible explanation for the aggressive manner in which the appellant had given evidence was his indignation at being suddenly remanded in custody. The effect of the judge's intervention to stop any such explanation and his own comment on the matter in summing up was such to render the conviction unsafe as there was a grave danger that the jury may have been given the impression that the appellant had been remanded in custody because he had been guilty of conduct justifying his incarceration.)

8.2.3.2 Problem of segregation during the short adjournment It may be a proper exercise of the judge's discretion to refuse bail during the short adjournment if the accused cannot otherwise be segregated from witnesses and jurors.

8.2.3.3 Overnight bail for defendants on bail pending trial A defendant who was on bail while on remand should not be refused overnight bail during the trial, unless in the opinion of the judge there are positive reasons to justify this refusal.

8.2.3.4 Exceptional reasons for withdrawing overnight bail from defendants on bail pending trial Such reasons are likely to be:

  (a) that a point has been reached where there is a real danger that the defendant will abscond, either because the case is going badly for the defence or for any other reason;

  (b) that there is a real danger that the defendant may interfere with witnesses or jurors.

8.2.3.5 Bail after start of summing-up There is no universal rule of practice that bail shall not be renewed when the summing-up has begun. Each case must be decided in the light of its own circumstances and having regard to the judge's assessment from time to time of the risks involved.

8.2.3.6 After the verdict Once the jury have returned a verdict, a further renewal of bail should be regarded as exceptional.

8.2.3.7 Nature of application Although the CCR 1982 provide that the jurisdiction of the Crown Court relating to the hearing of bail applications may be exercised by a judge in chambers (r. 27(1) and (2)(a)), judges seldom go into chambers to hear applications in the course of a trial or other proceedings. However, they may do so if there are special reasons for privacy.

8.2.3.8 Co-defendant absconding

Not dealt with in the 1974 practice direction is the situation where one of two or more defendants absconds during the trial. In such a case the judge has a discretion to continue the trial against the others: *R* v *Panayis (Charalambos)* [1999] Crim LR 84.

8.2.4 Pre-committal applications

Section 60 of the CJA 1982 amended the BA 1976, s. 5, and the SCA 1981, s. 81, so as to permit applications for bail to be made to the Crown Court prior to committal by a magistrates' court (see para. 5.5). The practice and procedure involved in such pre-committal applications is set out in *Practice Direction (Crown Court – Bail)* 77 Cr App R 69, issued 26 April 1983, the provisions of which follow immediately below.

8.2.4.1 Application of Crown Court Rules 1982 Rules 19 and 20 of the CCR 1982 (see para. 8.2.1) regulate these applications. The application form has been amended to cover the new procedure.

8.2.4.2 Full argument certificate necessary Before the Crown Court can deal with an application it must be satisfied that the magistrates' court has issued a certificate under s. 5(6A) of the BA 1976 certifying that it heard full argument on the application for bail before it refused the application.

8.2.4.3 Defence to submit full argument certificate to Crown Court A copy of the certificate of full argument will be issued to the applicant and not sent directly to the Crown Court. It will therefore be necessary for applicants' solicitors to attach a copy of the certificate to the bail application form. If the certificate is not enclosed with the application form it will be difficult to avoid some delay in listing. (The authors observe that many courts are content to receive a duplicate or faxed copy of the original certificate on the understanding that the original is produced at the hearing.)

8.2.4.4 Venue generally Applications should be made to the court to which the case will be or would have been committed for trial.

8.2.4.5 Venue in summary only cases In the event of an application in a purely summary case it should be made to the Crown Court centre which normally receives Class 4 work.

8.2.4.6 Hearing to be in chambers The hearing will be listed as a chambers matter unless a judge has directed otherwise.

8.2.4.7 Legal aid: existing order covers application If the applicant is legally aided in the magistrates' court (either under an ordinary order, or under an order limited to a bail application) the legal aid order covers pre-committal applications for bail.

8.2.4.8   No existing legal aid order: no power to grant legal aid purely for pre-committal Crown Court bail applications   If the applicant is not legally aided, neither the Crown Court nor the magistrates' court has power to grant a legal aid order for the purpose of applications for bail to the Crown Court alone.

8.2.4.9   Legal aid limited to solicitor representation   Legal aid for this purpose is limited to representation by a solicitor only, unless the legal aid order granted by the magistrates' court specifically includes representation by counsel. This does not preclude solicitors from instructing counsel to act on their behalf if they wish, though any costs determined cannot exceed those which would be allowed had the solicitor undertaken the case without counsel. The legal aid costs will be determined by the Legal Aid Board (the original *Practice Direction* referred to the Law Society) as part of the magistrates' court costs under the legal aid order.

8.2.4.10   Prosecution right of reply   The prosecution should be allowed to reply on bail applications in the Crown Court, particularly where there are, in the view of the prosecution, misstatements of fact in the application which require correction: *R* v *Isleworth Crown Court and D, ex parte Commissioners of Customs and Excise* [1991] COD 1, DC.

8.3   PROSECUTION APPEAL AGAINST GRANT OF BAIL ENACTED BY THE BAIL (AMENDMENT) ACT 1993

8.3.1   Offences carrying right of prosecution appeal against bail grant

Where a magistrates' court grants bail to a person who is charged with or convicted of:

(a)   an offence punishable by a term of imprisonment of five years or more; or
(b)   an offence under the Theft Act 1968, s. 12 (taking a conveyance without authority) or s. 12A (aggravated vehicle taking);

the prosecution may appeal to a judge of the Crown Court against the granting of bail: Bail (Amendment) Act 1993 (BAA 1993), s. 1(1).

8.3.2   Prosecutors who may appeal

Section 1(2) of the 1993 Act provides that the right of prosecution appeal applies only where the prosecution is conducted:

(a)   by or on behalf of the Director of Public Prosecutions; or
(b)   by a person falling within such class or description of person as may be prescribed for the purposes of s. 1 by order made by the Secretary of State.

The power to make such an order is exercisable by statutory instrument and any instrument is subject to annulment in pursuance of a resolution of either House of

Parliament: BAA 1993, s. 1(11). The Bail (Amendment) Act 1993 (Prescription of Prosecuting Authorities) Order 1994 (SI 1994 No. 1438) prescribes the following authorities for the purposes of s. 1:

(a) the Director of the Serious Fraud Office and any person designated under s. 1(7) of the CJA 1987;
(b) the Secretary of State for Trade and Industry;
(c) the Commissioners of Customs and Excise;
(d) the Secretary of State for Social Security;
(e) the Post Office; and
(f) the Commissioners of Inland Revenue.

8.3.3 Right dependent on opposition before grant

The prosecution may appeal against a grant of bail only if before bail was granted they made representations that it should not be granted: BAA 1993, s. 1(3).

8.3.4 Requirement for notice

8.3.4.1 Oral notice required at conclusion of proceedings when bail granted   In the event of the prosecution wishing to exercise the right of appeal, oral notice of appeal must be given to the magistrates' court at the conclusion of the proceedings in which such bail has been granted and before the release from custody of the person concerned: BAA 1993, s. 1(4) and MCR 1981, r. 93A(1); rule inserted by the Magistrates' Courts (Bail) (Amendment) Rules 1994 (SI 1994 No. 1481). Oral notice must also be given at that stage to the defendant: MCR 1981, r. 93A(1). A short delay, such as five minutes between the announcement and grant of bail and the prosecutor giving notice of appeal is acceptable providing the person concerned is still in custody: *R v Isleworth Crown Court, ex parte Clarke* [1998] 1 Cr App R 257. The magistrates do not need to be in court when the oral notice of appeal is given: *ibid.*

8.3.4.2 Clerk's public acknowledgement of giving of oral notice   When oral notice of appeal is given, the clerk of the magistrates' court shall announce in open court the time at which such notice was given: MCR 1981, r. 93A(2).

8.3.4.3 Written notice necessary within two hours of the grant of bail   In addition to the requisite oral notice, written notice of appeal must be served on the magistrates' court and on the person concerned within two hours of the conclusion of the proceedings at which bail was granted: BAA 1993, s. 1(5). Rule 11A(2) of the CCR 1982 provides that the written notice of appeal required by s. 1(5) shall be in the form prescribed in sch. 9 to the Rules or a form to the like and effect and shall be served on the clerk of the magistrates' court and the defendant. (Rule 11A and sch. 9 were inserted by the Crown Court (Amendment) Rules 1994 (SI 1994 No. 1480.)

8.3.4.4   Failure to serve the required notices within the period of two hours   Where the prosecution fail, within the period of two hours, to serve one or both of the required notices the appeal is deemed to have been disposed of: BAA 1993, s. 1(7).

8.3.4.5   Written notice of abandonment of appeal   Provision is also made for service of notice of abandonment of the appeal within the two-hour period after the proceedings when bail was granted (see MCR 1981, r. 93A(8)). Rule 11A(6) of the Rules of 1982 provides that at any time after the service of the written notice of appeal under BAA 1993, s. 1(5) the prosecution may abandon the appeal by giving notice in writing in the form prescribed by sch. 10 to the Rules or a form to the like effect (sch. 10 was inserted by the Crown Court (Amendment) Rules 1994). The notice of abandonment must be served on the defendant or the defendant's legal representative, the clerk of the magistrates' court, and the appropriate officer of the Crown Court: CCR 1982, r. 11A(7).

8.3.4.6   Records   A record of the prosecution's decision to appeal and of the time the oral notice of appeal was given must be made in the register and must contain the particulars set out in the appropriate form for the purpose: MCR 1981, r. 93A(3). A record of the receipt of the written notice of appeal shall be made in the same manner as that of the oral notice: MCR 1981, r. 93A(6). Where the prosecution fail to serve a written notice of appeal, or serve notice of abandonment, the clerk of the magistrates' court shall record the failure or the service of notice of abandonment in the appropriate form prescribed for the purpose: MCR 1981, r. 93A(9).

8.3.4.7   Service by magistrates' court of relevant records on Crown Court   A clerk of the magistrates' court upon whom written notice of appeal has been served is required by r. 93A(10) of the MCR 1981 to provide as soon as practicable to the appropriate officer of the Crown Court a copy of that written notice, together with:

(a)   the notes of argument made by the clerk of the court under r. 90A of the 1981 Rules; and

(b)   a note of the date, or dates, when the person concerned is next due to appear in the magistrates' court, whether released on bail or remanded in custody by the Crown Court.

8.3.5   Remand in custody by magistrates' court upon service of notice of appeal against grant of bail

The BAA 1993 provides that upon receipt from the prosecution of oral notice of appeal from its decision to grant bail the magistrates' court must remand in custody the person concerned, until the appeal is determined or otherwise disposed of: BAA 1993, s. 1(6). It is provided by the MCR 1981, r. 93A(4) that where an oral notice of appeal has been given the court shall remand the person concerned in custody by a warrant of commitment in the appropriate form prescribed for the purpose. There is no reference to the duration of the custody order, as there is in BAA 1993, s. 1(6). The rule goes on to provide that on receipt of the *written* notice of appeal required by s. 1(5) of the 1993 Act the court must remand the person concerned in custody by a warrant of commitment in the appropriate form prescribed for the purpose, until the appeal is determined or otherwise disposed of: MCR 1981, r. 93A(5). The distinction between paras (4) and (5) is in the duration of the remand. The custody order required by para. (4) to follow immediately upon the giving of oral notice of appeal would appear to be provisional and intended to await confirmation within two hours by the service of written notice. Thereafter the remand in custody is to have effect 'until the appeal is determined or otherwise disposed of' (para. 5). The regime is intended to allow for a prosecution 'cooling off' period, or a breathing space, of up to two hours, during which the question of an appeal can be reconsidered and the defendant held in custody in the meantime. The difference between s. 1(6) and r. 93A(4) is of no significance. The fact that the remand in custody required by BAA 1993, s. 1(6) is to have effect 'until the appeal is determined or otherwise disposed of' is not irreversible. If within the period of two hours the prosecution decide to accept the granting of bail and not to proceed with the appeal, it will have been 'otherwise disposed of' and the order for provisional custody can be discharged there and then. This is in the Act, s. 1(7) of which, as already mentioned, provides that where the prosecution fail, within the period of two hours, to serve one or both of the required notices the appeal is deemed to have been disposed of. Further, the MCR 1981, r. 93A(7) provides that if, having given oral notice of appeal, the prosecution fail to serve a written notice of appeal within the two-hour period referred to in s. 1(5) of the Act, the clerk of the magistrates' court shall, as soon as practicable, by way of written notice to the persons concerned, direct the release of the person concerned on bail as granted by the magistrates' court and subject to any conditions which it imposed. If the prosecution serve notice of abandonment of appeal on the clerk of the magistrates' court, the clerk shall, forthwith, by way of written notice to the governor of the prison where the person concerned is being held, or the person responsible for any other establishment where such a person is being held, direct release on bail as granted by the magistrates' court and subject to any conditions which it imposed: MCR 1981, r. 93A(8).

8.3.6 Children and young persons

In relation to a child or young person (within the meaning of the CYPA 1969) it is provided by the BAA 1993, s. 1(10) that:

(a)   the reference in s. 1(1) to an offence punishable by a term of imprisonment is to be read as a reference to an offence which would be so punishable in the case of an adult; and

(b)   the reference in s. 1(6) to remand in custody is to be read subject to the provisions of s. 23 of the Act of 1969 (remands to local authority accommodation).

(See also Chapter 11, paras. 11.1.6 to 11.1.8.)

8.3.7   The appeal

8.3.7.1   Notices to be give by the Crown Court   The appropriate officer of the Crown Court is required by r. 11A(3) of the CCR 1982 to enter the appeal and to give notice of the time and place of the hearing to:

(a)   the prosecution;
(b)   the defendant or defence legal representative; and
(c)   the clerk of the magistrates' court.

8.3.7.2   Time limit for commencing appeal hearing   The hearing of an appeal against a decision of the magistrates' court to grant bail must be commenced within 48 hours, excluding weekends and any public holiday (that is to say, Christmas Day, Good Friday, or a bank holiday), from the date on which oral notice of appeal is given: BAA 1993, s. 1(8).

8.3.7.3   Written notice of abandonment of appeal   At any time after the service of the written notice of appeal under BAA 1993, s. 1(5) the prosecution may abandon the appeal by giving notice in writing in the form prescribed by sch. 10 to the Rules or a form to the like effect: CCR 1982, r. 11A(6). The notice of abandonment must be served on the defendant or the defendant's legal representative, the clerk of the magistrates' court, and the appropriate officer of the Crown Court: CCR 1982, r. 11A(7).

8.3.7.4   Appeal is by way of re-hearing   At the hearing of any appeal by the prosecution under s. 1 of the 1993 Act the appeal is by way of re-hearing, and the judge hearing any such appeal may remand the person concerned in custody or may grant bail subject to such conditions (if any) as is thought fit: BAA 1993, s. 1(9).

8.3.7.5   Defendants not acting in person not normally permitted to be present at the hearing   The defendant shall not be entitled to be present at the hearing of the appeal unless acting in person, or in any other case of an exceptional nature, a judge of the Crown Court is of the opinion that the interests of justice require the defendant to be present and gives leave: CCR 1982, r. 11A(4).

8.3.7.6   Representation by the Official Solicitor   Where the defendant has not been able to instruct a solicitor for representation at the appeal, the defendant may give notice to the Crown Court requesting representation by the Official Solicitor and the court may, if it thinks fit, assign the Official Solicitor to act for the defendant accordingly: CCR 1982, r. 11A(5).

8.3.7.7 Records Any record required by s. 5 of the BA 1976 (together with any note of the reasons required by s. 5(4) to be included) is required by CCR 1982, r. 11A(8) to be made by way of an entry in the file relating to the case in question, and the record shall include the following particulars:

(a)   the effect of the decision;
(b)   a statement of any condition imposed in respect of bail, indicating whether it is to be complied with before or after release on bail;
(c)   where bail is withheld, as statement of the relevant exception to the right to bail (as provided in sch. 1 to the Act of 1976) on which the decision is based.

8.3.7.8 Notices to be sent by the Crown Court relating to the decision The appropriate Crown Court officer is required by the CCR 1982, r. 11A(9), as soon as practicable after the hearing of the appeal, to give notice of the decision and of the matters required by r. 11A(8) to be recorded to:

(a)   the defendant or defence legal representative;
(b)   the prosecution;
(c)   the police;
(d)   the clerk of the magistrates' court;
(e)   the governor of the prison or person responsible for the establishment where the person concerned is being held.

8.3.7.9 Rule 20 of the Crown Court Rules 1982 to apply Where the judge hearing the appeal grants bail to the defendant, the provisions of r. 20 of the 1982 Rules apply as if the defendant had applied to the Crown Court for bail: CCR 1982, r. 11A(10) (see generally para. 8.2).

8.3.7.10 Methods of transmitting notices The notices required to be sent by CCR 1982, r. 11A(3), (5), (7) and (9), may be sent by way of facsimile transmission and the notice required by r. 11A(3) may be given by telephone: r. 11A(11).

8.3.7.11 Period of remand upon successful prosecution appeal Although a remand in custody by a judge of the Crown Court is not subject to s. 128, s. 128A and s. 129 of the MCA 1980, the lawfulness of the detention of the person concerned has to be judged against those provisions because the person is still subject to the jurisdiction of the justices. The judge should therefore be invited to stipulate a period of remand in custody which complies with ss. 128 to 129: *R v Governor of Pentonville Prison, ex parte Bone, The Times*, 15 November 1998.

9 Bail Pending Appeal

The right to bail enacted by s. 4 of the BA 1976 is inapplicable to convicted offenders who have initiated appeal proceedings following the imposition of a custodial sentence. They may be granted bail but, in contrast with the statutory right, the decision lies within the discretion of the court enjoying jurisdiction to grant it.

9.1 APPEAL FROM A DECISION OF THE MAGISTRATES' COURT

9.1.1 Bail granted by the magistrates' court

9.1.1.1 Bail following notice of appeal to the Crown Court Where a person in custody has given notice of appeal to the Crown Court against the decision of a magistrates' court the magistrates' court, may, subject to s. 25 of the CJPOA 1994, grant bail: MCA 1980, s. 113(1), as amended by the CJPOA 1994, s. 168(2) and sch. 10, para. 44.

9.1.1.2 Bail following application for case stated Where a person in custody has applied to a magistrates' court, under s. 111 of the MCA 1980, to state a case for the opinion of the High Court on a question of law or jurisdiction, the magistrates' court may, subject to s. 25 of the CJPOA 1994, grant bail: MCA 1980, s. 113(1), as amended by the CJPOA 1994, s. 168(2) and sch. 10, para. 44.

9.1.1.3 Bail pending appeal to Crown Court unavailable from the magistrates' court where the defendant has been committed for sentence Section 113(1) of the MCA 1980 does not apply where the accused has been committed for sentence to the Crown Court under s. 38 of the 1980 Act: s. 113(3). As to the power to grant bail on committal for sentence, see Chapter 7.

9.1.1.4 Time and place for surrender in cases of appeal to the Crown Court A defendant who has given notice of appeal and has been granted bail under s. 113(1) of the 1980 Act must appear before the Crown Court at the time appointed for the hearing of the appeal: MCA 1980, s. 113(2).

9.1.1.5 Time and place for surrender where defendant has applied for case stated A defendant who has applied for the statement of a case and has been granted bail under s. 113(1) of the 1980 Act must appear at the magistrates' court at such time within 10 days after the judgment of the High Court as may be specified by the magistrates' court, except in the event of the determination in respect of which the case is stated being reversed by the High Court: MCA 1980, s. 113(2).

9.1.1.6 Recognizances Where persons appealing to the Crown Court or applying for a case to be stated by the magistrates' court have been granted bail, the magistrates' court has power to require an appellant or applicant, as the case may be, to enter into a recognizance, with or without sureties. In the case of an appeal to the Crown Court, any recognizance that may be taken from the appellant or from any surety shall be conditioned according to the date on which the appellant is required to appear at the Crown Court for the hearing of the appeal: MCA 1980, s. 113(2). Where bail is granted to a person applying for a case to be stated by the magistrates' court, any recognizance that may be taken from that applicant or from any surety shall be conditioned according to the date at which the person is required to appear at the magistrates' court after the High Court judgment. A recognizance, with or without sureties, may also be taken conditioned to prosecute the appeal without delay. The purpose of such a recognizance is to show good faith in pursuing the appeal as appeals might otherwise be abandoned at the time and expense of the respondent. There is no statutory duty to consider the means of an appellant or applicant in fixing the amount of the recognizance where the appeal is from a magistrates' court. However, in *R v Newcastle-upon-Tyne Magistrates, ex parte Skinner* [1987] Crim LR 113, the Divisional Court held that magistrates must have regard to the means of an applicant before requiring a recognizance or fixing the amount. Where the amount of the recognizance is unreasonable, that might prove counter-productive as the applicant might be encouraged to prosecute the appeal even though the chances of success were remote.

9.1.1.7 Currency of sentence when a defendant is released on bail by magistrates pending case stated appeal Section 113(4) of the MCA 1980 provides that s. 37(6) of the CJA 1948 (which relates to the currency and computation of a sentence while a person is released on bail by the High Court: see Chapter 10) applies to a person released on bail by a magistrates' court under s. 113 pending the hearing of a case stated as it applies to a person released on bail by the High Court under s. 22 of the CJA 1967.

9.1.2 Bail granted by the Crown Court

It has already been stated (in Chapter 8, at para. 8.1) that s. 81(1)(b) of the SCA 1981 empowers a Crown Court, subject to s. 25 of the CJPOA 1994, to grant bail to any person who is in custody pursuant to a sentence imposed by a magistrates' court and who has appealed to the Crown Court against conviction or sentence.

9.1.3 Bail granted by the High Court

9.1.3.1 Appeal to the Crown Court A defendant who has been convicted and sentenced by a magistrates' court and who has appealed to the Crown Court against such conviction or sentence, or both, may apply under s. 22 of the CJA 1967 to a High Court judge in chambers for bail pending appeal (for full consideration see Chapter 10, para. 10.1.1.1, *et seq.*).

9.1.3.2 Appeal by way of case stated Where a person who has received a custodial sentence from a magistrates' court has applied to that court to state a case for the opinion of the High Court on a question of law or jurisdiction, the High Court may grant bail pending the hearing (see Chapter 10, para. 10.1.1.1, *et seq.*).

9.1.4 Bail and short sentences

The vast majority of custodial sentences likely to be imposed by magistrates will necessarily be of comparatively or very short duration. In many such cases the vagaries of Crown Court listing will preclude the hearing of the appeal before all or most of the sentence is served if the appellant is refused bail pending appeal. This might be thought, therefore, to be a cogent argument in favour of promptly releasing the appellant on bail pending appeal against a short sentence. However, in *R* v *Imdad Shah* (1980) 144 JP 460 (see para. 9.3.3) Roskill LJ held that in short sentence cases it was undesirable to grant bail pending appeal merely in order to preclude the risk of all or most of the sentence being served before the appeal hearing could take place. The solution to that problem was to try to seek an early listing of the appeal. The decision related to the granting of bail by the Court of Appeal pending an appeal to that court, and it is not clear to what extent the judgment is applicable to bail pending appeal from the magistrates' court to the Crown Court. There would seem to be no good reason why it should not extend to such appeals in principle. Applying *R* v *Imdad Shah*, the question whether bail pending appeal might be granted in the case of a very short sentence would have to depend on how soon the Crown Court could hear the case. Since only the Crown Court would be in a position to know this, the question whether bail should be granted if the Crown Court were not able to accommodate the case expeditiously would properly be one for the Crown Court and not for the magistrates' court. As soon as the defendant wishing to appeal has been sentenced by the magistrates and has lodged notice of appeal, application should be made to the Crown Court for the case to be listed for mention and for a bail application pending appeal. On the application being heard the judge should consult the List Officer as to whether the appeal can be listed promptly; if not, only then ought bail to be considered.

Although the question of bail pending appeal to the Crown Court against a very short sentence is one which it may be proper only for the Crown Court to consider, the uncertainty of whether *R* v *Imdad Shah* applies to such appeals is such that it may usually be worth asking the magistrates' court to consider bail.

A defendant seeking to appeal against a conviction or sentence in the magistrates' court must serve on the prosecutor and on the court a notice in the appropriate form. Where a defendant wishes to appeal against a short sentence it is advisable to complete the necessary forms and serve them at court as soon as sentence has been imposed in order to provide the basis for an immediate application for bail pending appeal on the basis that the sentence is likely to be served before the appeal can be heard. Where a short custodial sentence is anticipated it will often be convenient to take instructions on the question of appeal and to complete the necessary appeal forms before the sentence hearing is called on. Then, if the defendant is sentenced as feared, the forms can be served before the defendant is taken down and a bail application can be made forthwith.

9.1.5 Military jurisdiction over civilians: the Standing Civilian Court

Civilians on active service are liable to prosecution for military and air force offences under the Army Act 1955 and the Air Force Act 1955, with appropriate modifications, and for civil offences. Many of those falling into this category will be the family members of service personnel. Before trial such persons may be held under close arrest (in custody), open arrest (on bail) or under no form of arrest. The Standing Civilian Court is the equivalent of the magistrates' court and has jurisdiction to deal with the less serious offences. It has power to imprison a defendant for a maximum of six months for a single offence (equivalent to MCA 1980, s. 31). Appeal lies by way of rehearing to a court-martial (equivalent to appeal by way of rehearing to the Crown Court). There is no power to grant bail pending appeal to a court-martial. For a powerful argument in favour of change in the law, see Judge-Advocate Camp, 'Post-Trial Bail for Civilians in Military Courts – Time for Change' [1998] Crim LR 123.

9.2 BAIL BY THE CROWN COURT PENDING APPEAL TO THE COURT OF APPEAL OR TO THE HIGH COURT

9.2.1 Appeal from the Crown Court to the Court of Appeal, Criminal Division

Under the CAA 1968, an appeal may lie to the Court of Appeal, Criminal Division, from the following categories of decision in the Crown Court:

(a) conviction on indictment (s. 1);
(b) sentence upon conviction on indictment (s. 9);
(c) verdict of not guilty by reason of insanity (s. 12);
(d) determination under s. 4 of the Criminal Procedure (Insanity) Act 1964, as amended by s. 2 of the Criminal Procedure (Insanity and Unfitness to Plead) Act 1991, of the question of a person's fitness to be tried (s. 15, as amended by sch. 3, para. 2 to the Act of 1991 and s. 1(5), Criminal Appeal Act 1995);

(e)   sentence following conviction by a magistrates' court and committal to the Crown Court to be dealt with (s. 10);

(f)   following conviction by a magistrates' court and the making of a probation order or an order of conditional discharge, or the imposition of suspended sentence of imprisonment, sentence by the Crown Court upon the appellant appearing or being brought before it to be dealt with for the original offence (s. 10).

9.2.2   Procedure relating to bail pending appeal to the Court of Appeal

9.2.2.1   Certificates of fitness for appeal from the Crown Court   Section 81(1)(f) of the SCA 1981 (as amended by s. 29(1) of the CJA 1982, and the CJPOA 1994, sch. 10, para. 48) empowers the Crown Court, subject to s. 25 of the CJPOA 1994, to grant bail to any person to whom the Crown Court has granted a certificate under:

(a)   s. 1(2), CAA 1968, that the case is fit for appeal on a ground which involves a question of fact or a question of mixed fact and law;

(b)   s. 11(1A), CAA 1968, that the case is fit for appeal against sentence; or

(c)   s. 81(1B), SCA 1981, that the case is fit for appeal on a ground which involves a question of law alone.

Section 81(1A) to (1G) of the 1981 Act, the provisions of which are set out in paras 9.2.2.2 to 9.2.2.7 immediately below, were inserted by s. 29(1) of the CJA 1982.

9.2.2.2   Finding of insanity or disability   The power to grant bail conferred by s. 81(1)(f) of the SCA 1981 does not apply to appeals against a verdict of not guilty by reason of insanity (s. 12 of the CAA 1968) or against a finding of disability (s. 15, CAA 1968) where the accused did the act or made the omission charged: s. 81(1A) as amended by the Criminal Procedure (Insanity and Unfitness to Plead) Act 1991, s. 7, and sch. 3, para. 6.

9.2.2.3   Who may exercise the power   Section 81(1C) of the 1981 Act provides that the power to grant bail pending appeal to the Court of Appeal is to be exercised:

(a)   where the appeal is under s. 1 or s. 9 of the CAA 1968 (appeal against conviction), by the judge who tried the case; and

(b)   where the application is under s. 10 of the CAA 1968, by the judge who passed the sentence.

It follows that if the judge is unavailable application for bail may only be made to the Court of Appeal (see Registrar of Criminal Appeals' guidance issued May 1983, referred to in para. 9.2.3).

9.2.2.4 Twenty-eight day time limit   The power may be exercised only within 28 days from the date of the conviction appealed against, or in the case of appeal against a sentence or order, from the date of the sentence or order: SCA 1981, s. 81(1D).

9.2.2.5 Application debarred by application for bail to the Court of Appeal
The Crown Court may not entertain an application for bail pending appeal if the appellant has made an application to the Court of Appeal for bail in respect of the offence or offences to which the appeal relates: SCA 1981, s. 81(1E).

9.2.2.6 Bail conditional on lodging of notice of appeal   Section 81(1F) of the SCA 1981 provides that it shall be a condition of bail granted in the exercise of the power under s. 81(1) that, unless a notice of appeal has previously been lodged in the Court of Appeal, Criminal Division, within the period laid down by s. 18(2) of the CAA 1968:

(a)   such a notice must be lodged within that period; and
(b)   not later than 14 days from the end of that period, the appellant must lodge with the Crown Court a certificate from the Registrar of Criminal Appeals that a notice of appeal was given within that period.

Section 18(2) of the 1968 Act provides that notice of appeal, or of application for leave to appeal, must be given within 28 days from the date of the conviction, verdict or finding appealed against, or in the case of appeal against sentence, from the date on which sentence was passed or, in the case of an order made or treated as made on conviction, from the date of the making of the order. The Court of Appeal may extend the time for giving notice under s. 18, either before or after it expires: CAA 1968, s. 18(3).

9.2.2.7 Directions to bailed person to appear   If the Crown Court grants bail in the exercise of the power under the SCA 1981, s. 81(1) it may direct the defendant to appear:

(a)   if a notice of appeal is lodged within the period specified in s. 18(2) of the CAA 1968, at such time and place as the Court of Appeal may require; and
(b)   if no such notice is lodged within that period, at such time and place as the Crown Court may require.

9.2.3 Guidance issued by the Registrar of Criminal Appeals, May 1983

In May 1983, the Registrar of Criminal Appeals issued *A Guide to Proceedings in the Court of Appeal Criminal Division*, which was published at (1983) 77 Cr App R 138. In a foreword, Lord Lane CJ commended the guide 'to the attention of all who practise in the Court of Appeal Criminal Division'. In *R v Howell* (1983) 78

Cr App R 195, Purchas LJ drew the attention of the Bar to the guide. Free copies may be obtained from the Criminal Appeal Office and from every Crown Court. Amended versions of this guide were issued in 1990 and again in February 1997 ([1997] 2 Cr App R 459) and include changes in law and practice since 1983.

Paragraph 17 summarises the diverse statutory provisions empowering the Crown Court to grant bail when the trial judge has issued a certificate of fitness to appeal against conviction or sentence. Reference should be made in particular to para. 17.5, which draws from s. 81(1C) of the SCA 1981 the inference that, if the judge who issued the certificate of fitness is unavailable, application for bail may only be made to the Court of Appeal, Criminal Division (see para. 9.2.2.3).

9.2.4 Practice Direction (Crown Court: Bail Pending Appeal)

9.2.4.1 Introductory *Practice Direction (Crown Court: Bail Pending Appeal)* [1983] 1 WLR 1292, issued on 10 November 1983, gives guidance to judges and practitioners on the power of the Crown Court to grant bail pending appeal to the Court of Appeal. Paragraph 1 refers to the fact that the procedure is described in *A Guide to Proceedings in the Court of Appeal Criminal Division* (see para. 9.2.3). Paragraph 2 states that the procedure is also set out in outline on Criminal Appeal Office Forms C (Crown Court Judge's certificate of fitness for appeal) and BC (Crown Court Judge's order granting bail), copies of which are held by the Crown Court. Further, para. 2 points out that the court clerk will ensure that the forms are always available when a judge hears an application for bail pending appeal to the Court of Appeal. The substantive terms of the *Practice Direction* are set out in the following paragraphs under the present head.

9.2.4.2 Hearing of the application Paragraph 3 of the *Practice Direction* states that the judge may well think it right:

(a) to hear the application in chambers with a shorthand writer present;

(b) to invite the defendant's counsel to submit before the hearing of the application a draft of the grounds which he will ask the judge to certify on Form C. It is observed that counsel for the Crown will be better able to assist the judge at the hearing if the draft ground is sent beforehand to him too.

9.2.4.3 Existence of particular and cogent ground of appeal The first question is whether there exists a particular and cogent ground of appeal. If there is no such ground there can be no certificate, and if there is no certificate there can be no bail (*Practice Direction*, para. 4). In *R v Williams, The Times*, 14 February 1985, Pain J commented that bail pending appeal against sentence was appropriate only in a case which was fit for appeal because the sentence was wrong and that sentencing judges must have the courage of their convictions. The idea that granting bail was a proper and normal course to take had to be dispelled. By his comment Pain J would appear to have meant that if sentencing judges are unsure of their ground in imposing a sentence they ought not to impose it, and that they should certainly not seek to resolve their uncertainty by granting a certificate in order to pass on responsibility to the Court of Appeal and at the same time granting bail.

9.2.4.4 Judge's view that due weight given to mitigation Judges should not grant a certificate with regard to sentence merely in the light of mitigation to which they have in their opinion given due weight (*Practice Direction*, para. 4 continued).

9.2.4.5 Judge's view that chance of successful conviction appeal is insubstantial Judges should not grant a certificate in regard to conviction on a ground where they consider the chance of a successful appeal is not substantial (*Practice Direction*, para. 4 continued).

9.2.4.6 Right to apply to Court of Appeal for leave to appeal and for bail should be borne in mind The judge should bear in mind that, where a certificate is refused, application may be made to the Court of Appeal for leave to appeal and for bail (*Practice Direction*, para. 4 continued).

9.2.4.7 Likely interval before appeal hearing The length of the period which might elapse before the hearing of an appeal is not a ground of appeal appropriate to the judge's certificate (*Practice Direction*, para. 5). That period, if there is otherwise good ground for a certificate, may be one factor in the decision whether or not to grant bail; but a judge who is minded to take this factor into account may find it advisable to have the court clerk contact the Criminal Appeal Office listing coordinator in order to obtain an accurate and up-to-date assessment of the likely waiting time (*Practice Direction*, para. 6). The coordinator will require a general account of the weight and urgency of the case (*ibid.*).

9.2.4.8 Urgent cases Where the defendant's representative considers that bail should be applied for as a matter of urgency, the application should normally be made, in the first instance, to the trial judge; and the Court of Appeal may decline to treat such an application as urgent if there is no good reason why it has not been made to the trial judge (*Practice Direction*, para. 7).

9.2.4.9 Proper process for appealing sentence The Court of Appeal has repeatedly drawn the attention of the Bar and the judiciary to the importance of adhering to this *Practice Direction*, and, in particular, to para. 4: see *R v Dawson*, *The Times*, 28 June 1984; *R v Page*, *The Times*, 22 January 1985; *R v Hescroff* (1990) 154 JP 1042; *R v Day*, *The Times*, 3 October 1991; and *R v Williams (P.D.)*, *The Times*, 28 October 1991. In *R v Hescroff*, the Court of Appeal emphasised that the proper process for anyone dissatisfied with a sentence was to lodge an application Court of Appeal, Criminal Division for leave to appeal, which would be considered by the single judge. In *R v Williams* the Court said that a certificate ought not to be issued 'unless very exceptional circumstances were present'.

9.2.5   Bail pending appeal by way of case stated to the High Court

Section 28 of the SCA 1981 permits an application to be made for the Crown Court to state a case for the opinion of the High Court with regard to any order, judgment or other decision of the Crown Court. The Crown Court may, subject to s. 25 of the CJPOA 1994, grant bail to any person who, after the decision of his case by the Crown Court, has applied to that court for the statement of a case for the High Court on that decision: SCA 1981, s. 81(1)(c).

9.2.6   Bail pending application to remove proceedings to the High Court

Section 81(1)(e) of the SCA 1981 empowers the Crown Court, subject to s. 25 of the CJPOA 1994, to grant bail to any person who has applied to the High Court for an order of *certiorari* to remove proceedings in the Crown Court into the High Court, or who has applied to the High Court for leave to make such an application.

9.3   JURISDICTION OF THE COURT OF APPEAL

9.3.1   The four contexts of jurisdiction

The Court of Appeal, Criminal Division, enjoys a discretion to grant bail in the following contexts:

(a)   where an appeal is pending to the Court of Appeal (see paras 9.3.2 and 9.3.3);

(b)   where following the quashing of a conviction on indictment an order is made for retrial or the issuing of a writ *venire de novo* (see para. 9.3.4);

(c)   where the Court allows an appeal against a finding under s. 4 of the Criminal Procedure (Insanity) Act 1964, as amended by s. 2 of the Criminal Procedure (Insanity and Unfitness to Plead) Act 1991, that the appellant is under a disability and is unfit to be tried, and orders the appellant to be tried for the offence (see para. 9.3.5);

(d)   where an appeal is pending to the House of Lords (see para. 9.4).

9.3.2   Bail pending appeal to the Court of Appeal

9.3.2.1   Basic statutory sources   Section 19 of the CAA 1968, as substituted by s. 29(2)(b) of the CJA 1982, and as subsequently amended by the CJA 1988, s. 170(1) and sch. 15, para. 26, and the CJPOA 1994, sch. 10, para. 22, confers on the Court of Appeal the three basic powers in relation to the granting of bail. The powers, which are subject to s. 25 of the CJPOA 1994 (restricting bail in certain very serious cases) are to grant bail pending appeal, to revoke bail and to vary the conditions on which an appellant is on bail pending appeal.

9.3.2.2 Discretionary grant of bail The Court of Appeal may if it thinks fit grant an appellant bail pending the determination of the appeal: CAA 1968, s. 19(1)(a).

9.3.2.3 Revocation of bail The Court of Appeal may if it thinks fit revoke bail granted to an appellant by the Crown Court under s. 81(1)(f) of the SCA 1981 or by the Court of Appeal under s. 19(1)(a) of the 1968 Act: CAA 1968, s. 19(1)(b). Clearly, an application for revocation will usually be made by the prosecutor.

9.3.2.4 Variation of conditions The Court of Appeal may if it thinks fit vary the conditions of bail granted to an appellant by the Crown Court in the exercise of the power conferred by s. 81(1)(f) of the SCA 1981, or granted by the Court of Appeal under s. 19(1)(a) of the 1968 Act: CAA 1968, s. 19(1)(c). It is contemplated that the prosecutor may apply for variation.

9.3.2.5 Application by the appellant The powers conferred by s. 19(1) of the 1968 Act, as amended, may be exercised on the application of an appellant: CAA 1968, s. 19(2)(a). (The circumstances in which an appellant might seek revocation of bail would seem to be rare.)

9.3.2.6 Application by the Registrar of Criminal Appeals The powers conferred by s. 19(1) of the 1968 Act may also be exercised on a reference to the court by the Registrar of Criminal Appeals if it appears to the Registrar that any of them ought to be exercised: CAA 1968, s. 19(2)(b).

9.3.2.7 Rôle of the single judge The powers of the Court of Appeal under s. 19 of the 1968 Act may be exercised by a single judge in the same manner as by the Court of Appeal: CAA 1968 s. 31(1) and (2), as amended by the BA 1976, s. 12 and sch. 2; and by the CJA 1982, s. 29(2)(c). The references in s. 31 to a single judge are to any judge of the Court of Appeal or of the High Court: s. 45(2). For the purpose of exercising any of the powers in s. 31 a single judge may appoint the place in which to sit and may sit otherwise than in open court: r. 11(1), Criminal Appeal Rules 1968 (CAR 1968), SI 1968 No. 1262, as amended by the Criminal Appeal (Amendment) Rules (SI 1978 No. 1118) and the Criminal Appeal (Amendment) Rules 1987 (SI 1987 No. 1977). *A Guide to Proceedings in the Court of Appeal Criminal Division*, (see para. 9.2.3), para. 6(1), advises that normally the single judge will consider an application for leave to appeal together with any ancillary applications, e.g., bail or legal aid, without hearing oral argument. However, an application for bail pending appeal may be made to the court orally: CAR 1968, r. 3(2). A party in any proceedings under s. 31 may be represented by counsel or solicitor: CAR 1968, r. 11(2).

In cases where it is considered that there is a compelling and urgent case for appeal it is occasionally sought to make an expedited application to the single judge for bail pending appeal. After notice of appeal is lodged the applicant's legal representatives will request a hearing before the single judge at short notice for the purpose of applying under s. 31 of the CAA 1968 for leave to appeal and for bail. Application will also be made for legal aid, the single judge having power to grant such an application in respect of proceedings in the Court of Appeal by virtue of the Legal Aid in Criminal and Care Proceedings (General) Regulations 1989 (SI 1989 No. 344), reg. 22(1). (The application for legal aid may be referred to the Registrar of Criminal Appeals where it was made orally to the judge: *ibid.*) If the single judge refuses an application for leave to appeal and any ancillary applications such as that for bail under s. 19 of the CAA 1968, or for legal aid, the appellant is entitled to have the application determined by the Court of Appeal: CAA 1968, s. 31(3) and CAR 1968, r. 12(1). The single judge may refer the case to the full court: see *R v Munns* (1908) 1 Cr App R 4, CCA, and *A Guide to Proceedings in the Court of Appeal Criminal Division*, para. 6.3. It is improper to ask a High Court judge to act under s. 31 until the proper application for leave to appeal has been lodged: *R v Suggett* (1984) 81 Cr App R 243, CA.

9.3.2.8 Jurisdiction of the Registrar of Criminal Appeals The Registrar of Criminal Appeals may vary the conditions of bail granted to an appellant by the Court of Appeal or the Crown Court provided that the Registrar is satisfied that the respondent does not object to the variation: CAA 1968, s. 31A(2)(c) and s. 31A(3). Subject to this, the power of variation is to be exercised by the Registrar in the same manner as by the Court of Appeal and subject to the same provisions: s. 31A(3). If the Registrar refuses an application on the part of an appellant to exercise the power of variation the appellant shall be entitled to have the application determined by a single judge: s. 31A(4). Section 31A was inserted by the CAA 1995, s. 6.

9.3.2.9 Application to the full court on refusal by the single judge Where a single judge has refused an application on the part of an appellant to exercise any of the powers under s. 31(1) and 31(2) of the CAA 1968, the appellant may have the application determined by the Court by serving a notice in Form 15 on the Registrar within 14 days, or such longer period as a judge of the Court may fix, from the date on which notice of refusal was served on the appellant by the Registrar: CAR 1968, r. 12(1). A notice in Form 15 must be signed by, or on behalf, of the appellant: r. 21(2).

9.3.2.10 Bail following recommendation for deportation In *R v Ofori and Tackie* (1994) 99 Cr App R 219, the Court of Appeal held that the power to grant bail includes a power to grant bail to an appellant subject to a recommendation for deportation who is detained by virtue of the Immigration Act 1971, sch. 3, para. 2(1). It was observed that if the appeal is dismissed the Court of Appeal may nevertheless direct the appellant's release under sch. 3, para. 2(1A). It was suggested that a court proposing to grant bail or to direct the release of an offender subject to a recommendation for deportation might, depending on the circumstances, consider it wise to give the Secretary of State an opportunity to make representations.

9.3.2.11 Time on bail pending appeal The time that the appellant is on bail pending appeal is disregarded in computing the term of any sentence to which the person is, for the time being, subject: CAA 1968, s. 29(3). Any sentence passed by the Court of Appeal shall, unless the Court otherwise directs, begin to run from the time it would have begun to run if passed in the proceedings from which the appeal lies: s. 29(4).

9.3.2.12 Time in custody Time is to be reckoned as part of the term of any sentence to which the appellant is subject, unless the Court of Appeal gives contrary direction: CAA 1968, s. 29(1). Where such a contrary direction is given the reasons must be stated: s. 29(2). No such direction shall be given where leave to appeal has been granted, a certificate of fitness for appeal was given by the trial judge or the case was referred by the Secretary of State under s. 17 of the Act: s. 29(2), and see *Practice Direction (Crime: Sentence: Loss of Time)* [1980] 1 WLR 270; *R* v *Howitt* (1975) 61 Cr App R 327 and see *Archbold*, para. 7–226.

9.3.3 Principles applying to bail pending appeal

9.3.3.1 Normal practice is to refuse bail It has already been noted that the presumption in favour of bail enacted in the BA 1976 does not apply to persons appealing against conviction or sentence. Rather the presumption is the other way, and the Court of Appeal has shown considerable reluctance to grant bail pending appeal. In *R* v *Gott* (1922) 16 Cr App R 86, the Court of Criminal Appeal declared that 'the rule of the court is to refuse bail pending appeal'.

9.3.3.2 Exceptional circumstances It follows that bail will be granted only in exceptional circumstances, those which would drive the court to the conclusion that justice can be done only by the granting of bail: *R* v *Watton* (1978) 68 Cr App R 293, *per* Lord Lane CJ. In that case, the Court of Appeal held that exceptional circumstances will exist where there are *prima facie* grounds for believing the appeal will be successful or where it is likely that the sentence will have been served before the appeal is heard. In *R* v *Landy* (1981) 72 Cr App R 237 (unreported on the point) the Court granted an appellant bail pending appeal, where it was satisfied that there was a 'substantial point' to be argued on misdirection 'and that it could result in the conviction being quashed'. A further determining factor was that the hearing of the appeal would be delayed for some months in order for the transcript to be prepared. Conversely to these examples, it might be difficult to establish the existence of exceptional circumstances where, although there is an arguable point of appeal against conviction, the evidence against the appellant is substantial, and the sentence imposed is within the normal tariff. (If, however, the sentencing court had failed to give due and proper weight to exceptionally strong mitigating factors this might bring the case within the 'exception' category.)

9.3.3.3   Policy of resistance to bail pending appeal and avoidance of the cruelty of returning unsuccessful appellants to prison   The reluctance of the Court of Appeal to grant bail pending appeal appears to stem in part from a belief that where bail is granted and subsequently no ground is upheld for setting aside the custodial sentence, it will be hard on appellants who must return to prison, particularly if the hearing has been delayed for an extended period through no fault of their own. In *R v Gruffyd* (1972) 56 Cr App R 585, CA, at p. 589, Edmund Davies LJ observed: '[O]nce bail has been granted bail pending an appeal, judges who later hear it are presented with an additionally heavy problem. Bail inevitably raises hopes and to wreck them by ordering a return to custody is a painful duty for any judge.'

In *R v Priddle* [1981] Crim LR 114, the appellant had been granted bail pending appeal in order to take up a place on a spray-painting course. In dismissing his appeal against sentence, the court emphasised that where the sentence is clearly appropriate to the offence, personal matters which are the basis for an appeal for clemency should not normally lead to the granting of bail. The normal approach of the court was that bail should not be granted in such cases, as defendants who have been sentenced and subsequently released on bail might go back to serve their sentences with greater difficulty. In *R v Markham*; *R v Cole*, *The Times*, 15 October 1982, the Court of Appeal held that the fact that an appellant had acquired a job while on bail pending appeal, and was working well, should not become a ground of appeal against immediate imprisonment. The cruelty argument is reinforced by clear pronouncements from the Court of Appeal that the fact that the granting of bail pending appeal may lead to delay in the hearing of the appeal is not a reason for not sending the appellant back to prison: see *R v Cullis and Nash* (1969) 53 Cr App R 162. In *R v Kalia and Others* (1974) 60 Cr App R 200, at p. 209, Roskill LJ said:

> This Court desires to say as plainly as possible that where (exceptionally), intending appellants or applicants are released on bail and delay follows in the hearing of the appeal, that delay cannot and must not be relied upon, whenever the appeal or application fails, as a reason for their not being sent back to prison to serve their sentence. That is usually made plain when bail is granted, and it must be clearly understood that that is so.

9.3.3.4   Short sentences   In cases in which a short custodial sentence is being appealed, the Court of Appeal has disavowed the argument that bail should be granted to avoid the sentence being served before the hearing of the appeal, the problem being capable of resolution by an expedited listing. In *R v Imdad Shah* (1980) 144 JP 460, CA, Roskill LJ observed:

> Where these short sentence cases [three months' detention centre] come up on applications for leave to appeal, bail in the ordinary way should not be granted, because these short cases can always, at short notice, be put in the list. A transcript is not necessary. With counsel's help, or sometimes without it, it is easy to find out what happened and therefore to decide whether the short

sentence is right or wrong. Therefore, we respectfully suggest to judges who are minded to grant leave, that rather than grant bail they should take steps to see that the case is expedited and that the attention of the registrar is brought to the need for expedition. Bail should only be granted in exceptional circumstances.

9.3.3.5 Further argument for not granting bail: bail precludes court from taking account of time spent in custody In *R* v *Neal*, *The Times*, 29 January 1986, Lawton LJ said that the experience of the Court had shown that it was not always wise for an application to be made for bail pending the hearing of an appeal against sentence, particularly if the application was made soon after conviction and the sentence was comparatively short. The Court had frequently taken the view that a period in prison pending the hearing of an appeal was enough, but when the appellant had been in custody for only a comparatively short time it was exceedingly difficult for the court on the hearing of the appeal to say that that period was enough for the purposes of justice. This case was decided before statute made it clear that 'a custodial sentence shall be for such term . . . as . . . is commensurate with the seriousness of the offence' (CJA 1991, s. 2(2)(a)). A rare example of the court taking a different approach is provided by *R* v *Kennison* [1997] RTR 421. The appellant had been sentenced to 28 days' imprisonment following her conviction for dangerous driving and was granted bail pending appeal after serving the equivalent of a fourteen day sentence. The court reduced her sentence to 14 days' imprisonment 'as an act of mercy'.

9.3.3.6 Adverse repercussions of bail on release date The undesirability of granting bail pending appeal was illustrated in *R* v *Jayes*, *Independent (CS)*, 8 January 1990. The appellant was granted bail by the single judge pending appeal against conviction and sentence but his appeal against conviction was dismissed by the full Court. If he had remained in custody, he would have been eligible for parole after a further two weeks. Were he to be returned to prison following the dismissal of his appeal it would take longer than two weeks to deal with his application for parole. In the circumstances, his appeal against sentence was allowed and a sentence permitting his release at the date of the grant of bail was substituted.

9.3.4 Bail following an order for retrial or writ of *venire de novo*

9.3.4.1 Retrial order Where the Court of Appeal allows an appeal against conviction and orders a retrial under s. 7 of the Act of 1968, it may make such orders as appear to the Court to be necessary or expedient for the custody or release on bail of the person ordered to be retried pending retrial: CAA 1968, s. 8(2)(a).

9.3.4.2 Retrial of persons detained under the Mental Health Act 1983 Where a retrial is ordered in the case of a person who immediately before the determination of the appeal was liable to be detained under an order or direction under Part V of the Mental Health Act 1959 or Part III of the Mental Health Act 1983, that order or direction must continue in force pending the retrial as if the appeal had not been allowed, and any order of the Court of Appeal under s. 8 for the person's custody or admission to bail shall have effect subject to that order or direction: CAA 1968, s. 8(3).

9.3.4.3 Writs of *venire de novo* It is provided that the Court of Appeal exercises the jurisdiction to issue writs of *venire de novo*: SCA 1981, s. 53(2)(d). They are awarded where a purported trial 'is actually no trial at all' because of an irregularity of procedure: *Crane* v *DPP* [1921] 2 AC 299; *R* v *Rose* [1982] AC 822, HL. In such a case the Court of Appeal can order the defendant to appear at the Crown Court and to plead to and answer the indictment: see *R* v *Ellis (J.)* (1974) 57 Cr App R 571. The power of the Court of Appeal to grant bail on the ordering of the issue of a writ of *venire de novo* is implied by r. 4(6) of the CAR 1968, which requires the Registrar in such a case to forward to the appropriate officer of the Crown Court a copy of any record made in pursuance of s. 5 of the BA 1976 relating to such bail and also all recognizances and statements required to be sent to the Registrar under r. 4(6).

9.3.4.4 Time in custody or on bail pending retrial Schedule 2, para. 2(3), to the CAA 1968 provides that where, following a retrial, the defendant is sentenced to imprisonment or other detention, the sentence shall begin to run from the time when a like sentence, passed at the original trial, would have begun to run; but in computing the term of the sentence or the period to be spent in detention, as the case may be, there shall be disregarded:

(a) any time before conviction on retrial which would have been disregarded in computing that term or period if the sentence had been passed at the original trial and the original conviction had not been quashed; and
(b) any time during which the defendant was released on bail under s. 8(2) of the Act.

The statutory requirement for deduction from certain sentences of time spent in custody before sentence, shall apply to any sentence imposed on conviction on retrial as if it had been imposed on the original conviction: *ibid.*, para. 2(4).

9.3.5 Bail pending trial upon quashing of a jury's finding of disability

Where there has been a determination under s. 4 of the Criminal Procedure (Insanity) Act 1964 of the question of a person's fitness to be tried, and the jury have returned findings that the person is under a disability and did the act or made the omission charged, the person may appeal to the Court of Appeal against either or both those findings: CAA 1968, s. 15(1). The Court of Appeal shall allow an appeal under s. 15 if it thinks that the finding is unsafe: s. 16(1). Where an appeal is allowed under s. 15(1) the appellant may be tried accordingly for the offence and the Court may, subject to s. 25 of the CJPOA 1994, make such orders as appear to the Court necessary or expedient pending any such trial for the person's custody, release on bail, or continued detention under the MHA 1983: s. 16(3). Section 16 is amended by the Act of 1983, s. 148 and sch. 3, para. 23(f); CJPOA 1994, sch. 10, para. 21; CJA 1991, s. 7 and sch. 3, paras 2 and 3; and the CAA 1995, s. 1(5).

9.3.6 Conditions and recognizances

9.3.6.1 Imposition of conditions Where the Court of Appeal imposes a requirement under s. 3(5) or (6) of the BA 1976 to be complied with before the appellant's release on bail, the Court may give directions as to the manner in which, and the person or persons before whom, the requirement may be complied with: CAR 1968, r. 4(3). Where under s. 3(5) or (6) of the BA 1976 the Court has imposed a requirement to be complied with before the appellant's release on bail, the Registrar must issue a certificate in Form 11 containing a statement of the requirement: r. 4(5). A person authorised to do anything in relation to the compliance with the requirement is not required to do it without production of such a certificate: r. 4(5). Where in pursuance of an order for the grant of bail made by the Court a requirement is complied with before any person, it is the duty of that person to cause a statement that the requirement has been complied with to be transmitted forthwith to the Registrar, and a copy of the statement must at the same time be sent to the governor or keeper of the prison or other place of detention in which the appellant is detained, unless the requirement is complied with before such a governor or keeper: r. 4(6). Where, under s. 3(5) or (6) of the BA 1976, the court has imposed any requirement to be complied with before the appellant's release on bail, the governor or keeper of the prison or other place of detention in which the appellant is detained must, on receipt of a certificate in Form 11 stating that all such requirements have been complied with or on being otherwise so satisfied, release the appellant: r. 4(8).

9.3.6.2 Recognizances Where the Court grants bail to the appellant, the recognizance of any surety required as a condition of bail may be entered into before the Registrar or, where the person who has been granted bail is in prison or other place of detention, before the governor or keeper of the prison or place as well as before the persons specified in s. 8(4) of the BA 1976: CAR 1968, r. 4(1). The recognizance of a surety must be in Form 8, or, in cases where a retrial is ordered or where a writ of *venire de novo* is issued, in Form 10: r. 4(2). A person who, in pursuance of an order for the grant of bail made by the court, proposes to enter into a recognizance as a surety or give security must, unless the Court or a judge thereof otherwise directs, give notice to the prosecutor at least 24 hours before entering into the recognizance or before giving security: r. 4(4). Where the Court has fixed the amount in which a surety is to be bound by a recognizance, the Registrar must issue a certificate in Form 11 showing the amount and conditions, if any, of the recognizance and a person authorised to take the recognizance is not required to take it without production of the certificate: r. 4(5). Where, in pursuance of an order for the grant of bail made by the court, a recognizance is entered into before any person, it is the duty of that person to cause the recognizance to be transmitted forthwith to the Registrar, and a copy of such recognizance must at the same time be sent to the governor or keeper of the prison or other place of detention in which the appellant is detained, unless the recognizance was entered into before such governor: r. 4(6). A person taking a recognizance in pursuance of such an order must give a copy thereof to the person entering into the recognizance: r. 4(7). Where the Court has fixed the amount in which a surety is to be bound by a recognizance, the governor or keeper of the prison or other place of detention in which the appellant is detained must, on receipt of a certificate in Form 11 stating that the recognizances of all sureties required have been taken or on otherwise being so satisfied, release the appellant: r. 4(8). Where the Court has granted bail pending retrial or on ordering the issue of a writ of *venire de novo*, the Registrar must forward to the appropriate officer of the Crown Court all recognizances and statements required to be sent to the Registrar under r. 4(6): r. 4(9).

9.3.6.3   Forfeiture of recognizance   Where a recognizance has been entered into in respect of an appellant and it appears to the Court that a default has been made in performing the conditions of the recognizance, the Court may order the recognizance to be forfeited and such an order may:

(a)   allow time for payment; or
(b)   direct payment by instalments; or
(c)   discharge the recognizance or reduce the amount due thereunder: CAR 1968, r. 6(1).

Where the Court is to consider making an order under r. 6(1) for a recognizance to be forfeited, the Registrar must give notice to that effect to the person by whom the recognizance was entered into indicating the time and place at which the matter will be considered: r. 6(2). No such order shall be made before the expiry of seven days after the notice required has been given: r. 6(2).

9.3.7   Procedural details

9.3.7.1   Form of notice of application   Notice of an application by the appellant to be granted bail pending the determination of an appeal or pending retrial shall be in Form 4 and must be accompanied by a notice of appeal or of an application for leave to appeal, unless such notice has previously been given: CAR 1968, r. 3(1)(a).

9.3.7.2   Service of notice of application on Crown Court officer   Where a notice of application for bail pending appeal is given together with a notice of appeal or notice of application for leave to appeal, the notice of application must be served on the appropriate officer of the Crown Court: CAR 1968, r. 3(1). Service may be effected by delivery or posting to the appropriate officer at the Crown Court centre at which the conviction, verdict, finding or sentence appealed against was given or passed: r. 21(1)(aa)(ii). Service on the appropriate Crown Court officer may be effected by delivery to the person having custody of the appellant: r. 21(1)(a)(i) or r. 21(1)(aa)(i). A person having custody of an appellant to whom notice is delivered must endorse on it the date of delivery and cause it to be forwarded forthwith to the appropriate Crown Court officer, as the case may be: r. 21(2).

9.3.7.3 Service of notice of application on Registrar of Criminal Appeals
Where the notice of application is not served together with a notice of appeal or of application for leave to appeal it must be served on the Registrar of Criminal Appeals: CAR 1968, r. 3(1). Service on the Registrar may be effected by delivery or posting to the Registrar's office in the Royal Courts of Justice, London WC2 (addressed to the Registrar): r. 21(1)(a). In the case of an appellant who is in custody, service on the Registrar may be effected by delivery to the person having custody of the appellant: r. 21(1)(a)(i) or r. 21(1)(aa)(i). A person having custody of an appellant to whom notice is delivered must endorse on it the date of delivery and cause it to be forwarded forthwith to the Registrar, as the case may be: r. 21(2).

9.3.7.4 Provision for oral application   As stated at para. 9.3.2.7, an application under r. 3 may be made to the court orally: CAR 1968, r. 3(2).

9.3.7.5 Other notices required to be served   Unless the court or judge thereof otherwise directs, notice in writing of intention to make an application to the court relating to bail must be served:

(a)   on the prosecutor; and
(b)   on the Director of Public Prosecutions (if conducting the prosecution); or
(c)   if the application is to be made by the prosecutor or a constable under s. 3(8) of the BA 1976 for a variation of the conditions of bail, on the appellant: CAR 1968, r. 3(3).

9.3.7.6 Minimum required notice   The notice required under r. 3(3) of the CAR 1968 must be served at least 24 hours before the application is made.

9.3.7.7 Records   Rule 4(10) of the CAR 1968 provides that any record required by s. 5 of the BA 1976 must be made by including in the case file:

(a)   where bail is granted, a copy of Form 11 issued under r. 4(5) and a statement of the day on which, and the time and place at which, the appellant is notified to surrender to custody;
(b)   in any other case, a copy of the notice of any determination by the court under s. 31 of the CAA 1968 required to be served under r. 15 of the CAR 1968.

Where the Court has granted bail pending retrial or on ordering the issue of a writ of *venire de novo*, the Registrar must forward to the appropriate officer of the

Crown Court a copy of any record made in pursuance of s. 5 of the BA 1976 relating to such bail: CAR 1968 r. 4(9).

9.4 BAIL ON APPEAL TO THE HOUSE OF LORDS

9.4.1 Appeal by the defendant or the prosecutor

9.4.1.1 Availability of appeal An appeal lies to the House of Lords, at the instance of the defendant or the prosecutor, from any decision of the Court of Appeal on an appeal to that court under Part I of the CAA 1968 or in respect of preparatory hearings: CAA 1968, s. 33(1).

9.4.1.2 Leave required The appeal lies only with the leave of the Court of Appeal or of the House of Lords, and leave shall not be granted unless it is certified by the Court of Appeal that a point of general public importance is involved in the decision and it appears to the court granting leave that the point is one which ought to be considered by the House of Lords: CAA 1968, s. 33(2). See *Practice Direction (House of Lords: Petitions: Leave to Appeal)* [1979] 1 WLR 498, and *Practice Direction (House of Lords: Petitions: Criminal)* [1979] 1 WLR 122.

9.4.1.3 Time limits An application to the Court of Appeal for leave to appeal to the House of Lords, must be made within 14 days after the decision, and an application to the House of Lords for leave must be made within 14 days after the refusal of leave by the Court of Appeal: CAA 1968, s. 34(1). The time may be extended: s. 34(2). An appeal to the House of Lords is treated as pending until any application for leave to appeal is disposed of and, if leave to appeal is granted, until the appeal is disposed of: s. 34(3). An application for leave to appeal is treated as disposed of at the expiration of the time within which it may be made, if it is not made within that time: s. 34(3).

9.4.1.4 Jurisdiction to grant bail On the application of a person appealing, or applying for leave to appeal, to the House of Lords (other than a person appealing or applying for leave to appeal against orders or rulings at preparatory hearings) the Court of Appeal may, subject to s. 25 of the CJPOA 1994, if it seems fit, grant bail pending the determination of the appeal: CAA 1968, s. 36(1), as amended by the CJA 1987, s. 15 and sch. 2, para. 4; the CJPOA 1994, sch. 10, para. 23; and the Criminal Procedure and Investigations Act 1996, s. 36(1).

9.4.2 Application for bail by defendant.

9.4.2.1 Oral application or application by notice to the Registrar An application to the Court of Appeal by a defendant for the granting of bail pending an appeal to the House of Lords:

(a) must made orally immediately after the decision of the court from which an appeal lies to the House of Lords; or

(b)   must be by way of notice in Form 17 served on the Registrar: CAR 1968, r. 23(1)(d).

Service on the Registrar of the Form 17 notice may be effected by delivering it to the Registrar, leaving it at the Registrar's office in the Royal Courts of Justice, London WC2 (addressed to the Registrar), sending it by post, or delivering it to the person having custody of the appellant: r. 21(1)(a). A person having custody of an appellant to whom the notice is delivered must endorse on it the date of delivery and cause it to be forwarded forthwith to the Registrar: r. 21(2).

9.4.2.2   Recognizance of a surety   The recognizance of a surety must be in Form 19: CAR 1968, r. 23(3).

9.4.2.3   Bail may be granted by a single judge   The power to grant bail may be exercised by a single judge of the Court of Appeal or of the High Court: CAA 1968, ss. 44(1) and 45(2).

9.4.2.4   Determination by the full court   Where a judge refuses bail the applicant is entitled to have the application determined by the full Court of Appeal: CAA 1968, s. 44(1). For the purpose of having an application determined by the Court in pursuance of s. 44, rr. 11 and 12 of the CAR 1968 (see paras 9.3.2.7 and 9.3.2.9) apply with the necessary modifications: CAR 1968, r. 23(6).

9.4.2.5   Procedural rules   With necessary modifications the procedure set out in rr. 4 and 6 of the CAR 1968 for the regulation of applications for bail pending appeal to the Court of Appeal applies also to applications for bail pending appeal to House of Lords: CAR 1968, r. 23(4).

9.4.3   Bail upon a prosecutor's appeal

Section 37(1) and (2) of the CAA 1968, provide that where, immediately after a decision of the Court of Appeal to allow an appeal, the prosecutor is granted or gives notice of an intention to apply for leave to appeal to the House of Lords and, but for the successful appeal the defendant would be liable to be detained, the Court of Appeal may order the defendant's detention or release on bail. Bail may be granted as under s. 36: s. 37(2). For persons detained in hospital under an order or direction under the MHA 1983 or the Criminal Procedure (Insanity) Act 1964, the order for detention shall be one of continued detention in that hospital: s. 37(4) and (4A). The court may order that the defendant shall be detained or not released except on bail for as long as the appeal to the House of Lords is pending: s. 37(2). Unless the appeal has previously been disposed of, an order under s. 37 of the 1968 Act ceases to have effect at the expiration of the period for which the defendant would have been liable to be detained but for the decision of the Court of Appeal: s. 37(3).

Where the Court of Appeal has power to make an order under s. 37, and either no order for detention is made or the defendant is released or discharged, by virtue of s. 37(3), before the appeal is disposed of, the defendant shall not be liable to be again detained as the result of the decision of the House of Lords on the appeal: s. 37(5). In *DPP* v *Merriman* [1972] AC 584, the House of Lord emphasised the desirability of the provisions of s. 37 being brought to the attention of the Court of Appeal in all cases in which the prosecution seek leave to appeal to the House of Lords from the quashing of a conviction and sentence of imprisonment. In *R* v *Hollinshead* [1985] AC 975, their Lordships held that an order under s. 37 should be made unless there were strong reasons for not so doing. The reason was: '. . . [to] ensure that, if the House takes a different view of the law from that taken in the Court of Appeal and therefore restores the quashed convictions, the offenders in question do not avoid all punishment . . .' (*per* Lord Roskill, at p. 999). In *Government of USA* v *McCaffery* [1984] 2 All ER 570, HL, this advice was applied to the case of fugitive offenders.

9.4.4   Time on bail to be disregarded for sentence

Where a person subject to a sentence is granted bail under s. 36 or s. 37 of the CAA 1968, any time on bail must be disregarded in computing the term of sentence: CAA 1968, s. 43(1).

9.5   APPEAL AGAINST COMMITTAL FOR CONTEMPT

9.5.1   Appellate jurisdiction

An appeal lies from any order or decision of a court in the exercise of its jurisdiction to punish for contempt of court (including criminal contempt): Administration of Justice Act 1960, s. 13(6). Section 13(5) provides that an appeal lies under this provision, to the exclusion of other rights of appeal, from the order or decision of:

(a)   an inferior court – to the High Court;

(b)   a county court or any other inferior court from which appeals generally lie to the Court of Appeal – to the Court of Appeal;

(c)   a single judge of the High Court (or any court having powers of the High Court or a judge of that court) – to the Court of Appeal;

(d)   the Crown Court – to the Court of Appeal;

(e)   the Divisional Court or the Court of Appeal (including an appeal relating to punishment for contempt of court) – to the House of Lords.

The offence of failing to surrender to bail is dealt with by the Crown Court as a contempt (see Chapter 4).

9.5.2 Bail

9.5.2.1 Availability In the case of an appeal to the Divisional Court or to the House of Lords from the Divisional Court, the High Court may order an appellant in custody to be released on the giving of security (whether with or without sureties, or otherwise and for such reasonable sums as the court may fix) for the appellant to appear within ten days after the judgment of the Divisional Court, or, as the case may be, the House of Lords, before the court from whose order or decision the appeal was brought, unless the order or decision is reversed by that judgment: RSC 1965, Ord. 109, r. 3.

9.5.2.2 Procedure and practice The procedure for application for bail is that laid down in the RSC 1965, Ord. 109, rr. 3 and 9. Evidence may be received by way of affidavit: *Crowley* v *Brown* [1964] 1 WLR 147, CA. Although statutory provision is made for the grant of bail, the Court of Appeal normally hears such appeals very expeditiously, usually within one or two days of the appeal being set down, rather than granting bail and setting a later date for the hearing (see Chatterton, C., *Bail: Law and Practice*, London: Butterworths, 1986, p. 227).

10 The Jurisdiction of the High Court

10.1 APPLICATION TO HIGH COURT JUDGE IN CHAMBERS

10.1.1 Magistrates' courts

10.1.1.1 Bail decision by magistrates Where a magistrates' court withholds bail in criminal proceedings or imposes conditions in granting bail in criminal proceedings, subject to s. 25 of the CJPOA 1994, the High Court may grant bail or vary the conditions: CJA 1967, s. 22(1). This provision is without prejudice to any other powers of the High Court to grant bail: s. 22(2). Section 22 of the 1967 Act will be used where the magistrates' court has refused bail after a person:

(a) ' has been remanded, a certificate of full argument having been issued (Form 151A, MCR 1981, rr. 66, 90);

(b) has been committed to the Crown Court for trial, or for sentence or to be 'dealt with';

(c) has been convicted and sentenced and has appealed to the Crown Court against the conviction or sentence; or

(d) has applied under s. 111 of the MCA 1980 to state a case for the decision of the High Court. (In such a case the bail decision will have been given under s. 113.)

In the cases of (a), (b) and (c) there is a parallel right to apply for bail to the Crown Court.

10.1.1.2 Bail on application for *certiorari* Subject to s. 25 of the CJPOA 1994, the High Court may grant bail to a person who has been convicted or sentenced by a magistrates' court and has applied to the High Court by way of judicial review for an order of *certiorari* to remove the proceedings in the magistrates' court into the High Court, or who has applied to the High Court for leave to make such an application: CJA 1948, s. 37(1)(d), as amended by the BA 1976, sch. 2, para. 11(d), and the 1994 Act, s 168(2) and sch. 10, para. 6. The magistrates' court has no jurisdiction to grant bail in such a case. Where the court so grants bail to a person the time at which the person must appear in the event of the conviction or sentence not being quashed by the High Court is such time within ten days after the judgment of the High Court has been given as may be specified by the High Court: s. 37(1A)(a). The place at which the person must appear in that event is a magistrates' court acting for the same petty sessions area as the court which convicted or sentenced the person: s. 37(1A)(b). In *Re Herbage, The Times*, 25 October 1985, DC, it was held that judicial review was not appropriate with regard to the grant of bail following a refusal by justices and a judge in chambers.

10.1.2 Crown Court

Where a Crown Court withholds bail in criminal proceedings or imposes conditions in granting bail in criminal proceedings, the High Court may grant bail or vary the conditions. Applications to the High Court for bail or for variation of conditions will be made in the various circumstances set out immediately below.

10.1.2.1 Crown Court refusal after a refusal by a magistrates' court An application to the High Court for bail might be made where, following the refusal of a magistrates' court to grant bail, an unsuccessful application to grant it is made to the Crown Court.

10.1.2.2 Case stated An application to the High Court for bail might be made after the Crown Court, having given a particular decision and having been asked to state a case on that decision for the opinion of the High Court, has, under s. 81 of the SCA 1981, refused to grant bail pending the High Court hearing. In such a case the High Court, subject to s. 25 of the CJPOA 1994, may grant bail: CJA 1948, s. 37(1)(b)(i).

10.1.2.3 *Certiorari* The High Court may, subject to s. 25 of the CJPOA 1994, grant bail to a person whose case is in the Crown Court and who has applied to the High Court for an order of *certiorari* to remove those proceedings into the High Court, or who has applied to the High Court for leave to make such an application: CJA 1948, s. 37(1)(b)(ii).

10.1.2.4 Appeal to the Court of Appeal (See Chapter 9, para. 9.3.) An appeal to the Court of Appeal against conviction in, or sentence imposed by, the Crown Court, or an application for leave of the court to appeal, must be preceded by the giving of notice of appeal or notice of application for leave to appeal in such manner as may be directed by rules of court: CAA 1968, s. 18. Notice of appeal or of an application for leave to appeal must be given by completing the prescribed form and serving it on the Registrar of Criminal Appeals: CAR 1968, r. 2. Following an application to appeal to the Court of Appeal a defendant may apply to the High Court for bail pending appeal: CAA 1968, ss. 1 and 9. A single judge

of the High Court may grant bail pending appeal: s. 31(1) and (2)(e). However, in
R v Suggett (1985) 81 Cr App R 243 it was held to be improper for counsel to ask
a judge, even a High Court judge on circuit, to act under s. 31 before the
appropriate application for leave to appeal has been made in accordance with
s. 18(1) of the 1968 Act. The reason was explained by Lord Lane CJ, at p. 245:

> It is improper for counsel to ask the judge even if he was a High Court judge
> on circuit to act under section 31 of the Criminal Appeal Act 1968 and to
> consider the question of bail and the question of leave to appeal. The result of
> this 'mis-procedure' is that the work of the Criminal Appeal Office is short
> circuited, the proper documents are not in existence and other cases, possibly
> more deserving cases, get pushed back in the pipeline.

10.1.3 Statutory right to bail

It has been suggested that bail by the High Court is not subject to the statutory
general right to bail enacted in s. 4 of the BA 1976 and that the issue falls to be
decided by exercise of judicial discretion (see Chatterton, *Bail: Law and Practice*,
London: Butterworths, 1986, p. 211). It is true that the power of the High Court
to grant bail arises from its inherent jurisdiction, preserved by s. 22 of the CJA
1967 (see *R v Reading Crown Court, ex parte Malik* [1981] QB 451). However,
s. 4 applies:

(a) where a person accused of an offence appears or is brought before a
magistrates' court or the Crown Court in the course of or in connection with
proceedings for the offence; or
(b) where the person 'applies to a court for bail in connection with proceedings': BA 1976, s. 4(2).

The distinction between (a) and (b) is that the former establishes the right to bail,
irrespective of the making of an application, when the accused appears before a
magistrates' court or Crown Court in the course of or in connection with
proceedings for the offence. Provision (b), by contrast, refers to purposive bail
applications. An application for bail to a High Court judge in chambers does not
take place in the course of proceedings but is *sui generis* for the purpose of bail.
This is the significance of the reference in (b) to bail applications made in the
proceedings to *a court*. The wording used in (b) studiously avoids limiting its ambit
to magistrates' courts and Crown Courts. Where, therefore, proceedings are
pending in the magistrates' court or Crown Court, s. 4 will apply to applications
for bail made to the High Court ('a court'). However, s. 4(2) also provides that the
'subsection does not apply as respects proceedings on or against a person's
conviction of the offence or proceedings against a fugitive offender for the
offence'.

10.1.4 Practice and procedure for applications to High Court judge in chambers

The practice and procedure involved in bail applications to a High Court judge in chambers are contained in the RSC 1965, Ord. 79, r. 9, as amended by The Rules of the Supreme Court (Amendment No. 2) of 1967 (SI 1967 No. 1809); RSC (Amendment No. 5) of 1971 (SI 1971 No. 1955); RSC (Amendment)(Bail) of 1978 (SI 1978 No. 251); and RSC (Amendment No. 3) of 1989 (SI 1989 No. 1307).

10.1.4.1 Defendant in custody Where a defendant is in custody in any criminal proceedings an application to the High Court for bail in those proceedings must be made by summons before a judge in chambers to show cause why the defendant should not be granted bail: RSC 1965, Ord. 79 r. 9(1)(a).

10.1.4.2 Defendant applying for variation of conditions of bail Where a defendant has been admitted to bail in criminal proceedings, an application to the High Court in respect of bail in those proceedings must be made by summons before a judge in chambers to show cause why the variation in the arrangements of bail proposed by the applicant should not be made: RSC 1965, Ord. 79, r. 9(1)(b). Such an application may be made by the defendant, or by the prosecutor or a constable under s. 3(8) of the BA 1976.

10.1.4.3 Service of summons At least 24 hours before the day specified for the hearing the summons (in Form No. 97 or 97A, Appendix A) must normally be served:

(a)   where the application was made by the defendant, on the prosecutor and on the Director of Public Prosecutions, if the prosecution is being carried on by that official;
(b)   where the application was made by the prosecutor or a constable under s. 3(8) of the BA 1976, on the defendant: RSC 1965, Ord. 79, r. 9(2).

10.1.4.4 Requirement for affidavit Every application must normally be supported by affidavit: RSC 1965, Ord. 79, r. 9(3).

10.1.4.5 Intervention of Official Solicitor A defendant in custody who desires to apply for bail but is unable through lack of means to instruct a solicitor may give notice to the judge in chambers requesting representation by the Official Solicitor in the application: RSC 1965, Ord. 79, r. 9(4). The judge may assign the Official Solicitor to act accordingly: *ibid.* Where the Official Solicitor has been so assigned the judge may dispense with the requirements of r. 9(1) to (3) and may deal with the application in a summary manner: RSC 1965, Ord. 79, r. 9(5).

10.1.4.6   Presence or absence of the parties   An application under r. 9 may be granted in either the presence or absence of the parties: RSC 1965, Ord. 79, r. 9(2), applying Ord. 32, r. 5.

10.1.4.7   Transmission of order granting bail   Where the judge in chambers by whom an application for bail in criminal proceedings is heard grants the defendant bail, the order must be in Form No. 98 in Appendix A and a copy of the order must be transmitted forthwith:

(a)   where the defendant has been committed to the Crown Court for trial or to be sentenced or otherwise dealt with, to the appropriate officer of the Crown Court;
(b)   in any other case, to the clerk of the court which committed the defendant: RSC 1965, Ord. 79, r. 9(6).

10.1.4.8   Recognizance of sureties   The recognizance of any surety required as a condition of bail imposed by a judge in chambers may, where the defendant is in a prison or other place of detention, be entered into before the governor of the prison or place as well as before the persons specified in s. 8(4) of the BA 1976: RSC 1965, Ord. 79, r. 9(6A), and see Chapter 2, para. 2.1.6.

10.1.4.9   Other conditions imposed   Where under s. 3(5) or (6) of the BA 1976 a judge in chambers imposes a requirement to be complied with before a person's release on bail, the judge may give directions as to the manner in which and the person or persons before whom the requirement may be complied with: RSC 1965, Ord. 79, r. 9(6B).

10.1.4.10   Requirement for notice by proposed surety or person proposing to give security   A person who in pursuance of an order for the grant of bail made by a judge under r. 9 proposes to enter into a recognizance or give security must, unless the judge otherwise directs, give notice (in Form No. 100 in Appendix A) to the prosecutor at least 24 hours before the recognizance is entered into or the security is given: RSC 1965, Ord. 79, r. 9(7).

10.1.4.11   Transmission to appropriate court of recognizance or statement of compliance with other requirement   Where in pursuance of an order under r. 9 imposing the requirement for a surety or any other requirement, a recognizance is entered into or the requirement is complied with before any person, it is the duty of that person to cause the recognizance or, as the case may be, a statement of the requirement complied with to be transmitted forthwith:

(a)   where the defendant has been committed to the Crown Court for trial or to be sentenced or otherwise dealt with, to the appropriate officer of the Crown Court;
(b)   in any other case, to the clerk of the court which committed the defendant: RSC 1965, Ord. 79, r. 9(8).

10.1.4.12 Copy of recognizance or compliance statement to be sent to the prison governor, etc A copy of the recognizance or compliance statement required to be transmitted to the appropriate court under r. 9(8) must at the same time be sent to the governor or keeper of the prison or other place of detention in which the defendant is detained, unless the recognizance was entered into or the requirement complied with before such governor or keeper: RSC 1965, Ord. 79, r. 9(8).

10.1.4.13 Variation of arrangements for granting bail An order by the judge in chambers varying the arrangements under which the defendant has been granted bail must be in Form 98A in Appendix A, and a copy of the order must be transmitted forthwith:

(a) where the defendant has been committed to the Crown Court for trial or to be sentenced or otherwise dealt with, to the appropriate officer of the Crown Court;

(b) in any other case, to the clerk of the court which committed the defendant: RSC 1965, Ord. 79, r. 9(10).

10.1.4.14 Record of decision to be filed The record required by s. 5 of the BA 1976 to be made by the High Court must be made by including in the file relating to the case in question a copy of the relevant order of the court and must contain the particulars set out in Form No 98 or 98A in Appendix A, whichever is appropriate; except that in the case of a decision to withhold bail the record must be made by inserting a statement of the decision on the Court's copy of the relevant summons and including it in the file relating to the case in question: RSC 1965, Ord. 79, r. 9(13).

10.1.4.15 Central Criminal Court Where a defendant is committed for trial to the Central Criminal Court, the application for bail to the High Court must be to a judge acting as a High Court judge and not to a judge in chambers at the Royal Courts of Justice: *Practice Direction (applications for bail: Central Criminal Court)* [1965] 1 WLR 710.

10.1.4.16 Enforcement of decision appealed against when bail granted pending appeal Where in pursuance of an order of a judge in chambers a person is released on bail in any criminal proceedings pending the determination of an appeal to the High Court or House of Lords, or an application for an order of *certiorari*, upon the abandonment of the appeal or application, or upon the decision of the High Court or House of Lords being given, any magistrate (being a magistrate acting for the same petty sessions area as the magistrates' court by which that person was convicted or sentenced) may issue process for enforcing the decision in respect of which such appeal or application was brought or, as the case may be, the decision of the High Court of House of Lords: RSC 1965, Ord. 79, r. 9(11).

10.1.5   Estreat of recognizances

10.1.5.1   Estreatment must be authorised by a judge No recognizance acknowledged in or removed into the Queen's Bench Division may be estreated without the order of a judge: RSC 1965, Ord. 79, r. 8(1). If it appears to the judge that a default has been made in performing the conditions of the recognizance, the judge may order estreatment: *ibid.* A surety who consents to a variation of conditions of bail does not thereby 'acknowledge' a recognizance: see *R* v *Warwick Crown Court, ex parte Smalley* (1987) 84 Cr App R 51, DC.

10.1.5.2   Procedure for estreatment Every application to estreat a recognizance in the Queen's Bench Division must be made by summons to a judge in chambers and must be supported by an affidavit showing in what manner the breach has been committed and proving that the summons was duly served: RSC 1965, Ord. 79, r. 8(2).

10.1.5.3   Summons to be served two clear days before hearing A summons must be served at least two clear days before the day named in it for the hearing: RSC 1965, Ord. 79, r. 8(3).

10.1.5.4   Trial by jury available On the hearing of the application the judge may, and if requested by any party must, direct any issue of fact in dispute to be tried by a jury: RSC 1965, Ord. 79, r. 8(4). It is not known if the rule is ever invoked.

10.1.6   Successive applications in the High Court and the Crown Court

10.1.6.1   High Court application followed by Crown Court application The RSC 1965, Ord. 79, r. 9(12) provides: 'If an applicant to the High Court in any criminal proceedings is refused bail by a judge in chambers, the applicant shall not be entitled to make a fresh application for bail to any other judge or to a Divisional Court.'

The paragraph and its impact on the relationship between the bail jurisdiction of the High Court and that of the Crown Court was considered in *R* v *Reading Crown Court, ex parte Malik* [1981] QB 451. The applicant had been committed for trial in custody by magistrates and had unsuccessfully applied for bail to a High Court judge in chambers. He then applied for bail to the Crown Court to which he had been committed for trial, but the circuit judge refused to entertain the application, apparently on the ground that the words 'any other judge' embraced circuit judges in the Crown Court. The applicant sought judicial review and the Divisional Court, holding that the judge was wrong not to have considered the applicant's claim on its merits, explained that the words 'any other judge' in r. 9(12) refer to the judge in chambers and not to the particular judge who considered the earlier application. Consequently, the paragraph was not an obstacle to the exercise by the circuit judge of the Crown Court's jurisdiction. The Divisional Court pointed out that the erroneous nature of the circuit judge's approach was demonstrated by its inconsistency with s. 5(6)(a) of the BA 1976, which requires justices on committal for trial (or after issuing a full argument certificate) to inform an unrepresented defendant of the right to apply for bail to the High Court or the Crown Court. Yet if the judge were correct there was no such right of application to the Crown Court if a previous application for bail had been refused by a judge of the High Court. The Divisional Court showed that the circuit judge's interpretation of r. 9(12) was inconsistent with another statutory rule. Rule 18(1) of the CCR 1971, as amended by the Crown Court (Amendment) Rules 1978 and subsequently by r. 20 of the CCR 1982, provides that: 'Every person who makes an application to the Crown Court relating to bail shall inform the court of any earlier application to the High Court or the Crown Court relating to bail in the course of the same proceedings.' The rule expressly presupposes the legitimacy of an application to the Crown Court after an earlier High Court application. In the view of the Divisional Court, the jurisdictions of the Crown Court and of the High Court in relation to bail remain quite distinct, notwithstanding that judges of the High Court are empowered to exercise the jurisdiction and powers of the Crown Court and, when doing so, are judges of the Crown Court. Thus, RSC 1965, Ord. 79, r. 9(12) relates exclusively to the High Court, while the power to grant bail is conferred on the Crown Court by s. 81 of the SCA 1981 (re-enacting s. 13(4) of the Courts Act 1971). The Crown Court jurisdiction arises only after magistrates have dealt with a person in one or another of the various ways specified in s. 81. The power of the High Court, on the other hand, exists both before and after committal and arises from its inherent jurisdiction and from s. 22(1) of the CJA 1967 (see para. 10.1.1) which preserves it. Giving the judgment of the court, Donaldson LJ, said (at p. 456):

> The origin of this rule is clear. There was at one time a widespread belief that the jurisdiction of the High Court to grant bail was not that of the High Court as such, but of the individual judges of that court. The logical consequence would be that the decision of one judge to refuse bail would not preclude another judge from entertaining the application immediately thereafter or perhaps even simultaneously. This belief should not have survived the [three decisions in *Re Hastings* [1958] 1 WLR 372; [1959] 1 QB 358; [1959] Ch 368]. However, it was resurrected in *Re Kray* [1965] Ch 736. Order 79, rule 9(12) was made in order to put the matter beyond doubt. It was also designed to affirm that the jurisdiction of the High Court was that of the court rather than the individual judges and that it was exercisable only by the judge in chambers.

10.1.6.2 Successive Crown Court applications While deciding that r. 9(12) did not disentitle a defendant from making an application for bail to the Crown Court after an earlier unsuccessful application to the High Court, the Divisional Court was anxious to dispel any notion that 'simultaneous or immediately consecutive applications for bail can be made to more than one Crown Court judge'. In the view of the court the principle of no renewed application for bail without a change of circumstances, which at that time prevailed in the magistrates' court as a result of *R* v *Nottingham Justices, ex parte Davies* [1981] QB 38 (see generally Chapter 5), was also applicable to the Crown Court.

10.1.6.3   Successive High Court applications   The RSC 1965, Ord. 79, r. 9(12) expressly precludes the right to make successive applications for bail to a High Court judge in chambers. This has been slightly ameliorated by the judgment in *Re Herbage, The Times*, 25 October 1985, in which Glidewell LJ applied the *Nottingham Justices* principle to concede that it was within the discretion of the judge in chambers who heard the original application to indicate a readiness to consider the matter further if there was a change in circumstances.

10.1.6.4   Crown Court application followed by High Court application   In *R* v *Reading Crown Court, ex parte Malik* (see para. 10.1.6.1) Donaldson LJ stated that under its inherent jurisdiction the High Court may hear an application for bail after an application has been refused by the Crown Court.

10.2   HABEAS CORPUS

10.2.1   Introduction

10.2.1.1   Origins and background   The ancient action, or writ, of habeas corpus – literally 'have the body' – is of the highest constitutional importance, safeguarding the liberty of the subject from any form of unwarranted imprisonment or detention, and is one of the key elements which came to mark out the English state as governed by the rule of law. There are a number of forms of the writ, but in applying for bail in criminal proceedings the writ used is *habeas corpus ad subjiciendum*, which, if granted:

> . . . commands the person to whom it is directed to produce the body of the person detained with the day and cause of his caption and detention, *ad faciendum, subjiciendum et recipiendum*, 'to do, submit to and receive' whatever the court shall direct. Its use is for testing the legality of imprisonment.
> (*Osborne's Concise Law Dictionary*, London: Sweet & Maxwell, 1993)

The ultimate force of the writ depends on the fact that it is only by ordering the person's physical presence in court itself can there be any guarantee that an order for release will be obeyed. The writ is embodied in statute (Habeas Corpus Acts 1679, 1816 and 1862, and the Administration of Justice Act 1960), but the right to the writ exists independently of statute: *Ex parte Besset* (1844) 6 QB 481. The 1679 Act made the granting of writs of habeas corpus compulsory where the person was imprisoned without lawful cause and provided for the trial without delay of those in custody for treason and felony. The 1816 Act provided for the issue and return of the writ in the vacation as well as in term. The 1862 Act precluded the writ from issuing out of England into any colony or dominion of the Crown which had a court of its own authorised to issue the writ, but subject to this constraint the jurisdiction of the writ extends to all parts of the Crown's dominion.

Because of the importance attached to the liberty of the subject applications for habeas corpus are always heard first in the list before any other court business.

10.2.1.2 Habeas corpus and the police One of the common uses of habeas corpus in the past was to secure the release of suspects held without charge by the police, but its use in this context has been largely superseded by the provisions of PACE 1984. Nevertheless, s. 51(8) of the 1984 Act specifically preserves the right of a person in police custody to apply for a writ of habeas corpus or other prerogative remedy.

10.2.1.3 Extension of custody time limit An application for habeas corpus will rarely be appropriate as a means of appeal against a decision of a magistrates' court to extend or further extend a custody time limit: *R v Governor of Canterbury Prison, ex parte Craig* [1991] 2 QB 195.

10.2.1.4 Other remedies exhausted Habeas corpus may not be sought until other remedies have been tried. In *Re Moles* [1981] Crim LR 170, it was held, refusing an application *ex parte* for a writ of habeas corpus where magistrates had refused to hear argument on a submission that there had been a change of circumstances warranting a fresh application for bail, that the proper course was to make an application to a judge in chambers (see also *R v Governor of Pentonville Prison, ex parte Gilliland* [1984] Crim LR 229, discussed at para. 10.2.1.5, below). An application for habeas corpus may not be used as a means of collateral attack upon a conviction by a court of competent jurisdiction: *Re Leachman* [1998] COD 466, DC.

10.2.1.5 Excessive conditions of bail Excessive bail, which at that time meant sureties, is prohibited by the Bill of Rights 1688. The writ may be appropriate where the amount of surety is excessive: *R v Thomas* [1956] Crim LR 119. The amount of a surety is not excessive merely because the defendant is unable to take advantage of it: *R v Goswami* [1969] 1 QB 453. In *R v Governor of Pentonville Prison, ex parte Gilliland* [1984] Crim LR 229, the applicant was granted bail in extradition proceedings on condition that he provided a security in the sum of £50,000. The prosecution applied to vary the condition in accordance with s. 8(3) of the BA 1976 on the grounds that the accused had in excess of £1.1 million in a Swiss bank account and he had corruptly received sums in excess of £6 million. The stipendiary magistrate varied the condition so as to require a security of £500,000. The defendant applied for a writ of habeas corpus on the grounds that the increase was so great as to amount to a revocation of bail and that the condition was excessive and contrary to the Bill of Rights. The Divisional Court refused the application on the ground that the correct procedure to adopt in complaining that the condition was excessive was to apply to a judge in chambers in the first instance, but took the view in any event that in the light of the additional material presented to the magistrate, it could not be said that the variation of the condition amounted to a revocation of the original order.

10.2.1.6 Allegation of ultra vires   Judicial review will be appropriate where it is submitted that in relation to bail the court has acted *ultra vires*. In *R* v *Governor of Ashford Remand Centre, ex parte Harris* [1984] Crim LR 618; 148 JP 584, the applicant was committed for trial and granted bail. As he was leaving the dock, he made a disparaging remark to a police officer. The stipendiary magistrate called him back to the dock and rescinded bail. The defendant sought habeas corpus on the ground that his detention was unlawful; that having committed him for trial and dealt with the question of bail, the magistrate was *functus officio* and had no power to rescind bail as jurisdiction had passed to the Crown Court. In dismissing the application, the Divisional Court held that it could not be said that as soon as he had finished speaking the magistrate was immediately *functus officio*. The occasion had not come to an end in practical terms and a commonsense approach had to be adopted. Although the court did not address the question whether the remark led to substantial grounds for believing that one or more of the exceptions to the right to bail applied, it might well have been the case that the making of a threat to the officer warranted the immediate withdrawal of bail.

10.2.2 Application for habeas corpus

Applications are regulated by the RSC 1965, Ord. 54.

10.2.2.1 Applications take precedence   Applications for habeas corpus are always heard first in the list before any other court business: *R* v *Home Secretary, ex parte Cheblak* [1991] 1 WLR 890.

10.2.2.2 Judge to whom application may be made   Applications for the writ must, and normally will, be made to a judge in the High Court, but they may be made to a Divisional Court of the Queen's Bench Division if the court so directs. If no judge is sitting in court at the time of the application, it may be made to any judge out of court.

10.2.2.3 Applications may be ex parte and must be made by or on behalf of the restrained person   The application may be made *ex parte* and must be supported by an affidavit by the person restrained showing that it is made at the instance of that person and setting out the nature of the restraint. Where the person restrained is unable for any reason to make the affidavit, it may be made by another person on behalf of the restrained person. The affidavit must in that case include a statement that the person restrained is unable to make the affidavit and must state the reason.

10.2.2.4 Minors   In the case of a minor the application must be made in the first instance to a judge in chambers. Applications made by parents or guardians relating to the custody, care or control of a minor must be made to the Family Division and the procedure set out for applications for writs of habeas corpus will apply in that court, subject to appropriate amendment: RSC 1965, Ord. 54, r. 11.

10.2.2.5 Lord Chancellor The Lord Chancellor has no power to grant a writ of habeas corpus: Administration of Justice Act 1960, s. 14(2) and *Re Kray* [1965] Ch 736.

10.2.3 Orders available on *ex parte* application

Orders available on an *ex parte* application are regulated by the RSC 1965, Ord. 54, r. 2.

10.2.3.1 Immediate order The court or judge to whom an *ex parte* application for habeas corpus is made may make the order forthwith for the writ to issue and for the release of the person restrained. Such an order must be regarded as exceptional since in practice the writ will be issued, according to the editors of the 'White Book' (the *Supreme Court Practice*, London: Sweet & Maxwell, 1999 p. 931), only 'where there is a likelihood that any delay may defeat justice, or where the facts and law are clear'. Where the writ is not issued forthwith bail may be granted, but the jurisdiction of the court is not affected: *Re Amand* [1941] 2 KB 239.

10.2.3.2 Application to a judge otherwise than in court Where the application is made to a judge, otherwise than in court, the judge may direct that (i) an originating summons for the writ be issued, or (ii) an application by way of originating motion be made to the Divisional Court or to a judge in court.

10.2.3.3 Application to judge in court An application made to a judge in court may be adjourned so that notice may be given or may be directed to be made by originating motion to a Divisional Court.

10.2.3.4 Application to the Divisional Court Where the application is made to the Divisional Court, that court may adjourn the application so that notice thereof may be given.

10.2.3.5 Service of summons or notice of motion Service of the summons or notice of motion must be made on:

(a) the person against whom the issue of the writ is sought; and
(b) such other persons as the court or judge directs.

10.2.3.6 Period of notice required Unless otherwise directed, eight clear days must be allowed between the service of the summons or notice and the date named therein for the hearing of the application.

10.2.3.7 Copy affidavits to be exchanged Copy affidavits which are to be used at the hearing must be supplied by each party to an application to every other party, on demand, and on payment of the proper charges.

10.2.3.8   Fresh evidence generally inadmissible   The applicant is not entitled to adduce fresh evidence which was not put before the lower court: *Re Nobbs* [1978] 1 WLR 1302, *per* Lord Widgery CJ, approving *Schtraks* v *Government of Israel* [1962] 3 All ER 529. In *Re Nobbs* the applicant had not raised in issue or called evidence before magistrates as to the fact that he would be sent back to Ireland, be prosecuted and detained for an offence of a political character, and was accordingly precluded from raising the issue in the High Court. Fresh evidence does not, in this context, mean different or additional evidence but 'evidence which the applicant could not have, or could not reasonably have been expected to put forward on the first application': *Re Tarling* [1979] 1 All ER 981, DC.

10.2.3.9   Refusal of application   Only a Divisional Court of the Queen's Bench Division and not a single judge may refuse an application: RSC 1965, Ord. 54, r. 2. Where, therefore, a court or judge declines to issue a writ/order the release of the person restrained, a direction shall be given that the application be made by originating motion to the Divisional Court. Once an application has been refused no further application may be made on the same grounds without fresh evidence: Administration of Justice Act 1960, s. 14(2).

10.2.3.10   Order for release   The court or judge hearing an application for a writ of habeas corpus may order that the person restrained be released, and such an order is sufficient warrant to any governor of a prison, constable or other person, for the release of the person under restraint: RSC 1965, Ord. 54, r. 4.

10.2.4   The writ issued

10.2.4.1   Directions for the return to the writ   Where a writ is issued the court or judge must direct before whom and the date on which the writ is returnable: RSC 1965, Ord. 54, r. 5 and see Forms 89, 91 or 92, whichever is appropriate.

10.2.4.2   Service of the writ   A writ must be served personally on the person to whom it is directed: RSC 1965, Ord. 54, r. 6. If it is not possible to effect personal service, or where it is directed to a governor of a prison or other public official, it must be served by leaving it with a servant or agent of the person to whom the writ is directed at the place where the person restrained is confined or restrained. Where the writ is directed to more than one person, it must be served on the person first named in the writ, and copies served in the same manner as the writ on each of those other persons.

10.2.4.3   Notice of hearing details to be served with the writ   A notice must be served with the writ detailing the court or judge before whom the person restrained is to be brought, together with details of the date and the time of that hearing: see Form 90. The notice must display that in default of obedience, proceedings for committal of the person disobeying will be taken.

10.2.4.4 Return to the writ The return to the writ must be indorsed or annexed to the writ and must state all the causes of the detainer of the person restrained: RSC 1965, Ord. 54, r. 7. If on its face the return to the writ shows a valid authority for detention, the applicant must show that the detention is *prima facie* illegal: *Re Hassan* [1976] 1 WLR 971. By leave of the court or judge before whom the writ is returnable the return may be amended or another return substituted.

10.2.4.5 Reading of the return and making of motions When the return of the writ of habeas corpus has been made it must first be read and then motion must be made for discharging or remanding the person restrained or amending or quashing the return: RSC 1965, Ord. 54, r. 8.

10.2.4.6 Order of submissions When the person restrained is brought up in accordance with the writ, counsel for that person is heard first, then counsel for the Crown and then one counsel for the person restrained in reply: RSC 1965, Ord. 54, r. 8.

10.2.5 Appeal

10.2.5.1 Appeal to the House of Lords, with leave There is no right of appeal from the decision of the single judge, but an appeal does lie to the House of Lords from a decision of the Divisional Court, with the leave of either court: SCA 1981, s. 18(1)(a); Administration of Justice Act 1960, ss. 1 and 15.

10.2.5.2 Parties who may appeal Both sides to an application may appeal: Administration of Justice Act 1960, s. 15(1). However, where the appeal is lodged by a party other than the person who, but for the Divisional Court's decision, would be restrained, then that person should not be made subject to an unqualified order of discharge as he will not be liable to be detained if the appeal is subsequently allowed: *United States Government* v *McCaffrey* [1984] 1 WLR 867.

10.2.5.3 Time for lodging appeal The appeal must be lodged within 14 days after the decision of the Divisional Court, but this may be extended in all cases of the person restrained: Administration of Justice Act 1960, s. 2(3).

10.3 JUDICIAL REVIEW

10.3.1 Introduction

The residual function of the Queen's Bench Division of the High Court in exercising its supervisory jurisdiction over the conduct of the inferior courts and of official bodies in general operates through the system of 'judicial review'. In the context of the law and practice of bail in criminal proceedings, judicial review provides a means by which the legitimacy of decisions relating to bail in magistrates' courts or Crown Courts can be challenged and determined. A successful application for judicial review will result in the issuing under RSC 1965, Ord. 53, r. 1, of one or more (as appropriate) of three 'prerogative' orders:

   (a) *certiorari* – an order to bring up into the High Court a decision of an inferior court for it to be quashed;
   (b) prohibition – an order restraining an inferior court from acting outside its jurisdiction; and
   (c) *mandamus* – an order requiring an inferior court to carry out its judicial order.

These originally took the form of prerogative writs, and applicants for such remedies were formerly obliged to select the prerogative writ most appropriate to the nature of the case. There were numerous technical differences between them and an error of selection or of procedure could result in a dismissal of the action having little relation to the merits of the case. Judicial review was introduced to provide a uniform, flexible and comprehensive means of access to administrative law by eliminating procedural technicalities and arcane distinctions between the remedies. Now, if the court upholds the application for judicial review it simply chooses the most suitable of the three available orders.

10.3.2   General principles

The general principles governing judicial review have been defined through a series of cases and may be summarised under the heads set out immediately below.

10.3.2.1   Review of the decision-making process, not the decision   Judicial review is concerned with reviewing not the merits of the decision about which complaint is made, but the decision-making policy, or the process of reasoning involved in it: see *Chief Constable of the North Wales Police* v *Evans* [1982] 1 WLR 1155, *per* Lord Brightman.

10.3.2.2   Ensuring fair treatment   In *Chief Constable of North Wales Police* v *Evans*, Lord Hailsham LC emphasised that the purpose of judicial review was: '. . . to ensure that the individual is given fair treatment by the authority to which he has been subjected and . . . it is no part of that purpose to substitute the opinion of the judiciary or of individual judges for that of the authority constituted by law to decide the matters in question.'

10.3.2.3   Failings for which judicial review is available   It was said in *Preston* v *Inland Revenue Commissioners* [1985] 2 All ER 327, *per* Lord Templeman, that judicial review is available where the decision-making authority has:

   (a) exceeded its powers (*ultra vires*);

    (b)   committed an error of law;

    (c)   committed a breach of natural justice;

    (d)   reached a decision which no reasonable tribunal could have reached (irrationality);

    (e)   abused its powers.

To these Lord Diplock, in *Council of Civil Service Unions* v *Minister for the Civil Service* [1985] AC 474, added the complaint that the decision-making authority has:

    (f)   committed a procedural impropriety.

10.3.2.4   Applicant must have a sufficient interest in the cause   An application for judicial review may be made only with the leave of the High Court, and leave will be granted only if the applicant has 'sufficient interest in the matter to which the application relates': SCA 1981, s. 13(3). The applicant will not have sufficient interest if the remedy has been obtained before the application is heard.

10.3.2.5   Other remedies must be unavailable or exhausted   It is a cardinal principle that save in exceptional circumstances the residual jurisdiction of the court to grant judicial review will not be exercised where other remedies are available and have not been used: *R* v *Epping and Harlow General Commissioners, ex parte Goldstraw* [1983] 3 All ER 257, CA. In *Preston* v *Inland Revenue Commissioners* [1985] 2 All ER 327, at p. 330, Lord Scarman observed: '. . . a remedy by way of judicial review is not to be made available where an alternative remedy exists. This is a proposition of great importance. Judicial review is a collateral challenge; it is not an appeal.'

10.3.2.6   When judicial review is available although other remedies have not been exhausted   The court may exercise its discretion to grant judicial review even if other rights of appeal have not been exhausted:

    (a)   where there has been a serious departure from procedure: *R* v *Chief Constable of Merseyside Police, ex parte Calveley and others* [1986] 1 All ER 257, CA;

    (b)   where there has been an identifiable breach of natural justice in criminal proceedings before magistrates, even though there existed a right of appeal to the Crown Court: *R* v *Bradford Justices ex parte Wilkinson* [1990] Crim LR 267.

10.3.3   Applicability of general principles to bail

10.3.3.1   Refusal of bail not of itself a matter for judicial review   It follows from the foregoing that in the absence of any suggestion of the kind of justiciable complaint specific to judicial review (see para. 10.3.2.3) the remedy is unavailable as a means of appealing against the decision of a court to refuse bail. In *Re Herbage, The Times*, 25 October 1985, DC, it was held that judicial review was not an appropriate means of seeking bail where bail had been refused by justices and then by a judge in chambers. It was said that the alternative was to reapply to a High Court judge under CJA 1967, s. 22, but, as the editors of *Archbold* observe at para. 3–194, the report failed to make clear why RSC 1965 Ord. 79, r. 9(12) – see para. 10.1.6.1 – was not thought to be an obstacle to such a fresh application. The learned editors conjecture that one possible explanation is that the application was not in fact an application for bail but an application to vary the conditions of bail imposed by the magistrates' court. However, in *R v Croydon Crown Court, ex parte Cox* [1997] 1 Cr App R 20, DC, it was held that judicial review was not appropriate to challenge the imposition of a bail condition by the Crown Court because there was the alternative remedy of an application to a High Court judge in chambers.

10.3.3.2 Available remedies should have been exhausted   The remedies available to a defendant in the Crown Court and in the High Court before a judge in chambers should have first been exhausted before an application in respect of bail is made to the Divisional Court: *R v Guildhall Justices ex parte Prushinowski, The Times*, 14 December 1985.

10.3.3.3 Refusal of justices to hear a bail application   Judicial review is generally unavailable where justices have refused to hear an application for bail. The correct approach is by way of an appeal to the Crown Court or a judge in chambers: *R v Dacorum Justices, ex parte Darker, The Times*, 14 October 1983. (See also *R v Blyth Juvenile Court, ex parte G* [1991] Crim LR 693.)

10.3.3.4 Possible exceptions to no other available remedies rule   Although it was held in *R v Guildhall Justices, ex parte Prushinowski*, above, that the available remedies should first have been exhausted before an application in respect of bail is made to the Divisional Court, Watkins LJ suggested that it might possibly be appropriate to give leave for review without other remedies having been pursued if bias, ill-will, prejudice or dishonesty were involved in the decision-making.

10.3.3.5 Judicial review admissible against bail practice policy   Judicial review will be appropriate where the complaint is against a policy rather than an individual decision, as in *R v Nottingham Justices, ex parte Davies* [1980] 2 All ER 775 (see generally Chapter 5) and [1985] 1 QB 613 (see Chapter 3, para. 3.2.2.1). In the latter case the court disapproved of the practice of affixing standard conditions to bail forms before the decision had been announced and while applications for unconditional bail were still being made. The decision was not, however, vitiated by the fact that the result of the application had been correctly anticipated.

10.3.3.6 Failure to apply relevant considerations in imposing bail conditions
It may be possible to obtain leave for judicial review where magistrates have failed to take into account relevant considerations when imposing conditions of bail: see *R* v *Mansfield Justices, ex parte Sharkey and others* [1985] QB 613.

10.3.3.7 Allegation of *ultra vires* Judicial review will be appropriate where it is submitted that in relation to bail the court has acted *ultra vires*. The case of *R* v *Governor of Ashford Remand Centre, ex parte Harris* [1984] Crim LR 618, already considered at para. 10.2.1.6, related to an application for habeas corpus but is relevant to judicial review generally as going to the issue of whether the magistrate had acted *ultra vires* in withdrawing bail after it was said that he was *functus officio*.

10.3.4 Judicial review following estreatment of bail in the Crown Court

The SCA 1981, s. 29(3), provides that decisions of the Crown Court may be subject to judicial review, except matters relating to trial on indictment. In *Smalley* v *Warwick Crown Court* [1985] 1 All ER 769, the Divisional Court, following previous case law, came to the conclusion that the subsection precluded them from reviewing a decision of the Crown Court estreating the recognizance of a surety. The decision was overturned by the House of Lords on the ground that the phrase 'relating to trial on indictment' meant 'affecting the conduct of the trial' and an order estreating a recognizance of a surety for a defendant who failed to surrender to bail at the Crown Court could not affect the conduct of the trial on indictment in any way. In the words of Lord Bridge of Harwich (at p. 779): 'If such an order is wrongly made, for example by denying the surety the right to be heard, I can see no sensible reason whatever why the aggrieved surety should not have a remedy by judicial review.'

An alternative view is proposed by James Richardson:

[T]he issue in relation to s. 29(3) is determined by reference to the answer to the simple question whether at the time of the decision in question, the judge of the Crown Court was dealing with proceedings on indictment or not; if he was, the High Court has no jurisdiction; if he was not, then it does. (*Criminal Law Week*, CLW/98/16/22, issue of 4 May 1998)

10.3.5 Procedure on application for leave to apply

The procedure to be followed on application for leave to apply for judicial review is regulated by the RSC 1965, Ord. 53, r. 3.

10.3.5.1 No application without leave It has already been mentioned that no application for judicial review may be made without the leave of the court (see para. 10.3.2.4).

10.3.5.2   Applicant must have sufficient interest in the matter   As already mentioned (in para. 10.3.2.4), the court must refuse leave to apply for judicial review unless it considers that the applicant has a sufficient interest in the matter. A wife is deemed to have sufficient interest in matters relating to bail: see *Re Herbage*, *The Times*, 25 October 1985, DC.

10.3.5.3   Filing of application   Application for leave must be made *ex parte* by filing a notice and supporting affidavit in the Crown Office.

10.3.5.4   Time for filing   The notice and affidavit must normally be filed within three months from the date when the grounds for the application first arose, unless the court considers that there is a good reason for granting an extension: RSC 1965, Ord. 53, r. 4.

10.3.5.5   Content of notice   The notice (in Form 86A) must contain a statement of:

  (a)   the name and description of the applicant;
  (b)   the relief sought;
  (c)   the grounds upon which the relief is sought;
  (d)   the name and address of the applicant's solicitor, if any; and
  (e)   the applicant's address for service.

The general rule on applications for judicial review is that they must comply with the *Practice Direction (Crown Office List: Preparation for Hearings)* [1994] 1 WLR 1551 (provision of a paginated, indexed bundle of documents with list of essential reading) and *Practice Direction (Crown Office List: Legislation Bundle)* [1997] 1 WLR 52. Applications which do not comply with these directions will not be accepted other than in exceptional cases such as urgency (notice issued by the head of the Crown Office: [1997] 1 Cr App R 472). It is submitted that applications relating to bail qualify as urgent.

10.3.5.6   Affidavit   The affidavit must set out the facts relied on.

10.3.5.7   Determination in chambers or in court   The judge may determine the application in chambers without a hearing, unless the notice states that a hearing is required.

10.3.5.8   Service of the judge's order   The Crown Office will serve a copy of the judge's order on the applicant.

10.3.5.9   Renewal of the application   Where a single judge has refused an application for leave to apply for judicial review or granted it subject to conditions, application for such leave may be renewed to the Divisional Court. Upon such a renewed application the court may allow the applicant to amend the statement in the notice by specifying different or additional grounds of relief or otherwise, on such terms, if any, as it thinks fit (see Form 86B). The amended statement must be lodged within ten days of the original judge's order.

10.3.5.10 Leave may be conditional Leave may be conditional as to terms relating to costs and such security as the court thinks fit.

10.3.5.11 Application for prohibition or *certiorari* Where an order of prohibition or *certiorari* is sought, the court may direct a stay of proceedings until either the determination of the application or such other time as it may direct.

10.3.5.12 Application for *mandamus* Where the relief sought is an order of *mandamus*, the court may at any time grant such interim relief as could be granted in an action begun by writ.

10.3.6 Procedure when leave to apply is granted (RSC 1965, Ord. 53, r. 5)

The procedure to be followed once leave is given to apply for judicial review is regulated by the RSC 1965, Ord. 53, r. 5.

10.3.6.1 Application to be by originating motion Where leave to apply is granted application must be entered within 14 days and is by originating motion to the High Court.

10.3.6.2 Service of notice of motion The notice of motion must be served with a copy of the statement at least ten days before the hearing, unless the court otherwise directs, on all persons directly affected. Where the notice relates to any proceedings in or before a court and the object of the application is either (i) to compel the court or an officer of the court to do any act in relation to the proceedings, or (ii) to quash those proceedings or any order made therein, the notice of motion must be served on the clerk or registrar of the court and, where any objection to the conduct of the judge is to be made, on the judge.

10.3.6.3 Affidavit of service of notice of motion An affidavit must be filed with the court before the motion is entered for hearing, setting out the names and addresses and the places and dates of service of all the persons who have been served with the motion. If the motion has not been served on a person who ought to have been served with it, the affidavit must state that fact and the reason for it.

10.3.6.4 Adjournment necessitated by failure to serve the motion Where the court is of the opinion that any person who ought to have been served has not been served, it may adjourn the motion. Where it does so, it may do so on such terms, if any, as it directs in order that the notice of motion may be served on that person.

10.3.6.5 Amendment of the statement   No ground which is not set out in the statement may be heard at the application: RSC 1965, Ord.1653, r. 6. However, the court has a discretion to allow the statement to be amended, whether by including different or additional grounds, or relief or otherwise, on such terms as the court thinks fit.

10.3.6.6 Further affidavits   The court may allow further affidavits to be used if they deal with new matters arising out of an affidavit of any other party to the application.

10.3.6.7 Notice of amendment   Where the applicant intends asking for leave to amend the statement or to rely on further affidavits, all other parties must be given notice of the proposed amendment.

10.3.6.8 Filing of respondent's affidavits   Where a respondent to the application intends using an affidavit at the hearing, it must be filed at the Crown Office as soon as practicable and in any event within 21 days after service of the notice of motion unless the court otherwise directs. The applicant and the respondent must supply to all other parties on demand and on payment of proper costs copies of the affidavits on which they intend to rely at the hearing.

10.3.6.9 *Certiorari*   In the case of the making of an order of *certiorari*, the court must direct that the proceedings be quashed immediately. Additionally, the court may remit the matter to the court concerned with a direction to reconsider it and reach a decision in accordance with the finding of the court.

10.3.6.10 Refusal of bail   The record of refusal of bail must be lodged in the Crown Office before the hearing of the motion where the relief sought is or includes an order of *certiorari* to remove any proceedings for the purpose of quashing them. The applicant may not question the validity of such a record unless before the hearing a copy has been lodged in the Crown Office, verified by affidavit or otherwise, or the applicant accounts for the failure to do so to the satisfaction of the court hearing the motion.

10.3.6.11 Expedited hearing list   Suitable applications in the Divisional Court for prerogative orders may be selected to go in the 'expedited hearing list', the main purpose of which is to dispose quickly of short and simple cases, and the procedure for dealing with which is set out in *Practice Note* [1974] 1 WLR 1219, CA *per* Lord Widgery CJ.

10.3.7 Procedure at the hearing

10.3.7.1 Persons who may be heard   The court may hear from any person who wishes to appear in opposition to the motion (RSC 1965, Ord. 53, r. 9) whom it considers a proper person to be heard, notwithstanding that that person has not been served with a copy of the motion.

10.3.7.2 Hearing proceeds by way of representation The content of the statement and affidavit and arguments on them will normally be presented by way of representation and not by way of adducing evidence. In *Re Herbage, The Times*, 25 October 1985, DC, Glidewell LJ observed that although under Ord. 53 there might be occasions when judicial review proceedings included the cross-examination of witnesses, as a generality such proceedings were totally inapt for the determination of questions of fact and certainly questions of fact, arising from bail proceedings.

11   Vulnerable Suspects and Defendants

11.1   CHILDREN AND YOUNG PERSONS

11.1.1   Definitions

11.1.1.1   Child   The definition of 'child' varies from statute to statute. Section 2(2) of the BA 1976 defines the term as denoting a person under the age of 14, but in the Children Act 1989 (CA 1989), which, *inter alia*, regulates the accommodation of those suspects or accused persons who might loosely be called non-adults, the term is defined in s. 105(1) as a person under the age of 18.

11.1.1.2   Young person   In contrast with the definition of a 'child' the statutory ambit of 'young person' somewhat confusingly varies within the context of the law relating to bail. Section 2(2) of the BA 1976 defines a young person as someone who has attained the age of 14 and is under the age of 17. This is the same definition as given in s. 23(12) of the CYPA 1969, which has application to bail. It is also consonant with the definition of 'arrested juvenile' given in s. 37(15) of PACE 1984, which provides that for the purposes of Part IV of the Act the term denotes a person arrested with or without warrant who appears to be under the age of 17. However, s. 29(2) of the CYPA 1969, which relates to children or young persons arrested in pursuance of a warrant, provides that for the purpose of the section the definition of a young person is someone who has attained the age of 14 and is under the age of *18*. The CA 1989, which contains provisions for the accommodation of children in police protection or detention or on remand, defines a 'child' as a person under the age of 18: s. 105(1). Outside the context of bail law, youth courts enjoy a generally exclusive jurisdiction to try young persons up to the age of 18 (CJA 1991, s. 18). For the purposes of sentence, young offenders are those under 21 years of age.

11.1.2   The right to bail and exceptions

11.1.2.1   Juveniles are no longer presumed inherently less likely to fail to surrender than adults   The BA 1976 applies to juveniles in the same way that it applies to adults, but until the passing of the CJA 1991 there was an important difference. The exception to bail which applies where there are substantial grounds for believing that the defendant will fail to surrender previously carried less force in the case of a young person if the reason for applying the exception was the nature and seriousness of the charge and the probable method of dealing with it. The reason was that by s. 123 of the CJA 1988 a court might sentence a person under the age of 21 to detention in a young offender institution only if the circumstances, including the nature and the gravity of the offence, were such that if the offender were aged 21 or over the court would pass a sentence of imprisonment, and that the defendant qualified for a custodial sentence. Offenders qualified for a custodial sentence if:

(a)   they had a history of failure to respond to non-custodial penalties and were unable or unwilling to respond to them; or

(b)   only a custodial sentence would be adequate to protect the public from serious harm from them; or

(c)   the offence of which they had been convicted or found guilty was so serious that a non-custodial sentence for it could not be justified.

There is no longer any difference between adults and young persons as regards the risk of failing to surrender to bail because the criteria for a custodial sentence are now the same for adults and young persons, the CJA 1991, s. 1(1) referring to '*a person*'.

11.1.2.2   Exceptions to the right to bail in the case of offences punishable with imprisonment   Schedule 1 (Part III, para. 1) to the BA 1976, provides that for the purposes of the schedule the question whether an offence is one which is punishable with imprisonment must be determined without regard to any enactment prohibiting or restricting the imprisonment of young offenders or first offenders.

11.1.2.3   Special exception to the right to bail   Schedule 1 to the BA 1976 provides that children or young persons accused or convicted of imprisonable offences (Part I, para. 3) or non-imprisonable offences (Part II, para. 3) need not be granted bail if the court is satisfied that they should be kept in custody for their own welfare. This special exception to the right to bail is incorporated in s. 38 of PACE 1984, which makes provision for the detention of persons following charge (see para. 6.1.3.2, above).

11.1.2.4   Remand in custody means remand to local authority care   In the BA 1976, sch. 1, Part III, para. 3 ('Interpretation'), it is provided that references in the schedule to a defendant's being kept in custody or being in custody include (where the defendant is a child or young person) references to his being kept or being in the care of a local authority in pursuance of a warrant of commitment under s. 23(1) of the CYPA 1969 (as to which see para. 11.1.8).

11.1.3 Sureties and conditional bail

11.1.3.1 Provision for surety to secure compliance with conditions of bail Section 3(7) of the BA 1976 provides that if a parent or guardian of a child or young person consents to stand as a surety for the child or young person for the purposes of the subsection, the parent or guardian may be required to secure that the child or young person complies with any requirement imposed by virtue of s. 3(6) or (6A), i.e. conditions of bail apart from surety.

11.1.3.2 Maximum recognizance The maximum amount of the recognizance allowed to secure compliance with conditions is £50: BA 1976, s. 3(7)(b).

11.1.3.3 Conditions not consented to by surety Parents or guardians must not be required to secure compliance with any condition to which they have not consented: BA 1976, s. 3(7)(b).

11.1.3.4 Young person likely to reach 17 by the surrender date No requirement to secure compliance with conditions may be imposed under s. 3(7) where it appears that the young person will turn 17 before the time to be appointed for the person's appearance: BA 1976, s. 3(7)(a).

11.1.4 Defendants accused of murder (or attempt), manslaughter and rape (or attempt)

Section 25 of the CJPOA 1994, as amended by s. 56 of the CDA 1998, provides that where defendants are accused or convicted of murder, attempted murder, manslaughter, rape or attempted rape, having previously been convicted by or before a court in any part of the United Kingdom of any such offence or of culpable homicide, they shall be granted bail in those proceedings only if there are exceptional circumstances which justify it. (It is provided only that in the case of a previous conviction of manslaughter or culpable homicide the person was then sentenced to imprisonment.) Importantly, for the purposes of the present chapter, this limitation applies in the case of a defendant who was then a child or young person, where the sentence for the previous conviction of manslaughter or culpable homicide was long-term detention under any of the relevant enactments: CJPOA 1994, s. 25(1) and (3). The relevant enactment as respects England and Wales is s. 53(2) of the CYPA 1933: CJPOA 1994, s. 25(5)(a).

11.1.5 Arrested juveniles and the police

11.1.5.1 Children under ten years of age Section 50 of the CYPA 1933 provides that there is a conclusive presumption that no child under the age of ten years can be guilty of an offence. It is consistent with this fundamental statutory principle that Part IV of PACE 1984, which deals with the detention of suspects, does not apply to a child under the age of ten. However, it may happen that a child under ten is arrested without warrant and brought to a police station in the mistaken belief that the child is ten or above. The child's true age is then determined. Such a child may be detained at a local authority community home or other place of safety under the CA 1989. The powers of such detention are beyond the scope of the present work.

11.1.5.2 Detention without charge following arrest without warrant Section 37 of PACE 1984 provides that where a juvenile who is in custody following an arrest without warrant is not charged because the custody officer determines that insufficient evidence has been presented, the juvenile (as in the case of an adult) must be released either on bail or without bail, unless the custody officer has reasonable grounds for believing that detention without charge is necessary to secure or preserve evidence relating to an offence for which the arrest was made, or to obtain such evidence by questioning (see generally para. 6.2).

11.1.5.3 Detention of charged juveniles in their own interest The duty of the custody officer under s. 38 of PACE 1984 to allow a person who has been charged with an offence to be released, either on bail or without, unless certain exceptions apply, was considered in para. 6.1.3, above, where the exceptions are listed. If the person is a juvenile within the meaning of Part IV of the Act a further exception applies where the custody officer has reasonable grounds for believing that detention ought to be authorised in the juvenile's own interests: PACE 1984, s. 38(1)(b)(ii).

11.1.5.4 Removal of charged juveniles to local authority accommodation Where an arrested juvenile has been charged and is kept in police detention under s. 38(1) of PACE 1984, the juvenile must be moved to local authority accommodation unless the custody officer certifies:

(a) that by reason of such circumstances as are specified in the certificate such a move is impracticable; or
(b) that in the case of an arrested juvenile who has attained the age of 12 years no secure accommodation is available and local authority accommodation would not be adequate to protect the public from serious harm: PACE 1984, s. 38(6).

Local authority accommodation means accommodation provided by or on behalf of a local authority within the meaning of the CA 1989, and secure accommodation means accommodation provided for the purposes of restricting liberty: PACE 1984, s. 38(6A), inserted by the CA 1989, s. 108(5) and sch. 13, para. 53. 'Local authority' has the same meaning as in the CA 1989: PACE 1984, s. 38(8). Any reference, in relation to an arrested juvenile charged with a violent or sexual offence, to protecting members of the public from serious harm from the juvenile is to be construed as a reference to protecting members of the public from death or serious personal injury, whether physical or psychological, occasioned by further such offences committed by the juvenile: PACE 1984, s. 38(6A), amended by s. 38 of the CJA 1991. 'Sexual offence' and 'violent offence' have the same meanings as in Part I of the CJA 1991: PACE 1984, s. 38(6A). An arrested juvenile moved to local authority accommodation under s. 38(6) of the 1984 Act, may be lawfully detained by any person acting on behalf of the authority. A certificate made under s. 38(6) must be produced to the court before which the arrested juvenile is first brought thereafter.

The CA 1989, s. 21(2), stipulates that every local authority must receive and provide accommodation for children (i.e. persons under 18) whom they are requested to receive under s. 38(6) of PACE 1984. In *R* v *Chief Constable of Cambridgeshire, ex parte Michel* (1990) 91 Cr App R 325, DC, the local authority had proposed to return the juvenile to a hostel where he had been living, but the custody officer was of the opinion that the accommodation was insecure and therefore inadequate. The juvenile applied for judicial review of the custody officer's refusal to release him to the care of the local authority in accordance with s. 38 of PACE 1984, submitting that it was not for the custody officer to decide on the quality of the accommodation being offered. Dismissing the application the Divisional Court held that although a custody officer had to ensure that everything practicable that could be done was done to ensure that the juvenile was put into the care of the local authority, where he was not satisfied with the proposed arrangements of the local authority for the secure detention of the juvenile he was entitled to refuse to transfer that juvenile to the local authority's care. This was particularly the case if the only accommodation available for the juvenile's detention was insufficient to avoid the very consequences which led to the decision to refuse bail in the first place. Since the time of this judgment, new para. 16.6 and *Note for Guidance* 16B have been inserted into PACE Code C, the *Code of Practice for the Detention, Treatment and Questioning of Persons by Police Officers* (issued under s. 66 of the 1984 Act; the first revision was issued in 1991 and the revision currently in force, SI 1995 No. 450, was issued on 10 April 1995). In accordance with PACE 1984, s. 38(6), as amended by CJA 1991, s. 59 and CJPOA 1994, s. 24, Code C, para. 16.6 provides that where a custody officer authorises the continued detention of a juvenile who has been charged with an offence, the officer must try to make arrangements for the juvenile to be taken into care of a local authority to be detained pending appearance in court unless the officer certifies that it is impracticable to do so. In the case of a juvenile of at least 12 years of age this need not be done if the officer certifies that no secure accommodation is available and there is a risk to the public of serious harm from the juvenile. *Note for Guidance* 16B advises that, except as provided for in Code C, para. 16.6, neither a juvenile's behaviour nor the nature of the offence charged provides grounds for the custody officer to decide that it is impracticable to seek to arrange transfer to the care of the local authority. Similarly, the lack of secure local authority accommodation shall not make it impracticable for the custody officer to arrange a transfer. The availability of secure accommodation is only a factor in relation to a juvenile aged 12 or over when the local authority accommodation would not be adequate to protect the public from serious harm from the juvenile. The obligation to transfer a juvenile to local authority accommodation applies as much to a juvenile charged during the daytime as it does to a juvenile to be held overnight, subject to a requirement to bring the juvenile before a court under PACE 1984, s. 46.

11.1.5.5 Remands to police detention The power of a magistrates' court under s. 128(7) of the MCA 1980 to remand persons whom it may remand in custody to detention in a police station for periods of not more than three days has effect in relation to a child or young person as if for the reference to three clear days there were substituted a reference to 24 hours: CYPA 1969, s. 23(18). The conditions for the making of such an order are the same as those in the case of an adult (see Chapter 7, para. 7.1.2.4).

11.1.5.6 Recognizance on release of juvenile arrested on warrant A child or young person arrested in pursuance of a warrant and detained at a police station must not be released unless the arrested juvenile's parent or guardian (with or without sureties) enters into a recognizance for such amount as the station custody officer considers will secure the juvenile's attendance at the hearing of the charge: CYPA 1969 s. 29(1). The recognizance so entered into may, if the custody officer thinks fit, be conditioned for the attendance of the parent or guardian at the hearing in addition to the child or young person: *ibid.* 'Young person' means a person who has attained the age of 14 and is under 18: CYPA 1969, s. 29(2). (Section 29 was amended by the PACE 1984, sch. 6, and the CJA 1991, s. 68 and sch. 8, para. 4(1), and repealed in part by the CJA 1988, s. 170(1) and (2), and sch. 15, para. 36, and sch. 16.)

11.1.6 Remand or committal by courts: secure places of remand for persons under 21 years

11.1.6.1 Provision of remand centres for persons aged 14 to 20 The Secretary of State is authorised to provide remand centres for the detention of persons of not less than 14 but under 21 years of age who are remanded or committed in custody for trial or sentence: Prison Act 1952, s. 43.

11.1.6.2 Remand to prison of persons aged 17 to 20 if no remand centre place available Section 27 of the CJA 1948 (as substituted by the CYPA 1969, sch. 5) makes provision for the detention of persons who are not less than 17 but under 21 years old, are charged with or convicted of an offence, are remanded or committed for trial or sentence and are not released on bail. In such cases the court will commit the person to prison unless it has been notified by the Secretary of State that a remand centre is available for the reception from the court of persons of the class and description of the defendant, in which case the defendant must be committed to a remand centre: s. 27(1). The centre must be specified in the warrant of committal and the person must be detained there for the period of the remand or until delivered from there in due course of law: s. 27(2). For the purposes of the section the term 'court' includes a justice, and nothing in the section affects the provisions of s. 128(7) of the MCA 1980 (which originally provided for remands to the custody of a constable – now to detention in a police station): s. 27(3), as amended by the MCA 1980, sch. 7.

11.1.6.3   Secretary of State's authority for detention of remand prisoners aged 17 to 20 in prison instead of a remand centre or *vice versa*   Notwithstanding the provisions of s. 27 of the 1948 Act, the Secretary of State may from time to time authorise the detention of a person under 21 but not less than 17 years of age in a prison instead of a remand centre, or *vice versa*, where that person is remanded in custody or committed in custody for trial or sentence: Prison Act 1952, s. 43(2).

11.1.7   Remand by the courts of persons under 17: old system of certificates of unruly character (now abolished)

Section 23 of the CYPA 1969 makes provision for the accommodation of children or young persons who are charged with or convicted of one or more offences and are remanded or committed for trial or sentence but not released on bail. ('Young persons' are defined as those aged not less than 14 and under the age of 17 years: s. 23(12).) The basic principle enunciated by the section is that such persons are remanded to local authority accommodation, that is, a community home, unless they are males aged at least 15 years whose behaviour warrants their being held in conditions of special security not provided by the local authority.

In the original form of the scheme provided for by s. 23(2) and (3) of the 1969 Act, persons in this special category would be made the subject of a certificate of unruly character, or 'certificate of unruliness', as it was commonly called. Involving two forms of risk defined in the Certificates of Unruly Character (Conditions) Order 1977, SI 1977 No. 1037, the scheme required the issuing of a certificate:

(a)   where the offence concerned was punishable in the case of an adult with imprisonment for 14 years, *or* the instant offence was one of violence or the defendant had been found guilty on a previous occasion of an offence of violence, *and* the court was remanding him for the first time in the proceedings and was satisfied that there had been insufficient time to obtain a written report from the appropriate local authority on the availability of suitable accommodation in a community home, or the court was satisfied on the basis of such a report that no suitable accommodation was available in a community home where he could be accommodated without substantial risk to himself or others; or

(b)   the defendant had persistently absconded from a community home or, while accommodated in a community home, had seriously disrupted the running of the home, and the court was satisfied on the basis of a written report from the appropriate local authority that accommodation could not be found for him in a suitable community home where he could be accommodated without risk of his absconding or seriously disrupting the running of the home.

If the court certified that the defendant fell into one of these categories and was therefore to be regarded as so unruly or out of control that he could not safely be placed in the care of a local authority then, if the court had been notified by the Secretary of State that a remand centre was available for the reception from the court of persons of his class of description, it was required to commit him to a remand centre; and if it had not been so notified, it was required to remand him to prison.

The White Paper, *Crime, Justice and Protecting the Public*, 1990, Cm. 965, proposed the abolition of the system of certificates of unruly character, and this was achieved by s. 61 of the CJA 1991. The section radically restructured the whole scheme and, while retaining the criterion of persistent absconding, perhaps most significantly dispensed with the element of disruptive behaviour in the community home. In amending s. 23 of the CYPA 1969, s. 60 of the 1991 Act made statutory provision for a court to impose on a local authority a 'security requirement', in respect of a young person who, in very broad terms, would formerly have been certified as 'unruly'. A security requirement imposed on the local authority an obligation to ensure that the person in question was placed and kept in secure accommodation, that is accommodation provided in a community home or a registered children's home for the purpose of restricting liberty. Further, s. 61 of the 1991 Act provided for the imposition of a duty on every local authority to ensure that it was in a position to comply with any security requirement made under s. 23 of the 1969 Act. The local authority was to be permitted to discharge this duty in one of a number of ways. It was envisaged that it might provide secure accommodation itself, or alternatively might make arrangements:

(a)   with other local authorities for the provision by them of such accommodation;

(b)   with voluntary organisations or persons carrying on a registered children's home for the provision or use by them of such accommodation; or

(c)   with the Secretary of State for the use by them of a home provided by the Home Office under s. 82(5) of the CA 1989.

It was intended to phase out the use of remand centres and prisons for such young persons, but many local authorities were not equipped to provide secure facilities, nor, it seemed, was there any likelihood of suitable facilities becoming available. Together, therefore, with the enactment of statutory provision for the scheme which it was hoped would eventually be brought into effect, s. 62 of the 1991 Act enacted in parallel what it termed 'temporary modifications'. These continued the resort for the time being to the use of remand centres or prisons for persons who under the new (but as yet inactive) scheme would be accommodated by the local authority under a statutory security requirement. The temporary modifications were to remain in force until such time as the Secretary of State might order under s. 62(1) of the 1991 Act, and they remained in force with no immediate prospect of giving way to the new scheme. Sections 97 and 98 of the CDA 1998 make further alterations to the scheme of s. 23 of the CYPA 1969 and presuppose that resort will continue to be necessary to remand centres and prisons in the case of males over 15 years of age. Provision is also made for the making of security requirements in appropriate cases of children as young as 12 years of age.

11.1.8   Local authority accommodation with no security requirement

11.1.8.1   Remand to local authority accommodation of children or young persons not posing a special risk to the community   Section 23(1) of the CYPA 1969 provides that where a child or young person charged with or convicted of one or more offences is remanded or committed for trial or sentence and is not released on bail, the remand or committal shall be to local authority accommodation. However, this will not apply in the case of any male person who is of the age of 15 or 16 and is not of a description prescribed for the purposes of s. 23(5) i.e. a description prescribed by reference to age or sex or both by an order of the Secretary of State (CYPA 1969, s. 23(12), as inserted by s. 97(4) of the CDA 1998) – and is remanded to a remand centre or a prison in pursuance of s. 23(4)(b) or (c): CYPA 1969, CYPA s. 23(1) as amended by CDA 1998, s. 98(2). (See para. 11.1.9.3 below.)

11.1.8.2   'Remand' includes committal   In s. 23 of the 1969 Act any reference (however expressed) to a remand is construed as including a reference to a committal.

11.1.8.3   Designation by the court of the local authority which is to receive the defendant   Section 23(2) of the CYPA 1969 provides that a court remanding a person to local authority accommodation must designate the local authority which is to receive the person and that authority must be:

   (a)   in the case of a person who is being looked after by a local authority, that authority; and
   (b)   in any other case, the local authority in whose area it appears to the court that the person resides or the offence or one of the offences was committed.

The reference to a person who is being looked after by a local authority is construed in accordance with s. 22 of the CA 1989: CYPA 1969, s. 23(13)(a).

11.1.8.4   Detention by person on behalf of the designated local authority   Children or young persons remanded to local authority accommodation may be detained lawfully by anyone acting on behalf of the designated authority: CYPA 1969, s. 23(3).

11.1.8.5 Defendant remanded to local authority accommodation may be required to comply with conditions akin to those under the Bail Act A court remanding a person to local authority accommodation without imposing a security requirement (that is to say, a requirement imposed under s. 23(4) of the 1969 Act that the person be placed and kept in secure accommodation) may, after consultation with the designated authority, require that person to comply with any such conditions as could be imposed under s. 3(6) of the BA 1976 if bail was then being granted: CYPA 1969, s. 23(7), as amended by the CDA 1998, s. 98(5). (For the definition of 'security requirement' see para. 11.1.9.3, below, and for the definition of 'secure accommodation' see para. 11.1.9.1.) Where a court imposes any such conditions, it must explain to the defendant in open court and in ordinary language why those conditions are being imposed, and a magistrates' court must cause a reason stated by it to be specified in the warrant of commitment and to be entered in the register: CYPA 1969, s. 23(8). Any reference to consultation shall be construed as a reference to such consultation (if any) as is reasonably practicable in all the circumstances of the case: CYPA 1969, s. 23(13)(b).

11.1.8.6 Requirement that the local authority ensures defendant complies with conditions imposed on being remanded to local authority accommodation A court remanding a defendant to local authority accommodation under s. 23 of the 1969 Act without imposing a security requirement may, after consultation with the designated authority, impose on that authority requirements for securing compliance with any conditions imposed on the defendant under s. 23(7): CYPA 1969, s. 23(9). (See para. 11.1.8.5 for s. 23(7).)

11.1.8.7 Prohibition on placement with a named person A court remanding a person to local authority accommodation may, after consultation with the designated authority, impose on that authority requirements stipulating that the defendant must not be placed with a named person: CYPA 1969, s. 23(9). This measure is evidently designed to prevent a child or young person being accommodated in the same establishment as another person who may previously have exercised an undesirable influence over the child or young person.

11.1.8.8 Conditions imposed on application by local authority Where a defendant is remanded to local authority accommodation, s. 23(10) of the 1969 Act provides that the relevant court:

(a) may, on the application of the designated authority, impose on the defendant any such conditions as could be imposed under s. 23(7) (see para. 11.1.8.5, above) if the court were then remanding the defendant to such accommodation; and

(b)   where it does so, may impose on that authority any requirements for securing compliance with the conditions so imposed.

A 'relevant court', in relation to a person remanded to local authority accommodation, means the court by which the person was so remanded, or any magistrates' court having jurisdiction in the place where the person is for the time being: CYPA 1969, s. 23(12).

11.1.8.9   Variation or revocation of conditions   Where a defendant is remanded to local authority accommodation, a relevant court (as defined in s. 23(12): see para. 11.1.8.8) may, on the application of the designated authority or the defendant, vary or revoke any conditions or requirements imposed under s. 23(7), (9) or (10): CYPA 1969, s. 23(11). (See paras 11.1.8.5, 11.1.8.7 and 11.1.8.8.)

11.1.8.10   Liability to arrest for breach of conditions attaching to a remand to local authority accommodation   A person who has been remanded or committed to local authority accommodation and in respect of whom conditions under s. 23(7) or (10) have been imposed, may be arrested without warrant by a constable if the constable has reasonable grounds for suspecting that that person has broken any of those conditions: CYPA 1969, s. 23A(1), inserted by the CJPOA 1994, s. 23. Except where such an arrest is made within 24 hours of the appointed time of appearance before the court in pursuance of the remand or committal, the person so arrested must be brought before a justice of the peace of the petty sessions area in which the arrest was made as soon as practicable, and in any event within 24 hours after the arrest: s. 23A(2)(a). Where an arrest under s. 23A(1) is made within 24 hours of the appointed time of appearance before the court in pursuance of the remand or committal, the arrested person must be brought before the court at which the appearance was to have been made: s. 23A(2)(b). In reckoning any 24-hour period no account must be taken of Christmas Day, Good Friday, or any Sunday: s. 23A(2). If a justice of the peace before whom a person is brought under s. 23A is of the opinion that that person has broken any condition imposed under s. 23(7) or (10) of the 1969 Act, the justice must direct a remand and s. 23 applies as if the person was then charged with or convicted of the offence for which the person had been remanded or committed: s. 23A(3)(b). (In other words, the general position must be considered *de novo*.) Alternatively, if the justice is not of the opinion that any of the conditions have been broken, there must be a remand or committal to the place to which the person had been remanded or committed at the time of arrest and subject to the same conditions as those which were in force at that time: s. 23A(3)(b).

11.1.9   Remand to secure accommodation

11.1.9.1   Order for security requirement (secure accommodation) after consultation with the designated authority   Section 23(4) of the CYPA 1969, as amended by s. 97(1) of the CDA 1998, provides that subject to s. 23(5) and (5A), a court remanding a person to local authority accommodation may, after consultation with the designated authority, require that authority to comply with a security requirement, that is to say, a requirement that the person in question be placed and kept in secure accommodation. 'Secure accommodation' means accommodation which is provided in a community home, a voluntary home or a registered children's home for the purpose of restricting liberty, and which is approved for that purpose by the Secretary of State: CYPA 1969, s. 23(12).

11.1.9.2 Security requirement permissible for 12 year olds and other young persons posing prescribed forms of risk to the community Section 23(5) of the CYPA 1969, as amended by s. 97(2) of the CDA 1998, provides that a court shall not impose a security requirement except in respect of a child who has attained the age of 12, or a young person, who (in either case) is of a prescribed description, and then only if:

(a) the child or young person is charged with or has been convicted of a violent or sexual offence, or an offence punishable in the case of an adult with imprisonment for a term of 14 years or more; or

(b) the child or young person has a recent history of absconding while remanded to local authority accommodation, and is charged with or has been convicted of an imprisonable offence alleged or found to have been committed while the child or young person was so remanded;

and (in either case) the court is of opinion that only such a requirement would be adequate to protect the public from serious harm from the child or young person in question.

Section 97(4) of the CDA 1998 inserts in s. 23(12) of the 1969 Act the definition of 'prescribed description', meaning a description prescribed by reference to age or sex or both by an order of the Secretary of State. The terms 'sexual offence' and 'violent offence' have the same meanings as in Part I of the CJA 1991: s. 23(12). Any reference, in relation to a person charged with or convicted of a violent or sexual offence, to protecting the public from serious harm from that person shall be construed as a reference to protecting members of the public from death or serious personal injury, whether physical or psychological, occasioned by further such offences committed by the person: CYPA 1969, s. 23(13)(c).

11.1.9.3 Males aged 15 or 16: eligibility for remand to secure local accommodation, remand centre, or prison In the case of any male person who is of the age of 15 or 16 and is not of a prescribed description for the purpose of s. 23(5) of the 1969 Act, s. 98(3) of the CDA 1998 enacts that the provisions in s. 23(4), (4A), (5) and (5A) applicable in the case of persons of both sexes of 12 years old and above are substituted by different provisions which are designated by the same numbers as the subsections they replace. 'Substitute' s. 23(5) applies to a person who:

(a)   is charged with or has been convicted of a violent or sexual offence, or an offence punishable in the case of an adult with imprisonment for a term of 14 years or more; or

(b)   has a recent history of absconding while remanded to local authority accommodation, and is charged with or has been convicted of an imprisonable offence alleged or found to have been committed while he was so remanded;

if (in either case) the court is of opinion that only remanding him to a remand centre or prison, or to local authority accommodation with a requirement that he be placed and kept in secure accommodation, would be adequate to protect the public from serious harm from him.

Substitute s. 23(4) provides that where a court, after consultation with a probation officer, a social worker of a local authority social services department or a member of a youth offending team, declares a person to be one to whom substitute s. 23(5) applies:

(a)   it shall remand him to local authority accommodation and require him to be placed and kept in secure accommodation if:

(i)   it also, after such consultation, declares him to be a person to whom substitute s. 23(5A) applies, namely a person who in its opinion it would, by reason of his physical or emotional immaturity or a propensity to harm himself, be undesirable to remand to a remand centre or a prison; and

(ii)   it has been notified that secure accommodation is available for him;

(b)   it shall remand him to a remand centre, if para. (a) above does not apply and it has been notified that such a centre is available for the reception from the court of persons to whom substitute s. 23(5) applies; and

(c)   it shall remand him to a prison if neither para. (a) nor para. (b) above applies.

11.1.9.4   Child or young person not legally represented   Where a person is not legally represented a court shall not impose a security requirement (CYPA 1969, s. 23(5A) – version applicable to children and young persons generally) or shall not declare that person to be a person to whom substitute s. 23(5) applies (substitute s. 23(4A)) unless:

(a)   the person applied for legal aid and the application was refused on the ground that it did not appear that the person's means were such that assistance was required; or

(b)   having been informed of the right to apply for legal aid and having had the opportunity to do so the person refused or failed to apply.

11.1.9.5   Pronouncement by the court that the person falls within section 23(5) and explanation   Where a court declares a person to be one to whom s. 23(5) applies, it must:

(a)   state in open court that it is of the opinion that the defendant is a person to whom that subsection applies; and

(b)   explain to him in open court and in ordinary language why it is of that opinion;

and a magistrates' court must cause a reason stated by it under para. (b) to be specified in the warrant of commitment and to be entered in the register: CYPA 1969, s. 23(6).

11.1.9.6   Defendants already remanded to local authority accommodation: application by designated authority for declaration under 'substitute' section 23(5)   Section 23(9A) of the 1969 Act, inserted by s. 98(6) of the CDA 1998, provides that where a person is remanded to local authority accommodation, a relevant court may, on the application of the designated authority, declare him to be a person to whom substitute s. 23(5) applies; and on its doing so, he ceases to be remanded to local authority accommodation and, in accordance with s. 23(4), he must be remanded to a remand centre, if the court has been notified that such a centre is available for the reception from the court of such persons, or to a prison, if the court has not been so notified.

11.1.10   Application by local authority to keep in secure accommodation a 'child' whom they are looking after

Where a child (i.e. a person under 18) has been remanded or committed to local authority accommodation by a youth court or a magistrates' court other than a youth court, the local authority looking after the child may apply to that court under s. 25 of the CA 1989 for authorisation to place the child in secure accommodation for a period greater than an aggregate of 72 hours in any 28-day period. The provision was brought into force on 14 October 1991, by the Criminal Justice Act 1991 (Commencement No. 1) Order 1991 (SI 1991 No. 2208). Such applications relate to children who are already subject to criminal process, whether under s. 38(6) of the PACE 1984 or remanded to local authority accommodation under s. 23 of the 1969 Act, but they do not themselves form part of the criminal process although their outcome will clearly have a bearing on what happens to the children concerned: see *Archbold*, para. 3–79, and see Children (Secure Accommodation) Regulations 1991 (SI 1991 No. 1505) as amended from 1 October 1992 by the Children (Secure Accommodation)(Amendment) Regulations 1992 (SI 1992 No. 2117).

11.1.11   Prosecution right of appeal in respect of bail

Where in the case of a child or young person (as defined in the CYPA 1969) the prosecution seek under s. 1 of the BAA 1993 to appeal to a Crown Court judge against the decision of a magistrates' court to grant bail, the magistrates' court, on receiving from the prosecution oral notice of appeal, must apply the provisions of s. 23 of the 1969 Act.

11.1.12 Abolition of power to commit juveniles with a view to sentence of detention in a young offender institution

Young offender institutions (for 15 to 17 year olds) under the CJA 1982, s. 1A, and secure training orders for 12 to 14 year old persistent offenders under CJPOA 1994, s. 1, are replaced by a single custodial sentence for 10 to 17 year old offenders – the detention and training order (CDA 1998, s. 73(1)). Magistrates are empowered to impose terms of up to 24 months: CDA, 1998, s. 73(5). Accordingly, s. 37 of the MCA 1980 (committal to the Crown Court with a view to a greater term of detention in a young offender institution for 15 to 17 year olds) was repealed by the CDA 1998, sch. 8, para. 41.

11.1.13 Time spent in custody to count towards sentence

The general principles on discount for time spent in custody before sentence were explained in Chapter 1 at para. 1.6. Time spent in custody at a remand centre or prison under s. 23 of the CYPA 1969 or under s. 37 of the MCA 1980 in connection with the offence for which a sentence of detention in a young offender institution is passed will count towards that sentence: CJA 1967, s. 67(5) and (6). Time spent in the care of a local authority will count towards sentence only where the defendant is held in secure accommodation: CJA 1988, s. 130.

11.2 PERSONS AFFECTED BY ADVERSE MENTAL CONDITION

11.2.1 Remand to hospital for report on the accused's mental condition

11.2.1.1 Section 35 of the Mental Health Act 1983 Under s. 35(1) of the MHA 1983, a magistrates' court or the Crown Court may order a remand to a hospital specified by the court for a report on the accused's mental condition.

11.2.1.2 Meaning of the 'accused' in the magistrates' court Section 35(2)(b) of the MHA 1983 provides that for the purposes of s. 35 an accused person in relation the magistrates' court is:

(a) anyone who has been convicted by the court of an offence punishable on summary conviction with imprisonment;

(b) anyone charged with such an offence if the court is satisfied that the person did the act or made the omission charged; or

(c) anyone charged with such an offence whom the court is satisfied has consented to the exercise by the court of the powers conferred by s. 35.

Persons in category (c) would include unconvicted defendants who have consented to a remand for a pre-trial examination and report on their medical condition.

11.2.1.3 Meaning of the 'accused' in the Crown Court For the purposes of s. 35, an accused in relation to the Crown Court is any person who is awaiting trial before the court for an offence punishable with imprisonment or who has been arraigned before the court for such an offence and has not yet been sentenced or otherwise dealt with for the offence concerned: MHA 1983, s. 35(2)(a).

11.2.1.4 Crown Court: offences carrying sentence fixed by law Section 35 of the 1983 Act has no application in the case of a person convicted before the Crown Court of any offence for which the sentence is fixed by law: MHA 1983, s. 35(3).

11.2.1.5 When the power of remand under section 35 may be exercised Section 35(3) of the 1983 Act provides that the power of remand to hospital for a report on the accused's mental condition may be exercised under s. 35 if:

(a)   the court is satisfied, on the written or oral evidence of a registered medical practitioner, that there is reason to suspect that the accused is suffering from mental illness, psychopathic disorder, severe mental impairment or mental impairment; and
(b)   the court is of the opinion that it would be impracticable for a report to be made if the accused were on bail.

The terms used in s. 35(3)(a) are defined in s. 1(2) of the 1983 Act. The court must not remand an accused person to a hospital under s. 35 unless satisfied, on the written or oral evidence of the registered medical practitioner who would be responsible for making the report, or of some other person representing the managers of the hospital, that arrangements have been made for the accused person's admission to that hospital: MHA 1983, s. 35(4).

11.2.1.6 Time limit on admission The court must also be satisfied, where arrangements have been made for the accused person's admission to hospital for the making of a report under the section, that those arrangements are for admission within the period of seven days beginning with the date of remand: MHA 1983, s. 35(4).

11.2.1.7 Detention in a place of safety pending admission to hospital
If the court is satisfied that the necessary arrangements have been made for the accused person's admission to hospital within seven days of the remand, it may, pending such admission, give directions for the accused to be conveyed to and detained in a place of safety: MHA 1983, s. 35(4).

11.2.1.8   Further remand necessary   An accused remanded under s. 35 of the 1983 Act may be further remanded if it appears to the court, on the written or oral evidence of the registered medical practitioner responsible for making the report, that a further remand is necessary for completing the assessment of the accused person's medical condition: s. 35(5). A further remand may take place in the absence of an accused who is represented by counsel or a solicitor and the legal representative is given an opportunity of being heard: s. 35(6).

11.2.1.9   Time limits on remands   The accused must not be remanded or further remanded under s. 35 for more than 28 days at a time or for more than 12 weeks in all: MHA 1983, s. 35(7). The court may at any time terminate the remand if it appears to that court that it is appropriate to do so: *ibid.*

11.2.1.10   Conveyance and admission to hospital   Section 35(9) of the 1983 Act provides that an accused person who is remanded under s. 35 will be conveyed to the hospital specified by the court by a constable or other person directed to do so by the court. The accused must be conveyed to the hospital within the period of seven days beginning with the date of the remand. The managers of the hospital must admit the accused within that period and thereafter detain the accused.

11.2.1.11   Arrest without warrant for absconding   Section 35(10) of the MHA 1983 provides that an accused person who is remanded to a hospital and absconds from it, or absconds while being conveyed to or from the hospital, may be arrested without warrant by any constable. The accused must then be brought, as soon as practicable, before the court of remand, which may thereupon terminate the remand and deal with the accused in any way in which it could have done if it had not remanded the accused to hospital under the section.

11.2.2   Remand by Crown Court of accused persons to hospital for treatment

11.2.2.1   Remand to hospital instead of in custody   Under s. 36(1) of the MHA 1983, the Crown Court may, instead of remanding an accused person in custody, remand the accused to a hospital specified by the court, for the purpose of medical treatment. In order to do so the court must be satisfied, on the written or oral evidence of two registered practitioners, that the accused is suffering from mental illness or severe mental impairment of a nature or degree which makes detention in a hospital for medical treatment appropriate: s. 36(1). Medical treatment is defined by s. 145(1) of the 1983 Act as including 'nursing' and 'care, habilitation and rehabilitation under medical supervision'.

11.2.2.2   Meaning of the 'accused'   For the purposes of s. 36 of the 1983 Act an accused person is any person who is in custody awaiting trial before the Crown Court for an offence punishable with imprisonment (other than an offence for which the sentence is fixed by law) or who at any time before sentence is in custody in the course of a trial before that court for such an offence: MHA 1983, s. 36(2).

11.2.2.3 Provisions regulating arrangements The provisions in s. 35 (see para. 11.2.1) concerning arrangements for admission to hospital, further remand, entitlement to an independent report and power of arrest, apply also to s. 36: MHA 1983, ss. 36(3) to (8), inclusively.

11.2.3 Committal to the Crown Court under sections 43 and 44 of the Mental Health Act 1983 with a view to a restriction order

11.2.3.1 Committal in custody Where a person aged at least 14 years is convicted by a magistrates' court of an offence punishable on summary conviction with imprisonment, and the conditions for the making of a hospital order under s. 37(1) and (2) of the 1983 Act are satisfied, the court may commit the offender in custody to the Crown Court to be dealt with for the offence, provided it appears to the court, having regard to the nature of the offence, the antecedents of the offender and the risk of the offender committing further offences if set at large, that if a hospital order is made a restriction order should also be made: MHA 1983, s. 43(1). Section 37(1) provides that where a person is convicted before the Crown Court of an offence punishable with imprisonment other than an offence the sentence for which is fixed by law, or is convicted by a magistrates' court of an offence punishable on summary conviction with imprisonment, and the conditions set out in s. 37(2) are satisfied, the court may by order authorise the person's detention in such hospital as may be specified in the order.

The conditions in s. 37(2) are as follows. The court must be satisfied, on the written or oral evidence of two registered medical practitioners, that the offender is suffering from mental illness, psychopathic disorder, severe mental impairment or mental impairment. Further, the court must be satisfied: either:

(a) the mental disorder from which the offender is suffering is of a nature or degree which makes detention in a hospital for medical treatment appropriate, and, in the case of psychopathic disorder or mental impairment, that such treatment is likely to alleviate or prevent a deterioration of his condition; or

(b) in the case of an offender who is aged at least 16 years, the mental disorder is of a nature or degree which warrants reception into guardianship under the Act.

Lastly, the court must be of the opinion, having regard to all the circumstances including the nature of the offence and the character and antecedents of, and the availability of other methods of dealing with, the offender, that the most suitable method of disposing of the case is by means of an order under s. 37.

11.2.3.2 Power of the Crown Court Section 43(2) of the 1983 Act provides that where an offender is committed to the Crown Court under s. 43, that court must inquire into the circumstances of the case, and may:

(a)   provided the conditions are satisfied, make a hospital order with or without a restriction order; or

(b)   deal with the offender in any other manner in which the magistrates' court might have dealt with the case.

11.2.3.3   Committal to hospital or in custody   A committal under s. 43 of the 1983 Act may be to hospital instead of in custody if the magistrates' court by whom the offender is committed is satisfied on the written or oral evidence of the registered medical practitioner who would be in charge of the offender's treatment or some other person representing the managers of the hospital, that arrangements have been made for the admission of the offender to a hospital in the event of an order being made under this section: MHA 1983, s. 44(1) and (2).

11.2.3.4   Power to make a hospital order in the detainee's absence   Where a person committed to the Crown Court to be dealt with under s. 43 of the 1983 Act is admitted to hospital in pursuance of an order under s. 44, s. 51(5) and (6) of the Act apply as if the person were subject to a transfer direction (see para. 11.2.4.6). The effect of this is that if it appears to the court that it is impracticable or inappropriate to bring the detainee before the court, a hospital order may be made in the detainee's absence (with or without a restriction order) if the court:

(a)   is satisfied, on the written or oral evidence of at least two registered medical practitioners, that the detainee is suffering from mental illness or severe mental impairment of a nature or degree which makes detention in a hospital for medical treatment appropriate; and

(b)   is of opinion, after considering any depositions or other documents required to be sent to the proper officer of the court, that it is proper to make such an order.

11.2.4   Removal to hospital of mental patients

11.2.4.1   Executive transfer to hospital of unsentenced prisoners   Section 48 of the MHA 1983 authorises the Secretary of State to direct the transfer to hospital of persons detained in a prison or remand centre, not being persons serving a sentence of imprisonment, and persons remanded in custody by a magistrates' court. The power under s. 48 may be exercised where the Secretary of State:

(a)   is satisfied by reports from at least two registered medical practitioners that the person is suffering from mental illness or severe mental impairment of a nature or degree that makes detention in hospital for medical treatment appropriate and that the person is in urgent need of such treatment; and

(b)   is of the opinion, having regard to the public interest and all the circumstances, that such detention is expedient.

11.2.4.2   Transfer direction ends after 14 days if not executed   A transfer direction ceases to have effect after 14 days unless it has been executed within that period: MHA 1983, s. 48(3). It has the same effect as a hospital order made in the case of the person in question: *ibid.*

11.2.4.3 Special restrictions of section 41 of the 1983 Act to apply Where a transfer direction is given in respect of a person coming within the MHA 1983, s. 48(2)(a) or (b), the Secretary of State must further direct that the person is subject to the special restrictions in s. 41 of the 1983 Act.

11.2.4.4 Effect of transfer direction ceases with disposal by the court The transfer direction ceases to have effect when the detainee's case is disposed of by the court having jurisdiction to try or otherwise deal with the detainee, but without prejudice to any power of that court to make a hospital order or other associated order: MHA 1983, s. 51(2).

11.2.4.5 Remittal where treatment no longer needed or possible Section 51(4) of the 1983 Act provides that if the court having jurisdiction to try or otherwise deal with the detainee is satisfied on the written or oral evidence of the responsible medical officer:

(a)   that treatment in hospital for mental disorder is no longer required; or

(b)   that no effective treatment for the disorder can be given at the hospital;

remittal may be ordered to a place where the detainee might have been detained but for the transfer direction, or, subject to s. 25 of the CJPOA 1994, released on bail. On arrival at that place, or with release on bail, the transfer direction ceases to have effect.

11.2.4.6 Power to make a hospital order in the detainee's absence Section 51(5) of the MHA 1983 provides that where no order has been made under s. 51(4) but it appears to the court having jurisdiction to try or otherwise deal with the detainee that it is impracticable or inappropriate to bring the detainee before the court, then, if the conditions set out in s. 51(6) are satisfied, a hospital order may be made (with or without a restriction order) in the detainee's absence. This also applies in the case of a person awaiting trial. The conditions set out in s. 51(6) are that the court must be:

(a)   satisfied, on the written or oral evidence of at least two registered medical practitioners, that the detainee is suffering from mental illness or severe mental impairment of a nature or degree which makes detention in a hospital for medical treatment appropriate; and

(b)   of the opinion, after considering any depositions or other documents required to be sent to the proper officer of the court, that it is proper to make such an order.

12 Custody Time Limits

12.1 BACKGROUND

Custody time limits were introduced by s. 22 of the Prosecution of Offences Act 1985 (POA 1985) in response to a recommendation of the House of Commons Home Affairs Committee in 1983–4 (*Remands in Custody*, HC 252). In the words of a Home Office researcher:

> Such limits were seen as a potential way of expediting the progress of cases through courts. Lengthy delay in hearing cases has a number of adverse effects: the quality of evidence deteriorates (due to failing memories, and the non-availability of witnesses); all parties – victims, suspects and witnesses – suffer a prolongation of anxiety; frequent adjournments increase courts' expenditure; the population of prisoners on remand awaiting trial increases and contributes to prison overcrowding. In addition, there is concern that long periods in prison on remand before conviction run counter to the ideal of justice, especially if defendants are ultimately given non-custodial sentences or acquitted. (Henderson, P., *Monitoring Time Limits on Custodial Remands*, Research and Planning Unit Paper 61, London: Home Office, 1991, p. 1)

12.2 OVERALL TIME LIMITS

12.2.1 Power of Secretary of State to set time limits

Section 22(1)(a) and (b) of the POA 1985 empower the Secretary of State to make provision by regulations with respect to any specified preliminary stage of proceedings for an offence as to the maximum period to be allowed to the prosecution to complete that stage ('overall time limits') and as to the maximum period during which the accused may, while awaiting completion of that stage, be in the custody of the magistrates' court or the Crown Court ('custody time limits').

12.2.2 Provisions for overall limits not yet implemented

No regulations have yet been made as to overall time limits although it is understood to be the Government's intention to pilot their use before implementing them nationally.

12.3 CUSTODY TIME LIMITS IN THE MAGISTRATES' COURT

12.3.1 Either-way offences

Except as provided by reg. 4(3) of the Custody Time Limits Regulations (Prosecution of Offences (Custody Time Limits) Regulations 1987 (SI 1987 No. 299), as amended by Prosecution of Offences (Custody Time Limits) (Amendment) Regulations 1995 (SI 1995 No. 555) and s. 71(4) of the CPIA 1996) in the case of an either-way offence the maximum period of custody between the accused's first appearance and the start of summary trial or the time when the court decides whether or not to commit the accused to the Crown Court for trial is 70 days: 1987 Regulations, reg. 4(2).

12.3.2 Either-way offences tried summarily

In the case of an offence triable either way if, before the expiry of 56 days following the day of the accused's first appearance, the court decides to proceed to summary trial, the maximum period of custody between the accused's first appearance and the start of the summary trial is 56 days: 1987 Regulations, reg. 4(3).

12.3.3 Indictable only offences

In the case of an offence triable on indictment only (except treason) the maximum period of custody between the accused's first appearance and the time when the court decides whether or not to commit the accused to the Crown Court for trial is 70 days: 1987 Regulations, (reg. 4(4)). The rule will be rendered otiose with the bringing into force nationally of s. 51(1) of the CDA 1998, which provides that where an adult appears or is brought before a magistrates' court charged with an offence triable only on indictment, the court must 'send him *forthwith* to the Crown Court for trial' (emphasis supplied).

12.3.4 Old-style committal

Where the committal is by way of s. 6(1) of the MCA 1980 (old-style committal), the time when the court decides whether or not to commit the accused for trial means the time when it begins to hear evidence for the prosecution at committal: 1987 Regulations, reg. 4(5)(a). Regulation 4(5) was considered in *Re Najam* [1998]

10 Archbold News 2. The applicant was committed for trial the day before the custody time limit expired but in quashing the committal the Divisional Court held that the question for the court was purely a factual one — has the court begun to hear evidence for the prosecution? If the answer is in the affirmative then there is no automatic entitlement to bail if the court had begun to hear the evidence within the pre-committal time limit.

12.3.5 Transfers

Where a notice of transfer has been given under s. 4(1)(3) of the CJA 1987, the time when the court decides whether or not to commit the accused for trial means the date at which notice of transfer was given: 1987 Regulations, reg. 4(5)(b)). It is to be noted that no reference is made to transfer under s. 3 of the CJA 1991 in relation to cases of sexual offences or offences of violence involving child victims or child witnesses.

12.3.6 Meaning of first appearance in magistrates' court

A person's first appearance in relation to proceedings in a magistrates' court is:

(a) on a defence application under s. 43B of the MCA 1980 (application to vary conditions imposed by a constable), the time when the application was made;

(b) where the defendant appears or is brought before the court in relation to an application under s. 5B of the BA 1976 (application by the prosecutor for decision to grant bail to be reconsidered in relation to a bail decision made by a constable), the time of that appearance or production before the court under that section;

(c) in any other case, when the defendant appears or is brought before the court: 1987 Regulations, reg. 2(2).

12.3.7 Application of custody time limits to young persons

Regulation 4 of the Prosecution of Offences (Custody Time Limit) Regulations (SI 1987 No. 299) states: 'The maximum period during which a person accused of an indictable offence other than treason may be in the custody of a magistrates' court in relation to that offence while awaiting completion of any preliminary stage of the proceedings . . . shall be . . . (4) [i]n the case of an offence triable on indictment exclusively the maximum period of custody between the accused's first appearance and the time when the court decides whether or not to commit the accused to the Crown Court for trial shall be fifty-six days.' In the case of an adult, robbery is triable on indictment exclusively. In the case of a child or young person, the offence is in general only triable summarily in consequence of s. 24, MCA 1980. The expression 'triable either way' is not defined in the Regulations. While robbery in the case of an adult is not triable either way, in the case of a child it is. Since s. 24 of the MCA 1980 is expressly referred to in reg. 4(3) it must have been intended that children and young persons accused of indictable offences other than homicide should be subject to the fifty-six day time limit there referred to (*R* v *Stratford Youth Court, ex parte S, The Times*, 28 May 1998).

12.4 CUSTODY TIME LIMITS IN THE CROWN COURT

12.4.1 The general rule

The maximum period of custody between committal and the start of the trial, or where a bill of indictment is preferred under s. 2(2)(b) of the Administration of Justice (Miscellaneous Provisions) Act 1933 (voluntary bill) between the preferment of the bill and the start of the trial, is 112 days: 1987 Regulations, reg. 5(3). In the case of a person who first appears in a magistrates' court before the commencement date of the new procedure, the Crown Court custody time is as above or 112 days, whichever is longer: Prosecution of Offences (Custody Time Limits) (Modification) Regulations 1998 (SI 1998 No. 3037) which adds new para. (6B) in reg. 5. The effect of the modification is that defendants sent for trial will be subject to the same custody time limits in total as those committed for trial.

12.4.2 Separate committals

The maximum period of custody applies in relation to each offence separately where, following a committal for trial, the bill of indictment (not being a voluntary bill) contains a count charging an offence for which the defendant was committed for trial at that committal together with a count charging an offence for which he was committed for trial on a separate occasion: 1987 Regulations, reg. 5(4).

12.4.3 Voluntary bill following committal

Where, following a committal for trial, a voluntary bill is preferred and the bill does not contain a count charging an offence for which the defendant was not committed for trial, the maximum period of custody between the preferment of the bill and the start of the trial is 112 days less any period, or the aggregate of any period, during which he has, since the committal, been in the custody of the Crown Court in relation to an offence for which he was committed for trial: 1987 Regulations, reg. 5(6).

12.4.4 Where indictment contains a new count

Where, following a committal for trial, the bill of indictment (not being a voluntary bill) contains a count charging an offence for which the accused was not committed for trial, the maximum period in custody (i) between the preferment of the bill and start of the trial, or (ii) if the count was added to the bill after its preferment, between that addition and the start of the trial, is 112 days less any period, or the aggregate of any period, during which the accused has, since the committal, been in the custody of the Crown Court in relation to an offence for which the committal took place: 1987 Regulations, reg. 5(6).

12.4.5 Application of the Regulations to transfers for trial

The foregoing provisions of reg. 5 of the 1987 Regulations have effect, where notice of transfer is given, as if references to committal for trial and to offences for which a person was or was not committed for trial included reference to the giving of notice of transfer and to charges contained or not contained in the notice of transfer (reg. 5(6A)).

12.4.6   Meaning of start of trial in the Crown Court

12.4.6.1   General rule   For the purposes of s. 22(11A) of the POA 1985, as inserted by s. 71 of the CPIA 1996, the trial starts when a jury is sworn to consider the issue of guilt or fitness to plead or, if a court accepts a plea of guilty before a jury is sworn, when the plea is accepted.

12.4.6.2   Preparatory hearings   A saving is provided for s. 8 of the CJA 1987 and s. 30 of the CPIA 1996 (preparatory hearings). Where a preparatory hearing is held, that hearing marks the start of the trial for the purpose of custody time limits.

12.4.7   Custody time limit does not end with arraignment

As a result of s. 71 of the CPIA 1996, custody time limits in the Crown Court now extend to the start of trial and do not end upon arraignment. This amendment puts an end to the practice of 'sham arraignments', the only purpose of which is to deprive the defendant of the expiry of the custody time limit (*R* v *Crown Court at Maidstone, ex parte Hollstein* [1995] 3 All ER 503), or to avoid an application for an extension of a custody time limit (*R* v *Maidstone Crown Court ex parte Clark* [1995] 1 WLR 831).

12.4.8   Measurement of the custody time limit

A custody time limit begins at the close of the day on which the defendant is first remanded and expires at midnight on the day of expiry: *R* v *Governor of Canterbury Prison, ex parte Craig* [1991] 2 QB 195.

12.4.9   Each offence attracts its own custody time limit

The 1987 Regulations refer to an 'offence' in the singular and not to 'a charge'. Each offence therefore attracts its own custody time limit (*R* v *Wirral District Magistrates' Court, ex parte Meikle* [1990] Crim LR 801).

12.4.10   Substitution of new charge

Where a charge is withdrawn and a new charge based on the same circumstances is substituted, a new custody time limit begins from the date of the preferment of the new charge: *R* v *Waltham Forest Justices, ex parte Lee and another* (1993) 97 Cr App R 287, where a charge of wounding with intent was substituted for a charge of attempted murder. The Divisional Court held *obiter* that it would no doubt be an abuse of process if the prosecution preferred a new charge based on the same facts merely as a device to circumvent the custody time limits.

The question whether a charge is a new one so as to attract a fresh custody time limit is one of substance, not of form. The legislative purpose would be defeated if relatively minor or unimportant amendments to existing charges were to result in the commencement of a new custody time limit: *R v Burton on Trent Justices, ex parte P* [1998] 3 *Archbold News* 1.

12.5 EXTENSION

12.5.1 Application for the extension of custody time limits

An application to a court for the extension or further extension of a custody time limit under s. 22(3) of the POA 1985 may be made orally or in writing: 1987 Regulations, reg. 7. Unless the accused or the accused's representative has informed the prosecution that notice is not required, the prosecution must give notice in writing to the accused or the representative and to the proper officer of the court stating that they intend to make such an application. Such notice must be given not less than five days before making such an application to the Crown Court and not less than two days before making such an application in a magistrates' court. The requirement as to notice may be waived or the minimum period may be reduced by the direction of the court if it is satisfied that it is not practicable in all the circumstances for the prosecution to comply with the requirement. Failure to comply with the notice requirements does not preclude the grant of an extension because such extension may be made at any time before the expiry of the custody time limit: *R v Governor of Canterbury Prison, ex parte Craig* [1991] 2 QB 195.

Regulation 7 was further considered in *R v Central Criminal Court, ex parte Marotta* [1998] 10 Archbold News 2. In order to establish the conditions necessary to justify an extension of a custody time limit, the Crown must specify in detail the reason for the delay. The fact that the case is large and complicated does not of itself justify an extension, without an adequately detailed explanation of what the prosecution had actually been doing. Although reg. 7 requires the prosecution to do no more than serve notice that they intend to apply for an extension to a time limit, it would be good practice for the factual basis on which the application relies to be set out.

Instruction for advocates appearing upon applications for extension has recently been given by Butterfield J in *Practice Direction (Application to extend custody time limits)*, unreported, 18 December 1998, Western Circuit, cited in CLW/99/1/3. There it was stated that all applications for an extension were to be listed in open court, with advocates (where possible, those instructed in the trial) to attend. They were to be fully instructed on all aspects of the case relating to the timetable, the nature of the case and any other matter relevant to the decision that has to be made. However short the extension sought, each application was to be fully considered.

Advocates were to inform the court at least 24 hours before the hearing of its anticipated length. All advocates would be expected to be fully conversant with the judgment in *R* v *Manchester Crown Court, ex parte McDonald*; *R* v *Leeds Crown Court, ex parte Hunt*; *R* v *Winchester Crown Court, ex parte Forbes*; *ex parte Wilson and Mason*, *The Times*, 19 November 1998, CA. (See para. 12.5.6 and 12.5.7, below.)

12.5.2   An application for extension must be made before the expiry of the custody time limit

A custody time limit cannot be extended after it has expired. An application for extension must be made before its expiry (*R* v *Governor of Winchester Prison, ex parte Roddie* [1991] 2 All ER 931) but the expiry of a pre-committal custody time limit is not a bar to the operation of a post-committal custody time limit: *R* v *Sheffield Justices, ex parte Turner* [1991] 2 QB 472. Where the Crown Court refuses an application for an extension, the Divisional Court is powerless to intervene once the time limit has expired: *R* v *Croydon Crown Court, ex parte Commissioner of Customs and Excise* [1997] 8 *Archbold News* 1.

12.5.3   Applications and orders must be made clearly

An application for the extension of a custody time limit must be made clearly and unmistakably so that the defence have the opportunity to raise any objections to the application. An order extending a custody time limit must be made clearly and unambiguously and cannot simply be inferred from other orders. The clerk of the court must keep a proper and permanent record: *R* v *Governor of Armley Prison, ex parte Ward*, *The Times*, 23 November 1990.

12.5.4   Method of application

The court may rely on assertions by the advocate and need not hear evidence, but may do so at its discretion. The prosecution must supply the court with full and accurate information: *R* v *Norwich Crown Court, ex parte Parker and Ward* [1992] Crim LR 500. As to the material which ought to be presented before the court, Lord Bingham CJ in *Ex parte McDonald, supra*, observed that it had always to be adequately and fully informed of the matters affecting the decision. Whether evidence would be necessary, or whether the court could rely on information supplied by counsel would depend on the nature and extent of any controversy.

12.5.5   Reasons to be given for making an extension order

Where a custody time limit is extended, the judge should not only state its decision but also reasons for concluding that there is good and sufficient cause for doing so and that the prosecution have acted with all due expedition: *R* v *Leeds Crown Court, ex parte Briggs*, *The Times*, 19 February 1998. Endorsing this principle in

Ex parte McDonald, supra, Lord Bingham CJ said that where an application was granted it was particularly important that the defendant should know why and that even where it was refused, the prosecution was entitled to know the reasons. In *R v Leeds Crown Court, ex parte Redfearn* [1998] COD 437, DC, it was held that the failure of the judge to give reasons why there was good and sufficient cause for a 10 week adjournment was not a basis for setting aside an extension order unless the failure was evidence that there really was not good and sufficient cause. James Richardson suggests that in the light of *Ex parte McDonald* such a failure would now appear to be difficult to sustain as being a good and sufficient cause: CLW/9901/4.

12.5.6 Standard of proof

The standard of proof is the civil standard: *White* v *DPP* [1989] Crim LR 375; *R v Governor of Canterbury Prison, ex parte Craig* [1991] 2 QB 195. In the latter decision the court observed (at p. 132): 'In our view the standard to be applied is that of the balance of probabilities. That is the standard for determining bail applications [*sic*].' See now also *Ex parte McDonald, supra.*

12.5.7 Grounds for extension or further extension of a custody time limit

The appropriate court may, at any time before the expiry of a time limit imposed by the Regulations, extend, or further extend, that limit if it is satisfied:

(a)   that there is good and sufficient cause for doing so; and
(b)   that the prosecution have acted with all due expedition: POA 1985, s. 22(3).

Whether these tests will be satisfied in any case will depend on factors which have been considered in a number of decisions, all of which must now be considered within the context of guidelines laid down by the Court of Appeal in *Ex parte McDonald, The Times,* 19 November 1998 (see also Lofthouse, J., 'Custody Time Limits after *ex parte McDonald,*' [1998] 10 *Archbold News* 6). There, it was held that on an application for extension of custody time limits, the court had to be careful to give full weight to the overriding purposes of s. 22(3) and reg. 5(3) of the 1987 Regulations, namely:

(i)   to ensure that the periods for which unconvicted defendants were held in custody awaiting trial were as short as reasonably and practicably possible;
(ii)   to oblige the prosecution to prepare cases for trial with all due diligence and expedition, and
(iii)   to invest the court with a power and duty to control any extension of the prescribed maximum of 112 days.

Giving judgment, Lord Bingham CJ said that as the burden on the prosecution of satisfying the statutory conditions in s. 22(3) was on the balance of probabilities, a court could never abdicate its responsibility by making orders for extension on the nod, or simply because the parties agreed or no objection was raised. Thus, according to Lofthouse (at p. 7), there can be no consent orders. The same learned commentator cites a passage from the judgment not quoted in the *Times* report, that 'the consent of experienced counsel will carry considerable weight and may relieve a judge of the need to go into all the details.' The court had to be seized of the question and address its mind to the subsection (see *R* v *Sheffield Justices, ex parte Turner* [1991] 2 QB 472). Lord Bingham further pointed out that any application will call for careful consideration and many will call for rigorous scrutiny. (Lofthouse, at p. 7, notes that no guidance is given as to what cases fall into which category.) It was, however, always for the court and not for the parties to be satisfied.

Even if satisfied of both limbs of s. 22(3) judges were not obligated to extend, enjoying an overriding discretion. (John Lofthouse suggests that they should give their reasons for exercising their discretion either way: p. 8.)

In *Ex parte McDonald. supra*, reference was made to cases decided by the European Court of Human Rights under art. 5 of the European Convention for the Protection of Human Rights and Fundamental Freedoms, Cmnd 8969, 1953, namely: *Wemhoff* v *Federal Republic of Germany* [1968] 1 EHRR 55; *Stögmüller* v *Austria* [1969] 1 EHRR 155; *Zimmerman and Steiner* v *Switzerland* [1983] 6 EHRR 17 (relating to art. 6(1)), and *W* v *Switzerland* [1993] 17 EHRR 60. When considering the effect of, and applying the domestic legislation of England and Wales, the court did not find anything in those cases which in any way threw doubt on the English law as it had been summarised in *Ex parte McDonald*. The term of 112 days prescribed by the regulations imposed what was, by international standards, an exacting one.

Following *Ex parte McDonald*, the Divisional Court in *R* v *Central Criminal Court, ex parte Bennett, The Times*, 25 January 1999, held that the judge had been wrong to extend a custody time limit notwithstanding that the prosecution's application was unopposed.

12.5.7.1 Good and sufficient cause In *R* v *Manchester Crown Court, ex parte McDonald; R* v *Leeds Crown Court, ex parte Hunt; R* v *Winchester Crown Court, ex parte Wilson and Mason, The Times*, 19 November 1998, CA, Lord Bingham CJ observed that whilst it was possible to rule that some matters were incapable in law of amounting to good and sufficient cause for granting an extension, there was an almost infinite variety of matters which might, depending on the facts of a particular case, be capable of doing so. It was neither possible nor desirable to attempt to define what might or might not do so in any given case and it would be facile to propose any test which would be applicable in all cases. All had to depend on the judgment of the court called on to make the decision, which would be made on its peculiar facts, always having regard to the over-riding purposes of the statutory provisions. In *R v Central Criminal Court, ex parte Abu-Wardeh* [1998] 1 WLR 1083, at p. 1090, it was pointed out that 'good' and 'sufficient' are separate tests. The following are factors which are likely to be taken into account:

(a) *Protection of the public.* The protection of the public is not a sufficient ground by itself for the extension of a custody time limit: *Ex parte McDonald*, following *R v Central Criminal Court, ex parte Abu-Wardeh*, *supra* (in which the contrary view expressed in *R v Luton Crown Court, ex parte Neaves* [1992] Crim LR 721, was disavowed). As all serious charges except treason are subject to custody time limits, and as any defendants facing serious charges are remanded in custody for the protection of others, Parliament could not have intended that the original reason for custody could in itself be a good cause for extending the custody time limit. The grounds for extending custody time limits are distinct from the reasons for refusing bail. The former relate to the preparation of the case and the latter to preventing any of the events which give rise to finding exceptions to the right to bail.

(b) *Protection of a witness.* In contradistinction to the protection of the public, the protection of a witness in conjunction with other factors may amount to good and sufficient cause: *R v Birmingham Crown Court, ex parte Bell and others, The Times*, 28 March 1997.

(c) *Seriousness of the offence.* The seriousness of the offence is not in itself a good and sufficient cause: *R v Governor of Winchester Prison, ex parte Roddie*; *R v Crown Court at Southampton, ex parte Roddie* (1991) 93 Cr App R 190; *Ex parte McDonald, supra*.

(d) *Shortness of the extension sought.* The shortness of the extension sought is not in itself a good and sufficient cause: *Ex parte Roddie, supra*; *Ex parte McDonald, supra*.

(e) *Complexity of case.* While the seriousness of the offence is not good and sufficient cause for extending a custody time limit, the complexity of the case may be: *R v Leeds Crown Court, ex parte Briggs, The Times*, 19 February 1998.

(f) *Defendant wanted by a foreign state.* Where a foreign state is seeking the return of a defendant and the English prosecuting authorities have decided that they will not continue proceedings in the event of an order for the defendant's return to the foreign state, this could amount to good and sufficient cause because it is in the interests of justice that the defendant is tried somewhere: *R v Gilligan*; *R v Crown Court at Woolwich, ex parte Gilligan* [1998] 2 All ER 1.

(g) *Unavailability of witness.* In *R v Leeds Crown Court, ex parte Redfearn* [1998] COD 437, DC, it was held that the non-attendance of a crucial prosecution witness, who had moved address several times before trial, was capable of amounting to a good and sufficient cause as the prosecution could not be expected to act as nursemaid to all prosecution witnesses between committal and trial and it was inappropriate for the Divisional Court, exercising its supervisory jurisdiction, to go into the detail of the causes of mishap which sometimes occurred when prosecution witnesses changed their address. It is to be supposed that in appropriate cases the illness of a witness may similarly provide good and sufficient cause and this does not seem to be at odds with the decision in *R* v *Central Criminal Court, ex parte Bennett, The Times*, 25 January 1999, DC, as to which see below, para. 12.5.7.3. (It is to be noted that the illness of a witness is one of the grounds for extension inserted in s. 22(3) by the CDA 1998, s. 45(2): see para. 12.7.2.2)

(h) *Administrative convenience.* Whilst it would be an exaggeration to suggest that a shortage of judges or of courtrooms is a phenomenon which 'plagues' the criminal justice system in England and Wales, such difficulties do undoubtedly cause a logjam of cases from time to time. In *R* v *Norwich Crown Court, ex parte Stiller and others* [1992] Crim LR 501, it was held that it is not a good and sufficient cause to extend a custody time limit because a courtroom and a suitable judge were not available. However, a less robust and more flexible response to the problem was preferred in *R* v *Norwich Crown Court, ex parte Cox* (1993) 97 Cr App R 145, in which it was held that because the words 'good and sufficient cause' are not defined in the statute and are not suitable for judicial definition, in special cases and on appropriate facts such reasons may constitute a good and sufficient cause, although each case had to be decided on its own merits. In *Ex parte McDonald, supra*, Lord Bingham referred with approval to the fact that courts had 'reluctantly' chosen this approach, warned of the need for great caution and adopted the following observations made by Toulson J in *R* v *Blair and Bryant* and *R* v *Taylor* at Winchester Crown Court (unreported, October 7, 1998) which John Lofthouse suggests will doubtless become the textbook reference in lack of suitable judge or courtroom cases (Lofthouse, J., 'Custody Time Limits after *ex parte McDonald*,' [1998] 10 *Archbold News* 6, at p. 7):

> If difficulties of providing a judge and courtroom are too readily accepted as being both a good and a sufficient reason [the word used in s.22(3) POA 1985 is 'cause'] for extending custody time limits, there is a real danger that the purpose of the statutory provisions would be undermined. There are provisions expressly designed to protect the liberty of the subject, assumed at the present stage not to be guilty. Of course, the decision to place him in custody involves a balance of his interests against those of the public; but to keep him in custody beyond the time reasonably necessary for his case to be prepared for trial, for administrative reasons which are essentially unconnected with his case, is another matter altogether. . . . [O]ne must be very careful that the exception is not allowed to grow so as to emasculate the primary provision. Of course there may be situations where the particular class of judge, where such a judge is only going to be available at a particular trial centre for a particular time, where other similar cases are already awaiting trial, and where there is no reasonable alternative but to make the defendant wait because the case cannot readily be transferred to another court centre . . .

Endorsed by the Divisional Court, this guidance, as Lofthouse remarks, may have gone some way towards 'forc[ing] governments of both parties to provide resources to meet their professedly libertarian statutory requirements: provide adequate resources or see defendants released under their own statutes' (p. 7). Where a trial date had been fixed three weeks hence this could amount to good and sufficient cause: *R* v *Norwich Crown Court, ex parte Cox, supra*. The position was otherwise where the earliest possible trial date was in 93 days and the trial judge had extended the custody time limit for 14 days in the hope that a date for trial would be fixed during that time: *R* v *Maidstone Crown Court, ex parte Schulz, The Times*, 2 December 1992. In *R* v *Blair and Bryant, R* v *Taylor, supra*, a serious but not exceptionally complex case was estimated to last no more than three weeks at worst and Toulson J refused an application to extend the 16 week time limit by an additional 17 weeks. The non-availability of a suitably qualified judge, in a case where counsel and the judge agreed that the trial should be heard by a circuit judge and not a recorder, was capable of amounting to a good and sufficient cause for adjourning the trial for 10 weeks: *R* v *Leeds Crown Court, ex parte Redfearn* [1998] COD 437, DC. (As in the case of failure to give reasons, James Richardson suggests that in the light of *Ex parte McDonald* the ready acceptance of the non-availability of an appropriately qualified judge at the particular Crown Court centre as being good and sufficient cause for such a lengthy adjournment now appears difficult to sustain: CLW/99/1/04.) Lack of a court and judge to try a case where the offence was not one which may only be tried by a particular class of judge cannot amount to 'good and sufficient cause': *R* v *Taylor*, unreported, 12 January 1999, Judge Walker, Recorder of Sheffield (cited in CLW/99/4/3).

12.5.7.2 Due expedition Extension is permissible if the court is satisfied that the prosecution have acted with all due expedition. The term 'prosecution' means both the police and the CPS: *R* v *Birmingham Crown Court, ex parte Ricketts* [1990] Crim LR 745. The effect of this decision is that whether the prosecution have acted with all due expedition includes the time before the CPS was seized of the case. In *R* v *Manchester Crown Court. ex parte McDonald*; *R* v *Leeds Crown Court, ex parte Hunt*; *R* v *Winchester Crown Court, ex parte Wilson and Mason, The Times*, 19 November 1998, CA, Lord Bingham CJ reiterated that the due expedition condition looked to the conduct of the prosecuting authority. To satisfy a court that the condition has been met, the prosecution did not have to show that every stage of preparation had been accomplished as quickly and efficiently as humanly possible. That would be an impossible standard to meet, particularly when the court which reviewed the history of the case enjoyed the immeasurable benefit of hindsight; nor should the history be approached on the unreal assumption that all involved on the prosecution side had been able to give the case their undivided attention. What the court had to require was such diligence and expedition as would be shown by a competent prosecutor conscious of the duty to bring the case to trial as quickly as reasonably and fairly possible. In considering whether that standard has been met, the court would have regard to the nature and complexity of the case, the extent of preparation necessary, the conduct of the defence, the extent to which there was dependence on the co-operation of others outside the prosecutor's control and other matters directly and genuinely bearing on the preparation of the case for trial. In the court's view it was undesirable and unhelpful to attempt to compile a list of matters which might be relevant to consider in deciding whether the condition was met. However, in deciding whether it was met, it would have to be borne in mind that the 112-day period specified in the regulations was a maximum, not a target; and that it was applicable in all cases. Attention would not be paid to pretexts such as chronic staff shortages, over work, sickness, absenteeism or matters of that kind. (Lofthouse, at p. 7, points to the irony that whilst shortage of CPS staff is not a consideration, shortage of judges may be!) This stricture is certainly not at odds with the European Court of Human Rights case of *Zimmerman and Steiner* v *Switzerland* (1983) 6 EHRR 17, in which it was held that whilst chronic lack of resources could not afford any excuse, a sudden problem swiftly remedied might do so. Lord Bingham's reference to the requirement for *diligence and expedition* are not necessarily at variance with earlier authority. Hitherto, the view was taken that due expedition was not the same as due diligence. In *R* v *Governor of Winchester Prison, ex parte Roddie* (1991) 93 Cr App R 190 it was said that the history of a particular case must be measured against an objective yardstick and that it was not sufficient that an understaffed police service was doing its best. In *R* v *Cardiff Crown Court, ex parte Reeves, The Independent,* 21 August 1996, it was held that a judge had been wrong to use the phrase 'due diligence,' but the Divisional Court declined to interfere because he had in fact applied the correct test. These strictures are not incompatible with Lord Bingham's inclusion of diligence within the test. He was simply observing that one of the factors involved in determining whether the objective test of due expedition has been satisfied is the diligence of prosecution officials. Expedition is relative and whether officials may be judged to have proceeded with due despatch must necessarily depend in part on the measure of their diligence in carrying out their duties in the circumstances. Lord Bingham was certainly not saying that the terms are interchangeable. Clearly, institutional shortcomings will not permit diligence to become a substitute for due expedition. Although s. 45(2) of the CDA 1998 makes due diligence an explicit criterion in addition to that of expedition (see para. 12.7.2.2, below) it cannot on the foregoing argument be said that Lord Bingham must have been applying the Act prematurely since due diligence on his reasoning was always a factor to be taken into account in determining the test of expedition. In other words, the Act merely expresses what was already implied.

The *dicta* in *ex parte Roddie* do not require the prosecution to act as if a custody case is their only task at hand: *R* v *Crown Court at Norwich, ex parte Parker and Ward* (1994) 96 Cr App. 16R 68. The prosecution had not acted with all due expedition where there had been a delay in serving evidence that was central to the Crown's case: *R* v *Central Criminal Court, ex parte Behbehani* [1994] Crim LR 352. The prosecution will have acted with all due expedition only if they have acted so as to allow of the possibility of a s. 6(1) committal within the time limit. It is not sufficient that they have merely acted with sufficient expedition so as to allow for a s. 6(2) committal: *R* v *Leeds Crown Court, ex parte Briggs (Ronald) (No. 2), The Times,* 10 March 1998. It is submitted that this decision is subject to the *dicta* in *ex parte Roddie* that the history of a particular case must be viewed against an objective yardstick. It has been observed that '[i]t seems perfectly possible that the prosecution may have acted with all due expedition but not be ready for any sort of committal within the time limit'. (*Criminal Law Week,* 98/10/4). In *R* v *Leeds Crown Court ex parte Whitbread, The Times,* 16

September 1998, DC, it was held that where a court is considering the test as to whether the prosecution have shown due diligence the decision must be made within the framework of the custody time limit under consideration. Thus the test is whether the prosecution have failed to act with due expedition so that an old-style committal cannot be achieved when it could otherwise have been, not whether or not the prosecution have at some point during the period failed to act with due expedition (as contended by counsel on the basis of *R* v *Central Criminal Court ex parte Behbehani*, above). It was observed that the Divisional Court was able to act with very considerable expedition when required to do so by custody time limit cases. Only rarely, therefore, would it be appropriate for leave to be granted to move for judicial review in a case, such as the instant, in which the outcome of the judicial review would be of no practical significance because by the time of the hearing the defendant would have been committed for trial and a new custody time limit started.

12.5.7.3 Requirement for separate consideration of (a) good *and* sufficient cause and (b) due expedition Since s. 22(3) of the POA 1985 requires the prosecution to establish both (a) good and sufficient cause and (b) due expedition, it has been held that this will necessitate separate consideration of the two limbs. In *R* v *Central Criminal Court, ex parte Bennett, The Times,* 25 January 1999, DC the prosecution had failed to conform with orders regarding the service of certain items on the defence within set time limits but on an unopposed application by the Crown the judge extended the custody time limit because the alleged victim was undergoing a throat operation. It was held that the judge should not have done so because although he had acknowledged the necessity of considering both limbs of s. 22(3) separately, he had done exactly the opposite in that he had considered the question of due expedition in the light of the test of good and sufficient cause and the concession by the defence that it was established by virtue of the principal prosecution witness's indisposition. In the view of the court the fact that the trial could not have gone ahead in any event because of the alleged victim's illness was an irrelevant consideration when deciding whether the prosecution had acted with all due expedition. Similarly, delay on the part of an independent forensic science laboratory is an irrelevant considation in determining whether the prosecution has acted with all due expedition: *R* v *Central Criminal Court, ex parte Johnson, The Independent (CS),* 25 January 1999, DC.

12.5.8 Judicial review

It follows from the principle that judges enjoy an overriding discretion that, as Lord Bingham emphasised in *Ex parte McDonald, supra,* where a court had heard full argument and given its rulings, the Divisional Court would be most reluctant to disturb that decision. The Divisional Court had no role in deciding whether an extension should be granted. Its only role, as in any other application for judicial review, was to see whether the decision in question was open to successful challenge on any of the familiar grounds which supported such an application. It was almost inevitable in cases of the present type that one or other party would disagree with the decision. Such disagreement, however strong, was not a ground for seeking judicial review. Those who made applications of that kind had to take care to ensure that there were proper grounds for doing so and that they were not inviting the Divisional Court to trespass into a field of judgment reserved to the court of trial.

In *R v Leeds Crown Court, ex parte Redfearn* [1998] COD 437, the Divisional Court held that there could be no judicial review on the issue of lack of due expedition where the point had not been taken in the court of first instance. This would appear to have been negated by Lord Bingham's statement that judges should not make extension orders simply because the parties agree or because no objection is raised. If now an error on a custody time limit issue is made which is justiciable on judicial review as a point of principle, a party will not be debarred from seeking intervention merely because no objection was taken at first instance.

An alternative remedy to seeking judicial review, and one probably more expeditious, would be to apply for bail to a High Court judge in chambers, rather as one might appeal to the Crown Court against conviction in the magistrates' court, as an alternative to appealing to the Divisional Court by way of case stated.

In the light of the willingness of the Divisional Court to interfere with decisions by judges only on classic judicial review grounds, John Lofthouse has suggested a number of practical suggestions arising from the principles which have emerged on the foregoing authorities:

> [I]t is essential for both sides to make sure that the application is properly heard. The prosecution must apply in time; the defence should not ordinarily consent to short service or inadequately drafted applications. A realistic time estimate should be given; courts should not routinely list matters such as this for brief hearings. If necessary, insist on proper evidence or testable material, even the cross-examination of the listing officer; do not automatically accept what someone (even the judge) says he has been told by someone in the list office (who may or may not be well informed). The prosecution should support any reasonable request by the defence if they do not wish to end up with a quashed decision. Make sure a good note of everything is taken. If the judge will not hear the case properly or reaches a decision which is challengeable, apply for leave to seek judicial review, using first a good note for the leave application, and obtaining a transcript as soon as possible of the relevant parts of the hearing. (Lofthouse, J., 'Custody Time Limits after *ex parte McDonald*,' [1998] 10 *Archbold News* 6, at p. 8.

12.6 APPEAL

12.6.1 By the defendant

Where a magistrates' court decides to extend, or further extend, a custody or overall time limit, the defendant may appeal against the decision to the Crown Court: POA 1985, s. 22(7).

12.6.2 By the prosecution

12.6.2.1 Right of appeal Where a magistrates' court refuses to extend a custody or overall time limit, the prosecution may appeal to the Crown Court against the refusal: POA 1985, s. 22(8).

12.6.2.2 Time limit on appeal An appeal by the prosecution may not be commenced after the expiry of the limit in question, but where such an appeal is commenced before the expiry of the limit, the limit is deemed not to have expired before the determination or abandonment of that appeal: POA 1985, s. 22(9).

12.6.3 Procedure

12.6.3.1 Appeals to be heard by a Crown Court judge in chambers Appeals by both defence and prosecution are heard by a judge of the Crown Court sitting in chambers: CCR 1982, r. 27(2)(f).

12.6.3.2 Ambit of rule regulating the issuing of notices of appeal The procedure regulating the issuing of notices of appeal against an extension of, or a refusal to extend, a custody time limit is set out in r. 27A of the CCR 1982. The rule applies to any appeal brought by:

(a) an accused, under s. 22(7) of the POA 1985, against a decision of a magistrates' court to extend, or further extend, a time limit imposed by regulations made under s. 22(1); and
(b) the prosecution, under s. 22(8) of that Act, against a decision of a magistrates' court to refuse to extend, or further extend, such a time limit.

12.6.3.3 Commencement of appeal Rule 27A(2) of the CCR 1982 provides that an appeal to which r. 27A applies must be commenced by the appellant's giving notice in writing of appeal:

(a) to the clerk to the magistrates' court which took the decision;
(b) if the appeal is brought by the accused, to the prosecutor and, if the prosecution is to be carried on by the CPS, to the appropriate Crown Prosecutor;
(c) if the appeal is brought by the prosecution, to the accused; and
(d) to the appropriate officer of the Crown Court.

12.6.3.4 Contents of notice of appeal A notice of appeal under r. 27A must state the date on which the time limit applicable to the case is due to expire and, if the appeal is brought by the accused under s. 22(7) of the POA 1985, the date on which the time limit would have expired had the court decided not to extend or further extend the time limit: CCR 1982, r. 27A(3).

12.6.3.5 Notice of hearing On receiving notice of an appeal to which this rule applies, the appropriate officer of the Crown Court shall enter the appeal and give notice of the time and place of the hearing to:

   (a) the appellant;

   (b) the other party to the appeal; and

   (c) the clerk to the magistrates' court which took the decision: CCR 1982, r. 27A(4).

12.6.4 Abandonment of appeal

Rule 27A(5) of the CCR 1982 provides that without prejudice to the power of the Crown Court to give leave for an appeal to be abandoned, an appellant may abandon an appeal to which this rule applies by giving notice in writing to any person to whom notice of the appeal was required to be given by para. (2) not later than the third day preceding the day fixed for the hearing of the appeal. For the purpose of determining whether notice was properly given in accordance with para. (2), there shall be disregarded any Saturday and Sunday and any day which is specified to be a bank holiday in England and Wales under s. 1(1) of the Banking and Financial Dealings Act 1971.

12.7 EFFECT OF EXPIRY OF CUSTODY TIME LIMIT

12.7.1 Modification of Bail Act 1976

Where a custody time limit has expired, the BA 1976 is modified in the following respects by the Prosecution of Offences (Custody Time Limits) Regulations 1987 (SI 1987 No. 299), regs 8(1) and 8(2):

   (a) *Right to bail applies.* A person to whom the BA 1976, s. 4, applies (general right to bail) shall be granted bail: s. 4(8A). This requirement is subject to s. 41 of the MCA 1980 (restrictions on the grant of bail to persons charged with treason) and s. 25 of the CJPOA 1994 (curtailment on right to bail in the case of defendants charged with or convicted of homicide or rape after previous conviction for such offences).

   (b) *Surety and security prohibited.* No requirement for surety or security may be imposed: BA 1976, s. 3A(a).

   (c) *Other conditions prohibited.* The court may not impose pre-release conditions of bail: BA 1976, s. 3A(b).

   (d) *No power to arrest where failure to surrender likely.* There is no power of arrest on the ground that the person is not likely to surrender to custody.

12.7.2 Crime and Disorder Act 1998

The provisions of the POA 1985 are extensively amended by the CDA 1998, the relevant provisions of which had neither come into effect, nor been given any date for coming into effect, at the time of going to press.

Section 43(1) empowers the Secretary of State:

(a)   to set time limits only in relation to proceedings instituted in specific areas, or in relation to persons of specified classes or descriptions; and

(b)   to make regulations to set different time limits in relation to proceedings in different areas, to proceedings of different classes or descriptions, or to proceedings against different classes or descriptions of person.

12.7.2.1   Additional time limits for persons under the age of 18   The main purpose of the changes listed above appears to be to enable the Secretary of State to set more exacting time limits for juveniles, and particularly strict limits for persistent young offenders (*cf.*, the White Paper, *No More Excuses: A New Approach to Tackling Youth Crime in England and Wales* (Cm 3809)). Section 22A(1) of the POA 1985, as inserted by s. 44 of the CDA 1998, empowers the Secretary of State to make provision for the maximum period to be allowed for the completion of the stage:

(a)   from arrest to the date fixed for first appearance ('the initial stage'); and

(b)   from conviction to sentence.

The Government appears to intend to use these powers to set particularly strict time limits for persistent young offenders. The Government proposes to define a persistent young offender as 'a young person aged ten to seventeen who has been sentenced by any criminal court in the UK on three or more separate occasions for one or more recordable offence, and within three years of the last sentencing occasion, is subsequently arrested or has an information laid against him for a further recordable offence'. (The definition comes from *The Crime and Disorder [HL] [Bill 167 of 1997–98]: Youth Justice, Criminal Procedures and Sentencing,* House of Commons Library Research Paper 98/43, House of Commons Library, p. 67, citing Crime and Disorder Bill, Notes on Clauses, House of Commons.) It is intended that this definition will be set down in the regulations which establish the time limits. Section 22A(2) of the POA 1985, as inserted by s. 44 CDA 1998, provides that the Secretary of State may make regulations (*inter alia*) to make such provision with respect to the procedure to be followed in criminal proceedings as is considered appropriate in consequence of any other provisions of the regulations. This will allow application of the provisions of s. 22(2) of the POA 1985, as inserted by s. 43 of the CDA 1998, to young offenders.

12.7.2.2   Grounds for extending time limits   Section 45(2) of the CDA 1998 substitutes a new s. 22(3) in the POA 1985. The new subsection empowers a court to extend or further extend a time limit only if:

(a)   it is satisfied that the need for the extension is due to the illness or absence of the accused, a witness, a judge or a magistrate;

(b)   the court has ordered separate trials of co-defendants, or of one defendant charged with more than one offence; or

(c)   the court is satisfied that there is some other good and sufficient cause and that the prosecution have acted with all due diligence as well as expedition.

John Lofthouse (Lofthouse, J., 'Custody Time Limits after *ex parte McDonald*,' [1998] 10 *Archbold News* 6, at p. 8) has argued that the amended wording of the section has achieved the government's aim of a tighter regime of criteria for granting extensions (see Lord Williams of Mostyn, Second Reading of the Bill, HL Deb, vol. 584, col 535) by referring to the illness or absence of *a* judge. It thereby excludes the unavailability of *any* judge (*ie* a question of resources) and concentrates on the absence of a *particular* judge (*eg* ill on the day, snowed in, *etc*). If the judge is not soon available, then the lack of a substitute will not, surely, be capable of being a good or sufficient cause. He observes that this will be on all fours with *Zimmerman and Steiner* v *Switzerland* [1983] 6 EHRR 17, in which it was held that whilst chronic lack of resources is not an excuse, a sudden problem swiftly remedied may be.

12.7.2.3   Grounds for extending the initial stage time limit in relation to persons under the age of 18   Section 22A(3) of the POA 1985, as inserted by s. 44 of the CDA 1998, empowers a magistrates' court at any time before the expiry of an initial stage time limit to extend or further extend that limit, but only if the court is satisfied:

(a)   that the need for the extension is due to some good and sufficient cause; and
(b)   that the investigation has been conducted, and (where applicable) the prosecution have acted, with all due diligence as well as expedition.

12.7.2.4   Effect of expiry of initial stage time limit   Section 22A(1) of the POA 1985, as inserted by s. 44(4) of the CDA 1998, provides that where the initial stage time limit (whether as originally imposed or as extended or further extended under s. 22(3)) expires before the person arrested is charged with the offence, the person shall not be charged with the offence unless further evidence relating to it is obtained. A person under arrest at that stage should be released. Where the person is on bail under Part IV of PACE 1984, that bail, and any duty or conditions to which it is subject, must be discharged. Section 22A(5), as inserted by s. 44 of the CDA 1998, provides that where the initial stage time limit (whether as originally imposed or as extended or further extended under s. 22(3)) expires after the person arrested is charged with the offence but before the date fixed for his first appearance in court, the court shall stay the proceedings.

12.7.2.5   Effect of escape or failure to surrender to bail   Section 22(6A) of the POA 1985, as inserted by s. 43(5) of the CDA 1998, provides that where a person is unlawfully at large through escape or failure to answer to bail, the time limits are suspended rather than seized for the period during which the defendant is unlawfully at large. This means that the time limits are maintained throughout the remainder of the proceedings. Section 22(6A) provides that the time limit for the completion of the preliminary stage is to be suspended at the point at which a defendant escapes from the custody of the court or (if on bail) fails to appear at the specified time. The court may direct that the overall time limit may be suspended to take account of any delay due to the absconding of the defendant. The determining factor in deciding whether to further suspend the time limit is the extent to which the prosecution has been disrupted by the defendant's absence and the length of time that the defendant was unlawfully at large. Thereafter, the remainder of the relevant time limit will reapply. Directions given by the court under s. 22(6A) may be the subject of appeal by either defence or prosecution (POA 1988, s. 22(7) and (8), as inserted by s. 43(6) and (7) of the CDA 1998).

12.7.3 Commencement of proceedings

Section 22(11ZA) of the POA 1985, as inserted by s. 43(8) of the CDA 1998, defines the commencement of proceedings for the purposes of this section. It provides that proceedings are to begin when the accused is charged with the offence or when an information is laid charging him with the offence. Time limits can be set under s. 22 from that point up until the start of trial.

12.8 CUSTODY TIME LIMITS IN PRACTICE

12.8.1 Routine extension

Rule 24(b) of the CCR 1982 (SI 1982 No. 109) provides that the maximum period between committal (or transfer) and the start of trial shall, unless the Crown Court has ordered otherwise, be eight weeks. The maximum period is routinely extended. In 1996, 83,328 cases were received for trial at the Crown Court, an increase of 3 per cent on the 1995 total (*Judicial Statistics*, 1996, Annual Report, Cm 3716, London: Lord Chancellor's Department, 1996). In 1997, 91,110 cases were received for trial at the Crown Court, an increase of 9 per cent on the 1996 total (*Judicial Statistics*, 1997, Annual Report, Cm 3980, London: Lord Chancellor's Department, 1997, p. 61). Committals for trial disposed of during 1997 totalled 90,096, an increase of 8 per cent. As receipts exceeded disposals, the number of cases outstanding rose 3 per cent to 25,916 compared with 25,048 at the end of 1996 (*ibid.*). The average waiting time for custody cases in 1996 was 9.5 weeks; it 1997 it was 8.7 weeks. The 1996 average for bail cases was 14.3 weeks; in 1997 it was 13.7 weeks. Only two circuits – Wales and Chester, and Midland and Oxford – met the eight weeks target for those in custody. The waiting times were 6.2 and 8.0 weeks respectively. Only Wales and Chester met the target for those on bail (8.0 weeks): *ibid.*, p. 69. The longest average waiting time was in London (20.5 weeks for bail cases and 12.6 weeks for custody cases).

These figures support the view of one commentator that custody time limits 'have been set at levels encompassing the careers of the vast majority of current cases; they reflect, in effect, the *status quo*': Morgan, R., 'Remands in Custody: Problems and Prospects' [1989] Crim LR 481, at p. 491. The House of Commons Public Accounts Committee was critical of the 'consistent failure of the courts to meet the waiting time limit' and noted that the Lord Chancellor's Department had introduced:

> . . . less demanding and more realistic targets to provide a greater incentive to improve court performance. They have set average waiting time limits of eight weeks for custody cases and twelve weeks for bail cases. (*Administration of the Crown Court*, Committee of Public Accounts, Session 1994–5, HC 173, pp. vi–viii)

12.8.2 Empirical findings

In 1987 and 1988 a study on custody time limits was conducted by the Home Office in the ten areas in which they were first introduced (Henderson, P., *Monitoring Time Limits on Custodial Remands*, Research and Planning Unit Paper 61, London: Home Office, 1991). The following findings are taken from the study.

12.8.2.1 Proportion of cases in which custody time limits were extended Of the cases in which custody time limits were extended the proportions were:

(a) 5 per cent before summary trial;
(b) 8.5 per cent before committal;
(c) 2.6 per cent in the Crown Court from committal to arraignment (custody time limits now extend to the start of trial, see para. 12.4.7).

12.8.2.2 Reasons for applications for the extension of custody time limits The most commonly cited reasons for extending a custody time limit were the following:

(a) *Before summary trial*: problems with listing (more than one-third of all applications).
(b) *Before committal*: the general reason given was 'committal delays' (60 per cent); nearly 20 per cent of the applications were based on delays by the defence.
(c) *From committal to arraignment*: 74.4 per cent of those cases in which reasons were cited gave listing difficulties as the cause of the application for extension.

12.8.2.3 Applications for extension which were refused There is no record of any application for extension being refused in 1987. In 1988, 2 per cent of applications were refused in the magistrates' court (all of which were committal cases) and 2 per cent in the Crown Court. As the study states, 'There is some indication that extensions were treated as an almost automatic part of the process' (at p. 24).

13 The Rôle and Duties of the Advocate on Matters of Bail

13.1. THE PROSECUTING ADVOCATE

13.1.1 Duty irrespective of whether objection is raised against bail

13.1.1.1 Court to be informed expressly that bail is unopposed Where the prosecution have no objection to bail the prosecuting advocate should make this quite clear to the court. The duty should not be fudged by a prosecutor who personally feels that on balance bail can safely be granted but who, on the other hand, wishes to avoid incurring criticism for not opposing bail if subsequently the defendant should abscond or break conditions in some other way.

13.1.1.2 Acknowledging that the bail decision is exclusively the court's It is essential for the prosecutor to approach and address the court on the basis of explicitly recognising that the bail decision is a matter for the court and not for the prosecution.

13.1.1.3 Duty to provide the court with all relevant information As a matter of law it is the court which in its discretion makes the judgment of whether the right to bail is to stand or whether any of the exceptions are to prevail. The view of the prosecution is influential, and there is some evidence to suggest that in the vast majority of cases it is decisive, see para. 7.9.4.2, above). But it is the court which makes the decision, irrespective of whether bail is unopposed or not requested. Accordingly, even if bail is unopposed the prosecution must be prepared in any event to provide the court with any information that may be required to enable the court to decide whether to refuse bail notwithstanding the Crown's attitude.

13.1.1.4 Indicating the strength of the evidence Even if there are no objections, the prosecutor should indicate the strength of the evidence against the accused, for example, evidence identifying the accused as perpetrator, any admissions, and recovery of relevant property as a result of such admissions or in circumstances indicating a connection with the accused. In addition to admissions relating to the offence charged, the prosecutor should refer to any offences for which the accused has expressed to the police a desire to have taken into account.

13.1.1.5 Antecedents and convictions Details should be given of the accused's antecedents, that is, family and educational background and employment history and previous convictions. The last should normally be submitted to the court in writing to avoid inadvertent publication in the press, an eventuality which it is particularly important to prevent since, although clearly undesirable and unfortunate, it would not constitute a ground for quashing any subsequent conviction: see *R* v *Dyson* (1943) 107 JP 178; *R* v *Fletcher* (1949) 113 JP 365, CCA; *R* v *Armstrong* [1951] 2 All ER 219, CCA.

13.1.1.6 Past bail breaches The prosecutor should inform the court of any convictions for failing to surrender or any past incidents of bail breach, if known, or any outstanding cases, and of any court orders such as suspended sentences of which the defendant will be in breach if convicted.

13.1.2 Raising objections and duties in contrast with the position in relation to sentencing

Section 36 of the CJA 1988 allows the Attorney General to refer unduly lenient sentences to the Court of Appeal, and prosecutors bear the duty of reminding the court of its maximum sentencing power in a given case and of adverting to the error if the court should purport to exceed that power (*R* v *Clarke* (1974) 59 Cr App R 298; *R* v *O'Neill* (1977) 65 Cr App R 318; *R* v *Komsta and Murphy* (1991) 12 Cr App R (S) 63; *R* v *Richards, The Times*, 1 April 1993; *R* v *Hartley* [1993] Crim LR 230; *R* v *Johnstone (Darren), The Times*, 18 June 1996; *R* v *Bruley* [1996] Crim LR 913; *R* v *McDonnell* [1996] Crim LR 914; *R* v *Street* (1997) 161 JP 281). Apart from this very limited rôle the prosecution has no say in matters of sentence. By contrast, in cases in which the Crown objects to bail, it is the prosecuting advocate's duty to address the court as to the objections raised. This is a duty regarded by many practitioners as distasteful, because although the refusal of bail is not a sentence, many practitioners feel it is analogous. The *Code of Conduct of the Bar of England and Wales* (5th ed., London: General Council of the Bar 1990, adopted by the GCB 27 January 1990; Amendment No. 5, effective 14 April 1997) makes it clear that prosecuting counsel should not attempt by advocacy to influence the court in regard to sentence ('standards applicable to criminal cases', para. 11.8). However, this does not apply to the issue of bail, and it is therefore important for prosecuting advocates to overcome any feeling of distaste and to act in accordance with their instructions.

13.1.3 Duty of disclosure to the defence

As a matter of professional etiquette, the prosecutor should be prepared to disclose the bail objections to the defence and to furnish any documents, pre-eminently a list of previous convictions, upon which it is sought to rely.

13.1.4 Mode of presenting objections

The presentation of bail objections should be succinct and to the point. It has been suggested that prosecutors should begin by placing the circumstances of the offence before the court before drawing the court's attention to those statutory considerations of bail which in the prosecutor's view are relevant to the application, and then concluding from them the ground or grounds and reason or reasons on which bail is opposed: Chatterton, *Bail: Law and Practice*, London: Butterworths, 1986, p. 50. It is submitted, however, that the reverse order of presentation may carry more impact. The prosecutor should begin by outlining which exceptions under the BA 1976, sch. 1, Part I, para. 2, it is contended apply and should then develop the representations by expounding upon the supporting reasons for applying the exceptions by reference to the contents of para. 9. Where the offence is non-imprisonable, the objection would be put in accordance with the contents of sch. 1, Part II, to the Act.

The prosecutor should at all times use moderate language. Principle 21.19 of the *Guide to the Professional Conduct of Solicitors* (7th ed., London: Law Society, 1996) states: 'Whilst a solicitor prosecuting a criminal case must ensure that every material point is made which supports the prosecution, in presenting the evidence he must do so dispassionately and with scrupulous fairness. '

13.1.5 Duty to reply when appropriate

Despite the informal nature of bail applications, there will be occasions when it is right for the prosecution to reply, especially where the Crown is of the view that there have been misstatements by the defence: *R v Isleworth Crown Court, ex parte Commissioners of Customs and Excise*, *The Times*, 27 July 1990.

13.2 THE DEFENDING ADVOCATE

13.2.1 Professionalism

The defending advocate will need to take special care when making a bail application to ensure that nothing is done to depart from the highest professional and ethical standards required. On the rare occasions when lapses do occur, they are usually the result of over-enthusiasm and lack of attention rather than of any deliberate intention to mislead the court.

13.2.2   Special difficulties involved in bail applications

For the following reasons the bail application presents the advocate with special difficulties:

(a)   instructions are often taken in a hurry just before going into court;

(b)   many courts (particularly those in older buildings) do not have proper interview facilities and instructions have to be taken through the wicket hatch in the cell door;

(c)   there is insufficient time to check or verify instructions;

(d)   the advocate will be under pressure from the client to obtain the desired result;

(e)   additional pressure may be levied by the family and friends of the client;

(f)   an advocate's reputation amongst clients will often depend on an ability to make successful bail applications.

13.2.3   The duty to present the client's case without knowingly misleading the court

The *Guide to the Professional Conduct of Solicitors* (7th ed., London: Law Society, 1996) provides, at para. 21.07, that: 'Solicitors who act in litigation, whilst under a duty to do their best for their client, must never deceive or mislead the court.'

Contained within the *Guide* is a Code for Advocacy, which provides, at para. 2.2, that: 'Advocates have an overriding duty to the court to ensure in the public interest that the proper and efficient administration of justice is achieved: they must assist the court in the administration of justice and must not deceive or knowingly or recklessly mislead the court.'

As the bail application is inquisitorial rather than accusatory and the strict rules of evidence do not apply when the court is considering whether there are substantial grounds for believing something in relation to the BA 1976 (see *Re Moles* [1981] Crim LR 170), the outcome will depend essentially on the assertions of the advocates involved and the impressions to be derived from those assertions rather than on evidence to be assessed independently of advocacy. In this situation the representations by advocates potentially assume much more significance than is perhaps the case in ordinary adversarial process, and the need for advocates to be vigilant against their being used as mouthpieces to mislead the court is particularly acute.

The defending advocate's duty is to present the client's case in accordance with the instructions given. It is almost a triteness to state that the duty to act on the client's instructions can never be conditional on a belief in their truth, from which it must follow that the advocate is neither required nor expected to inquire into the instructions for the purpose of establishing whether or not they are true. So much is straightforward and uncontroversial. However, difficulty may arise where the instructions are inconsistent or contradictory. A common such example is where the client is unemployed for the purpose of a legal aid application but in full-time employment for the purpose of the bail application. Another example is where the client insists that his domestic partner is pregnant but the lady herself appears to be unaware of her condition! In cases of inconsistency, the advocate must be firm with the client in clarifying the instructions in order to avoid involvement in an attempt knowingly to misleading the court. The *Guide to the Professional Conduct of Solicitors* provides (in Principle 21.20.4) helpful assistance in resolving the sort of conflicts of duty which are liable to arise from time to time in situations of inconsistency. The Principle states:

> In general, there is no duty upon a solicitor to inquire in every case as to whether the client is telling the truth. However, where instructions or other information are such as should put the solicitor upon inquiry, he or she must, where practicable, check the truth of what the client says to the extent that such statements will be relied upon before the court, or in pleadings or affidavits.

13.2.4 The difficulty over previous convictions

It is in the area of previous convictions that the greatest difficulty over divided loyalty arises. Lists of convictions are not always available to the prosecution, especially at short notice such as at the first hearing of the case in the magistrates' court after the defendant has been charged. The file may have been taken out of the Criminal Records Office for updating purposes, the list may not contain a recent conviction, it may omit some convictions, or it may be inaccurate in some other way.

A defendant's previous convictions are obviously of importance to a court making a decision about bail. It will need to know if the defendant has previously failed to surrender, or whether the record is such that there are substantial grounds for believing that the defendant will commit an offence while on bail.

It is important to establish the defending advocate's duty where the information presented by the prosecution is known to be inaccurate or false. At one time the *Code of Conduct for the Bar of England and Wales* gave fairly specific guidance as to the conundrum which counsel often face. Rule 24.11 of the edition of the code superseded in 1990 stated:

> Defending counsel is not under any duty to correct any misstatement of fact made by the prosecution. If the court has been led by the prosecution to believe that the accused has no previous convictions, defence counsel is under no duty to disclose facts to the contrary which are known to him, nor correct any information given by the prosecution if such disclosure or correction would be to his client's detriment. Defending counsel must take care not to lend himself to any assertion that his client has no convictions or no more than a limited number of convictions or to ask a prosecution witness whether there are previous convictions against his client in the hope that he will receive a negative answer.

For reasons which are unclear this rule no longer appears in the current edition of the code. However, para. 5.2 of the 'General Standards' section of Appendix H to the Code, ('Written Standards for the Conduct of Professional Work') states that '[a] barrister must assist the Court in the administration of justice and, as part of this obligation and the obligation to use only proper and lawful means to promote and protect the interests of his client, must not deceive or knowingly or recklessly mislead the Court'. In general terms, this would seem to encapsulate the essence of the former para. 24.11, but the principle enunciated in para. 5.2 is evidently now left to the barrister to apply to the facts of the particular case, a discretion which appears to be in keeping with the statement in para. 5.3 of the 'General Standards' that '[a] barrister is at all times individually and personally responsible for his own conduct and for his professional work both in Court and out of Court'. This seems to express the general principle that the advocate is under no duty to correct incorrect information about previous convictions provided that the court is not actively misled.

Principle 21.07 of the *Guide to the Professional Conduct of Solicitors* follows similar lines. It states that solicitors owe a duty to their clients to do their best for them but that they must never deceive or mislead the court. Principle 21.20 declares that solicitors are under a duty to say on behalf of their clients what clients should properly say for themselves if they possessed the requisite skill and knowledge. Principle 21.20.1 makes it clear that solicitors must not, without instructions, disclose facts known to them regarding a client's character and antecedents, nor must they correct any information given by the prosecution if such correction would be to the client's detriment. However, they must not knowingly put forward or let the client put forward false information with intent to mislead the court. Similarly, they must not indicate their agreement with information that the prosecution put forward which they know to be false. Annex 21G to the *Guide to the Professional Conduct of Solicitors* explains that:

A solicitor takes part in a positive deception of the court when he or she puts forward to the court information, or lets the client put forward information, which the solicitor know to be false, with the intent of misleading the court. The defence solicitor need not correct information given to the court by the prosecution or any other party which the solicitor knows will have the effect of allowing the court to make incorrect assumptions about the client or the case, provided the solicitor does not indicate in any way his or her agreement with that information. The solicitor can, as it were, sit back and do nothing about it, as opposed to participating actively in misleading the court by adopting that false information.

The application of these principles presents particular difficulty where the list of convictions is wrong not because of a mistake on the part of the prosecution, but because the defendant has given false particulars. This was the situation facing Mr John Bridgwood, a solicitor, when he was instructed to represent a client whose true identity he knew, having acted for her on many previous occasions. When charged again in criminal proceedings she had given a false name and date of birth. Bridgwood advised her to give her true particulars, but she did not act on his advice and instructed him that she wished to plead guilty using the false name. He mitigated on her behalf but made no reference to her character and did not refer to her by her assumed name. He was convicted of acting in a manner tending and intending to pervert the course of justice and was sentenced to nine months' imprisonment suspended for two years and fined £2,000 by the Solicitors' Disciplinary Tribunal. As a result of the case, The Law Society issued appropriate advice to practitioners in the *Guide to the Professional Conduct of Solicitors*, since re-issued in Annex 21G in slightly amended form as follows:

- Where, to the knowledge of the solicitor, the client seeks to give to the court a false name and address and date of birth, the solicitor's first duty is to discuss the matter with the client to try to persuade the client to change his or her mind. The solicitor should explain that unless the client changes his or her mind the solicitor will have to withdraw from acting. The client should be advised further that if the solicitor withdraws from acting there could be problems with the client's legal aid order, if one is in existence. If, having explained this to the client, it is clear that the client does not accept this, then the solicitor should cease to act. The solicitor's duty to say on the client's behalf all that the client would wish to say is in clear conflict with the solicitor's duty not to participate in a positive deception of the court.

- Sometimes the client will give his or her correct name to the court, but will put forward a false address or a false date of birth. The solicitor should cease to act in these circumstances. It is arguable that the client is not attempting to conceal his or her identity, but the solicitor should be aware of the importance of the correct date of birth and correct address to the course of the administration of justice. The date of birth is the key to the record of previous convictions. The correct address is essential to the proper administration of justice as it is required for the purposes of consideration of bail, and it is the point of contact between the court, the solicitor, the police and the client.

- There are special difficulties for a solicitor who feels obliged to withdraw from the case where the client is in receipt of legal aid. The solicitor must apply to the court to be released from the legal aid order. The duty of confidentiality prevents the solicitor from revealing the reason for this request. The Committee considered that solicitors in these circumstances must be firm. The court must be advised that because of the solicitor's duty of confidentiality he or she cannot give the court reasons for the request to be released from the legal aid order, but the court must accept that a matter has arisen making it impossible for him or her to continue to act. The solicitor should explain the situation to the client so that the client is not taken unawares.

- Solicitors should endeavour to obtain a list of their client's previous convictions in good time to take the client's instructions upon them before going into court.

Solicitors are frequently asked by magistrates' clerks to confirm the accuracy of previous convictions on the client's behalf, or to confirm that the previous convictions are a full list of previous convictions. Whilst these are perfectly proper questions to ask, serious problems arise for solicitors where they know that the list does not accurately reflect the number or type of convictions recorded against the client, or the sentences previously imposed. To confirm such an inaccurate list as 'accurate', or as a 'full list' could amount to a positive deception of the court. As a matter of professional conduct the solicitor must not disclose facts known to him or her regarding the client's character or previous convictions without the client's express consent. Therefore it is advised that in the future solicitors and their clients should decline to comment on the accuracy of such lists. It can be seen that if solicitors do obtain a list of previous convictions in good time before going into court, these problems can be discussed in good time with the client and it can be pointed out to the client the difficulties which could arise if the client were to mislead the court by confirming the accuracy of a list known by both solicitor and client to be inaccurate. If the client insists that, if asked he will contribute to a positive deception of the court by pretending that the list is accurate, the solicitor must cease to act.

The contents of the last paragraph of the advice represent a fundamental change from previously accepted practice. The essential part of the advice is that solicitors should decline to comment, and should decline to be a party to their clients commenting, on the accuracy of lists of convictions.

It has been reported by the Law Society that some magistrates have complained that, by refusing to comment on their client's previous convictions, solicitors are failing in their duty to assist in the smooth administration of justice (*Criminal Practitioners Newsletter*, November 1989). The Law Society's counter-argument is that it is the solicitor's duty of confidentiality towards the client which is of importance to the general administration of justice. The Law Society also reported that solicitors have even been threatened with contempt of court proceedings for refusing to comment on the accuracy of a list of a client's previous convictions (*Criminal Practitioners Newsletter*, November 1989). In the view of the Law Society, such conduct can never amount to contempt of court, having regard to the Contempt of Court Act 1981 which makes it an offence wilfully 'to insult the justices . . . or wilfully [to] interrupt the proceedings or otherwise misbehave'. In *Justices' Clerks Society News Sheet* No. 98/11, 17 February 1998, the following statement was circulated to members of the society:

In the light of the Law Society guidance, it has been agreed to recommend to members that, in relation to the citing of previous convictions, one question only should be put to the defence by the bench or clerk, namely: 'Have you seen this list?' All other questions are superfluous and inappropriate.

The Bridgwood case and the consequent advice by The Law Society deal with the solicitor's duty more particularly where the inaccuracy is to the defendant's advantage. There will, however, be situations where the client will wish to comment on the accuracy of the list of convictions because it will be his disadvantage not to comment. The prosecution may be portraying the defendant as a person of bad character when the defendant is claiming to have no convictions or many fewer than alleged. If no comment is made on the list tendered to the court then it will doubtless make its bail decision on the basis of that list. Solicitors will be failing in their duty to the client if they allow the court to make a decision on the basis of inaccurate information. If convictions are disputed, the prosecution should be put to proof, although this may involve delay. Section 7 of PACE 1984 provides that disputed convictions may be proved by:

(a)   producing a certificate of conviction signed by the clerk of the court where the conviction was recorded; and

(b)   adducing evidence to prove that the person named in the certificate is the person whose conviction it is sought to establish.

Such evidence may be adduced by a police officer who was in court when the defendant was convicted to prove that it is the same person, or by proving that the defendant's fingerprints are the fingerprints of the person named on the certificate of conviction. In the event of dispute, new computer systems for the searching and matching of fingerprints will do much to speed up the process of proof.

The 'Bridgwood guidelines' raised doubts as to the future of *Practice Direction (Crime; Antecedents)* [1966] 1 WLR 1184, which was accordingly superseded by *Practice Direction (Crime: Antecedents)* [1997] 4 All ER 350. The new *Practice Direction* makes new arrangements for the provision of antecedent information following the introduction of computerised information from the Police National Computer. Such information should include details and background, convictions, cautions, and outstanding cases.

13.2.5   Influence on performance of costs regulations

Mention must be made of the question of costs. In interviews with solicitors, Brink and Stone ('Defendants who do not ask for bail' [1988] Crim LR 152) found that a few practitioners consider that their duty to protect the legal aid fund overrides their duty to protect the interests of their clients. These solicitors reported that they do not make an application for bail on behalf of a legally-aided client if they consider the application is unlikely to succeed. This view arises out of a misunderstanding of the regulations controlling the award of costs under legal aid and (it might be said) of the professional rôle of the solicitor. The practitioner's personal view of the client's case is of no importance. A legally-aided client is entitled to the same degree of care and attention as a private client. The solicitor is not under a duty, as in civil proceedings, to report to the Legal Aid Board clients who require their case to be conducted unreasonably, nor is the solicitor in criminal proceedings required to keep under constant review the reasonableness of such proceedings continuing at the public expense. Instead, '[t]he appropriate authority . . . shall allow such work as appears to it to have been actually and reasonably done': Legal Aid in Criminal and Care Proceedings (Costs) Regulations 1989 (SI 1989 No. 343), reg. 6(2)(a), as amended by Legal Aid in Criminal and Care Proceedings (Costs) (Amendment) Regulations 1992 (SI 1992 No. 592) which inserted the words 'actually and'. The latter words had originally been in the Legal Aid in Criminal Proceedings (Costs) Regulations 1988 (SI 1988 No. 423), reg. 6, but for some reason were deleted in the 1989 Regulations.

A judge of the Crown Court or the Court of Appeal may make observations for the attention of the taxing authority where it appears that a 'legally assisted person's case may have been conducted unreasonably so as to incur unjustifiable expense': *Practice Direction (Costs in Criminal Proceedings)* (1991) 93 Cr App R 89, para. 10.1, *per* Lord Lane CJ. It is almost inconceivable that a judge would consider a bail application to be unreasonable or an 'unjustifiable expense'. The situation might possibly arise with repeated bail applications where there is no fresh argument, but, even then, such applications are unlikely to be adjudged unreasonable if they were allowed by the court (because 'the court need not hear arguments as to fact or law which it has heard previously': BA 1976, sch. 1, Part IIA, para. 3). Conduct which gives rise to the court's inherent jurisdiction to order that a solicitor personally pay the costs of proceedings is that which involves a serious dereliction of duty on the part of that solicitor or his duty to the court: *Holden & Co. and Others* v *Crown Prosecution Service* (1990) 90 Cr App R 385.

13.2.6   Reluctance to make unmeritorious applications

Brink and Stone also found that some solicitors were reluctant to make unmeritorious bail applications lest their own reputation with the court should suffer. Some practitioners try to overcome this difficulty by prefacing an unmeritorious application with the euphemistic preamble 'I am instructed to apply for bail', clearly implying 'I know my client does not deserve bail and I appreciate you will not grant it but I have to go through the motions of making an application'. Fear of disrepute is quite unfounded and the coded disavowal is unnecessary. Any reasonable tribunal will respect advocates who act in the interests of their clients, but will not respect those who put self-interest first. Brink and Stone make the point that:

> . . . the assumption that the solicitor is personally and professionally responsible for assuring that only deserving defendants are granted bail . . . is generally regarded as a corruption of the adversary system of justice. Lawyers, as officers of the court, have an obligation to serve the cause of justice, but in an adversary system justice is served by the strongest possible arguments being put in every case.

Recent research indicates that little has changed since the time of Brink and Stone's study. Anthea Hucklesby has observed that 'it became apparent that an important consideration for defence solicitors in advising their clients on whether or not a bail application should be made was their credibility in the court' (Hucklesby, A., *Bail or Jail? The Magistrates' Decision*, unpublished Ph.D. thesis, 1994, p. 354).

13.2.7 Preparation

The importance of adequate preparation can hardly be understated. Preparation will involve ascertaining the full details of the allegation, in order the better to anticipate the grounds upon which the prosecution are likely to oppose bail.

It was formerly very common that on a first appearance in custody the defending advocate would have little more than the sketchiest of details of the case and would be dependent on the willingness of the prosecuting advocate to supply the salient facts before the court session that morning. Although the Magistrates' Court (Advance Information) Rules 1985 (SI 1985 No. 601) provide that in 'either way' offences the prosecution must, as soon as practicable, furnish the defence either with material parts of every witness statement or with a summary (unless disclosure might lead to intimidation of witnesses or interference with the course of justice), it is very often impracticable to serve this material until a later hearing. However, the 'inferences from silence' provisions of the CJPOA 1994 have made it customary for the police to give details of the allegation to a defending solicitor during the investigative stage of a case in order to trigger the operation of the Act in relation to questioning of the defendant at the police station. The basis of this broad policy of disclosure is that it would not in general be reasonable to expect the defendant, during questioning, to mention a fact on which reliance is later placed if the defendant is not put on notice of the relevance of that fact beforehand (*R v Roble* [1997] Crim LR 449). Defending solicitors who have been in attendance at the police station will generally have kept notes of the salient facts taken from the police in the briefing before interview (see Shepherd, E., *Becoming Skilled: A Resource Book*, Police Station Skills for Legal Advisers series, Law Society Criminal Law Committee, 2nd ed., London: Law Society, 1997, *passim*; Shepherd, E., and Ede, R. , *Active Defence*, London: Law Society, 1997). These will either be available for the use of the advocate applying for bail at court, or their content passed on orally if it has not been practicable at short notice to transmit them by messenger or fax.

The advocate must obtain the fullest information about the defendant's background and current circumstances: e.g., age; place of birth; address; type of accommodation; *de facto* marital status; number of dependent relatives (in particular children) and their ages; work history; current employment; whether custody will mean immediate loss of job; if currently unemployed, job prospects (unemployed defendants will not uncommonly have a job starting on Monday); and previous convictions.

Most importantly of all, it is as well to have full details, if practicable, of proposed sureties. If candidates have come to court it may often assist a bail application to call them in support. To this end, proposed sureties should be asked for full details of such of their assets as they are willing to disclose and of their ability to keep in close touch with the accused. An impressive surety may so inspire the court's confidence as to be decisive.

13.2.8 The hearing

It is not proposed to expound at length on points of advocacy here. Suffice to say that although the court should need no reminding, it may well be appropriate before a lay bench for the defending advocate to weave into any submissions a reference to the presumption in favour of bail. Further, the defence should always anticipate the fact that although the prosecutor has not raised a particular ground of objection the court may nevertheless be minded to invoke it anyway. This is not necessarily to say that the defence should mention it before the court does. On the other hand, an impressive advocate who inspires the confidence and trust of the court is one who is sometimes prepared to grasp the nettle and deal with potential obstacles to the granting of bail which the bench may well have in mind even though they have not been mentioned by the prosecutor. The problem with this approach is that the advocate can sometimes appear to raise an objection that would never have occurred to the magistrates had it not been for the defending advocate's style of raising a potential objection in order to shoot it down. Moreover, the risk of anticipating a possible objection not raised by the prosecution is that, if the application for bail is refused, the defendant and any relatives or friends who happen to be at court may feel aggrieved that the advocate appeared to be acting against the interests of the defence.

13.2.9 Advocate's duty where client fails to attend court

13.2.9.1 Solicitors The Law Society's Standards and Guidance Committee and Criminal Law Committee have issued guidance on the duties of solicitors with regard to the attendance of clients for hearings in court (*The Guide to the Professional Conduct of Solicitors*, London: Law Society, 1996, Annex 21F (originally issued 1988; updated January 1996)). The guidance states:

> It is accepted that there is a duty to provide reasonable assistance in the smooth running of the court lists, but the duty of confidentiality and the right of privilege override the duty to the court and, therefore, the solicitor should provide only such assistance to the court as is consistent with the duty to the client.
>
> The Society has received inquiries from solicitors as to the lengths to which they should go to ensure that clients receive notification of listing arrangements of matters to be tried in the Crown Court. The Society's view is that, while a solicitor ought to take reasonable steps to ensure that the client is aware of the

date for attendance at the Crown Court and of the client's duty to attend, the solicitor is not under an obligation to take all possible steps to secure attendance.

Should a client fail to attend for trial, a solicitor should, as mentioned above, consider the limitations imposed upon him or her by the duty of confidentiality and the client's privilege when deciding what information might be revealed to the court. There would be no objection to a solicitor stating that he or she had written to the client about the hearing and that the letter had not been returned undelivered. Where a solicitor believes that a client is unlikely to attend court it is reasonable for the solicitor to advise the court accordingly, although he or she might not be able to state the grounds for this belief. If the client has failed to respond to requests to attend the solicitor's office, it might be reasonable, depending on the facts, for the solicitor to advise the court that he or she is without instructions and/or that it would be desirable to list the case.

With reference to the above guidance, the Criminal Law Committee take the view that different circumstances will make different steps reasonable. The following are some examples.

Notification by post will be reasonable if the client can read English or such other language as the solicitor might reasonably be expected to use; and only if there are sufficient days between the date of posting and date of hearing for the client to be warned in time (bearing in mind postal conditions at the time) and to advise the solicitor that he or she has received the notice.

A request to clients to telephone daily after a case appears in the warned list should be used with great caution. It will only be appropriate for clients with ready access to a private telephone and for offices where a responsible fee-earner will be readily available to take the calls.

If it is not reasonable to expect the client to telephone the solicitor's office daily to check the position of the case in the warned list, then some other method may be reasonable, such as delivery of a letter by taxi or courier. These should also be considered if there has been no acknowledgement of a written notice.

In cases where personal service is reasonable the solicitor may need to consider who should or can effect such service. It may need to be done by a person who knows the client; the time of day or type of area in which the client lives, or some other factor, may make it unreasonable to expect a junior or female employee or colleague, or perhaps any person alone, to undertake the task.

The Criminal Law Committee are continuing to press for an end to short-notice listing of cases for hearing in the Crown Court. Although there have been some improvements in some places, the position remains far from satisfactory.

The Criminal Law Committee were concerned at the incidence of judicial criticism of defendants' solicitors in public, particularly where such criticism was unjustified, and asked the Lord Chancellor's Department (LCD) to remind members of the judiciary that these issues should be dealt with in chambers.

Practitioners are reminded that the Society's support is available to solicitors who are unjustly criticised or penalised by the court; or who, after taxation, wish to take further a claim against unjustified disallowance or reduction of costs. In appropriate cases, financial assistance from the Society will be given if the Courts and Legal Services Committee should so agree.

With reference to the LCD guidance . . . the Criminal Law Committee take the view that 'several days' normally means four to six days and 'very short notice' normally means three days or less; and that Sundays cannot count for this purpose.

In regard to criminal legal aid costs generally, practitioners are reminded of the need to record every telephone call to ensure that none is forgotten when drawing the bill. Dealing with a telephone call from the client or from witnesses, for example, is normally done by a fee-earner and, if reasonable, is normally paid for.

The Professional and Legal Policy Directorate wish to be kept informed of any disallowances thought to be unfair of items of costs claimed in Crown Court cases; in particular, please inform the Directorate of any difficulties encountered concerning items of costs or disbursements claimed for informing or attempting to inform the client of the date for attendance at court.

The guidance, in Annex 21F, reproduces the Lord Chancellor's Department guidance to circuit taxing coordinatators and determining officers concerning notification of the defendant for court hearings (dated 1988). The guidance is set out as follows:

The Law Society has written to the department expressing the concern of many practitioners about the seeming lack of consistency between Crown Courts when considering claims by solicitors for notifying defendants of court hearings.

This subject was discussed at the recent circuit taxing coordinators meeting. Those present were surprised by the letter, being under the impression that in cases where it was reasonable to make payment for warning the defendant, determining officers were doing so.

I would ask you to bring this matter to the attention of all determining officers reminding them of the tests to be applied when considering such a claim.

Where a case is included in a fixed list which is published far enough in advance for the defendant to be warned by correspondence then a letter (allowed at unit cost) should usually suffice. But it might also be reasonable to allow an occasional telephone call in from the defendant to the solicitor to check that the position is unchanged.

Where a case is brought into a list at shorter notice and assuming the defendant is not on the telephone the determining officer should consider:

(a)   was there reasonably sufficient time for the solicitor to warn the defendant by letter;
(b)   if not, was the method of warning chosen reasonable?

As to (b), if the notice of listing is several days in advance it might be considered:

(a) that notification should have reasonably been covered by adequate arrangements made by the solicitor for the defendant to telephone or call in at the office;

(b) that a form of notice other than personal service would have been reasonable (e.g. a letter sent by taxi);

(c) that in the circumstances of the particular case personal service was reasonable.

If a case is brought into a list at very short notice then personal service would normally be reasonable and should be allowed. Personal service should generally be regarded as fee-earner work and in normal circumstances would be appropriate to a grade C fee-earner. It is, as always, for the solicitor to provide the determining officer with full details in support of his claim.

13.2.9.2 Counsel's duty when the defendant absconds during the trial Where the defendant absconds during the trial, the question as to whether counsel can participate in the trial is for counsel's judgment and within counsel's absolute discretion: *R* v *Shaw* (1980) 70 Cr App R 313. The position is also addressed in the *Code of Conduct for the Bar of England and Wales*, 5th ed., London General Council of the Bar, 1990, 'Standards for the Conduct of Professional Work applicable to Criminal Cases', paras 5.3.1 and 5.3.2.

Appendix

TEXT OF THE BAIL ACT 1976

Bail Act 1976

Preliminary

Meaning of 'bail in criminal proceedings'

1.—(1) In this Act 'bail in criminal proceedings' means—

(a) bail grantable in or in connection with proceedings for an offence to a person who is accused or convicted of the offence, or

(b) bail grantable in connection with an offence to a person who is under arrest for the offence or for whose arrest for the offence a warrant (endorsed for bail) is being issued.

(2) In this Act 'bail' means bail grantable under the law (including common law) for the time being in force.

(3) Except as provided by section 13(3) of this Act, this section does not apply to bail in or in connection with proceedings outside England and Wales.

. . .

(5) This section applies—

(a) whether the offence was committed in England or Wales or elsewhere, and

(b) whether it is an offence under the law of England and Wales, or of any other country or territory.

(6) Bail in criminal proceedings shall be granted (and in particular shall be granted unconditionally or conditionally), in accordance with this Act.

Other definitions

2.—(1) In this Act, unless the context otherwise requires, 'conviction' includes—

(a) a finding of guilt,

(b) a finding that a person is not guilty by reason of insanity,

(c) a finding under section 30(1) of the Magistrates' Courts Act 1980 (remand for medical examination) that the person in question did the act or made the omission charged, and

(d) a conviction of an offence for which an order is made placing the offender on probation or discharging him absolutely or conditionally, and 'convicted' shall be construed accordingly.

(2) In this Act, unless the context otherwise requires—

'bail hostel' and 'probation hostel' have the same meanings as in the Powers of Criminal Courts Act 1973,

'child' means a person under the age of fourteen,

'court' includes a judge of a court or a justice of the peace and, in the case of a specified court, includes a judge or (as the case may be) justice having powers to act in connection with proceedings before that court,

'Courts-Martial Appeal rules' means rules made under section 49 of the Courts-Martial (Appeals) Act 1968,

'Crown Court rules' means rules made under section 15 of the Courts Act 1971,

'magistrates' courts rules' means rules made under section 15 of the Justices of the Peace Act 1949,

'offence' includes an alleged offence,

'proceedings against a fugitive offender' means proceedings under section 9 of the Extradition Act 1870, section 7 of the Fugitive Offenders Act 1967 or section 2(1) or 4(3) of the Backing of Warrants (Republic of Ireland) Act 1965,

'Supreme Court rules' means rules made under section 99 of the Supreme Court of Judicature (Consolidation) Act 1925,

'surrender to custody' means, in relation to a person released on bail, surrendering himself into the custody of the court or of the constable (according to the requirements of the grant of bail) at the time and place for the time being appointed for him to do so,

'vary', in relation to bail, means imposing further conditions after bail is granted, or varying or rescinding conditions,

'young person' means a person who has attained the age of 14 and is under the age of 17.

(3) Where an enactment (whenever passed) which relates to bail in criminal proceedings refers to the person bailed appearing before a court it is to be construed unless the context otherwise requires as referring to his surrendering himself into the custody of the court.

(4) Any reference in this Act to any other enactment is a reference thereto as amended, and includes a reference thereto as extended or applied, by or under any other enactment, including this Act.

Incidents of bail in criminal proceedings

General provisions

3.—(1) A person granted bail in criminal proceedings shall be under a duty to surrender to custody, and that duty is enforceable in accordance with section 6 of this Act.

(2)   No recognisance for his surrender to custody shall be taken from him.

(3)   Except as provided by this section—

(a)   no security for his surrender to custody shall be taken from him,

(b)   he shall not be required to provide a surety or sureties for his surrender to custody, and

(c)   no other requirement shall be imposed on him as a condition of bail.

(4)   He may be required, before release on bail, to provide a surety or sureties to secure his surrender to custody.

(5)   He may be required, before release on bail, to give security for his surrender to custody.

The security may be given by him or on his behalf.

(6)   He may be required to comply, before release on bail or later, with such requirements as appear to the court to be necessary to secure that—

(a)   he surrenders to custody,

(b)   he does not commit an offence while on bail,

(c)   he does not interfere with witnesses or otherwise obstruct the course of justice whether in relation to himself or any other person,

(d)   he makes himself available for the purpose of enabling inquiries or a report to be made to assist the court in dealing with him for the offence,

(e)   before the time appointed for him to surrender to custody, he attends an interview with an authorised advocate or authorised litigator, as defined by section 119(1) of the Courts and Legal Services Act 1990;

and, in any Act, 'the normal powers to impose conditions of bail' means the powers to impose conditions under paragraph (a), (b) or (c) above.

(6ZA)   Where he is required under subsection (6) above to reside in a bail hostel or probation hostel, he may also be required to comply with the rules of the hostel.

(6A)   In the case of a person accused of murder the court granting bail shall, unless it considers that satisfactory reports on his mental condition have already been obtained, impose as conditions of bail—

(a)   a requirement that the accused shall undergo examination by two medical practitioners for the purpose of enabling such reports to be prepared; and

(b)   a requirement that he shall for that purpose attend such an institution or place as the court directs and comply with any other directions which may be given to him for that purpose by either of those practitioners.

(6B)   Of the medical practitioners referred to in subsection (6A) above at least one shall be a practitioner approved for the purposes of section 12 of the Mental Health Act 1983.

(7)   If a parent or guardian of a child or young person consents to be surety for the child or young person for the purposes of this subsection, the parent or guardian may be required to secure that the child or young person complies with any requirement imposed on him by virtue of subsection (6) or (6A) above but—

(a)   no requirement shall be imposed on the parent or the guardian of a young person by virtue of this subsection where it appears that the young person will attain the age of 17 before the time to be appointed for him to surrender to custody; and

(b)   the parent or guardian shall not be required to secure compliance with any requirement to which his consent does not extend and shall not, in respect of those requirements to which his consent does extend, be bound in a sum greater than £50.

(8)   Where a court has granted bail in criminal proceedings that court or, where that court has committed a person on bail to the Crown Court for trial or to be sentenced or otherwise dealt with, that court or the Crown Court may on application—

(a)   by or on behalf of the person to whom bail was granted, or

(b)   by the prosecutor or a constable,

vary the conditions of bail or impose conditions in respect of bail which has been granted unconditionally.

(8A)   Where a notice of transfer is given under a relevant transfer provision, subsection (8) above shall have effect in relation to a person in relation to whose case the notice is given as if he had been committed on bail to the Crown Court for trial.

(8B)   Subsection (8) above applies where a court has sent a person on bail to the Crown Court for trial under section 51 of the Crime and Disorder Act 1998 as it applies where a court has committed a person on bail to the Crown Court for trial. [This subsection is inserted by the CDA 1998, sch. 8 and is in force from 4 January 1999 only in certain pilot areas where s. 51 of the CDA 1998 is in force.

(9)   This section is subject to subsection (2) of section 30 of the Magistrates' Courts Act 1980 (conditions of bail on remand for medical examination).

(10)   This section is subject, in its application to bail granted by a constable, to section 3A of this Act.

(10)   In subsection (8A) above 'relevant transfer provision' means—

(a)   section 4 of the Criminal Justice Act 1987, or

(b)   section 53 of the Criminal Justice Act 1991.

Conditions of bail in case of police bail

3A.—(1)   Section 3 of this Act applies, in relation to bail granted by a custody officer under part IV of the Police and Criminal Evidence Act 1984 in cases where the normal powers to impose conditions of bail are available to him, subject to the following modifications.

(2)   Subsection (6) does not authorise the imposition of a requirement to reside in a bail hostel or any requirement under paragraph (d) or (e).

(3)   Subsection (6ZA), (6A) and (6B) shall be omitted.

(4)   For subsection (8), substitute the following—

'(8)   Where a custody officer has granted bail in criminal proceedings he or another custody officer serving at the same police station may, at the request of the person to whom it was granted, vary the conditions of bail; and in doing so he may impose conditions or more onerous conditions.'.

(5)   Where a constable grants bail to a person no conditions shall be imposed under subsections (4), (5), (6) or (7) of section 3 of this Act unless it appears to

the constable that it is necessary to do so for the purpose of preventing that person from—

(a) failing to surrender to custody, or

(b) committing an offence while on bail, or

(c) interfering with witnesses or otherwise obstructing the course of justice,

whether in relation to himself or any other person.

(6) Subsection (5) above also applies on any request to a custody officer under subsection (8) of section 3 of this Act to vary the conditions of bail.

Bail for accused persons and others

General right to bail of accused persons and others

4.—(1) A person to whom this section applies shall be granted bail except as provided in schedule 1 to this Act.

(2) This section applies to a person who is accused of an offence when—

(a) he appears or is brought before a magistrates' court or the Crown Court in the course of or in connection with proceedings for the offence, or

(b) he applies to a court for bail or for a variation of the conditions of bail in connection with the proceedings.

This subsection does not apply as respects proceedings on or after a person's conviction of the offence or proceedings against a fugitive offender for the offence.

(3) This section also applies to a person who, having been convicted of an offence, appears or is brought before a magistrates' court to be dealt with under part II of schedule 2 to the Criminal Justice Act 1991 (breach of requirement of probation, community service, combination or curfew order).

(4) This section also applies to a person who has been convicted of an offence and whose case is adjourned by the court for the purpose of enabling inquiries or a report to be made to assist the court in dealing with him for the offence.

(5) Schedule 1 to this Act also has effect as respects conditions of bail for a person to whom this section applies.

(6) In schedule 1 to this Act 'the defendant' means a person to whom this section applies and any reference to a defendant whose case is adjourned for inquiries or a report is a reference to a person to whom this section applies by virtue of subsection (4) above.

(7) This section is subject to section 41 of the Magistrates' Courts Act 1980 (restriction of bail by magistrates' court in cases of treason).

(8) This section is subject to section 25 of the Criminal Justice and Public Order Act 1994 (exclusion of bail in cases of homicide and rape).

Supplementary

Supplementary provisions about decisions on bail

5.—(1) Subject to subsection (2) below, where—

(a) a court or constable grants bail in criminal proceedings, or

(b)   a court withholds bail in criminal proceedings from a person to whom section 4 of this Act applies, or

(c)   a court, officer of a court or constable appoints a time or place or a court or officer of a court appoints a different time or place for a person granted bail in criminal proceedings to surrender to custody, or

(d)   a court or constable varies any conditions of bail or imposes conditions in respect of bail in criminal proceedings,

that court, officer or constable shall make a record of the decision in the prescribed manner and containing the prescribed particulars and, if requested to do so by the person in relation to whom the decision was taken, shall cause him to be given a copy of the record of the decision as soon as practicable after the record is made.

(2)   Where bail in criminal proceedings is granted by endorsing a warrant of arrest for bail the constable who releases on bail the person arrested shall make the record required by subsection (1) above instead of the judge or justice who issued the warrant.

(3)   Where a magistrates' court or the Crown Court—

(a)   withholds bail in criminal proceedings, or

(b)   imposes conditions in granting bail in criminal proceedings, or

(c)   varies any conditions of bail or imposes conditions in respect of bail in criminal proceedings,

and does so in relation to a person to whom section 4 of this Act applies, then the court shall, with a view to enabling him to consider making an application in the matter to another court, give reasons for withholding bail or for imposing or varying the conditions.

(4)   A court which is by virtue of subsection (3) above required to give reasons for its decision shall include a note of those reasons in the record of its decision and shall (except in a case where, by virtue of subsection (5) below, this need not be done) give a copy of that note to the person in relation to whom the decision was taken.

(5)   The Crown Court need not give a copy of the note of the reasons for its decision to the person in relation to whom the decision was taken where that person is represented by counsel or a solicitor unless his counsel or solicitor requests the court to do so.

(6)   Where a magistrates' court withholds bail in criminal proceedings from a person who is not represented by counsel or a solicitor, the court shall—

(a)   if it is committing him for trial to the Crown Court, or if it issues a certificate under subsection (6A) below inform him that he may apply to the High Court or to the Crown Court to be granted bail;

(b)   in any other case, inform him that he may apply to the High Court for that purpose.

(6A)   Where in criminal proceedings—

(a)   a magistrates' court remands a person in custody under any of the following provisions of the Magistrates' Courts Act 1980—

(i)   section 5 (adjournment of inquiry into offence);

(ii)   section 10 (adjournment of trial);

(iii)   section 18 (initial procedure on information against adult for offence triable either way); or

(iv)   section 30 (remand for medical examination),

after hearing full argument on an application for bail from him; and

(b)   either—

(i)   it has not previously heard such argument on an application for bail from him in those proceedings; or

(ii)   it has previously heard full argument from him on such an application but it is satisfied that there has been a change in his circumstances or that new considerations have been placed before it,

it shall be the duty of the court to issue a certificate in the prescribed form that they heard full argument on his application for bail before they refused the application.

(6B)   Where the court issues a certificate under subsection (6A) above in a case to which paragraph (b)(ii) of that subsection applies, it shall state in the certificate the nature of the change of circumstances or the new considerations which caused it to hear a further fully argued bail application.

(6C)   Where a court issues a certificate under subsection (6A) above it shall cause the person to whom it refuses bail to be given a copy of the certificate.

(7)   Where a person has given security in pursuance of section 3(5) above, and a court is satisfied that he failed to surrender to custody then, unless it appears that he had reasonable cause for his failure, the court may order the forfeiture of the security.

(8)   If a court orders the forfeiture of a security under subsection (7) above, the court may declare that the forfeiture extends to such amount less than the full value of the security as it thinks fit to order.

[Subsections (8A) to (9A) detail procedure for taking and forfeiting a security. For a full discussion of these procedures, see paras. 2.2.6.6 and 2.2.6.7.]

(10)   In this section 'prescribed' means, in relation to the decision of a court or an officer of a court, prescribed by Supreme Court rules, Courts-Martial Appeal rules, Crown Court rules or magistrates' courts rules, as the case requires or, in relation to a decision of a constable, prescribed by direction of the Secretary of State.

(11)   This section is subject, in its application to bail granted by a constable, to section 5A of this Act.

Supplementary provisions in cases of police bail

5A.—Section 5 of this Act applies, in relation to bail granted by a custody officer under part IV of the Police and Criminal Evidence Act 1984 in cases where the normal powers to impose conditions of bail are available to him, subject to the following modifications.

(2)   For subsection (3) substitute the following—

'(3)   Where a custody officer, in relation to any person,—

(a)   imposes conditions in granting bail in criminal proceedings, or

(b)   varies any conditions of bail or imposes conditions in respect of bail, in criminal proceedings,
the custody officer shall, with a view to enabling that person to consider requesting him or another custody officer, or making an application to a magistrates' court, to vary the conditions, give reasons for imposing or varying the conditions.'.

(3)   For subsection (4) substitute the following—

'(4)   A custody officer who is by virtue of subsection (3) above required to give reasons for his decision shall include a note of those reasons in the custody record and shall give a copy of that note to the person in relation to whom the decision was taken.'.

(4)   Subsections (5) and (6) shall be omitted.

Reconsideration of decisions granting bail
5B.—(1)   Where a magistrates' court has granted bail in criminal proceedings in connection with an offence, or proceedings for an offence, to which this section applies or a constable has granted bail in criminal proceedings in connection with proceedings for an offence, that court or the appropriate court in relation to the constable may, on application by the prosecutor for the decision to be reconsidered,—

(a)   vary the conditions of bail,

(b)   impose conditions in respect of bail which has been granted unconditionally, or

(c)   withhold bail.

(2)   The offences to which this section applies are offences triable on indictment and offences triable either way.

(3)   No application for the reconsideration of a decision under this section shall be made unless it is based on information which was not available to the court or constable when the decision was taken.

(4)   Whether or not the person to whom the application relates appears before it, the magistrates' court shall take the decision in accordance with section 4(1) (and schedule 1) of this Act.

(5)   Where the decision of the court on a reconsideration under this section is to withhold bail from the person to whom it was originally granted the court shall—

(a)   if that person is before the court, remand him in custody, and

(b)   if that person is not before the court, order him to surrender himself forthwith into the custody of the court.

(6)   Where a person surrenders himself into the custody of the court in compliance with an order under subsection (5) above, the court shall remand him in custody.

(7)   A person who has been ordered to surrender to custody under subsection (5) above may be arrested without warrant by a constable if he fails without reasonable cause to surrender to custody in accordance with the order.

(8)   A person arrested in pursuance of subsection (7) above shall be brought as soon as practicable, and in any event within 24 hours after his arrest, before a justice of the peace for the petty sessions area in which he was arrested and the justice shall remand him in custody.

In reckoning for the purposes of this subsection any period of 24 hours, no account shall be taken of Christmas Day, Good Friday or any Sunday.

(9)   Magistrates' court rules shall include provision—

(a)   requiring notice of an application under this section and of the grounds for it to be given to the person affected, including notice of the powers available to the court under it;

(b)   for securing that any representations made by the person affected (whether in writing or orally) are considered by the court before making its decision; and

(c)   designating the court which is the appropriate court in relation to the decision of any constable to grant bail.

Offence of absconding by person released on bail
6.—(1)   If a person who has been released on bail in criminal proceedings fails without reasonable cause to surrender to custody he shall be guilty of an offence.

(2)   If a person who—

(a)   has been released on bail in criminal proceedings, and

(b)   having reasonable cause therefor, has failed to surrender to custody, fails to surrender to custody at the appointed place as soon after the appointed time as is reasonably practicable he shall be guilty of an offence.

(3)   It shall be for the accused to prove that he had reasonable cause for his failure to surrender to custody.

(4)   A failure to give to a person granted bail in criminal proceedings a copy of the record of the decision shall not constitute a reasonable cause for that person's failure to surrender to custody.

(5)   An offence under subsection (1) or (2) above shall be punishable either on summary conviction or as if it were a criminal contempt of court.

(6)   Where a magistrates' court convicts a person of an offence under subsection (1) or (2) above the court may, if it thinks—

(a)   that the circumstances of the offence are such that greater punishment should be inflicted for that offence than the court has power to inflict, or

(b)   in a case where it commits that person for trial to the Crown Court for another offence, that it would be appropriate for him to be dealt with for the offence under subsection (1) or (2) above by the court before which he is tried for the other offence,
commit him in custody or on bail to the Crown Court for sentence.

(7)   A person who is convicted summarily of an offence under subsection (1) or (2) above and is not committed to the Crown Court for sentence shall be liable to imprisonment for a term not exceeding three months or to a fine not exceeding level 5 on the standard scale or to both and a person who is so committed for

sentence or is dealt with as for such a contempt shall be liable to imprisonment for a term not exceeding 12 months or to a fine or to both.

(8) In any proceedings for an offence under subsection (1) or (2) above a document purporting to be a copy of the part of the prescribed record which relates to the time and place appointed for the person specified in the record to surrender to custody and to be duly certified to be a true copy of that part of the record shall be evidence of the time and place appointed for that person to surrender to custody.

(9) For the purposes of subsection (8) above—

(a) 'the prescribed record' means the record of the decision of the court, officer or constable made in pursuance of section 5(1) of this Act;

(b) the copy of the prescribed record is duly certified if it is certified by the appropriate officer of the court or, as the case may be, by the constable who took the decision or a constable designated for the purpose by the officer in charge of the police station from which the person to whom the record relates was released;

(c) 'the appropriate officer' of the court is—

(i) in the case of a magistrates' court, the justices' clerk or such other officer as may be authorised by him to act for the purpose;

(ii) in the case of the Crown Court, such officer as may be designated for the purpose in accordance with arrangements made by the Lord Chancellor;

(iii) in the case of the High Court, such officer as may be designated for the purpose in accordance with arrangements made by the Lord Chancellor;

(iv) in the case of the Court of Appeal, the registrar of criminal appeals or such other officer as may be authorised by him to act for the purpose;

(v) in the case of the Courts-Martial Appeal Court, the registrar or such other officer as may be authorised by him to act for the purpose.

Liability to arrest for absconding or breaking conditions of bail

7.—(1) If a person who has been released on bail in criminal proceedings and is under a duty to surrender into the custody of a court fails to surrender to custody at the time appointed for him to do so the court may issue a warrant for his arrest.

(2) If a person who has been released on bail in criminal proceedings absents himself from the court at any time after he has surrendered into the custody of the court and before the court is ready to begin or to resume the hearing of the proceedings, the court may issue a warrant for his arrest; but no warrant shall be issued under this subsection where that person is absent in accordance with leave given to him by or on behalf of the court.

(3) A person who has been released on bail in criminal proceedings and is under a duty to surrender into the custody of a court may be arrested without warrant by a constable—

(a) if the constable has reasonable grounds for believing that that person is not likely to surrender to custody;

(b) if the constable has reasonable grounds for believing that that person is likely to break any of the conditions of his bail or has reasonable grounds for suspecting that that person has broken any of those conditions; or

(c)   in a case where that person was released on bail with one or more surety or sureties, if a surety notifies a constable in writing that that person is unlikely to surrender to custody and that for that reason the surety wishes to be relieved of his obligations as a surety.

(4)   A person arrested in pursuance of subsection (3) above—

(a)   shall, except where he was arrested within 24 hours of the time appointed for him to surrender to custody, be brought as soon as practicable and in any event within 24 hours after his arrest before a justice of the peace for the petty sessions area in which he was arrested; and

(b)   in the said excepted case shall be brought before the court at which he was to have surrendered to custody.

In reckoning for the purposes of this subsection any period of 24 hours, no account shall be taken of Christmas Day, Good Friday or any Sunday.

(5)   A justice of the peace before whom a person is brought under subsection (4) above may, subject to subsection (6) below, if of the opinion that that person—

(a)   is not likely to surrender to custody, or

(b)   has broken or is likely to break any condition of his bail,

remand him in custody or commit him to custody, as the case may require, or alternatively, grant him bail subject to the same or to different conditions, but if not of that opinion shall grant him bail subject to the same conditions (if any) as were originally imposed.

(6)   Where the person so brought before the justice is a child or young person and the justice does not grant him bail, subsection (5) above shall have effect subject to the provisions of section 23 of the Children and Young Persons Act 1969 (remands to the care of local authorities).

Bail with sureties

8.—(1)   This section applies where a person is granted bail in criminal proceedings on condition that he provides one or more surety or sureties for the purpose of securing that he surrenders to custody.

(2)   In considering the suitability for that purpose of a proposed surety, regard may be had (amongst other things) to—

(a)   the surety's financial resources;

(b)   his character and any previous convictions of his; and

(c)   his proximity (whether in point of kinship, place of residence or otherwise) to the person for whom he is to be surety.

(3)   Where a court grants a person bail in criminal proceedings on such a condition but is unable to release him because no surety or no suitable surety is available, the court shall fix the amount in which the surety is to be found and subsections (4) and (5) below, or in a case where the proposed surety resides in Scotland subsection (6) below, shall apply for the purpose of enabling the recognisance of the surety to be entered into subsequently.

(4)   Where this subsection applies the recognisance of the surety may be entered into before such of the following persons or descriptions of persons as the

court may by order specify or, if it makes no such order, before any of the following persons, that is to say—

(a) where the decision is taken by a magistrates' court, before a justice of the peace, a justices' clerk or a police officer who either is of the rank of inspector or above or is in charge of a police station or, if magistrates' courts rules so provide, by a person of such other description as is specified in the rules;

(b) where the decision is taken by the Crown Court, before any of the persons specified in paragraph (a) above or, if Crown Court rules so provide, by a person of such other description as is specified in the rules;

(c) where the decision is taken by the High Court or the Court of Appeal, before any of the persons specified in paragraph (a) above or, if Supreme Court rules so provide, by a person of such other description as is specified in the rules;

(d) where the decision is taken by the Courts-Martial Appeal Court, before any of the persons specified in paragraph (a) above or, if Courts-Martial Appeal rules so provide, by a person of such other description as is specified in the rules; and Supreme Court rules, Crown Court rules, Courts-Martial Appeal rules or magistrates' courts rules may also prescribe the manner in which a recognisance which is to be entered into before such a person is to be entered into and the persons by whom and the manner in which the recognisance may be enforced.

(5) Where a surety seeks to enter into his recognisance before any person in accordance with subsection (4) above but that person declines to take his recognisance because he is not satisfied of the surety's suitability, the surety may apply to—

(a) the court which fixed the amount of the recognisance in which the surety was to be bound, or

(b) a magistrates' court for the petty sessions area in which he resides, for that court to take his recognisance and that court shall, if satisfied of his suitability, take his recognisance.

(6) Where this subsection applies, the court, if satisfied of the suitability of the proposed surety, may direct that arrangements be made for the recognisance of the surety to be entered into in Scotland before any constable, within the meaning of the Police (Scotland) Act 1967, having charge at any police office or station in like manner as the recognisance would be entered into in England or Wales.

(7) Where, in pursuance of subsection (4) or (6) above, a recognisance is entered into otherwise than before the court that fixed the amount of the recognisance, the same consequences shall follow as if it had been entered into before that court.

Miscellaneous

Offence of agreeing to indemnify sureties in criminal proceedings

9.—(1) If a person agrees with another to indemnify that other against any liability which that other may incur as a surety to secure the surrender to custody of a person accused or convicted of or under arrest for an offence, he and that other person shall be guilty of an offence.

(2)   An offence under subsection (1) above is committed whether the agreement is made before or after the person to be indemnified becomes a surety and whether or not he becomes a surety and whether the agreement contemplates compensation in money or in money's worth.

(3)   Where a magistrates' court convicts a person of an offence under subsection (1) above the court may, if it thinks—

(a)   that the circumstances of the offence are such that greater punishment should be inflicted for that offence than the court has power to inflict, or

(b)   in a case where it commits that person for trial to the Crown Court for another offence, that it would be appropriate for him to be dealt with for the offence under subsection (1) above by the court before which he is tried for the other offence,

commit him in custody or on bail to the Crown Court for sentence.

(4)   A person guilty of an offence under subsection (1) above shall be liable—

(a)   on summary conviction, to imprisonment for a term not exceeding 3 months or to a fine not exceeding the prescribed sum or to both; or

(b)   on conviction on indictment or if sentenced by the Crown Court on committal for sentence under subsection (3) above, to imprisonment for a term not exceeding 12 months or to a fine or to both.

(5)   No proceedings for an offence under subsection (1) above shall be instituted except by or with the consent of the Director of Public Prosecutions.

[**10** and **11**   Repealed.]

[**12**   Amendments, repeals and transitional provisions.]

[**13**   Short title, commencement, application and extent.]

SCHEDULE 1   PERSONS ENTITLED TO BAIL: SUPPLEMENTARY PROVISIONS

PART I   DEFENDANTS ACCUSED OR CONVICTED OF IMPRISONABLE OFFENCES

Defendants to whom part I applies

1.   Where the offence or one of the offences of which the defendant is accused or convicted in the proceedings is punishable with imprisonment the following provisions of this part of this schedule apply.

Exceptions to right to bail

2.   The defendant need not be granted bail if the court is satisfied that there are substantial grounds for believing that the defendant, if released on bail (whether subject to conditions or not) would—

(a)   fail to surrender to custody, or

(b)   commit an offence while on bail, or

(c) interfere with witnesses or otherwise obstruct the course of justice, whether in relation to himself or any other person.

2A. The defendant need not be granted bail if—
    (a) the offence is an indictable offence or an offence triable either way; and
    (b) it appears to the court that he was on bail in criminal proceedings on the date of the offence.

3. The defendant need not be granted bail if the court is satisfied that the defendant should be kept in custody for his own protection or, if he is a child or young person, for his own welfare.

4. The defendant need not be granted bail if he is in custody in pursuance of the sentence of a court or of any authority acting under any of the Services Acts.

5. The defendant need not be granted bail where the court is satisfied that it has not been practicable to obtain sufficient information for the purpose of taking the decisions required by this part of this schedule for want of time since the institution of the proceedings against him.

6. The defendant need not be granted bail if, having been released on bail in or in connection with the proceedings for the offence, he has been arrested in pursuance of section 7 of this Act.

Exception applicable only to defendant whose case is adjourned for inquiries or a report
7. Where his case is adjourned for inquiries or a report, the defendant need not be granted bail if it appears to the court that it would be impracticable to complete the inquiries or make the report without keeping the defendant in custody.

Restriction of conditions of bail
8.—(1) Subject to subparagraph (3) below, where the defendant is granted bail, no conditions shall be imposed under subsections (4) to (7) (except subsection (6)(d) or (e)) of section 3 of this Act unless it appears to the court that it is necessary to do so for the purpose of preventing the occurrence of any of the events mentioned in paragraph 2 of this part of this schedule.
    (2) Subparagraph (1) above also applies on any application to the court to vary the conditions of bail or to impose conditions in respect of bail which has been granted unconditionally.
    (3) The restriction imposed by subparagraph (1) above shall not apply to the conditions required to be imposed under section 3(6A) of this Act or operate to override the direction in section 30(2) of the Magistrates' Courts Act 1980 to a magistrates' court to impose conditions of bail under section 3(6)(d) of this Act of the description specified in the said section 30(2) in the circumstances so specified.

Decisions under paragraph 2

9.   In taking the decisions required by paragraph 2 or 2A of this part of this schedule, the court shall have regard to such of the following considerations as appear to it to be relevant, that is to say—

(a)   the nature and seriousness of the offence or default (and the probable method of dealing with the defendant for it),

(b)   the character, antecedents, associations and community ties of the defendant,

(c)   the defendant's record as respects the fulfilment of his obligations under previous grants of bail in criminal proceedings,

(d)   except in the case of a defendant whose case is adjourned for inquiries or a report, the strength of the evidence of his having committed the offence or having defaulted,

as well as to any others which appear to be relevant.

9A.—(1)   If—

(a)   the defendant is charged with an offence to which this paragraph applies; and

(b)   representations are made as to any of the matters mentioned in paragraph 2 of this part of this schedule; and

(c)   the court decides to grant him bail,

the court shall state the reasons for its decision and shall cause those reasons to be included in the record of the proceedings.

(2)   The offences to which this paragraph applies are—

(a)   murder;

(b)   manslaughter;

(c)   rape;

(d)   attempted murder; and

(e)   attempted rape.

Cases under section 128A of Magistrates' Courts Act 1980

9B.   Where the court is considering exercising the power conferred by section 128A of the Magistrates' Courts Act 1980 (power to remand in custody for more than 8 clear days), it shall have regard to the total length of time which the accused would spend in custody if it were to exercise the power.

PART II   DEFENDANTS ACCUSED OR CONVICTED
OF NON-IMPRISONABLE OFFENCES

Defendants to whom part II applies

1.   Where the offence or every offence of which the defendant is accused or convicted in the proceedings is one which is not punishable with imprisonment the following provisions of this part of this schedule apply.

Exceptions to right to bail

2.   The defendant need not be granted bail if—

(a)   it appears to the court that, having been previously granted bail in criminal proceedings, he has failed to surrender to custody in accordance with his obligations under the grant of bail; and

(b)   the court believes, in view of that failure, that the defendant, if released on bail (whether subject to conditions or not) would fail to surrender to custody.

3.   The defendant need not be granted bail if the court is satisfied that the defendant should be kept in custody for his own protection or, if he is a child or young person, for his own welfare.

4.   The defendant need not be granted bail if he is in custody in pursuance of the sentence of a court or of any authority acting under any of the Services Acts.

5.   The defendant need not be granted bail if, having been released on bail in or in connection with the proceedings for the offence, he has been arrested in pursuance of section 7 of this Act.

PART IIA   DECISIONS WHERE BAIL REFUSED ON PREVIOUS HEARING

1.   If the court decides not to grant the defendant bail, it is the court's duty to consider, at each subsequent hearing while the defendant is a person to whom section 4 above applies and remains in custody, whether he ought to be granted bail.

2.   At the first hearing after that at which the court decided not to grant the defendant bail he may support an application for bail with any argument as to fact or law that he desires (whether or not he has advanced that argument previously).

3.   At subsequent hearings the court need not hear arguments as to fact or law which it has heard previously.

PART III   INTERPRETATION

1.   For the purposes of this schedule the question whether an offence is one which is punishable with imprisonment shall be determined without regard to any enactment prohibiting or restricting the imprisonment of young offenders or first offenders.

2.   References in this schedule to previous grants of bail in criminal proceedings include references to bail granted before the coming into force of this Act; and so as respects the reference to an offence committed by a person on bail in relation to any period before the coming into force of paragraph 2A of part I of this schedule.

3.   References in this schedule to a defendant's being kept in custody or being in custody include (where the defendant is a child or young person) references to his being kept or being in the care of a local authority in pursuance of a warrant of commitment under section 23(1) of the Children and Young Persons Act 1969.

4.   In this schedule—
     'court', in the expression 'sentence of a court', includes a service court as defined in section 12(1) of the Visiting Forces Act 1952 and 'sentence', in that expression, shall be construed in accordance with that definition;
     'default', in relation to the defendant, means the default for which he is to be dealt with under section 6 or section 16 of the Powers of Criminal Courts Act 1973;
     'the Services Acts' means the Army Act 1955, the Air Force Act 1955 and the Naval Discipline Act 1957.

TEXT OF THE BAIL (AMENDMENT) ACT 1993

Bail (Amendment) Act 1993, s. 1

(1)   Where a magistrates' court grants bail to a person who is charged with or convicted of—
     (a)   an offence punishable by a term of imprisonment of 5 years or more, or
     (b)   an offence under section 12 (taking a conveyance without authority) or 12A (aggravated vehicle taking) of the Theft Act 1968,
the prosecution may appeal to a judge of the Crown Court against the granting of bail.
     (2)   Subsection (1) above applies only where the prosecution is conducted—
     (a)   by or on behalf of the Director of Public Prosecutions; or
     (b)   by a person who falls within such class or description of person as may be prescribed for the purposes of this section by order made by the Secretary of State.
     (3)   Such an appeal may be made only if—
     (a)   the prosecution made representations that bail should not be granted; and
     (b)   the representations were made before it was granted.
     (4)   In the event of the prosecution wishing to exercise the right of appeal set out in subsection (1) above, oral notice of appeal shall be given to the magistrates' court at the conclusion of the proceedings in which such bail has been granted and before the release from custody of the person concerned.
     (5)   Written notice of appeal shall thereafter be served on the magistrates' court and the person concerned within two hours of the conclusion of such proceedings.
     (6)   Upon receipt from the prosecution of oral notice of appeal from its decision to grant bail the magistrates' court shall remand in custody the person concerned, until the appeal is determined or otherwise disposed of.
     (7)   Where the prosecution fails, within the period of two hours mentioned in subsection (5) above, to serve one or both of the notices required by that subsection, the appeal shall be deemed to have been disposed of.

(8) The hearing of an appeal under subsection (1) above against a decision of the magistrates' court to grant bail shall be commenced within forty-eight hours, excluding weekends and any public holiday (that is to say, Christmas Day, Good Friday or a bank holiday), from the date on which oral notice of appeal is given.

(9) At the hearing of any appeal by the prosecution under this section, such appeal shall be by way of re-hearing, and the judge hearing any such appeal may remand the person concerned in custody or may grant bail subject to such conditions (if any) as he thinks fit.

(10 In relation to a child or young person (within the meaning of the Children and Young Persons Act 1969)—

(a) the reference in subsection (1) above to an offence punishable by a term of imprisonment is to be read as a reference to an offence which would be so punishable in the case of an adult; and

(b) the reference in subsection (5) above to remand in custody is to be read subject to the provisions of section 23 of the Act of 1969 (remands to local authority accommodation).

Index